Public Utilities, Second Edition

Dedicated to the men and women who devote their lives to providing the essential services that make modern life possible for the rest of us.

Public Utilities, Second Edition

Old Problems, New Challenges

David E. McNabb

Water and Wastewater District Commissioner and Professor Emeritus, Pacific Lutheran University, USA

Edward Elgar
PUBLISHING

Cheltenham, UK • Northampton, MA, USA

Published by
Edward Elgar Publishing Limited
The Lypiatts
15 Lansdown Road
Cheltenham
Glos GL50 2JA
UK

Edward Elgar Publishing, Inc.
William Pratt House
9 Dewey Court
Northampton
Massachusetts 01060
USA

Paperback edition 2018

A catalogue record for this book
is available from the British Library

Library of Congress Control Number: 2016942176

This book is available electronically in the **Elgar**online
Social and Political Science subject collection
DOI 10.4337/9781785365539

ISBN 978 1 78536 552 2 (cased)
ISBN 978 1 78536 553 9 (eBook)
ISBN 978 1 78897 049 5 (paperback)

Typeset by Servis Filmsetting Ltd, Stockport, Cheshire
Printed and bound in the United States.
Printed on ECF recycled paper containing 30% Post Consumer Waste.

Contents

PART V   PUBLIC UTILITIES: NEW CHALLENGES

About the author

David E. McNabb is Professor Emeritus at Pacific Lutheran University and the audit commissioner of a local water and wastewater utility. He has taught graduate and undergraduate business administration courses at Oregon State University, the Stockholm School of Economics–Riga, Evergreen State College, the University of Maryland-UC (Europe), and the University of Washington–Tacoma. He is an Adjunct Professor at Olympic College and a recent consultant on aspects of survey methodology for an agency of the U.S. government. He earned his PhD at Oregon State University, an MA at the University of Washington, and a BA at California State University, Fullerton. He served as Director of Communications for a caucus of the Washington House of Representatives and as Director of Economic Development for the City of Fullerton, California. He has authored twelve books and nearly one hundred articles and conference papers. The first edition of *Research Methods in Public Administration and Nonprofit Management: Quantitative and Qualitative Approaches* received the Grenzebach Research Award for Outstanding Published Scholarship.

Acronyms

AAR	Association of American Railroads
ADA	Americans with Disabilities Act 1990
AI	Artificial Intelligence
AMWA	Association of Metropolitan Water Agencies
APGA	American Public Gas Association
APPA	American Public Power Association
APTA	American Public Transportation Association
APWA	American Public Works Association
ASCC	Alaska Systems Coordinating Council
ASCE	American Society of Civil Engineers
AWWA	American Water Works Association
BE	Business Ecology
BEPC	Basin Electric Power Cooperative
BPA	Bonneville Power Administration
CAA	Clean Air Act
CAMS	Customer Application Maintenance System
CAO	Control Area Operator
CBIS	Computer-based Information System
CCGT	Combined-Cycle Gas Turbine
CCT	Corridor Cities Transit
CEP	Competitive Electricity Provider
CERCLA	Comprehensive Environmental Response, Compensation, and Liability Act
CHP	Combined Heat and Power
CIP	Capital Improvement Plan
CIP	Critical Infrastructure Protection
CIS	Customer Information System
CIWMB	California Integrated Waste Management Board
CLV	Customer Lifetime Value
COU	Consumer-owned Utilities
CPP	Contract Power Project
CRM	Customer Relationship Management
CSAPR	Cross-State Air Pollution Rule
CSCMP	Council of Supply Chain Management Professionals

CSO	Combined Sewer Overflow
CTAA	Community Transportation Association of America
CWA	Clean Water Act
DOE	Department of Energy
DOT	Department of Transportation
DPU	Department of Public Utilities
DSM	Demand-side Management
DSS	Decision Support System
ECAR	East Central Area Reliability Coordination Agreement
ECRM	Electronic Customer Relationship Management
EDC	Endocrine Disrupting Chemicals
EIA	Energy Information Administration
EIS	Environmental Impact Statement
EMI	Emergency Management Institute
EMRF	Electric Markets Research Foundation
EPA	Energy Policy Act of 2005
EPA	Environmental Protection Agency
EPAct	Energy Policy Act of 1992
EPCRA	Emergency Preparedness and Community Right to Know Act
EPE	El Paso Electric
EPWU	El Paso Water Utilities
ERCOT	Electric Reliability Council of Texas
ERWoW	Evergreen Rural Water of Washington
EWG	Exempt Wholesale Generator
FCM	Federation of Canadian Municipalities
FEMA	Federal Emergency Management Agency
FERC	Federal Energy Regulatory Commission
FGU	Florida Gas Utility
FIFRA	Federal Insecticide, Fungicide and Rodenticide Act
FPA	Federal Power Act of 1935
FPC	Federal Power Commission
FRA	Federal Railroad Administration
FRCC	Florida Reliability Coordinating Council
FTA	Federal Transportation Administration
FWQA	Water Quality Administration
GAISP	Generally Accepted Information Security Principles
GHG	Greenhouse Gas
HMI	Human–Machine Interface
HOV	High-occupancy Vehicle
HPWSD	Harstene Pointe Water and Sewer District
HRM	Human Resources Management

HSWA	Hazardous and Solid Waste Amendments 1984
HVAC	Heating, Ventilation and Air Conditioning
ICC	Interstate Commerce Commission
ICS-CERT	Industrial Control Systems Cyber Emergency Response Team
IOU	Investor-owned Utilities
IPCC	Intergovernmental Panel on Climate Change
IRP	Integrated Resource Planning
ISAC	Information Sharing and Analysis Center (water and wastewater)
ISO	Independent Service Operator
ISO	Independent System Operator
ISO	International Organization for Standardization
ISSA	Information Systems Security Association
IST	Information System Technology
ISTEA	Intermodal Surface Transportation Efficiency Act of 1991
ISWM	Integrated Solid Waste Management
IT	Information Technology
ITM	Information Technology Management
KEU	Kissimmee Electric Utility
LDC	Local Distribution Company
LEA	Local Enforcement Agency
LMIS	Lean Management Information System
LNG	Liquefied Natural Gas
LNG	Liquid Nitrogen Gas
MAAC	Mid-Atlantic Area Council
MACT	Maximum Available Control Technology
MAIN	Mid-America Interconnected Network
MAPP	Mid-Continent Area Power Pool
MARC	Maryland Area Regional Commuter
MATA	Metropolitan Area Transit Authority
MATS	Mercury and Toxics Rules
MBTA	Massachusetts Bay Transportation Authority
MIS	Management Information System
MOU	Municipally-owned Utilities
MPP	Merchant Power-producing Project
MPSC	Maine Public Service Company
MRSC	Municipal Research and Services Center
MSW	Municipal Solid Waste
MSWLF	Municipal Solid Waste Landfill
MTA	Maryland Transit Administration

MWL	Municipal Water Law
NAAQS	National Ambient Air Quality Standards
NAICS	North American Industry Classification System
NACWA	National Association of Clean Water Agencies
NAGA	National Association of Government Accountants
NAE	National Academy of Engineering
NAPCA	National Air Pollution Control Administration
NARUC	National Association of Regulatory Utility Commissioners
NAWC	National Association of Water Companies
NCDENR	North Carolina Department of Environment and Natural Resources
NCSL	National Conference of State Legislatures
NDMC	National Drought Mitigation Center
NEP	National Energy Policy Act
NEPA	National Environmental Policy Act of 1969
NERC	North American Electric Reliability Council
NGA	National Gas Act of 1938
NGCC	Natural Gas Combined Cycle
NGD	Natural Gas Distribution
NGL	Natural Gas Liquid
NGPA	Natural Gas Policy Act of 1978
NGWA	National Ground Water Association
NGWDA	Natural Gas Wellhead Decontrol Act of 1989
NIEHS	National Institute of Environmental Health Sciences
NIIMS	National Interagency Incident Management System
NIMS	National Incident Management System
NOAA	National Oceanic and Atmospheric Administration
NPCC	Northeast Power Coordinating Council
NPDES	National Pollutant Discharge Elimination System
NRDC	Natural Resources Defense Council
NRECA	National Rural Electric Cooperative Association
NRP	National Response Plan
NTSSA	National Transit Systems Security Act
NWRA	National Waste and Recycling Association
NYCT	New York City Transit
NYMTA	New York Metropolitan Transit Authority
NYSPA	New York State Power Authority
OASIS	Open Access Same-time Information System
OCIPEP	Office of Critical Infrastructure Protection and Emergency Preparedness
OEDER	Office of Electricity Delivery and Energy Reliability

OMM	Operation and Maintenance Management
PHMS	Pipeline and Hazardous Materials Safety Administration
PNPRIS	Pacific Northwest Partnership for Regional Infrastructure Security
PPIFU	Power Plant and Industrial Fuel Use Act
PSC	Public Services Commission
PUC	Public Utility Commission
PUD	Public Utility District
PUHCA	Public Utility Holding Company Act of 1935
PURPA	Public Utilities Regulatory Policies Act
QF	Qualifying Facility
R&R	Repair and Replacement
RCAC	Rural Community Assistance Corporation
RCRA	Resource Conservation and Recovery Act
ROR	Rate of Return
RRA	Resource and Recovery Act 1976
RS	Reporting System
RTO	Regional Transmission Organization
RUS	Rural Utilities Service
SCADA	Supervisory Control and Data Acquisition
SDWA	Safe Drinking Water Act
SEC	Securities and Exchange Commission
SERC	Southwestern Electric Reliability Council
SMD	Standard Market Design
SMM	Sustainable Materials Management
SOES	Service Order Entry System
SPP	Southwest Power Pool
SPU	Seattle Public Utilities
SST	Sea Surface Temperature
SWANA	Solid Waste Association of North America
SWDA	Solid Waste Disposal Act
TCRM	Technology-enabled Customer Relationship Management
TEA 21	Transportation Equity Act for the 21st Century
TGF	The Groundwater Foundation
TMDL	Total Maximum Daily Load
TPS	Transaction Processing System
TVA	Tennessee Valley Authority
UACOG	Utility Advisors and Collaborating Organization Group
UBA	Utility Business Architecture
UCA	Utility Communications Architecture
UMTA	Urban Mass Transportation Administration
URC	Utility Regulatory Commission

USCDCP	United States Center for Disease Control and Prevention
USDA	United States Department of Agriculture
USDA ARS	United States Department of Agriculture, Agricultural Research Service
USDOE EIA	United States Department of Energy, Energy Information Administration
USGCRP	United States Global Change Research Program
USGS	United States Geological Survey
UST	Underground Storage Tank
VIU	Vertically Integrated Utility
VPN	Virtual Private Network
WASWD	Washington Association of Sewer and Water Districts
WECC	Western Electric Coordinating Council
WEF	Water Environment Federation
WEP	Water and Environmental Program
WMD	Weapons of Mass Destruction
WRDC	Western Rural Development Center
WSCC	Western Systems Coordinating Council
WSDOH	Washington State Department of Health
WSDOT	Washington State Department of Transportation
WUE	Water Use Efficiency

USCDCP	United States Center for Disease Control and Prevention
USDA	United States Department of Agriculture
USDA ARS	United States Department of Agriculture, Agricultural Research Service
USDOE EIA	United States Department of Energy, Energy Information Administration
USGCRP	United States Global Change Research Program
USGS	United States Geological Survey
UST	Underground Storage Tank
VIU	Vertically Integrated Utility
VPN	Virtual Private Network
WASWD	Washington Association of Sewer and Water Districts
WECC	Western Electric Coordinating Council
WEF	Water Environment Federation
WEP	Water and Environmental Program
WMD	Weapons of Mass Destruction
WRDC	Western Rural Development Center
WSCC	Western Systems Coordinating Council
WSDOH	Washington State Department of Health
WSDOT	Washington State Department of Transportation
WUE	Water Use Efficiency

PART I

Public utilities: old problems

1. Public utilities: essential services, critical infrastructure

During the writing of the first edition of this series on public utilities it was apparent that a transformation was taking place in the way public utilities were managed, regulated, and governed. That managerial transformation had been largely accomplished by the middle of the second decade of the new century. Traditional bureaucratic administration had been or was being replaced by market-driven managerial and entrepreneurial leadership. The historical method of government regulation of utilities as natural monopolies best kept under tight government control was still extant, although it was being replaced by deregulation and privatization, just as it had happened in many other industries. By the late 1990s many publicly owned utilities had to either give way to investor-owned governance or find and implement the economic efficiencies that were expected to accrue from free market competition. However, not all of the changes to the regulatory system were as successful as had been hoped. The collapse of a number of deregulated and privatized utilities, a growing number of brownout and blackouts in the electricity sector, and natural gas and water shortages that followed were attributed to the difficulties associated with utility restructuring.

For public utilities in general, many, but not all, of the problems they faced in the last several decades of the twentieth century have been solved. However, new challenges to maintaining sustainability have arisen to replace those that have been resolved. For example, shortages in energy supplies have been replaced by relatively secure supply of oil and natural gas resources. Regulation of the electric and natural gas utility distribution segments of the industry appear to be little changed, but with federal regulators concerned with the need to ensure the security of the nation's electric energy grid and extensive gas and fuel pipeline system. Water and wastewater utilities, nearly exclusively publicly owned enterprises, remain under the often heavy-handed oversight of federal, state and local governments. Like all the sector, water utilities are faced with the need to acquire the funds necessary for repair and replace aging infrastructure while encouraging consumers to use less of what is becoming an increasingly scarce resource.

Solid waste utilities are running out of sites for ecologically sound landfills while also having to dispose of larger amounts of waste products.

While some hesitancy in the willingness to apply greater regulatory restrictions on utility operations is apparent, the regulatory movement has not disappeared, nor has it eased. Rather, the regulatory focus appears to be more focused on rules and regulations to enhance the sustainability of the public utility system than on rate equability. Regardless of the intent, regulatory changes require investments. The external challenges to the industry brought on by population growth and changing climate conditions have resulted in water shortages and stresses on wastewater and solid waste treatment and disposal facilities. Regulatory developments in these sectors are also leaning toward maintaining and monitoring compliance with public health standards in the face of the climate and environmental stresses that now affect the sustainability of the sector. The telecommunications and cable television sectors, while not discussed in this text, remain overwhelmingly competitive private-sector businesses that remain under federal oversight.

THE PUBLIC UTILITIES CONCEPT

The term *public utilities* refers to the collection of specific services provided by public and private organizations and institutions that make up the public services industry. At the broadest level, the services provided have been long been denominated according to the essential services they perform (Glaeser 1957): (1) public transportation, (2) communication services, (3) energy for light, heat and refrigeration services, (4) water, wastewater, drainage, flood protection, and irrigation, and (5) resource conservation through solid and hazardous waste collection and disposal. The products or services provided by the public utility industry include electrical energy, natural gas, water, sanitation, waste disposal and recycling, communications, public rail and bus transportation, and certain types of storage facilities, including public warehouses, and grain elevators, among others. In brief, these are the organizations and institutions that build and maintain the nation's critical infrastructure while providing the essential services necessary for modern civilization. A more detailed definition of public utilities published in the *Encyclopedia of Law and Economics* in 1999 (online) is included in Box 1.1.

Regardless of their form of ownership, to be regarded as a public utility the entities providing the service utilities are organizations that are *affected with a public interest*, as called for by Justice Waite in 1877 (Farris and Sampson 1973). Public utilities provide essential services needed by every individual and every other institution in a society. The organizations

---

BOX 1.1   WHAT ARE "PUBLIC UTILITIES"?

"The term 'public utility' encompasses a wide variety of industries including, among others, airlines, telecommunications, oil, natural gas, electricity, trucking, cable television [water and wastewater, solid waste collection and disposal, and public transit]. . . .These industries share a common 'network' structure, in that they have an extensive distribution system of lines, pipes, or routes requiring the use of public rights of way, often with strong physical linkages between component parts. In some cases, such as airlines, government owns a part of the infrastructure. Public utilities typically have substantial sunk costs because of [their extensive infrastructure.]

"Historically, utilities, where privately owned, have been rate-of-return regulated. Utilities are government-owned in some jurisdictions. In almost all cases, utilities have been granted legally enforced monopolies over their service territories.

"Utilities typically create a good or service at one location, and then distribute it over a 'network' where it is delivered to numerous customers for end use. The use of a network structure creates special issues for utilities. The network often exhibits economies of scale and involves substantial sunk costs, so the issue of natural monopoly has played an important role in utility literature. The network may require the use of public streets or other rights of way, so government involvement is of particular concern. Since several firms often utilize the network, there are 'network externalities' or congestion if its use is not properly priced. The activities of utilities can be broken down into three components: production, transmission, and distribution. While the production component has, in the U.S., been almost exclusively privately owned, the transmission and distribution stages have been either private or government-owned."

Source: Geddes (2000).

---

operating within the various sectors of this industry have the responsibility for seeing that their services are available when and where the public desires them. Collectively, the set of services are referred to as the *social capital* of a society. Without them, there can be no cities, no nations. More than seventy years ago, Yale economist Irston Barnes suggested the following definition for public utilities:

> Those industries are public utilities which are required to render service as reasonable and nondiscriminatory prices to all who apply for it. The measure of regulation thought necessary to insure universal service at reasonable prices will differ widely from one industry to another, but it characteristically begins with prescribing standards of service and price. (Barnes 1942: 1)

For all editions of this book, then, the term public utilities refers to the large group of public service organizations that exist to locate, produce or collect, transmit, distribute and/or process and store, a variety of products and services that are vital to modern life. These products and services are ubiquitous. They include the electric energy that lights our workspaces and powers computers, appliances, and motors in offices, stores, factories, and homes. These services also include the natural gas we use to heat our residences, cook our meals, and supply raw material for industrial processes. And, they include the water we drink and the treatment and disposal of our wastewater and household and commercial waste, including the organizations that collect, process, and store our solid and liquid waste, including toxic waste. Also included in this discussion are the many organizations that provide some aspect of public transportation and/or storage are also classified public utilities. It was government regulation of this class of activity—transportation of the public waterways and railroads—that were among the first public utility industries to be brought under government regulation.

Why and How Utilities are "Different"

Two key factors which distinguish the majority of the utility industry from other economic endeavors are: (1) elements of the utility industry operate under socially-sanctioned conditions of monopoly competition, and (2) one or more element of the organizations' operations or supply chain are regulated by one or more levels of government. U.S. laws require that regulated businesses be managed in ways different in many respects from that of the nonregulated businesses. For example, management decisions in regulated businesses are often subject to public oversight at public utility commission hearings. Public policy and public opinion expect different conduct in many managerial matters, including the setting of prices, the mandate to meet all service-area demand, and restrictions on allowed operating profits, among others.

Because public utilities provide essential public services that are considered to be endowed with a public interest, utilities management requires both public and private sector management knowledge. Market economies must often balance conflicting social and private interests. This is paramount in the utility industry, where there exists a variety of conditions under which economic activities take place. At one end of the range of conditions are the privately owned, nonregulated businesses that range in size from General Electric and General Motors to the independent corner grocery store. At the opposite end of this continuum are the government-owned organizations such as the U.S. Post Office, TVA, and Bonneville Power; extreme examples at this pole include the nationalized industries that were often found in many Third World countries, the Soviet Bloc of nations, and socialist economies such as were found in Great Britain, Sweden, New Zealand, and others. Municipally owned and operated utilities are near to this tradition of public ownership.

Somewhere between the opposite poles of this economic continuum are free-enterprise businesses such as banks, investment brokers, and insurance companies that are subject to varying degrees of special economic regulation. Also in this group are the privately owned public utilities; these have been on the receiving end of the most complete government regulation of any industry in the group. These regulated industries are a diverse group of public service organizations ranging in size and scope from multinational, vertically integrated energy corporations to local water and power cooperatives. These utilities have been subject to government regulation at either the federal, state, or local, or all three levels at once.

Most energy utilities and waste collection operations are privately owned businesses—commonly referred to as *investor-owned utilities* (IOUs). On the other hand, local governments own most of the nation's water, wastewater, and solid waste disposal site utilities. These governments may operate the utility themselves, or they may contract with private operators for the day-to-day operations; in either case, the government utility may also contract with private firms to perform their billing and customer service functions, among others.

Public utilities differ from other business organizations in many other ways. Six of these differences are: (1) utilities are legally required to serve all customers in their market area without discrimination; (2) they are generally neither exclusively profit or nonprofit; a mix of both types of organizations exist, often side-by-side; (3) utility income often includes a mix of earnings from rates charged customers, stocks and bonds, and/or taxes; (4) utilities are economic organizations because there is a cost to produce and a price for supply of the products, regardless of what form of ownership or governance that characterizes the organization involved in the industry; (5) utilities often practice legally sanctioned price discrimination; and (6) prices for the utility's product or service often do not reflect supply and demand market forces.

These differences from other industries occur for a number of reasons. First, unlike other types of businesses, utilities are legally required to serve all customers in their market area without discrimination; they are limited in this requirement only by their capacity, and may be required to construct additional capacity if demand warrants.

A Mix of Governance Models

Second, they are generally neither exclusively profit or nonprofit; a mix of both types of organizations exist, often side-by-side, functioning in at this time began in Europe with reforms proposed by Max Weber (Christensen and Lægreid 2002). Weber called for the traditional spoils system approach to government employment to be replaced by a cadre of professional civil servants, selected by merit, organized into bureaucracies, and motivated by an ethos of public service. The spoils system lasted longer in the United States but was finally subsumed by a system of professional public servants, organized according to skill categories spelled out in a rule-based civil service code. These changes in public administration were almost fully in place by the onset of the First World War.

The Utility Reform Movement

The utility reform movement underway in the last two decades of the twentieth century was founded on four main components: (1) limits to civil service autonomy to make government more responsive to political influence; (2) introduction of performance-based private sector management principles and practices to improve operational efficiency, effectiveness, and accountability; (3) greater transparency in operations, with increased participation by individuals, consumer groups, and local communities in the design and delivery of all public services; and (4) widespread deregulation of investor-owned utilities. Collectively, these four forces are the foundation stones of what has been referred to as the *New Public Management* (NPM).

Many European governments, including Sweden, Italy, France, and Germany, among others, have adopted elements of NPM. Other Western nations, such as New Zealand, Canada, Brazil, and Australia, have also implemented NPM policies. The nations that have adopted NPM have done so with a number of similar purposes; these include the reduction of public spending and reduced public employment, reduction of deficits and debt service, meeting a perceived need to modernize and improve the management of government services, and bringing about a turnaround in the global trend of citizens' distrust in government.

Organizations such as the World Bank and the EU encouraged their lesser developed client states to adopt NPM policies designed to shift public sector operations from their traditional hierarchical, rule-based, process-oriented, bureaucratic structures toward a flatter, performance-based, organizational model in which public managers are willing to take risks, including contracting with private industry for the provision of public utility services. In addition, the public service deliverers—public and private—had to expand and upgrade their earlier infrastructure, while at the same time continuing to provide quality services. The global payoff sought for the reforms were development of ethical, motivated, public servants trained in the skills of risk-taking, public–private sector partnerships, management of scarce resources, strategic planning, and continuous learning required by a global economy. The ultimate promise was a revitalized, modern, public service and utility governance system that is responsible and responsive to the needs of all stakeholders.

Twentieth Century Reforms

A series of paradigm shifts in the way public utility services function in the United states and other Western democracies occurred over the last hundred years. Calls for change in economic systems first appeared near the start of the last century as laissez faire economic principles were replaced by federal and state legislative controls. The next big change occurred during the Great Depression of the 1930s. The latest call for replacement for the bureaucratic model of public administration developed by Max Weber and added to by Woodrow Wilson first appeared in New Zealand, was then adopted in the United Kingdom in the 1970s under the leadership of Prime Minister Margaret Thatcher (Barzelay 2001). Known as the New Public Management (NPM), it was made popular shortly afterward in the United States by President Ronald Reagan. This shift away from the bureaucratic management model began in the twentieth and early twenty-first century as a search for ways to implement transformational changes in the traditional bureaucratic model of public administration.

Over the last two decades of the twentieth century, the authoritative administrative system with detailed federal and state government regulation was replaced by a market-oriented management system characterized by privatization and increased user fees for public services, the appearance of more and more public and private sector partnerships, management's adoption of long-term strategic planning and programs, evaluation and accountability, and a flattening of the administrative hierarchy. The interest of public administration reformers in the NPM management paradigm, while not dead, has stagnated at best.

Forces that Shaped the Modern Utilities Sector

Three operating environmental forces combined in the last half of the twentieth century and the early decades of the twenty-first century to bring about a deep reaching transformation in the economic structure of most of the industrialized nations of the world. The first was a shift in their demographic makeup and urbanization of their populations. An aging population and concentration of people in cities eventually made possible a truly reachable mass market. At the same time, population megatrends that impact all utilities, regardless of size, location, or sector, and which function as major barriers to their continued sustainability. The first trend includes the changes occurring in the source and type of product and service supplied. On one hand, the once abundant water supplies are declining rapidly, droughts are longer and occurring more often, wastewater and solid waste disposal methods and sites are becoming more restricted, while on the other, the availability and use of once-scarce domestic supplies of energy supplies have increased dramatically, resulting in deep declines in prices. The second trend involves the supply and delivery changes made necessary by changing climate conditions and for replacement and repair of aging and obsolete infrastructure.

A third is the growing difficulty of coming up with funds needed to pay for the improvements needed to meet the needs of demographic changes to society; federal financial support continues to decline while the ability to impose increases in rates is more problematic. A fourth trend is the operational changes imposed upon all public service organizations because of the security threat imposed by domestic terrorist activity.

For many public utilities, the financial challenges are exacerbated by the significant drop in service income brought about by successful conservation developments. Financial needs are growing faster than income for nearly all utilities. The ability to implement changes in rates or to use a different rate structure for different classes of users is becoming problematic due to court-instituted changes and restrictions.

This new edition of the challenges and opportunities facing public utilities was planned as a way to help bring to public awareness the challenges facing public and private utilities. In the long run, rate payers are responsible for providing utility managers with the wherewithal to overcome these and other challenges. However, the book does not address technical issues; rather it focuses on the administrative legal, political and economic issues that commissioners and administrators of large and small public utilities must deal with every day. It is also intended for the leaders of communities, and for the students of utility operations that will be the managers and commissioners of the future.

Investor-owned utilities and those owned by community groups, municipalities, counties, and regional organizations in the United States and elsewhere in the world continue to go far in surmounting many of the challenges they faced in the first decade of the new century. However, they know their work is not done; the many new challenges they face a decade later may be even more difficult to overcome. Many of these issues appear to be attributable to what many scientists believe to be the warming of the climate. A warmer climate in some regions has resulted in severe drought and overstressed water resources, while in others the changes have resulted in more severe rainstorms, hurricanes and cyclones. Arid areas such as the western U.S. and Asia have become more arid while population growth is beginning to over-tax limited water supplies in many of these regions. There is just so much freshwater available and many supplies are already under strain. Parts of the U.S. and elsewhere are undergoing a long-term drought, one for which no early end is in sight. At the opposite end of the scale, other areas are forced to deal with the effects of weather trends that are increasingly severe and damaging to existing infrastructure. Added to the supply problem is that much of the country's water and wastewater infrastructure is one to several hundred years old and buried under metropolitan streets. In the U.S., for example, many of the major mains serving cities were constructed in the nineteenth century. In Europe and Asia, many are even older. Much of that infrastructure is beginning to fail at the same time that supplies are reaching or beyond their sustainability.

SUMMARY

The term *public utility* is used to describe a variety of publicly and investor-owned organizations that provide certain specific essential services to residential consumers, industrial and commercial customers, and government organizations. U.S. Supreme Court decisions dealing with the services provided by utilities have resulted in those services being 'affected with the public interest,' and therefore deserving of government regulation.

Utilities are supposed to provide a common benefit to each class of users, but users do not always enjoy equal benefit from the products of the utility. Moreover, homeowners are often charged a higher rate for the service than are industrial users, for example. Despite this legally sanctioned price discrimination, prices charged by utilities to all their customers must be seen as "reasonable" by regulators and the general public. In the case of publicly owned utilities, prices are often kept artificially low for political purposes and do not take into consideration the true cost of the service. With investor-owned utilities, commissions weigh all the cost data provided by the firm to justify their rates. Regulated utilities are allowed to add a legislatively established minimum rate of return to the accepted cost of their operations.

A fundamental economic principle that differentiates utilities from all other forms of economic organizations is that of the *natural monopoly*. Natural monopolies occur when a single firm is able to supply a market at a cost and price far lower than would be possible if several firms served the market. The concept of utilities being a *natural monopoly* came into general use during the Progressive Era reform movement, when the federal government began its first experiments with ways to control the perceived excesses of the very large and growing businesses, cartels, trusts, and early utilities.

ADDITIONAL READING

Coe, Charles K. (2015), *Urban Services: A Basic Guide for Local Governments*. New York: Routledge.

Colburn, David R. and George E. Pozzetta (eds) (1983), *Reform and Reformers in the Progressive Era*. Westport, CT: Greenwood Press.

Glaeser, Martin G. (1957), *Public Utilities in American Capitalism*. New York: Macmillan.

Lambert, Jeremiah D. (2015), *The Power Brokers: The Struggle to Shape and Control the Electric Power Industry*. Cambridge, MA: MIT Press.

Morgan, C.S. (2010), *Regulation and the Management of Public Utilities*. Boston: Gale (Cengage).

Pond, Oscar L. (2012), *Municipal Control of Public Utilities; a Study of the Attitude of Our Courts Toward an Increase in the Sphere of Municipal Activity*, Lenox, MA: HardPress.

2.   Public utility policy issues

The range of the decision alternatives available to public utility managers is framed by the policies that exist at the time the decisions must be made. Public utility managers are guided in their everyday organizational activities by two levels of policy: internal and external. Internal policy includes the normal levels of organizational and management policies and procedures that shape the business enterprise. Internal policy is a product of the vision of senior management and board of directors, the organization's mission, its resources, and the existing organizational climate and culture. Elements of internal policy are discussed in Chapters 14 through 17. This chapter focuses on external policy forces.

External policy is a reflection of the environment that shapes and constraints the range of choices from which management policy may be selected. External policy is formed by the influences resulting from the political and public-attitude environment of the period. Examples included tax policy, investment policy, anti-trust policy, environmental policy, and the like.

The external public utility policy is neither static nor a single-sourced construct. Rather, it changes with time and is shaped by the changing and often competing attitudes, intentions, and actions of elected government officials, the public served, regulatory organizations and agencies, financial institutions, and the citizen action groups within society. There are many types of policies that affect public utility operations and management. Examples include a nation's welfare policies, public safety and security policies, and the policies pertaining to public health, the environment, energy, conservation, and fiscal policy, among others. These policies shape the types of laws passed by federal, state, and local governments. They also provide a framework for the rules and regulations developed by the government agencies charged with implementing the laws—as well as the court decisions that often follow implementation.

One of the most powerful forces shaping governments' policy toward public utilities is public opinion; it was used effectively by supporters of public electric utility ownership in Seattle, Washington in the first quarter of the twentieth century and again against power holding companies in the 1930s (McNabb 1968; Lambert 2015). Since the earliest stages of the

the economic system. By 2015, technological advances had resulted in a surplus of oil and gas, together with steep drops in the price of these products. On the other hand, a long-term drought in the West-Central United States has caused water shortages and higher prices for water.

EVOLVING PUBLIC UTILITY POLICY

Public policy toward utilities has undergone many changes over the 200-plus years of the nation's history. Formation of a federal policy toward utilities was not an important issue until the closing years of the nineteenth century. During the period between the Civil War and the end of the 1800s, America drifted steadily away from its agricultural foundations toward the urbanized industrial nation it would be by the start of the twentieth century. During those transition years the economy of the young nation came to be controlled to a large degree by a few large industrial, transportation, and financial giants (Chandler and Tedlow 1985). Among these giants were segments of what was to become the energy supply portion of the utility industry.

From its beginnings in the 1880s until the end of the century, the utility industry had received little public attention. Governments and the courts adopted the opinion that utilities were natural monopolies that provided essential public services. As long as the services continued unabated and remained generally affordable, government tended to follow the same hands-off policy it followed with all businesses. This was a time of city building across America, and city growth required an ample supply of reliable energy, water, and sanitation.

The leading industries driving the economy in the last half of the nineteenth century were railroads, iron and steel, and coal. Unbridled capitalism was the law of the land. By 1900 a dual economy had evolved in the United States, dominated by big business at the center with small businesses existing at the periphery. The power held by the leaders of these giant industries was phenomenal. For example, in 1883 it was the nation's railroads that established the four time zones in the country as a way of standardizing their schedules. The federal government simply acquiesced in the decision, as it would again three years later when railroad managers got together to agree on a standard-gauge track. Eventually, however, some actions of railroads and the financial houses behind them were considered harmful to the overall economy of the nation and required government intervention and control. Based on court opinions that railroads and associated services such as grain elevators were "affected with a public interest," the federal government endorsed early state regulatory activities.

Railroads were the first industry to be regulated by both state and federal governments.

EARLY UTILITY POLICY

The initial government policy toward public utilities took shape within the broader framework of a shift in governments' attitudes toward business in general that occurred in the last decades of the nineteenth century. Steps taken in a few states to regulate some activities of railroads forced the federal government to examine its traditional laissez faire policy toward business. State legislatures passed laws aimed at redressing perceived issues of restraint of trade, unfair and discriminatory pricing, and the anti-competition activities of trusts.

Collectively, these and similar policy changes became incorporated under the label of *Progressive Era* reforms. They resulted in passage in the states in the upper Midwest of the *Granger Laws*, named after the sponsoring organization, the National Grange of the Patrons of Husbandry, or the Grangers. The laws created state commissions to regulate railroad pricing and end discriminatory business practices (Bryant and Dethloff 1990). The early state laws were subsequently upheld by the U.S. Supreme Court in the 1877 *Munn v. Illinois* case. However, by 1886 the power of the states to regulate railroads had been severely curtailed by appeals and by subsequent court decisions. In 1887, the federal government responded to public demands for additional regulation with passage of the Interstate Commerce Act, which established the Interstate Commerce Commission (ICC). The ICC was given the responsibility for regulating the rail system.

Developers of early privately financed railroads and utility services were enthusiastically courted by civic leaders, many of whom discovered that essential services also provided a way of personal enrichment. Franchises were often sold to the highest bidder, while kickbacks, payoffs, and bribes were considered a normal cost of doing business. Private citizens had little or no say in the design and construction of network systems. Based on the territory they were located in, customers were told which water, gas, or electricity organization would provide their service, and how much they would have to pay for the service.

The establishment of utility services in the nation took three major forms of ownership: private (later called 'investor-owned'), public (typically municipal), and cooperative. Municipal ownership was the path followed for most water and sanitation services, while manufactured and natural gas systems, telecommunications systems, and electrical energy networks, including traction and street lighting, tended to be established by private individuals or corporations, although in some cities, particularly in the west and upper middle west, municipal ownership was the norm for all utilities. The third form of organization—cooperative ownership—occurred in small markets, where little profit potential existed to attract commercial interests, and local governments lacked the financial strength or size to warrant municipal ownership. Cooperatives exist today, but mostly for small water and sanitation systems.

Decisions were made by utility company directors and managers meeting in secret on such issues as: (1) the form of ownership (holding company or subsidiary); (2) the amount, type, and timing for the sale of securities; (3) on how the service was produced (that is, should it be self-produced or bought for re-sale); (4) whether new facilities would be constructed and when; (5) if new capacity was needed, where it should be located; (6) the type and location of new transmission lines, pipelines, and distribution network facilities; and (7) how much should be charged to each class of customer. Little or no competition existed because policymakers believed that it would be inefficient to build overlapping systems within the same service territories. There were no state public utility commissions and no public hearings to provide oversight services.

According to Federal Reserve Bank economist Richard Mattoon (2002), there were good reasons for maintaining this structure. Utilities in general have always been a capital intensive industry. Large sums are required for prospecting, drilling, pumping, and storing natural gas; for constructing reservoirs, water treatment plants, aqueducts and pipelines; and for building power plants, transmission lines, street traction and lighting systems. Proper maintenance of extensive distribution networks once they are up and running is also costly. Utility infrastructure is expensive and requires long-lived investments. In order to meet their mandated requirements for provision of service when and where it is required in their operating areas, utilities need to be assured that they would always be able to amortize their large, long-term investments.

The first wave of trust forming in traditional public utility sectors—electricity, manufactured and natural gas, water and sanitation, and telecommunications—began in 1866 with the nation's three leading telegraph companies merged to form Western Union. Telephones, manufactured gas, oil, and the electricity industries followed similar patterns a few years later. The early entrepreneurs in these fields formed businesses to capitalize on their inventions and discoveries. Charles F. Brush, inventor of the arc-light system, formed the Brush Electric Company in the 1870s. Elihu Thomson and E. H. Houston, high school science teachers, developed improvements on the Brush system and formed the Thomson-Houston Electric Company in 1883 to manufacture electrical equipment. The Thomson-Houston

Company soon absorbed many smaller manufacturers and quickly dominated their industry.

Thomas Edison, inventor of the incandescent electric light bulb in 1879, acquired a half million dollars in investment capital and formed the Edison Lamp Company to make and sell light bulbs and the Edison Electric Light Company to install generating and lighting systems. In 1892 the two Edison firms merged to become Edison General Electric. The Edison Company opened a steam electricity generating plant in New York City in 1882, supplying direct current to light streets, businesses, and a few residential customers. Thomson-Houston eventually merged with Edison General Electric in 1892.

National, state, and local governments were eventually forced by unbridled growth and technical problems to develop and implement standard policies toward utilities. For electricity, the major problem was that electricity cannot efficiently be stored; generating plants must always be constructed at least 15 percent greater capacity than needed. In the industry's early years, Edison's direct current systems competed with the George Westinghouse alternating current system. Manufactured gas was so expensive that only businesses, municipalities, and a few wealthy private citizens could afford it.

Very few pipelines existed to move natural or gas manufactured from coal from where it was found to where it was needed. Until safe supplies could be secured for water systems, water pumped from shallow wells often spread disease. Eventually, civic leaders and reformers forced the federal government, state legislatures, and city councils to recognize their responsibility for provision of safe, secure, stable supplies of utility services. Public utility policy became one of governments' chief concerns thereafter.

Utilities grew rapidly during the first quarter of the twentieth century. Fueled by floods of low-wage immigrants from Europe, the nation's industries became world leaders during this period. The early immigrants flocked to the nation's cities. Industry required uninterrupted energy supplies and raw materials; workers required reliable supplies of utility services, including light, water, and transportation. Utilities grew to meet these demands.

Government's policy response to the demands for uninterrupted service at affordable prices was to recognize the monopoly status of utility companies, assign them well-defined geographic service territories, and guarantee a reasonable return on their investments. However, because of the potential for abuses inherent in monopolies, the utility companies were eventually subjected to rigorous regulation so as to prevent the exercise of monopoly pricing power. The same rationale was eventually applied to all network industries, including, water, sanitation, manufactured and natural gas, and telecommunications. For the most part, this led to a favorable regulatory environment in which utilities were granted monopoly status in return for a pricing structure based on rates that were "just and reasonable"; prices agreed upon reflected the utilities' cost of production and delivery, with provision for a fair rate of return on invested assets (Mattoon 2002).

A shift in public policy toward utilities occurred after the stock market crash of 1929 and the economic depression that followed. One of the victims of the collapse was the Chicago-based holding company empire of electricity and gas utilities put together by Samuel Insull, an industry leader who strongly supported state regulation of utilities as natural monopolies. At its peak, the Insull utility holding company empire controlled a collection of utility operating and service companies with something like 600,000 investors and 500,000 bondholders. By 1930, his companies had a net worth of more than $3 billion and served customers in 5,000 towns in 32 states. The empire collapsed in 1932, bringing financial ruin to thousands of investors. The Public Utility Holding Company Act (PUHCA) enacted in 1935 effectively ended the utility holding company, and brought the federal government into greater regulatory control of the utility industry. During the next decade, government increased its level of control over businesses of all types; it played a particularly important role in the utility industry in this period.

Under President Franklin Delano Roosevelt, the federal government became heavily involved in the utility industry, developing huge utility projects and networks, including the Tennessee Valley Authority (TVA) and the Bonneville Power Administration (BPA). These were established as government corporations rather than government agencies. Passage of the Rural Electrification Act in 1936 brought power to distant farms, villages, and small towns across the country; from less than 10 percent in 1935, farms with electricity increased to nearly 94 percent in 1955 (Farris and Sampson 1973).

The first major Act regulating natural gas appeared several years before the United States' entry into the Second World War. The 1938 Natural Gas Act (NGA) created the Federal Power Commission (FPC) in order to regulate natural gas pipelines, although the price of gas at the wellhead was left unregulated. Economic growth after the war resulted in demand for gas outpacing pipeline capacity, which, in turn, saw excessive retail price volatility and shortages of gas through most of the 1940s and 1950s. The FPC refused to establish price caps, believing that it did not have the power to participate in pricing decisions. Public demands to ease the price and supply problems resulted in a 1954 Supreme Court decision (the *Phillips Decision*) that the NGA could regulate pipelines and wellhead prices of gas. The decision solved price problems, but did nothing to resolve supply problems.

Another major shift in public policy toward the utility industry began in the 1970s. The natural gas industry was one of the first utilities to be affected by the new policy shift. The FPC was replaced when passage of the 1978 Natural Gas Policy Act (NGPA) established a new regulatory body, the Federal Energy Regulatory Commission (FERC). Natural gas wellhead gas prices were deregulated as powers allotted to the NGPA reversed the 1954 Phillips decision. As a result, gas production increased dramatically, prices dropped, and by 1985, the decades-long shortage was replaced by a surplus of natural gas.

A second piece of legislation passed in 1978 that affected the natural gas industry was the Outer Continental Shelf Lands Act (OCSLA). This law opened up gas pipeline operations to competition by requiring that pipelines provide open, non-discriminatory access to all shippers, regardless of whether they held any ownership in the pipeline.

The trend toward open access of pipelines was extended in 1985 with release of FERC Order 436, which required pipelines to provide open access to transit of gas produced by other firms. It unbundled natural gas supply from gas transportation by allowing gas buyers to negotiate prices directly with producers and then contract separately with a pipeline company for shipment of the gas. FERC Order 500 issued in 1987 established take-or-pay contracts between suppliers and customers. Take-or-pay contracts provide long-term stability for both parties by requiring the buyer to pay some portion of the cost even if gas is not accepted. As a result of these developments, gas market firms were established. Often without ties to any gas company, market firms provide an intermediary service between gas buyers and other industry segments.

The final natural gas policy statement to come out of the 1980s was the Natural Gas Wellhead Decontrol Act of 1989. This Act resulted in a phasing out of the regulation of all wellhead prices; it required that all price controls be eliminated by January 1, 1993. Gas prices were from then on to be freely set in the market.

Two major policy developments took place in the early 1990s. The first was the 1991 Mega-Notice of Proposed Rulemaking (MegaNOPR). With this notice the FERC formally requested gas consumers and the gas industry to submit proposals and comments about ways to further structure gas pipeline transportation. MegaNOPR was followed the next year by FERC Order 636—the *Restructuring Rule*. This order was a more comprehensive unbundling of the gas supply and transportation segments of the industry; it resulted in a major restructuring of the interstate pipeline industry by separating sales from transportation services. Customers could now choose supply services and transportation services from any competitor in any quantity and any combination. This essentially eliminated the need for take-or-buy contracts. The most important byproduct of Order 636 was dramatic increases in gas exploration, pipeline construction, falling prices, and greater profits for industry participants.

In 2000, FERC Order 637 resolved several discrepancies in the restructuring of the industry by addressing inefficiencies in the capacity release market. Customers can now negotiate supply and transposition contracts while simultaneously negotiating better terms in other markets as a price hedge. The natural gas commodity market is now traded on the New York Mercantile Exchange (NYMEX).

Deregulation of the U.S. natural gas market is considered to be a success and is used as a policy model for the restructuring of other public utilities. Today, the industry includes something like 8,000 independent producers, 160 pipeline operators with 285,000 miles of pipes, and 1,500 local distribution utilities with 833,000 miles of pipes.

POLICY IN THE TWENTY-FIRST CENTURY

Current public policy toward water utilities is less intrusive than the deregulation programs underway in the power and gas industries. There are no federal agencies pushing for restructuring, deregulation, or unbundling of services in the water utility industry today. However, the pressures for restructuring in those industries are likely to put increased pressure on managers and workers in water utilities to become more efficient (Beder 2003. This does not mean to say that water utilities are not subject to government regulation. Indeed, the opposite is true; water utilities are subject to regulatory actions on three separate planes: water quality, quantity, and price. The point is that government regulation is simply different for water utilities than it is for electricity and natural gas. One of the major reasons for this is the different ownership picture. Whereas something like 75 percent of the electricity industry and 80 percent of the gas industry is investor owned, less than 10 percent of the nation's 53,400 water utilities are investor owned; most water systems are municipal operations.

Restructuring of the energy industry was seen as a way to reduce the cost of electricity generation by substituting low-cost generation process for older, higher cost, large capacity plants, many of which were approaching the end of their useful life and needed either replacement, augmentation, or extensive revamping. In addition, smaller plants could be brought on line much faster than hydroelectric, nuclear, or coal-fired generating plants. The water utility industry faced different problems. Construction of new water production plants is more costly than those they are designed to replace. A major reason for this is the greater treatment requirements required by major shifts in public policy. For these and other underlying technological reasons, the water industry does not enjoy the same benefits from restructuring enjoyed by electricity and natural gas. Increasing competition in the water industry would not result in a cost savings to consumers.

The electricity industry can gain cost savings because new, smaller energy sources can be constructed at less than the average cost of existing sources. Savings in the gas industry are possible because production costs may vary greatly among the many independent producers. The ability of a gas user to gain transmission access for the gas purchased from a low-cost producer enables that gas user to substantially lower the overall acquisition cost of the gas. On the other hand, in the water industry new plants are far more expensive to build than it costs for the average existing plants. To control water supply costs, production must be centralized as much as possible. Scott Rubin summarized these differences in a speech given in Pennsylvania:

> In summary, both the technology of water production and the characteristics of water itself make it very unlikely that the water industry will be restructured in the same way as the energy industries. Multiple water suppliers serving a single market and competing for customers is very unlikely. (Rubin 1998: 10)

Restructuring of the water industry meant the separation of water-production plant ownership from the transmission and distribution of water. This occurred in several locations, as new water treatment plants were constructed by companies independent of the distribution operators. Treatment services were then sold to the distributor, who is not saddled with the need to construct new facilities to meet growing demand. Little new separation of services in this way has followed the initial experiments.

ENERGY SECTOR POLICY

Policy for the United States electric utility sector began a new chapter during the administration of President Jimmy Carter. Three important pieces of utility legislation were signed by President Carter: (1) the Power Plant and Industrial Fuel Use Act (PPIFU), (2) the Natural Gas Policy Act (NGPA), and (3) the Public Utility Regulatory Policies Act (PURPA). The Fuel Use Act prohibited the use of oil or natural gas to power any new electric energy plants; the intent was to reserve natural gas for heating and other high value uses. The Natural Gas Act deregulated the price of newly discovered natural gas. Passage of PURPA in 1978 opened the wholesale

Mixed Results for Restructuring

Regardless of their product or service, public utility services are composed of three similar components: production, transmission, and distribution. For electricity, production means power generation. Power is generated by falling water in hydroelectric systems, by steam-powered turbines using fossil fuel, geothermal, or nuclear power energy, by wind-power generators, and by gas turbines using natural gas or propane fuels, solar collectors, and fuel cells, among others. Natural gas is collected at wells, often as a byproduct of petroleum production. Water is either pumped from wells that tap into underground aquifers or released from reservoirs, rivers, or streams.

Transmission is similar for all three utilities. Electric power is moved over high voltage transmission lines; gas is transported by large volume pipelines; water is pumped through pipelines or moved by aqueduct. Distribution is also similar. Electric power is distributed over low voltage overhead or underground power lines; gas and water is distributed via underground pipe networks.

Traditionally, utility networks have tended to be vertically integrated firms that provided all three services: generation, transmission, and distribution. Some observers and policymakers felt that this system resulted in higher rates to residential customers in order to subsidize costs of production and/or transmission of product to large industrial customers. Residential customers were thought to be subjected to price discrimination as commercial and industrial prices for utility products were lower than they were for residential customers. Furthermore, integrated utilities were able to deny competitors access to their private transmission and distribution facilities. This was seen as resulting in scale inefficiencies, which further raised the price of utility products.

The utility industry restructuring actions that occurred during the 1980s and 1990s were implemented in order to redress perceived price discrimination and to reduce what were believed to be unnecessarily high prices for utility services. This policy shift that brought about restructuring was driven by a global trend that combined elements of minimalism in government, accountability, and market efficiencies in the management of public services. This multifaceted movement is reflected in the global drive toward deregulation, restructuring of utilities, and market competition appears to be somewhat in limbo. A number of states put their restructuring plans on hold after the problems encountered by California in the year 2002 and particularly after the deep recession of 2008 and 2009.

A New Energy Policy Bill

Congress failed to pass the Energy Policy Act of 2003. That Act would have designated "national interest electric transmission corridors," and authorized the Department of Energy (DOE) to issue permits for transmission line construction in the corridors. The right of eminent domain for acquisition of affected private property was included to facilitate the construction process. Parties other than utilities or transmission operators were to be allowed to finance construction of the new DOE-owned transmission lines. Repayment was to occur through rates charged to customers. In addition, in order to ensure that terms and conditions of transmission rates are not discriminatory, the FERC would have been given jurisdiction over unregulated transmitting utilities. Unregulated transmitting utilities are publicly owned, and include such organizations as Bonneville Power. If passed, the 2003 Act would have required unregulated transmission utilities to provide the same transmission rates, terms, and conditions as regulated utilities, thus eliminating any competition between the two.

A new bill, the Energy Policy Act of 2005 (EPA), made it through the next session of Congress and was signed into law by President George W. Bush on August 8, 2005. Incorporating many of the features of the failed 2003 legislation, the Policy Act focused on the following aspects of energy production:

1. Energy efficiency and renewable energy
2. Oil, gas and coal production
3. Tribal energy
4. Nuclear matters and nuclear generation security
5. Vehicles and motor fuels, including ethanol and hydrogen
6. Electricity
7. Energy tax incentives
8. Hydropower and geothermal energy
9. Climate change technology.

The Act provided loan guarantees for organizations that develop or use innovative technologies that avoid the byproduction of greenhouse gases. Another provision of the Act increased the amount of biofuel such as ethanol that must be mixed with gasoline sold in the United States. One little-remarked feature of the 2005 Act was the provision that repealed the New Deal-era Public Utility Holding Act of 1935.

managed. At the federal level, one analyst identified 50 different agencies involved with water issues, including the Environmental Protection Agency, the Forest Service, Department of Agriculture, the Bureau of Land Management, Corps of Engineers, The Department of the Interior, Native American tribes, and the Department of Energy. According to one count, in the Department of the Interior alone eight sub-agencies have some involvement with water. Congressional oversight of water issues is also varied; more than 40 committees and subcommittees are involved with some aspect of water policy.

WASTE SECTOR POLICY

Government interest in a national policy for the collection and disposal of municipal and industrial solid waste and hazardous liquids from all sources was the latest utility sector to come under the nation's interest in conservation and environmental protection that occurred during the 1960s and 1970s. For nearly all of the first 200 years of the United States, the national government paid little attention to the solid waste problem; it was looked upon as a local problem, finding an affordable answer to the question of what to do with the growing mountains of garbage generated in cities. In New York City, garbage was loaded on barges and dumped into New York harbor. In Seattle, garbage was dumped onto a low marsh on the shores of Lake Washington, in sight of the University of Washington's football stadium. Or, it was trucked to privately owned landfills or barged under private contract to a marshy area of a Native American island in the middle of Puget Sound. But in most towns and cities across America garbage and industrial wastes were simply indiscriminately tossed into the town dump where it was openly burned or left to sit while poisons leached into nearby streams and rivers or into underground water supplies.

A comprehensive policy for dealing with hazardous and household solid waste did not appear until 1965 when the federal government enacted the Solid Waste Disposal Act (SWDA). Congress passed the SWDA as part of the amendments to the Clean Air Act. It was the first federal law that required environmentally sound methods for the disposal of household, municipal, commercial, and industrial waste. Later amendments to the SWDA substantially increased the federal government's involvement in solid waste management.

Government's policy shifted from disposal to conservation and resource recover with passage of the Resource Conservation and Recovery Act (RCRA) in 1976. The RCRA's objectives were to regulate collection and disposal of solid waste "to protect human health and the environment from the potential hazards of waste disposal, conserve energy and natural resources, reduce the amount of waste generated, and ensure that wastes are managed in an environmentally sound manner" (EPA 2013a). The goals of the RCRA were environmental protection, resource conservation, and reduction in the amount of waste being generated. Two key sections of the RCRA are sections C and D: Section C covers requirements for solid waste agencies for establishing comprehensive plans for the complete waste generation-disposal life cycle; Section D covers regulations for locating nonhazardous wastes and solid waste disposal facilities.

The Environmental Protection Agency (EPA) tightened its hazardous waste disposal policies in 1980 with amendments to the RCRA that required identifying hazardous wastes, set production standards for producers and transporters of hazardous wastes, standards for disposal facilities and required permits for storage of hazardous wastes. Box 2.1 illustrates how violators of the permit requirements are subject to steep fines.

BOX 2.1   EPA FINES ALASKA BOROUGH FOR UNLAWFUL STORAGE OF HAZARDOUS WASTE

In 2015, the EPA fined Alaska's North Slope Borough nearly $500,000 for alleged violations of hazardous waste requirements under the Resource Conservation and Recovery Act (RCRA). EPA alleged that the North Slope Borough failed to perform required hazardous waste determinations for at least five separate waste sources at a facility in Barrow, Alaska.

The Borough allegedly stored more than 45,000 pounds of hazardous waste without the required RCRA storage permit. The waste included acids, alkalis, anti-freeze contaminated with benzene, corrosive solvents and paint, and other related materials stored in more than 200 metal drums and five gallon buckets for more than 90 days. RCRA permits are required prior to operating any hazardous waste storage facility. The process is designed to prevent harm to the environment or human health.

The Consent Agreement and Final Order, signed by EPA and the North Slope Borough covered RCRA violations that occurred from 2012 to 2014. They were subsequently removed from the site. As part of this agreement, the North Slope Borough will pay a $445,336 penalty and remove metal drums and containers of hazardous waste from the site.

The RCRA federal law governs the treatment, storage, and disposal of hazardous waste. RCRA is designed to protect public health and the environment, and avoid costly cleanups, by requiring the safe, environmentally-sound storage and disposal of hazardous waste. The RCRA requires the use of safe practices to greatly reduce the chance that hazardous waste will be released into the environment.

Source: ERC (2015).

been publicly owned, relatively small systems, constructed and operated by municipalities. Because water is so essential for maintaining life, quality has long been a major concern in this industry. It has resulted in an insertion of an additional step in the production–transmission–distribution chain: water treatment. Restructuring of the U.S. water industry is proceeding much slower than what has occurred in the energy fields. Rather than unbundling of services, the dominant trend seems to be privatization of complete systems. A typical example of the privatization of utilities is the former municipal water system in Cambridge, England, that for nearly a decade has been owned by a Spanish multinational corporation. This same pattern exists across the European Union, Australia, New Zealand, and Canada, as well as in Latin America and Asia.

These differences in governance have important ramifications for regulatory outcomes. While large investor-owned utilities (IOUs) are subject to review by state public utility commissions, many public power authorities are exempt from these requirements. This fragmented structure makes electricity a policy area with many participants and little central planning or review authority, except within the Balkanized areas served and regulated by a public authority.

The national and some cases, international, associations of electric, gas, water, and sanitation utilities are forums for addressing the big issue policy questions faced by all utilities collectively, and each industry independently. Associations meet early each year to identify the more pressing issues they feel will have the greatest impact upon their operations. An example was the January 20–21, 2003 summit meeting of the National Association of Regulatory Utility Commissioners (NARUC). Commissioners met to discuss the major regulatory policy issues they faced and to consider the options available to them for dealing with the issues that would most affect the states in 2003 and beyond. Five key concerns were identified in a report on the conference produced by the National Regulatory Research Institute; other public utility associations produce similar policy issue platforms. For example:

1. The Federal Energy Regulatory Commission's initiative for establishment of a Standard Market Design (SMD), and particularly the jurisdictional implications of the concept.
2. State perspectives on government telecommunications policy.
3. The impact that competition in the utility supply chain will have on consumer protection and service quality regulation.
4. The implications for oversight of transactions between affiliate organizations resulting from reform of the Public Utility Holding Company Act (PUHCA) of 1935.

5. The impact that implementation and changes in energy and environmental policies will have upon state regulatory commissions.

SUMMARY

The activities of public utility managers are influenced by public policy,
corporate policy, and company or organization policy. *Public policy* is a
reflection of particular attitudes, intentions and actions of policymakers
that affect society; examples include industrial policy, education policy,
welfare policy, public safety policy, environmental policy, energy policy,
water policy, and the like. Public policy shapes the types of laws passed
by federal, state, and local governments and provides a framework for the
rules and regulations developed by government agencies for implementing
the laws.

Public policy is itself shaped by public opinion. Public policy also
influences the amount and shape of regulatory content and procedures,
locating decisions, utility taxation, and other public service functions and
operations.

Corporate policy refers to the operational guidelines that shape and
frame the corporate mission and fundamental operations of an organization. Corporate policy is shaped by the actions of an organization's directors and by the CEO. Corporate policy is manifested in the vision of the
leadership and the mission statement of the organization.

Company policy refers to the specific rules, regulations, procedures,
and practices that guide managers and workers in their interpersonal and
inter-organizational actions. Because policy exists at more than one level in
all organizations, managers often face difficulties when making decisions
when the guiding policies conflict.

The results of public policy on utilities is seen in the character of the
laws enacted, regulatory actions taken, court decisions handed down,
and the behaviors and attitudes expressed by legislatures and the public
on utility operations and issues. Moreover, public policies seldom if ever
remain permanent; they are always subject to change. Policy changes are
often as a result of some catastrophic event.

From its beginnings in the 1880s until the end of the century, the utility
industry received little public attention. Governments and the courts felt
that utilities were natural monopolies providing essential public services.
As long as the services continued unabated and remained generally affordable, government tended to follow the same hands-off policy it followed
with all businesses.

Government policy toward public utilities took its initial shape within the framework of a shift in government's attitudes toward business in general that occurred in the last decades of the nineteenth century. These policy changes occurred as part of what we now call Progressive Era reforms. A few states' efforts to regulate railroads forced the federal government to examine its traditional laissez faire policy toward business. State legislatures passed laws aimed at redressing perceived issues of restraint of trade, unfair and discriminatory pricing, and the anti-competition activities of trusts.

A second wave of changes in public policy toward utilities occurred after the stock market crash of 1929. The Securities Act of 1933, Securities and Exchange Act of 1934, and the Public Utility Holding Company Act of 1935 severely restricted the power and scope of action of utility holding companies. These laws also brought the federal government into greater regulatory control of the utility industry.

A third wave of changes in public utility policy in the United States began in the late 1970s.

The utility industry restructuring actions of the 1980s and 1990s were implemented to redress perceived price discrimination and reduce what were believed to be unnecessarily high prices. This policy shift that brought about restructuring was driven in large part by a global trend that combined elements of minimalism in government, public accountability, performance appraisal, and market efficiencies in the management of public services.

ADDITIONAL READING

Brennan, Timothy J., Karen L. Palmer and Salvador A. Martinez (2002), *Alternating Currents*. Washington, DC: Resources for the Future.

Brown, Matthew H. and Richard P. Sedano (2003), *A Comprehensive View of U.S. Electric Restructuring with Policy Options for the Future*. Washington, DC: National Council on Electricity Policy.

Jacobson, Charles David (2000), *Ties that Bind: Economic and Political Dilemmas of Urban Utility Networks, 1800–1990*. Pittsburgh: University of Pittsburgh Press.

Kraft, Michael E. and Scott R. Furlong (2015), *Public Policy: Politics, Analysis and Alternatives* (5th edn). Thousand Oaks, CA: Sage.

Wickwar, W. Hardy (1938), *The Public Services: A Historical Survey*. London: Cobden-Sanderson.

3. Public utility regulatory environment

Public utilities are subject to a wide variety of local, state, and federal government regulations. These regulations have evolved from a body of laws passed over the last eighty-plus years that deal with such business functions as ownership and governance, raising capital, transactions between company units, environment, and the methods of producing utility products. Additional regulations deal with health and safety issues, environmental concerns, and many other aspects of utility operations. As "natural monopolies," utilities are considered to be holders of a special public trust and therefore legitimately subject to government oversight. This chapter discusses some of the more important of the regulations under which utilities operate.

The rationale for regulation of business activities lies in our reliance upon market competition to set and control prices (Brennan, Palmer, and Martinez 2002). Businesses often use price competition to better their competitors. Consumers pay what it costs to produce and distribute goods, with suppliers' profits limited by these competitive actions of businesses. Moreover, market competition helps provide consumers with an increasing number of options from which to choose how they spend their money. The key to making the system work is that enough competition exists to drive down prices to a level close to the cost of production. If this is not the case, producers are free to raise prices without worrying that customers will find other sellers, or that new sellers will enter the market to take advantage of the high profits available. If only one seller exists, the firm will enjoy monopoly power over the marketplace. When such monopoly situations develop, governments step in and use regulations as a substitute for market forces to limit the market power exercised by the firm.

Portions of the public utility industry function under monopolistic conditions; a single provider is the most efficient way to serve consumers. Economists call this state of affairs a natural monopoly. A natural monopoly occurs when a single firm can supply a product or service to all buyers at a lower cost than would occur if two or more sellers tried to serve the market. In a natural monopoly, the average cost of production falls, as the firm benefits from economies of scale (Chandler 1990).

Decisions by the U.S. Supreme Court have recognized the beneficial outcomes of single provider operations in natural monopoly situations. However, they have also recognized that, without government oversight, a firm in a monopoly position may be tempted to raise prices above what the firm would probably charge if it were not operating in a monopoly condition. To make sure that overpricing does not occur, the courts have sanctioned the imposition of federal, state, and local controls over utility operations. While these controls are designed to guarantee that price gouging does not occur, they also ensure a steady source of the utility product and a reasonable, or "fair," rate of return for utility investors. Problems arise when federal and state utility commissioners and staff are required to determine the level of investment upon which to base the return, and what constitutes a "fair" rate of return. These topics are discussed in greater detail in the chapter on pricing.

THE BEGINNINGS OF UTILITY REGULATION

Utility regulations are the outgrowth of the many state railroad commissions formed after the Civil War to control what was seen as discriminatory pricing practices for shipping and storage of agricultural products. Those early state public utility commissions (PUCs) gradually extended their oversight operations to also control manufactured and natural gas, telegraph and telephone systems, water and wastewater treatment programs, and electric utilities. Today, some PUCs also regulate such diverse services as intrastate transportation, television cable companies, the shipping and storage activities of moving companies, and fuel oil sale and distribution, among other disparate public services.

Utility regulation at the federal level began with the Granger laws passed in the late 1800s to provide for interstate public oversight of the nation's railroads and related services, although it was not until the 1920s and 1930s that government regulation grew in scope to the point where it eventually reached into every aspect of the utility industry.

Federal regulation of public utilities has been traced to the year 1920, when Congress passed the Water Power Act, after a long and acrimonious battle. The Act set licensing requirements for the development of waterpower and included provisions for improvement of navigation on the nation's inland waterways. It also established rules for the use of public lands connected with such development. Its chief regulatory provisions, however, result from establishment of the Federal Power Commission (FPC). The Commission was given jurisdiction over all construction, operation, and maintenance of dams, water conduits, reservoirs, powerhouses, transmission lines, and other facilities association with the development, transmission, and use of hydroelectric power. The structure of the federal power commission was streamlined in 1930, with the appointment of a full-time board of five commissioners.

The Commission's jurisdiction applied to all navigable waters and public lands. The Act required everyone wanting to develop a power project to apply for a federal license, which was to remain in effect for a period no longer than fifty years. When it expired, the license could then be either renewed or the property be taken over by the government for its own use.

The federal regulatory system grew dramatically under the New Deal legislative program of President Franklin D. Roosevelt. The two pieces of legislation that had the greatest impact on utility regulation by the federal government were the Securities and Exchange Commission (SEC) Act of 1934 and the Public Utility Holding Company Act of 1935. Most of the regulations that were put in place during that period remain in effect today, although they have, in many instances, been revised extensively.

Modern government involvement in the regulation of the business practices of public utilities came into effect during the sweeping changes made during the 1930s. That trend in increased government oversight received a kick-start in the 1960s and 1970s, but this time tended to be more concerned with public health and safety. The Environmental Protection Agency (EPA) was established in December 1970, culminating a decade of growing public interest in their physical environment and public safety. Most of the regulatory laws passed after that landmark legislation, although often modified, still guide the U.S. public utilities. At the same time that government regulation was increasing, a movement toward greater privatization of utilities was underway in many of the developed countries. The conflicting influences of great regulation and privatization resulted in a reduction in the regulation of telecommunications and energy-related utilities. However, the water, wastewater and solid waste sectors of the utility industry saw an increase in regulation at the federal, state and often local levels of government. The energy sectors have always been predominantly investor-owned organizations and as such, enjoyed a more laissez faire approach to regulation. Moreover, at the same time that the EPA was being planned, the nation was faced with a shortage in oil and gas. Water and wastewater utilities, both of which are predominantly municipally owned, are concerned with maintenance of public health. As a result, their operations have long been closely watched by federal, state and local agencies.

FEDERAL REGULATION OF UTILITIES

The rationale for close regulation of public utilities rests in the concept of their being granted status as natural monopolies. As monopolies, as long as they met their service obligations utilities were protected from the power of market competition to control their prices. They are guaranteed the right to earn what the community believes is a reasonable profit. In return, laws and overseers are used to ensure that utility operators do not take advantage of that protection while continuing to provide a public service. Thus, all segments of the utility industry are affected by federal, state and local rules and regulations. Some of the more important federal regulations for the energy and water segments are discussed in the following pages.

Early Regulatory Actions

Four federal regulatory actions dealing with electric power were adopted during the 1930s. The first two were incorporated into the 1935 two-part law that (1) created federal regulation of wholesale dealings of electricity, and (2) established the Public Utility Holding Company Act (PUHCA). The PUHCA ordered changes in the governance of utilities and gave the Securities and Exchange Commission (SEC) control of utility financing. The PUHCA declared that all holding companies of gas and electric utilities were "affected with the national public interest because they sell their securities in interstate commerce and use the mails to transact business" (Glaeser 1957: 153).

An earlier law, the Securities Act of 1933, gave the federal government jurisdiction over issuance of all securities sold in interstate commerce. The Securities and Exchange Commission was established a year later with passage of the Securities and Exchange Act of 1934. The SEC was established with three main divisions: a Trading and Exchange Division, a Corporation Finance Division, and a Public Utilities Division.

The third set of actions established federal power supply systems. The two most important of these new federal systems were the Tennessee Valley Authority (TVA) and the Bonneville Power Administration (BPA). The fourth action provided low interest loans to cooperatives for developing power systems in rural areas, thus paving the way for the New Deal's rural electrification program.

Federal regulatory actions during the 1930s also involved the natural gas industry. A new law dealing with regulation of the gas industry was passed in 1938: the Natural Gas Act of 1938. The Federal Power Act and the Natural Gas Act expanded federal control over both energy industries by giving the commission power to regulate the rates and service of electric and gas utilities when their transactions are in interstate commerce.

The Public Utility Holding Company Act of 1935

Prior to the Great Depression that began with the stock market crash of 1929 the public utility industry was highly concentrated, with control in the hands of only a few multi-tiered holding companies. One of the largest of these was the holding company empire formed by Samuel Insull of Chicago. A small number of very large companies owned the controlling stock of other holding companies, which eventually owned one or more operating utilities. The pyramid of holding companies reached absurd heights; in one case the pyramid was six tiers high. The collapse of many of these pyramid empires during the Depression resulted in calls for stiff regulation—with some critics going so far as to call for government owner-ship of all utilities (Kent 1993).

Before the regulatory sweep of the New Deal, controlling utility holding companies was limited by problems inherent in the constitutional division of power between the states and the federal government. Because operat-ing companies tended to serve relatively small, homogeneous markets, regulating local utilities was seen as a local problem. As utilities grew, however, operating companies expanded across state lines or acquired operations far beyond their original service areas. To help finance that growth, holding companies were established. As they expanded, regulation remained almost exclusively in the hands of the states or, in some states, even to the municipalities in which the utilities operated. Decisions by the U.S. Supreme Court restricted state utility commissions from regulating holding companies that were engaged in interstate commerce. As a result, the transmission of electricity or natural gas from one state to another was interstate commerce which states could not directly regulate.

Utility holding companies were a product of the financial booms of the late 1800s. With cartels and trusts, they were a way of countering the effects of cut-throat competition and of using financial leverage to gain control of vast business empires. In a wave of mergers and acquisitions, holding company empires grew dramatically until the 1929 Crash. In 1926 alone, there were more than 1,000 utility mergers.

Two related reasons have been given for the growth of the holding company. First, the amount of cash needed to grow by acquiring other companies was greatly reduced. A controlling share of the voting stock was purchased, not the entire company. The purchase was usually made with borrowed money or from the proceeds from the flotation of new stock issues that established the holding company. The assets of the holding companies were the securities of other holding companies. Second, the income gained by the holding company at the peak of the pyramid was far greater than could be gained from operating one or a few utilities.

Investors employed the process of leveraging to finance their new holdings. With leveraging, relatively small investments and debt can often earn exceptionally high returns for investors. However, leveraging also increased the ratio of debt to equity to capitalize a firm. This created a situation that made it possible for the holding company scheme to collapse like a house of cards with the financial crisis of 1929.

When several of the nation's largest holding company empires collapsed after the stock market crash of 1929, subsequent federal investigations uncovered widespread corruption and shady dealings in utility financing, intracompany sales, bribery of local officials, and other unethical activities. These and other problems with the system resulted in passage of the Public Utility Holding Company Act (PUHCA). This Act was the most far-reaching federal regulatory legislation to be passed during the Great Depression. In the years since its passage, the utility industry and owners of utilities lobbied Congress heavily to repeal PUHCA, claiming that it was outdated. Their efforts finally succeeded in 2015 when the U.S. Congress failed to renew the law.

The holding company law was designed to eliminate problems associated with the practice of building layer upon layer of holding companies in the electric and gas energy industries. Under PUHCA, any company that owned or controlled 10 percent or more of the outstanding voting stock of a public utility company, or of a holding company of public utilities, had to register with the Securities and Exchange Commission.

Holding companies subject to SEC registration were required to limit their utility operations to a single integrated utility system. The holding company also had to divest itself of any operations that did not functionally relate to the operation of the utility. SEC approval was required for nearly all financial and business activities of registered holding companies. SEC registration had to include copies of the firm's articles of incorporation, partnership agreements, bylaws, mortgages, underwriting arrangements, and voting trust agreements. Registration also required full disclosure of the firm's financial structure, names of all officers and directors, any contracts for materials, services, or construction, explanations of bonus and profit sharing arrangements, and consolidated balance sheets and comparable information (Kent 1993).

The SEC was given power to approve only those securities which it felt were "reasonable," and which were adapted to the firm's existing financial structure. Approved securities had to reflect both the earning power of the holding company and be shown to be necessary to promote the economical and efficient operation of the utility. Fees and commissions for the sale of securities also had to be "reasonable." Prior to the 1929 Crash, underwriting of utility securities issues had been an extremely lucrative business for a select few investment banking houses, most of which were headquartered in New York. A few underwriters charged fees as high as 50 percent of the value of the issue. For securities to be sold after 1934, the SEC had to be able to establish that the terms and conditions were not detrimental to the interests of the general public, the firms' investors, or to operating company consumers.

REGULATING THE ELECTRIC POWER INDUSTRY

The Public Utility Regulatory Policies Act of 1978 (PURPA) represented the most far-reaching body of changes to the utility regulatory system since the Holding Company Act in 1935. One of the primary goals of PURPA was to ease the nation's dependence upon foreign energy sources. PURPA required the new Federal Energy Regulatory Commission (FERC) to provide incentives for the development of cogeneration facilities and small power generating facilities (less than 80 megawatts capacity) that use renewable fuels, including biomass, wind power, geothermal, and other fuels.

The small and alternative fuel generating facilities named in PURPA are known as *Qualifying Facility* (QF) generating units and are exempt from certain holding company regulations. In addition to receiving some rate benefits, QFs are exempt from most provisions of the Federal Power Act of 1992 (FPA). For a cogeneration unit to qualify as a qualifying facility, it must produce useful thermal energy as well as electricity. The energy can be used in industrial or commercial processes and for heating and cooling. The output must make up a stated percentage of the user's total energy consumption and meet established energy efficiency standards.

A QF is eligible to receive two major benefits. First, they are exempt from federal and state controls on ownership and from the prices and terms they can charge for their generated power. Second, utilities must purchase electricity generated by a QF at a price based on the utility's *avoided cost*, and the utility must sell back-up power to the QF on a non-discriminatory basis. Avoided cost refers to the incremental cost of electricity which, except for the QF, the utility would have to pay to generate the power itself or buy from another source. QFs and a utility can also negotiate rates that are below that of the utility's avoided cost. Furthermore, as a result of changes to the law made in 1978, any electrical generating operation considered a Qualifying Facility under FERC regulations is not considered to be a utility company under PUHCA rules, and can therefore be owned by a holding company.

The Energy Policy Act of 1992

The Energy Policy Act of 1992 (EPAct) provided an additional incentive for developing small generating facilities. These facilities do not have to quality as QFs for benefits if all their produced energy is sold for resale rather than to end users; this type of facility is termed an Exempt Wholesale Generator (EWG). EPAct permitted EWGs to own and operate non-qualifying generating facilities, without the units being subject to PUHCA registration and regulation. The incentives for developing small power plants may end soon, however. Congress has been considering repealing the PUHCA, and amending PURPA to limit the rule that requires public utilities to purchase QF and EWG power.

The Federal Power Act of 1992

Under the Federal Power Act, also enacted in 1992, the FERC was authorized to regulate electricity transmission and the sale of wholesale electric energy in interstate commerce. FERC regulation was expanded to include approval of the disposition of utility property, sales of securities, and regulation of the rates, terms, and conditions for the transmission or sale of electric energy in wholesale markets. FERC also regulates interlocking directorates and imposes a uniform system of accounts and reporting requirements.

Three subsequent FERC developments have had a significant impact on the transmission segment of the power industry. FERC issued orders 888 and 889 in the summer of 1996, and order 2000 in December 1999. Orders 888 and 889 called for the utilities under its jurisdiction to unbundle generation and transmission functions (organizations such as the Bonneville Power Administration and TVA are not subject to FERC jurisdiction). Under Order 888, transmission-owning utilities were required to adopt open access and non-discriminatory pricing for their transmission services, including generator interconnection. Order 889 required transmission-owning utilities to publish information about the availability of transmission capacity and make that capacity available to anyone. The orders also set forth operational requirements for a new institution in the system, the Independent System Operator (ISO). ISOs were given the authority to operate the transmission systems formerly operated by vertically integrated utilities.

Regional Transmission Organizations

Order 2000 further refined the way the nation's transmission institutions were to function. The order required utilities with transmission systems (grids) to either enter into an agreement with an ISO, or to join another new organization, a Regional Transmission Organization (RTO). The RTO would then control the company's transmission facilities. Order 2000 also spelled out governance procedures for RTOs. Compliance with the ISO/RTO directives has been irregular; many state governments have objected to the concept, and have successfully fought divestiture of transmission facilities.

The United States is divided into 15 separate regional transmission territories, almost all of which include more than one state. As of 2003, five of the new RTOs were functioning: only the New York, New England, Midwest, California, and the PJM (Pennsylvania, New Jersey, Maryland) RTOs were fully organized and operational.

In addition to setting up the ISO/RTO concepts, the FERC attempted to bring order to the transmission sector by introducing what they term a Standard Market Design (SMD). The SMD clarifies the rights and obligations of owners and users of the interstate transmission grid. The objective of the SMD is to form a set of standard rules for the following purposes:

- To allow transmission-owning utilities to develop a revised tariff schedule.
- To establish a system for allocating transmission capacity.
- To determine how transmission capacity will be allocated given system constraints.
- To coordinate system upgrades and allocation of the costs of the upgrades.
- To allocate costs for constructing special facilities needed to interconnect generators to the grid.
- And other transmission-related issues.

REGULATING THE NATURAL GAS INDUSTRY

Despite several decades of successful implementation of segments of the U.S. natural gas arm of the energy industry, this sector remains subject to extensive regulation by federal, state, and local governments. More than one federal agency exercises some degree of control over exploration, drilling, and interstate pipeline transmission activities.

Government regulation of the natural gas industry began with passage of the Natural Gas Act of 1938 (NGA). This legislation gave the Federal Power Commission the right to regulate interstate sales for resale of gas purchases by pipelines from producers. From its inception, the Commission required that natural gas sales take place under long-term contracts for dedicated reserves. Prices were set by the commission and were based on average production costs in several different regions. As a result, lowest cost producers benefited disproportionately, which in turn provided incentives for all producers to lower their costs, thus driving the price of gas down for everyone.

The goal of the Commission was to see that prices remained stable, in line with prices charged ten years earlier. This system remained effective until the 1970s, when energy shocks in 1972, 1974, 1978, and 1980 resulted in price increases of 20 percent per year for unregulated natural gas. Very quickly, price controls on regulated gas caused shortages which, in turn, caused losses by consumers in excess of $23 billion, and producers' losses greater than $44 billion (MacAvoy 2000).

The Federal Energy Regulatory Commission, which replaced the Federal Power Commission, was placed under control of the new Department of Energy. The Commission was charged with coming up with a plan that eliminated shortages without causing excessive price increases. Passage of the Natural Gas Policy Act of 1978 (NGPA) was the first salvo in the government's efforts to deregulate the natural gas industry. Price controls were to be phased out on new production but remained in effect for large segments of the industry. Although the Act identified more than 30 different classifications of natural gas, only three of the classifications were deregulated. The most important of these were new production and high cost production, types that fell under a larger scheme based on depth and location (on or offshore production). Prices of offshore gas sold after April 20, 1977, were decontrolled. Onshore new gas was decontrolled only if it came from wells 1000-feet deeper than existing wells in the field.

The NGPA was part of the plan of the administration of President Jimmy Carter to make the country less dependent upon foreign energy sources. Elimination of controls on wellhead prices—scheduled by NGPA to occur over six years—was seen as a way to encourage greater production. At the time, gas supplies were short and little new exploration was taking place. Gas producers were reluctant to sell gas to interstate pipelines, which were subject to price controls. Instead, producers targeted sales to nearby intrastate distributors and industrial users that were not subject to federal price controls.

A consequence of price controls at the time was a decline in interstate reserves. This, in turn, produced shortages in the old industrial northeast and far west portions of the country. Many industries moved south to take advantage of uncontrolled gas supplies. Over the first four years after passage of the NGPA, the volume of gas reserves under contract for interstate shipment increased dramatically. Passage of the Fuel Use Act in 1979 restricted growth in industrial usage by requiring power plants to use coal or nuclear fuel instead of natural gas for all new generation capacity. The shortages in the northeast and far west disappeared, and the flight of industry to the south ended.

Deregulation in the natural gas industry began in earnest in 1985 when the Federal Energy Regulatory Commission took steps to restructure the buyers–seller relationships within the producing, transmission, and distribution portions of the industry. Prior to this time, gas was traditionally sold by pipeline companies to local distributors in a gas-plus-transportation package priced for delivery at "the city gate." Pipeline companies purchased gas from producers at the wellhead, collected and stored, and, if necessary, processed the gas to remove impurities. The city gate delivery price included the cost of these services.

The Natural Gas Wellhead Decontrol Act of 1989

FERC Order 436 issued in 1985 was the first attempt to unbundle gas and transportation. Under an open access rule, wholesale buyers and large industrial users of gas could buy their gas directly from the producer, bypassing the pipeline companies. The orders also enabled buyers to purchase space in pipelines for shipment of their gas at published FERC regulated prices. To deal with some still unresolved issues, four years later Congress passed the Natural Gas Wellhead Decontrol Act of 1989. This Act called for removal of all controls on wellhead gas pricing by January 1993. This meant that gas purchasers could from then on negotiate with producers for the best price possible from any producer.

FPA Regulation of Pipelines

As fracturing activities produce more and more natural gas, regulation is exercised over activities that do not involve construction of interstate pipelines. However, interstate pipeline rates, terms, and conditions remain subject to FERC oversight. The Federal Power Act of 1992 gave the FERC jurisdiction over the transportation and storage of natural gas in interstate commerce. At the state and local levels, agencies and commissions regulate drilling, production, and processing activities. Each state has its own licensing, permitting, and bonding requirements, as well as its own system for enforcing local rules and regulations, assessing fines for perceived discrepancies, and for valuing properties for taxation purposes.

Pipeline companies were still permitted to follow their old system, and many still provided gas to wholesale customers as they had for years. That system ended completely in 1992, when FERC Order 636 took unbundling of the industry to its final position: pipelines from then on could only offer transportation. Transportation prices remained under FERC regulation, however. Pipeline firms offer prices for spot (interruptible), short-term, and long-term space in their pipelines.

Deregulation Developments

A result of deregulation of a portion of the gas industry in the 1970s and 1980s, together with availability of gas from new Canadian sources, resulted in an oversupply of gas for most of the decade of the 1990s. Prices dropped accordingly. That glut and low prices resulted in many industry conversions to gas from other, dirtier or more expensive fuels, and a major market expansion effort by gas distributors. A new technology developed by the Boeing Company for aviation use—the gas turbine—made it possible to quickly construct small, efficient, gas turbine powered electric generators almost anywhere. Gas turbine generators are the first choice for the addition of peak-period power generating capacity.

These developments resulted in a rapid run-up in the consumption of natural gas, so much so that soon a shortage replaced the former glut. As a result, gas prices increased dramatically over the first years of the twenty-first century. Once again gas producers began looking for additional supplies, including applying the fracturing process to old wells. The distribution utilities considered the most promising of these alternative supplies to be imported liquefied natural gas. Other alternative fuels examined include synthetic natural gas and coal gas (Costello and Burns 2003). By the end of the decade, however, the industry found itself with a surplus of gas; fracturing had put an end to importation of LNG and, instead, the industry developing liquefying facilities for exporting rather than importing LNG.

REGULATING WATER AND WASTEWATER UTILITIES

Other than laws pertaining to water rights, the foundation of regulation of the operations of water utilities is the Safe Drinking Water Act of 1974 (SDWA). A list of the major water laws in the U.S. is shown in Table 3.1. The provisions of the SDW law are managed by the Federal Environmental Protection Agency (EPA) with monitoring utilities' operations under the

Table 3.1 Selected environmental protection and water pollution legislation, 1948–1990

Year	Act	Public Law No.
1948	Federal Water Pollution Act	P. L. 80–845
1956	Federal Water Pollution Control Act Amendments	P. L. 84–660
1961	Federal Water Pollution Control Act Amendments	P. L. 87–88
1965	Water Quality Act	P. L. 89–234
1966	Clean Water Restoration Act	P. L.89–753
1969	National Environmental Policy Act	P. L. 91–190
1970	Water Quality Improvement Act	P. L. 91–224*
1972	Federal Water Pollution Control Act (Clean Water Act)	P. L. 92–500
1974	Safe Drinking Water Act	P. L. 93–523
1977	Safe Drinking Water Act Amendments	P. L. 95–190
1977	Clean Water Act Amendments	P. L. 95–217
1978	Great Lakes Water Quality Agreement (amended)	P. L. 101–596
1980	Safe Drinking Water Act Amendments	P. L. 96–502
1981	Municipal Wastewater Treatment Grants Amendments	P. L. 97–117
1986	Safe Drinking Water Act Amendments	P. L. 99–339
1987	Water Quality Act of 1987	P. L. 100–4
1990	Oil Pollution Act (amended Clean Water Act)	P. L. 101–380
1990	Water Resources Development Act	P. L. 101–640
1996	Safe Drinking Water Act Amendments	P. L. 104–482
2011	Reduction of Lead in Drinking Water Act	P. L. 111–380

Notes: * Available sources assign the same Public Law number to both acts.

Source: Data from EPA and other sources.

provisions of the law generally left to the states. Additional and often more onerous regulation of water utilities is administered by state environmental and public health agencies. Box 3.1 describes the early formation of the EPA in 1970 and how its many and varied responsibilities were first brought together.

The Safe Drinking Water Act

The objective of the Safe Drinking Water Act was protection of public health by regulating the nation's public drinking water supply. The law required the U.S. Environmental Protection Agency (EPA) to set national health standards for drinking water to protect against naturally occurring and human-made contaminants. The law has been amended twice, the first

BOX 3.1   BIRTH OF THE ENVIRONMENTAL PROTECTION
           AGENCY

The components of the new agency proposed by President Richard Nixon in his
July 9, 1971 message to Congress were pieced together from various programs
at other departments to form a new agency responsible for all aspects of environmental protection, the Environmental Protection Agency (EPA). From the
Department of Health, Education and Welfare (HEW) came several special function bodies: the National Air Pollution Control Administration, the bureaus of Water
Hygiene and Solid Waste Management, and some functions of the Bureau of
Radiological Health. The Food and Drug Administration of HEW gave to EPA
control over pesticide tolerance levels. The Department of the Interior contributed
the Federal Water Quality Administration and portions of its pesticide research
responsibilities. EPA also gained functions including pesticide registration from the
Department of Agriculture. From the Atomic Energy Commission and the Federal
Radiation Council, the new agency gained responsibility for radiation criteria and
standards.

   Two of these programs—HEW's National Air Pollution Control Administration
(NAPCA) and Interior's Water Quality Administration (FWQA)—represented the
core of the federal government's pollution-control activities. The air program,
founded in 1955 in reaction to such problems as the blanket of smog covering
greater Los Angeles; the 1948 atmospheric inversion that temporarily raised the
death rate in Donora, PA, by 400 percent; a London "fog" in 1952 that killed 4,000
people over a four-day period. Equally severe water pollution problems—untreated
sewage and industrial waste, dying rivers and lakes—led to the founding of the
predecessor of the FWQA in 1948.

   Originally, NAPCA was a research body with no regulatory powers. Only after
the Clean Air Act of 1963 was enacted did NAPCA gain enforcement authority to
attack interstate air pollution problems. Two years later, the Act was amended to
permit NAPCA to set air pollution standards for new motor vehicles. In reality,
however, little effective use was made of these powers in the 1960s, and they were
further diluted by the Air Quality Act of 1967, which re-emphasized the principle of
state and local control over air pollution. FWQA began in the Public Health Service
of HEW but was transferred to Interior in 1966 when it was authorized to give
technical assistance to states and localities and to distribute construction grants
for municipal waste treatment programs. Like NAPCA, FWQA gained enforcement
and standard-setting powers in the 1960s.

Source: Lewis (1985).

in 1986 and again in 1996. The 1996 amendment recognized source water
protection, operator training, funding for water system improvements and
for public information as important components of a safe drinking water
system. SDWA applies to every public water system in the nation. The only
systems excluded are those with fewer than 15 service connections or which
serve fewer than 25 customers per day for at least 60 days of the year. At the

end of the twentieth century, more than 170,000 public water systems fell under SDWA jurisdiction. Most of the regulatory oversight of water systems is carried out by state drinking water programs. States are able to apply to the EPA for "primacy," which is the authorization to implement and control SDWA programs within their jurisdictions, provided they can show that their standards are at least as stringent as the federal standards. They must also ensure that all their water systems meet those requirements. Only Wyoming and the District of Columbia had not received primacy status by 2000.

Water standards are established through a three-step process. First, EPA identifies harmful water contaminants. Second, EPA determines a maximum goal for each contaminant, below which there is no known or expected risk to health. Third, EPA specifies a maximum permissible contaminant level for drinking water delivered to any customer of a public water system. These levels are enforceable standards and are set as close to the goals as possible. EPA also proposes appropriate treatment techniques. Water utilities must follow EPA standards and provide an annual report of their progress, including measurements of all listed contaminants found in their water supplies.

Regulating Wastewater Utilities

The Clean Water Act (CWA) establishes the basic structure for regulating discharges of pollutants into the waters of the United States and regulating quality standards for surface waters. The basis of the CWA was enacted in 1948 as the Federal Water Pollution Control Act, but the Act was significantly reorganized and expanded in 1972. *Clean Water Act* became the Act's common name with amendments in 1972. The CWA functions as the foundation for the subsequent regulation of all wastewater utilities, and includes control over discharge into the nation's waterways.

The individual states have also enacted legislation that controls wastewater treatment and discharge. The Clean Water Act established rules regulating the discharge of pollutants into the waters of the nation. Utilities must file for wastewater and storm water discharge permits for wastewater and runoff at some of their facilities. They must also monitor and control such discharges. In addition, many utilities are required to maintain spill prevention and countermeasure programs. The CWA was passed after the public became alerted to the fact that the nation's rivers and lakes were rapidly becoming polluted, and that many wetlands were drying up; other irreplaceable wetlands were disappearing under real estate developments. Wetlands came to be recognized as valuable areas that filter and strain harmful pollutants from the water, provide flood control during storms, and provide vital habitat for plants and animals (EPA 2016a).

The Clean Water Act

Under Clean Water Act rules, individual states are required to monitor the Total Maximum Daily Loads (TMDLs) of a variety of substances and chemicals in their waterways. In addition, states must ensure that water does not exceed the TMDLs set forth in the Act. Not all states have the ability to comply with these provisions. For those that do not, the EPA is supposed to perform the service. However, because the EPA is also limited in what it can do, this section of the Act usually is not implemented (Bellenger 2002).

The Clean Water Act has been modified several times since its passage. A 1981 change improved the capabilities of treatment plants constructed under a city grants program. Changes in 1987, however, eliminated the grants program, substituting the State Water Pollution Control Revolving Fund (also called the Clean Water State Revolving Fund), which used EPA-state partnerships to fund projects. A 2003 EPA announcement provided the following summary of the Clean Water Act's focus:

> Evolution of CWA programs over the past decade has . . . included something of a shift from program-by-program, source-by-source, and pollutant-by-pollutant approach to more holistic watershed-based strategies. Under the watershed approach equal emphasis is placed on protecting healthy waters and restoring impaired ones. A full array of issues are addressed, not just those subject to CWA regulatory authority. Involvement of stakeholder groups in the development and implementation of strategies for achieving and maintaining state water quality and other environmental goals is another hallmark of this approach. (EPA 2016a)

Under CWA rules, it is unlawful to discharge any pollutant into navigable waters, unless a permit is obtained. EPA's National Pollutant Discharge Elimination System (NPDES). This program controls discharges from such sources as pipes or man-made ditches. Individual homes do not need an NPDES permit; however, industrial, municipal, and other facilities must obtain permits if their discharges go directly to surface waters. The EPA, with the U.S. Army Corps of engineers was unsuccessful in a 2015 attempt to expand control over selected streams, tributaries and wetlands. A North Dakota federal judge issued an injunction against the proposal. The law suit was brought by thirteen states: North and South Dakota, Alaska, Arizona, Arkansas, Colorado, Idaho, Missouri, Montana, Nebraska, New Mexico, Nevada, and Wyoming.

REGULATING THE SOLID WASTE SECTOR

The broadly-based Resource Conservation and Recovery Act of 1976 (RCRA) was enacted to protect human health and the environment from the potential dangers of waste disposal, conserve energy and natural resources, reduce the amount of waste generated by people and industries, and ensure that all wastes were managed in an environmentally sound manner (EPA 2013b). Section D of the law regulates management of non-hazardous solid waste and sets minimum standards and guidelines for waste disposal, including waste disposal sites. Section D regulates handling and disposal of the following materials:

- Garbage (municipal solid waste), including disposal methods;
- Refuse, such as metal scrap, wall board, and empty boxes, crates and containers;
- Sludge from waste treatment plants, water supply plants, and pollution control facilities;
- Non-hazardous industrial waste, including process wastewater and nonwastewater sludge and solids; and
- Other discarded materials, including solids, semisolids, liquid or contained gaseous materials resulting from industrial and commercial activities. Also included are wastes from mining, oil and gas production, construction and demolition, medical operations, agriculture and household hazardous wastes.

The 1984 Hazardous and Solid Waste Amendments to Section D of the RCRA Act established a framework for planning and implementing federal, state and local level standards for municipal solid waste landfills. EPA regulations of the water, wastewater, and solid waste sectors of the public utilities industry continue to be proposed and implemented. In 2015, for example, the EPA was collecting information from interested parties on revisions or amendments to the Toxic Substances Control Act of 1976 and the reporting requirements criteria for classification of solid waste disposal facilities and practices contained in the Resource Conservation and Recovery Act.

PUBLIC TRANSIT REGULATION

Regulation of heavy rail, light rail, and bus transit operations in the United States are monitored and administered by several different agencies; several of the most important are the U.S. Department of

Transportation (DOT), the Federal Transit Administration (FTA), and the Federal Railroad Administration (FRA). The mission of the DOT is ensuring a fast, safe, efficient, accessible and convenient transportation system. The federal government, through the FTA, provides financial assistance to develop new transit systems and improve, maintain, and operate existing systems. The FTA oversees grants to state and local transit providers, primarily through its ten regional offices. These grantees are responsible for managing their programs in accordance with federal requirements, and the FTA is responsible for ensuring that grantees follow federal mandates along with statutory and administrative requirements. The FRA establishes and enforces heavy-rail safety regulations; administers railroad assistance programs, conducts research and development in support of improved railroad safety and national rail transportation policy, and administers government rail transportation programs. Some of the major federal transit regulation legislation and the dates they were adopted are (FTA 2015a):

- 1964: Congress passed the Urban Mass Transportation Act, the nation's first comprehensive public mass transportation. Included are buses, subways, light rail, commuter rail, monorail, passenger ferry boats, trolleys, inclined railways, and people movers.
- 1990: The Americans with Disabilities Act of 1990 (ADA) required transit agencies to provide service accessible to persons with disabilities.
- 1990: The Clean Air Act Amendments of 1990 recast transportation planning to provide for improved air quality.
- 1991: The Federal Transit Act Amendments of 1991, Title III of the Intermodal Surface Transportation Efficiency Act of 1991 (ISTEA) extended public transportation assistance through FY 1997, increased the amounts authorized, re-named the transit law the Federal Transit Act and the Urban Mass Transportation Administration the Federal Transit Administration.
- 1991: The Omnibus Transportation Employee Testing Act of 1991 mandated the establishment of anti-drug and alcohol misuse programs for safety-sensitive employees of recipients and contractors to recipients of public transportation funds.
- 1992: The Energy Policy Act of 1992 increased the tax-free amount of the public transportation commuter fringe benefit to $60 per month with an inflation provision, and extended the benefit to vanpools.
- 1994: The Federal Transit Act was codified as Title 49, Chapter 53— Mass Transportation, of the United States Code.

- 1997: Intermodal Surface Transportation Efficiency Act of 1991 (ISTEA) was extended through March 31, 1998.
- 1998: The Federal Transit Act of 1998, Title III of the Transportation Equity Act for the 21st Century (TEA 21) extended the public transportation program through 2003. TEA 21 increased public transportation funding authorizations. A total of $41 billion was authorized for the six-year period, of which $36 billion was guaranteed. Guaranteed amounts are protected in the budget process and can only be appropriated for public transportation uses, but remain subject to annual appropriation by the Congress.
- 2012: The Federal Public Transportation Law reauthorized public transportation, Federal-aid highway, and highway safety programs for fiscal years 2013 and 2014.

The FTA also has environmental protection responsibilities, as established by the National Environmental Policy Act (NEPA) of 1969. Many different federal laws, rules, and regulations govern environmental reviews of all federally assisted mass transportation projects. NEPA establishes a process for coordinating compliance with these laws by the requirement to prepare an Environmental Impact Statement (EIS) for all major transportation actions significantly affecting the environment. Other special purpose statutes and procedures may apply as well, depending on specific circumstances, for example, protective measures for historic properties, wetlands, floodplains, and so on. If related environmental review requirements apply, they are to be undertaken as part of the NEPA compliance process. Many of the policies followed as a result of passage of NEPA are the result of actions supported by the environmental citizens group, the Natural Resources Defense Council (NRDC). This group has been particularly successful in the nation's actions to ensure the safety and sustainability of the U.S.'s water resources.

STATE AND LOCAL UTILITY REGULATION

State regulations occur on four different levels. One, the states are the only regulators of some business operations, such as business licensing (sometimes referred to as *charters*), insurance, workers' compensation, and occupational licensing, such as for real estate sales. Two, the states share some level of regulation with the federal government. This occurs most often where the demarcation between intrastate and interstate business blurs, such as with telecommunications, some transportation activities, and the public utility industry. Three, state agencies are often the implementers of federal regulation and standards, such as occupational safety and environmental programs, where states are often permitted to seek different ways of implementing federal programs. Finally, the states sometimes share overlapping jurisdictions with the federal government. Examples of areas where this occurs include such programs as consumer protection, advertising regulation, and some financial regulatory programs (Teske 2003).

Individual states have long had the authority to regulate the activities of public utilities that operate within their borders. This authority includes power to regulate rates charged and the financial activities of utilities. The federal government also assigned states the authority to implement the regulations set forth by PURPA. Distribution utilities purchase their power from independent producers. Power purchases are thus a part of the utility's cost structure. Operating costs are a major component in the construction of the rates paid by retail consumers. Operating costs are also included in the compilation of the PUC-established rate of return utilities are allowed. The *Wall Street Journal* article discussed in Box 3.2 illustrates the power of local utility regulators to shape the operations of public utilities.

Under normal conditions, public utilities pass the cost of purchasing

---

BOX 3.2   DISTRICT REGULATORS BLOCK SALE OF UTILITY HOLDING COMPANIES

On August 26, 2015, the Public Service Commission (PSC) of the District of Columbia rejected Exelon Corporation's $6.8 billion bid to purchase Pepco Holdings, Inc. after regulators in Delaware, Maryland, New Jersey and Virginia had approved the proposal. The Federal Energy Regulatory Commission had also approved the deal. The PSC regulates utilities in Washington, DC, where Pepco is based, and was the last regulatory body's appeal needed to allow the deal to come to fruition.

Exelon owns a large number of modern power plants and distribution utilities that serve the Chicago, Philadelphia and Baltimore metropolitan areas. Pepco owns electric utilities in Maryland, Delaware, New Jersey, and the nation's capital.

In announcing their decision, Regulators in DC said they were unhappy with the management structure that would result from the merger of the two firms. They added that the new company would "diminish Pepco's influence and make [the commission's] job of regulating the utility more difficult." They also said they believed that "a conflict of interest at the company could prevent Pepco from becoming a cleaner and greener utility that uses more renewable energy . . . and that management redundancy could constrain Pepco from adapting to current changes in the energy industry."

Source: Sweet (2015: B6).

power from an independent power producer, including power purchased from a QF or from a EWG, through to its retail customers. However, some state public utility commissions do not always allow full reimbursement to a utility for the purchase of this, often higher-priced, QF power. In one sense, this has negated the objective of the FERC to support development of non-traditional generating facilities. Some states consider QFs and EWGs to be public utilities and subject to state PUC regulation. PUC control includes requiring a certificate of public convenience and necessity, and regulation of organizational, accounting, financial, and other corporate matters. States also exercise control over siting and building generating facilities and over the sales of securities and asset transfer.

DEREGULATION OR RE-REGULATION?

For more than a century, deregulation has been a preeminent policy in the regulatory, economic, and political environments of businesses both in the United States and abroad. As a result, less than 6 percent of American business is now affected by some form of direct regulation; in 1975, more than 16 percent of the U.S. economy was covered by government regulation. As the following statement suggests, except for the utility industry, policy has shifted dramatically away from economic regulation of business:

> The dominant view about much economic regulation . . . is that it was either a bad idea from the start or a practice that failed over time, except in cases of ongoing monopoly power that required ongoing regulation. (Teske 2003: 294)

Since the 1970s, the rationale underlying utility regulation in the United States and elsewhere has been undergoing extensive revision. Efforts to deregulate the utility industry followed a trend toward smaller and less intrusive government, privatization of government owned businesses, and freeing management from many restrictive rules and regulations that seemed to be stifling economic growth. The deregulation movement was brought to a rapid slowdown in 2002 and 2003, however, after problems in California's deregulation program resulted in alleged price gouging and the bankruptcies of firms like Pacific Gas and Electric (PG&E) and Enron, among others. As a result of this crisis, a number of changes in the way energy markets are regulated have been proposed at both the federal and state levels. A number of states have put their proposed deregulation proposals on hold. Congress failed to pass the 2003 Energy Act. Before California's experience in 2000, deregulation of the power industry was proceeding rapidly; from 1995 to 2000, fully half of the states chose to deregulate. Since the California and Enron problems, there is great uncertainty in the future scope and scale of utility regulation. The pace of utility deregulation has slowed significantly, as failure to pass the 2003 energy bill illustrates.

SUMMARY

Public utilities are subject to a wide variety of local, state, and federal government regulations. These regulations deal with ownership and governance, raising capital, transactions between company units, environment, the methods of producing utility products, health and safety issues, environmental concerns, and many other aspects of utility operations. As "natural monopolies," utilities are considered to be legitimately subject to government oversight.

Utility regulation at the federal level began with the Granger laws passed in the late 1800s. In the 1920s and 1930s, government regulation grew to where it eventually reached into every aspect of the industry. Modern federal regulation of utilities first appeared in 1920, when Congress passed the Federal Water Power Act. The Act set licensing requirements for the development of waterpower and included provisions for improvement of navigation on inland waterways. It also established the Federal Power Commission (FPC), which was given jurisdiction over all construction, operation, and maintenance of dams, water conduits, reservoirs, powerhouses, transmission lines, and facilities associated with development, transmission, and use of hydroelectric power.

The federal regulatory system grew dramatically under President Franklin D. Roosevelt. The two pieces of federal legislation that had the greatest impact on utility regulation were the Securities and Exchange Commission (SEC) Act of 1934 and the Public Utility Holding Company Act of 1935. SEC approval was required for nearly all financial and business activities of registered holding companies. Holding companies required to register with the SEC in this way had to limit their utility operations to a single integrated utility system, while divesting themselves of any operations that were not functionally related to the operation of that utility. In 2015, this law was allowed to die when Congress did not approve its renewal.

Since the 1970s, the rationale underlying utility regulation in the United States and elsewhere has been undergoing extensive revision. Over the last quarter-century, deregulation of the utility industry has dominated policymakers' thinking. This follows a trend toward smaller and less intrusive government, privatization of government owned businesses, and freeing management from many restrictive rules and regulations.

ADDITIONAL READING

Bauer, John (2010), *Effective Regulation of Public Utilities*. Boston: Gale (Cengage Learning).

Hempling, Scott (2015), *Regulating Public Utility Performance: The Law of Market Structure, Pricing and Jurisdiction*. Chicago: American Bar Association.

MacAvoy, Paul W. (2000), *The Natural Gas Market: Sixty Years of Regulation and Deregulation*. New Haven: Yale University Press.

Morgan, C.S. (2010), *Regulation and the Management of Public Utilities*. Boston: Gale (Cengage Learning).

Robinson, Colin (ed.) (2007), *Utility Regulation in Competitive Markets: Problems and Progress*. Cheltenham, UK and Northampton, MA, USA: Edward Elgar Publishing.

PART II

Sectors of the public utility industry

4. Electric energy utilities

A few minutes after 4:00 pm, Eastern Daylight Time, on the afternoon of August 14, 2003, an enormous electricity blackout hit much of the eastern United States and Canada. A section of North America with something like 50 million people was suddenly and completely without electric power. In little more than half an hour, nearly 62,000 megawatts of electricity had fallen off-line. Affected were the Canadian Province of Ontario and the states of Connecticut, Massachusetts, Michigan, New Jersey, New York, Ohio, Pennsylvania, and Vermont. In some areas, the power was out for two full days; parts of Ontario suffered rolling blackouts for more than a week before full restoration of power (McCann 2004).

An investigation under the direction of a joint U.S. and Canadian task force reported that the power outage was probably caused by the failure of the Ohio grid operator to adequately control tree growth in its transmission rights-of-way. This was cited as the cause of an outage of three local transmission lines over 36 minutes beginning at 3:05 p.m. EDT. This caused congestion overloads on other parts of the grid. In addition, the grid regulators failed to diagnose the problem in time to avoid the loss at 4:06 p.m. of an overloaded major transmission line. Loss of this line, in turn, resulted in too heavy loads placed on other lines. To avoid permanent damage to the grid and related equipment, automatic shutdowns fell into place across the entire interconnected grid. By 4:13 p.m., the blackout was complete.

Why the blackout occurred is as much a result of the fundamental nature of electricity as it is any other reason. The most important feature is known as *loop flow*. Loop flow means that electricity takes all available routes to get from one point to another; the flow of electricity across a transmission network cannot economically be directed along a particular line. When one line is shut down for any reason, as occurred in Ohio in 2003, electricity continues to flow across all available transmission lines. This can cause overloads on the other lines, which are themselves then shut down to avoid damage to the system. Moreover, loop flow means that the use of the transmission grid by any one generator or power customer has an effect on the amount of transmission capacity available to all users. This is why the FERC requires that transmission systems be constantly monitored. Monitoring is particularly important when all parts of the system are congested. This occurs on hot summer afternoons when air conditioning demand is high. This is what happened on that hot August afternoon.

Another particularity of electricity is that it cannot be economically stored. Power must be used as it is produced, and produced as it is used. However, the capacity of all transmission lines in the national grid has an absolute upper limit. The transmission grid must have sufficient capacity to move the generated electricity to load or demand centers. Insufficient capacity results in line overloads. When overloads happen, automatic safeguards shut down generators. Personnel charged with monitoring the grid must ensure that the system is always balanced within a narrow band of tolerances.

THE CHANGING ENERGY INDUSTRY

The use of electric power for lighting purposes was first put to a test in 1858 when an arc lamp was installed in a lighthouse near Dover, England. Arc lights were far brighter than gas streetlights. It was not long before civic leaders saw the advantages of using arc lights to illuminate their alleys and streets, and contracts were negotiated with new entrepreneurs to rig and operate municipal lighting systems. The first manufacturers of electrical equipment in the United States began by constructing arc light equipment; they also formed the companies that operated the new systems. Soon, small generators located in storefront power stations generated power for municipal streetlight systems. Private companies were granted licenses to string power lines on poles installed on the public right of way; this became the standard means of distributing power within municipalities (Bryant and Dethloff 1990).

The electric power industry is in the last stages of radical change. Historically, regulated investor-owned utilities served specified markets under exclusive franchise. State regulators monitored operations and regulated rates, approving only the rates that they believed were the lowest possible prices for consumers while still granting the utilities a "fair" rate of return on their investment. The service areas of regulated utilities were usually restricted to either (1) a single region within a given state, (2) more than one region but in contiguous areas outside the state, or (3) both. The vertically integrated utilities, in turn, were required to provide electric services to any and all customers in their areas of operation and to maintain extra capacity ready to bring online at any moment it was needed.

For many years, this system worked just fine. However, the fuel price shocks and shortages that occurred during the 1970s ushered in changes that are still going on today. The monopolistic, tightly regulated utilities created under New Deal trust-busting legislation more than 60 years ago are becoming increasingly exposed to competition, particularly in the generation and wholesale power markets. Even greater changes were brought about by the National Energy Policy Act (NEP) of 1992. Passage of this bill brought deregulation and restructuring of the industry to front stage. Box 4.1 illustrates how these forces changed one formerly vertically integrated utility in the state of Texas.

The shocks that occurred in the nonregulated power marketing and trading field during 2000 and 2001 in California resulted in cessation of the move toward deregulation in that state. Nonetheless, industry analysts expect that, over the long term, there will be a revival of heightened competitive activity with more privatization activity. The deep recession that began in 2008 also helped curtail the privatization movement. Analysts believe that the power industry will become increasingly consolidated, with eventually only a few dominant "powerhouse companies" in control of most of the market. They cautioned, however, that this concentration could result in a "market environment that is notably less competitive than regulators initially intended; it should still allow electricity buyers to choose the supplier from which they purchase power" (McCann 2004).

In December 2003, restructuring was underway in 18 of the original 24 states where it began and the District of Columbia. In those 24 states, legislatures had either enacted enabling legislation or issued a regulatory order to implement retail access. Retail competition was available to some or all customers in all of the 18 except Oregon. Oregon State law allowed nonresidential customers access, but customers were slow in participating in the retail access program. California was the only state in which retail access to competitive suppliers was completely suspended.

COMPONENTS OF THE POWER INDUSTRY

The electric power industry is made up of a number of different participants, the majority of which are investor owned. At the most basic level, the segments can be grouped into two broad categories: buyers and sellers. Buyers of power are divided into three classes: residential (single family residences and individually metered apartment units), commercial, and industrial. On the seller side are five main types of organizations: investor-owned utilities (IOUs), publicly owned energy utilities, rural electric cooperatives, federally owned utilities, and independent power producers (also known as non-utility generators). In 2015, investor-owned utilities supplied electricity to 68.4 percent of the total number of customers U.S.

BOX 4.1   CENTERPOINT ENERGY, A TEXAS ENERGY
          HOLDING COMPANY

CenterPoint energy is a public utility holding company. Operating subsidiaries own and operate natural gas distribution facilities and electric transmission and distribution facilities, and own interests in Enable Midstream Partners, LP (Enable). Wholly owned subsidiaries include:

- CenterPoint Energy Resources Corporation (CERC) and its subsidiaries own and operate natural gas distribution systems. A subsidiary offers variable and fixed-price natural gas supplies to commercial and industrial customers and electric and natural gas utilities. As of 2014, CERC also owned close to 55.4 percent of the limited partner industries in Enable, which owns, operates and develops natural gas and crude oil infrastructure assets.
- CenterPoint Energy Houston Electric, LLC engages in the electric transmission and distribution business in an area of the Texas Gulf coast that includes the City of Houston.

The company's business segments are Electric Transmission & Distribution, Natural Gas Distribution, Energy Services, Midstream Investments and Other Operations.

Natural Gas Distribution
CERC Corp's natural gas distribution business (NGD) engages in regulated intrastate natural gas sales to, and natural gas transportation for, approximately 3.4 million residential, commercial, industrial and transportation customers in Arkansas, Louisiana, Minnesota, Mississippi, Oklahoma and Texas. The largest metropolitan areas served in each state by NGD are Houston, Texas; Minneapolis, Minnesota; Little Rock, Arkansas; Shreveport, Louisiana; Biloxi, Mississippi; and Lawton, Oklahoma. In 2014, approximately 42 percent of NGD's total throughput was to residential customers and approximately 58 percent was to commercial and industrial and transportation customers. NGD also provides unregulated services in Minnesota consisting of residential appliance repair and maintenance services along with heating, ventilating and air conditioning (HVAC) equipment sales. NGD owns and operates an underground natural gas storage facility with a capacity of 7.0 billion cubic feet (Bcf). It has a working capacity of 2.0 Bcf available for use during the heating season and a maximum daily withdrawal rate of 50 million cubic feet (MMcf). It also owns eight propane-air plants with a total production rate of 180,000 Dekatherms (DTH) per day and on-site storage facilities for 12 million gallons of propane (1.0 Bcf natural gas equivalent). It owns a liquefied natural gas plant facility with a 12 million-gallon liquefied natural gas storage tank (1.0 Bcf natural gas equivalent) and a production rate of 72,000 DTH per day.

Source: CenterPoint Energy (2014).

Table 4.1   Number and size of electric providers by type in the U.S. in 2014

Type	Number	% of Total	No. Customers	% of Total
Publicly Owned	2,013	60.9	21,394,336	14.5
Investor Owned	189	5.7	101,151,671	68.4
Cooperatives	877	26.5	18,920,001	12.8
Federal Agencies	9	0.3	38,870	0.0
Power Marketers	218	6.6	6,344,231	4.3
Totals	3,306	100	147,849,109	100

Source: Publicpower.org (2015), used with permission.

generating capacity and were responsible for 74 percent of all retail sales of electricity. Publicly owned utilities and cooperatives accounted for 27.3 percent of the total number of customers served with electric power (APPA 2015). Publicly owned utilities include municipal utilities, public power districts, irrigation districts, and state authorities. Rural electric cooperatives consist of distribution systems cooperatively owned by rural farmers and communities that primarily distribute power to residential customers. Rural cooperatives also provide power for irrigation pumping. Cooperatives serve about 10 percent of the U.S. population and have the lowest generation capacity of all providers. Table 4.1 lists the numbers and percentages of all categories of private and publicly owned electric utilities.

Federally owned utilities consist of five federal wholesale power producers and four federal power-marketing administrations. Most of these agencies market their power through one of four administrations, the largest of which is the Bonneville Power Administration. The exception is the TVA, which markets its own electricity. TVA is the largest federally owned producer of electricity. Federal power agencies had 6.4 percent of the generating capacity in 2015. Finally, independent (that is, non-utility generators) power producers include more than 2,000 generators not owned or operated directly by a utility within a designated franchise service area. However, they may be owned by a utility holding company affiliate. Collectively, they account for about 39.9 percent of U.S. generating capacity.

Regardless of their system of governance or where on the globe they are located, electric power systems consist of four major functional components: (1) power generation, (2) transmission of high voltage power from where it is generated to where it is needed, (3) distribution of low voltage power to various types of customers, and (4) a marketing function. Marketing includes such ancillary services as retail marketing, connection and disconnection, meter reading, repair and upgrading, billing, and increasingly, conservation programs and trading in derivatives.

Table 4.2   Fuels used to generate electricity in the U.S., 1990–2045 (percent of total)

Fuel Source	1990	2011	2014	2045 (projected)
Coal	53	42	39	35
Natural Gas	13	25	27	30
Renewables	11	13	14	16
Nuclear	19	19	19	17
Other	4	1	1	2
Totals	100.0	100.0	100.0	100.0

Source: U.S. Energy Information Administration (EIA 2015b).

Power Generation—Suppliers of Bulk Power

Electric power is generated by revolving a magnet within a coil of copper wire. A variety of technologies and fuels are used to turn the magnets, including falling water, wind power, heat from beneath the surface of the earth (geothermal), and steam and gas turbines powered by fossil fuels and nuclear reactors. Table 4.2 displays the distribution of fuels used to generate power in 2002 and the percentage distribution that is expected in 2045. Coal-fired steam turbine plants generated over half of all the investor-owned electricity in the United States; this percentage is expected to become even greater in the decade ahead. Coal is followed by natural gas and nuclear generation, each with close to 20 percent of the total.

According to Brennan, Palmer, and Martinez (2002), the average coal-fired steam turbine has a capacity of roughly 250 megawatts, which is roughly the amount of power needed to supply a town of 60,000 homes. As a rule, coal-fired plants which contain multiple steam turbines require a capacity of 300–600 megawatts to produce at an output that roughly minimizes the average cost of producing a kilowatt-hour. Construction costs at the beginning of the twenty-first century were about $1,100 a kilowatt. Operating costs ranged from less than 2 cents to a little more than 3 cents per kilowatt hour, depending upon the age of the plant and the types of environmental controls it is required to have.

From 2002 to 2014 natural gas was the second most popular choice of fuel to power electric generators. Two technologies use natural gas: standard gas turbines (similar to those found on jet aircraft) and combined-cycle gas turbines. In gas turbines, hot gases from the combustion of natural gas (or fuel oil) pass directly through the turbines that spin the electric generator. These account for roughly 10 percent of total generating capacity. Gas turbines are often used to meet peak demands. They have relatively low capital costs, but high operating costs. The average generating capacity is 35 megawatts. New gas turbines have a construction cost of roughly $260 per kilowatt and operating costs that are 30 to 50 percent higher than a typical coal plant.

The second type is the combined-cycle gas turbine, or CCGT, system. CCGT generators use both combustion turbine and steam turbine technologies. The hot gases drive a turbine in the same way that gas turbine generators function. However, the heat from CCGT systems is not dissipated immediately. Rather, it is collected and used to create steam that is then used to drive a steam turbine in the same system. About two-thirds of the power in a CCGT system is generated by the gas turbine, and one-third is generated by the steam turbine. CCGT systems are compact, reliable, and versatile; they also require short installation times. The energy efficiency or the amount of electricity produced per unit of fuel for a CCGT can be as much as 70 percent greater than typical coal plant and 40 percent higher than a gas turbine plant. CCGT plants now produce about 8 percent of all electricity. According to Brennan, Palmer, and Martinez (2002), new CCGT plants can be constructed for about $450 per kilowatt, and they also have low pollution emissions.

Nuclear plants now generate about 20 percent of the nation's electricity. This percentage is expected to drop to something like 17 percent by 2010, although high natural gas prices and rising prices of coal may change this prediction. Nuclear fission creates heat to produce steam, which is then used to turn the power plant turbines in much the same way as steam generated from coal, gas, or oil burning generating systems. No new nuclear plants have been constructed since 1979; they are among the most expensive plants to build, and they have high maintenance costs. However, the cost of operating the plants is quite low, something in the neighborhood of 1 to 2 cents per kWh. The nation's energy resources in August 2015 and the net changed from the same month in 2014 are shown in Table 4.3.

Fossil fuels are also used to power internal combustion generators. The systems burn either diesel fuel or natural gas much like power is created in a diesel electric locomotive. The internal combustion engine drives a generator (similar to an automobile alternator). These systems are compact and able to start up and shut down almost instantaneously. As a result, they are often used primarily for generating power for short periods when peak demand exceeds normal generating capacity. They range from 1 to 3 MW in size. They generate only a very small fraction of power in the United States or Canada.

Renewable resources constitute a little more than 9 percent of the power generated in the United States. Of these fuels, by far the most important is hydroelectric power. About 8 percent of U.S. electricity

Table 4.3   Shifts in electricity generation fuels, 2002–2014 (percent)

Fuels Used	2002	2010	2014
Coal	50.2%	51.9%	39.0%
Natural gas	17.9	20.9	27.0
Nuclear power	20.3	17.3	19.0
Renewable fuels (hydroelectric, solar, geothermal, wind, etc.)	9.1	9.2	13.0
Petroleum	2.3	0.7	1.0
Other	0.002	0.01	1.0

Source: EIA (2015a).

comes from hydropower. Most hydroelectric generators are located in the west and northwestern sections of the country. Two types of hydropower dominate this sector of the industry: falling water stored behind dams, and river-current driven generators (called run-of-river generators). A third system is pumped storage, in which falling water is used in low-demand periods to power pumps that lift the water back to storage areas above the generators. The water is then reused to generate power to meet peak demand requirements. The fuel costs for these types of hydroelectric generators are zero, but construction costs are high. Other, nonhydroelectric renewables include wind, solar, geothermal, and biomass combustion. Together, these technologies produce about 2 percent or less of the nation's electricity.

The Impact of Distributed Generation

One of the fastest growing parts of the generation industry is the *distributed generation* or *distributed energy* segment. Distributed generation is defined as small generators that are located near or at the consumer site, but which stay within the control of the distribution utility. These small generators are usually not connected to the transmission grid, but supply power directly to the customer. They are typically used to supplement power from the grid during peak demand periods, when prices tend to escalate rapidly. According to the Energy Information Administration, technological advances have improved the economics of small generators. Fuel cells and photovoltaic systems are also becoming available as alternative sources.

Until the recent rapid increases in the price of natural gas, distributed generation was seen as a viable alternative to mandated reductions in power use or constructing new large central generating plants. Locating a number of small, very efficient and cost-effective natural gas powered jet-engine turbines was seen as the best alternative to building new, large, fossil fuel-powered steam generators. The economics have forced utilities to take another look at this alternative, however. A number of utilities are considering adding new natural gas-powered or nuclear powered plants over the next decade or so.

UNCERTAIN FUTURE FOR ELECTRIC UTILITIES

As we enter the second half of the second decade of the twenty first century, electric energy utilities find themselves facing what has been described as an uncertain future. On the one hand, large coal-fired generating plants that for decades constituted the major production arm of the industry are on the way out. Electric sales growth is largely stagnant. An aging workforce is retiring and fewer men and women are deciding to enter this career field. Old infrastructure is giving way to new. On the other hand, the industry is faced with a number of significant, new opportunities. Among these are the new and readily available supplies of natural gas for power generation; renewables are slowly replacing older and less clean energy resources. Information technology and the smart grid are turning the old one-way supply system into a two-way interconnected grid that promises new business opportunities as well as greater operational efficiency. Solar panels are readily available for private and commercial rooftops and electric cars are now becoming a commonly encountered sight. From a technology standpoint the long impossible dream of cost-effective energy storage is now just on the horizon. This does not mean to say that the industry is without a wide variety of challenges. A 2014 survey of a sample of the U.S. electric utility industry identified 12 problems respondents reported to be most pressing for their utility. In this new addition I plan to address these issues as much as possible. The problems across the industry and how often they were mentioned were:

1. Aging infrastructure   48%
2. Existing regulatory model   32%
3. Aging workforce   31%
4. Distributed generation   30%
5. Flat demand growth   28%
6. Smart grid deployment   23%
7. Grid dependability   21%
8. Coal plant retirements   17%
9. Renewable portfolio standards 17%

10. Energy efficiency mandates   16%
11. Emission standards   12%
12. Cyber security   11%

Power Transmission Operators—Providers of Long Distance Distribution

Transmission is the movement of electric power over relatively large distances from where the power is generated to where the power is put to use. An interconnected network of transmission lines is referred to as a transmission grid. Transmission grids consist of interconnected high voltage overhead and underground lines made of copper or aluminum. The power is stepped up to a higher voltage at the site of its generation. It is then transmitted, sometimes over very long distances. Transformers at substations then step down the high voltage power to the low voltage needed by distribution lines in major load centers. Load centers are concentrations of residential, commercial, industrial power users, or all three.

In the U.S., investor-owned utilities own nearly three-fourths of existing transmission lines; federal utilities own 13 percent, and public utilities and cooperatives own 14 percent. Not all utilities own transmission lines; nor are transmission lines owned by any independent power producers or power marketers. This picture is changing, however, as the FERC continues to push for more wholesale competition and efficiency in the transmission sector. Box 4.2 describes a cross-border interconnect arrangement between El Paso Electric and its bordering state in Mexico.

Three major transmission grids or *interties* have been formed to ensure efficient transmission of power across all of North America: the *Eastern Interconnected System*, which serves the majority of the eastern U.S. and parts of Canada; the *Western Interconnected Grid*, which serves the west side of the Rocky Mountain area, part of Texas, and parts of western Canada and Mexico; and the *Texas Interconnected System*, which serves most of the state of Texas. The Texas grid is also partially connected to the other two North American grids. Both the western and Texas interconnects are linked with Mexico; the eastern and western interconnects are completely integrated with most of Canada. Interconnected utilities in the grids coordinate their operations and buy and sell power to each other (Box 4.2).

Control of the National Grid

The Federal Energy Reliability Council (FERC) maintains oversight control over the three extra-high voltage grids. Within these three electric grids are about 150 control areas, most of which are operated by the dominant investor-owned utility in the region (Brennan, Palmer, and

---

BOX 4.2   CROSS-BORDER INTERCONNECT IN TEXAS AND
MEXICO

El Paso Electric (EPE), an investor-owned public utility engaged in the generation, transmission, and distribution of electricity in West Texas and southern New Mexico, has had a long and mutually beneficial relationship with Mexico's *Comisión de Electricidad* (CFE). El Paso Electric has negotiated a contract to sell up to 150 megawatts of power during the summer months. The sales improved the company's earnings during 2002 by about 3 cents per share.

The relationship between El Paso Electric and its Mexican neighbors goes beyond just selling power. For example, in 2002, EPE and city officials in Juarez, Mexico, just across the river from El Paso, received approval from the Texas Commission on Environmental Quality on a joint proposal to improve air quality in the region. EPE is replacing older, high-polluting brick kilns in Juarez with new, cleaner kilns developed by a former professor at New Mexico State University. Emissions from each new kiln are about 80 percent lower than the kilns they replace. EPE receives emission credits from Texas.

Gary R. Hedrick, EPE's president and CEO, said about the relationship, "EPE looks forward to continuing its partnership with the Republic of Mexico on other binational issues that affect the border region."

Source: Shareholder Statement, EPE 2002 Annual Report (EPE 2002).

Martinez 2002). These are electric geographic areas with control operators that balance electric load while maintaining reliability. Most of these control areas are in the Eastern Interconnection; only 12 in the Texas Interconnection. Control Area Operators (CAOs) dispatch power from a central control center to balance supply and demand and maintain system safety and reliability.

Ten North American Electric Reliability Council regions have been formed within the three major national grids. The Reliability Council is a voluntary, nonprofit corporation formed by members from all segments of the industry, including utilities, power producers, power marketers, and power customers. The Reliability Council was formed in 1965 after the catastrophic northeast blackout. Individual councils are responsible for the coordination of bulk power policies that affect reliability and adequacy of service in their regions. The boundaries of these NERC regions follow the service areas of the utilities in the region and, as a result, do not exactly follow state boundaries. They also share operating and planning information. The ten area councils are:

- ECAR: East Central Area Reliability Coordination Agreement
- ERCOT: Electric Reliability Council of Texas

- FRCC: Florida Reliability Coordinating Council
- MAAC: Mid-Atlantic Area Council
- MAIN: Mid-America Interconnected Network
- MAPP: Mid-Continent Area Power Pool
- NPCC: Northeast Power Coordinating Council
- SERC: Southeastern Electric Reliability Council
- SPP: Southwest Power Pool
- WSCC: Western Systems Coordinating Council

Changes in the Grid

Prior to the late 1990s, most electric power was supplied to customers by vertically integrated public utilities. About 75 percent of these utilities were investor owned; the remaining 25 percent were publicly owned. Municipally-owned utilities served customers in urban areas; organizations operating as special districts served rural areas (Public Utility Districts, for example). The large investor-owned utilities tended to be vertically integrated. They owned and operated power generating plants, transmission lines, local distribution systems, and did their own meter reading, billing, and other ancillary service activities.

Beginning with passage of the Public Utility Regulatory Policies Act (PURPA) of 1978, transmission owners were required to allow open access to their lines by alternative energy producers, including small dams, solar, and biomass generators. To encourage their growth, these small generators were exempt from state regulation. The National Energy Policy Act (NEP) of 1992 carried open access a step farther. The vertically integrated utilities were to be "unbundled," under a plan designed to replace utility monopolies with competition. Unbundling meant separating the functions of generation, transmission, and distribution. These were to function as separate competitive businesses. The first plan was to establish competition at the wholesale level.

The FERC issued two Orders in 1996 that further enabled open access: Order 888, which required open-access transmission; and Order 889, which required establishment of electronic systems to share information about transmission capacity. Order 888 had two goals: (1) elimination of anti-competitive practices by transmission line owners, including elimination of owner discrimination in granting access to the grid by requiring a universally applied open access transmission tariff; and (2) to enable the utilities that constructed the lines to recover what were called their *stranded costs* (also called *sunk costs*, or *transition costs*). These are the costs of certain specific capital improvements made by a utility before restructuring. According to the EIA (1996), the rationale for allowing stranded cost recovery is that utilities have invested billions of dollars in facilities under a regulatory regime that allowed cost recovery of all prudent investments. FERC endorsed the idea in the belief that recovery of sunk costs was needed if the move toward competition was going to succeed. At the same time, they recognized that recovery of sunk costs would delay lower prices that were expected to accrue from competition.

Order 888 required owners of transmission lines to separate the lines from their other business, a practice called *unbundling*. This meant that transmission owners were required to use transmission service on lines they owned under the same tariff and access conditions as other transmission users—in what was called a *comparability standard*.

Order 889 was issued in order to make the pricing and access process more transparent. All investor-owned utilities were required to participate in an Open Access Same-time Information System (OASIS). This interactive Internet-based database contains information on the availability of transmission capacity, capacity reserved for one or more users, other services, and transmission prices. As of 2003, 166 transmission line owners participated by providing information about the transmission facilities.

Order 2000 issued in 1999 encouraged all public and investor-owned electric utilities to place their transmission systems under the independent control of a regional transmission organization or RTO. The RTO concept has been described as:

> FERC Order 2000 was meant to build upon the ISO concept by encouraging smaller transmission entities to join together into larger RTOs, and by pushing all transmission operators and regions to develop plans for participation in an RTO. While Order 2000 did not technically mandate participation in an RTO, the Order required all transmission owners to submit progress reports detailing their plans to participate in an RTO by October 16, 2000. The deadline was extended by three months to January 16, 2001 for existing ISOs. (Marshall et al. 2001)

Compliance with the RTO order has been slow; most of the national transmission grid is still not under control of an independent RTO. In consequence, in July 2002 the FERC proposed its standard market design (SMD) rule. This would have established a single set of rules for the entire North American wholesale market. The SMD proposal was revised in April 2003 to allow for regional opposition and renamed the *wholesale power market platform*. The revised SMD proposal was part of the federal energy bill of 2003, which Congress failed to pass. The energy bill called for a delay of three years before the FERC could require utilities to join a regional transmission organization or before it could mandate a standard market design. The 2003 bill would also have made grid reliability standards mandatory and would have required federal permits for transmission lines. A key section of the failed bill would have repealed the Public Utility Holding Company Act of 1935.

McCann (2004) described the FERC's Order for a standard market design as one of the most far-reaching of its proposals governing the transmission of wholesale electric power. The SMD would have established and monitored a set of consistent transmission rules applicable to all participants. The FERC was convinced that the lack of a clear set of rules governing the wholesale electric industry was responsible for failure of a truly competitive power market to emerge in North America.

The FERC's SMD concept was strongly opposed by state regulators and utilities in the U.S. northwest and southeast. Opponents of the concept believed that the SMD plan might work for the changing transmission markets in the northeast, but it was not right for their own areas. The service territories of the northwest are much larger than those in the east. There are relatively few but very long transmission lines in the west. State regulators and market participants did not believe there was a need for new lines for trading by power marketers. Also, the northwest depends heavily on publicly owned hydroelectric power, which usually is not open to competitive market pricing. In the southeast, there was great concern that the imposition of the SMD would result in those regions losing their low-cost advantage, as nationwide trading could possibly force an increase in power prices in that region. Loss of that advantage would, it was felt, limit their ability to attract new industries to the region, thus severely curtailing economic development.

The Distribution Sector: Reliable Power at Home

Distribution is the process of moving electricity from the high-voltage transmission grid to lower voltages and delivering it to customers' meters. This aspect of the industry is still considered to be a "natural monopoly" and, as such, remains under the control of state Public Utility Commissions (PUCs). Distribution is considered to be an intrastate function, even when power suppliers serve customers in more than one state. The process of providing the electric energy to ultimate customers is called *retail marketing* or *retail sale*. Investor-owned utilities that provide power distribution services are to remain the regulated portion of the utility industry, serving residential, commercial, and industrial customers, sometimes in competition with nonregulated firms.

Under the regulated system, state PUCs approve retail rates for electricity based on the cost of service plus an allowed "fair" rate of return. Utilities present information at rate hearings when seeking approval for a

proposed rate change. The total cost of service includes the cost of generated and purchased power, the capital cost of the utility's generating plants
(called stranded costs), the cost of transmission, installed distribution
infrastructure, all operations and maintenance, as well as the cost of programs required by the PUC to maintain consumer safety, energy efficiency,
and environmental protection. In addition, federal, state, and local taxes
are generally included in the rate base.

The major challenge facing utility distribution companies may be
learning how to effectively and efficiently operate their businesses under
conditions of competition rather than as regulated monopolies. In the few
states that have adopted retail competition, some commercial and large
industrial power users have taken the opportunity to choose from among
two or more competing suppliers for the power delivered to their premises.
However, very few residential customers have opted to change electricity
suppliers. Residential retail competition is not moving forward as quickly
as federal regulators had hoped.

RESTRUCTURING THE ELECTRIC UTILIITY INDUSTRY

The electric power industry remains somewhat in a state of flux. On one
side, investor-owned utilities and some federal legislators see great hopes
for the plan to bring competition to the industry. Events taking place in the
industry have been described in these terms: Possibly the most important
changes in the history of the electric utility industry during the first decade
of this century. The industry was being restructured from one that was
highly regulated to one in which competition in power generation and sales
to consumers are becoming the norm.

Opponents of restructuring in the industry see it in a different light.
Australian professor and privatization critic Sharon Beder provided this
version of the process in her book *Power Play: The Fight to Control the
World's Electricity*:

> The term 'deregulation,' when referring to electricity is essentially a misnomer,
> since the changes involved are not really about getting rid of regulations: they
> are about replacing the regulations that protect the public and the environ-
> ment with rules to ensure the smooth running of the market and the electricity
> system. 'Privatization' is the more accurate term, because what is happening in
> the case of deregulation is the privatization of control over electricity provision.
> The use of the term is endorsed by the US Department of Energy (DOE), which
> says: "We treat privatization . . . as any movement that diminishes public owner-
> ship and control and increases private ownership and control." (Beder 2003: 2)

The drive toward restructuring the electric power industry began in 1978 with passage of the Public Utility Regulatory Policies Act (PURPA). This was passed in response to the unstable energy climate of the 1970s; it was triggered by the actions of the OPEC cartel to refuse to sell oil to the United States. PURPA encouraged conservation of electrical energy. More importantly, it created a new class of organizations in the energy supply chain: non-utility generators. Established utilities were required to buy power from these small independent power producers and qualified cogenerators. PURPA also gave the Federal Energy Regulatory Agency the authority to require owners of transmission lines to wheel power generated by independents over the privately owned transmission lines.

As a result of the 2000–2001 energy crisis that began in California and included the collapse of the energy trading company Enron, the move toward restructuring has lost its momentum. When Congress failed to pass the Energy Bill, it left many questions still unresolved, including the following restructuring issues:

1. Mandatory participation in a regional transmission organization (RTO)
2. Bulk power reliability
3. Nuclear decommissioning provisions
4. Transmission grid expansion and construction
5. Reform of TVA and federal power marketing administrations
6. Federal authority to regulate retail sales, protect retail consumers, and regulate local grid interconnections
7. Utility mergers
8. Public benefits fund
9. Retail net metering
10. Emissions caps and standards for generators
11. IRS restrictions on "private use" of municipal electric systems
12. State/federal jurisdiction clarification
13. Retail sales to federal agencies
14. Retail reciprocity
15. Extension of Order 888 wholesaling wheeling rules to transmission by municipals, cooperatives, federal power marketing administrations, and TVA
16. Renewable energy source portfolio standards
17. Repeal of PUHCA and Section 210 of PURPA.

TOP TO BOTTOM OVERSIGHT

As this chapter has indicated, agencies of the federal government play a major role in protecting the national electric grid against cyberattacks. What has not been emphasized is the collaborative role that the individual states also play. The several federal agencies involved include the Federal Energy Regulatory Commission (FERC), the North American Electric reliability Corporation (NERC), the U.S. Department of Energy (DOE) the Department of Homeland Security (DHS), and the National Institute of Standards and Technology (NIST), which is part of the U.S. Department of Commerce. Also involved in this collaborative effort is Canada's state public utility commissions (PUCs) provide oversight of the private and public utilities that distribute electric power to homes, industries and commercial users—the final link in the electricity supply chain. In this role, these distribution organizations, their several trade associations such as the National Association of Regulatory Utility Commissions and the National Rural Electric Cooperative Association (NRECA), also have an important position in protecting the safe and reliable operation of the national grid.

SUMMARY

The electric power industry is in the midst of a complete overhaul. The changes taking place are having the greatest impact upon investor-owned utilities. Deregulation, restructuring, and competition have forced these utilities to make drastic shifts in their strategic direction. Restructuring has brought on unbundling of the industry. Former vertically integrated utilities have had to divest themselves of major components. The biggest change has been the selling off of generating plant. Most of this generation capacity has been acquired by independent power producers. The FERC is also trying to have the utilities place their transmission assets into nonprofit regional organization designed to control all transmission within a given market area. Finally, in those states where retail competition is allowed, some utilities have spun off their marketing units as separate, nonregulated meter-reading and billing businesses.

Despite these major changes, vertical integration remains a viable strategy. A spate of mergers has produced some very large, vertically integrated regional utilities. One result of the upsurge in mergers and acquisitions has been a concentration in the ownership of power generation among a small number of firms; the 20 largest investor-owned utilities now own about 72 percent of total generation capacity. The consolidation taking place in the industry has also seen some electric utilities merging with natural gas production and pipeline companies to form vertically integrated *energy* companies, which may be the predominant form of the industry in the future.

Electric power systems have four major functional components: (1) power generation, (2) transmission of high voltage power from where it is generated to where it is needed, (3) distribution of low voltage power to various types of customers, and (4) a marketing function. A variety of technologies and fuels are used to generate electricity, including falling water, wind power, heat from beneath the surface of the earth (geothermal), and steam and gas turbines powered by fossil fuels (coal and petroleum), and nuclear reactors. Coal-fired steam turbine plants generated over half of all the investor-owned electricity in the United States. Coal is followed by natural gas and nuclear generation, each with close to 20 percent of the total.

Transmission is the movement of electric power over relatively large distances. An interconnected network of transmission lines is referred to as a transmission grid. Transmission grids consist of interconnected high voltage overhead and underground lines of copper or aluminum. The power is stepped up to a higher voltage at the site of its generation. It is then transmitted, sometimes over very long distances. Transformers at substations then step down the high voltage power to the low voltage needed by distribution lines in major load centers.

Three major transmission grids or *interties* have been formed to ensure efficient transmission of power across all of North America: the *Eastern Interconnected System*, the *Western Interconnected Grid*, and the *Texas Interconnected System*. There are about 150 control areas within the three interties to balance electric load and maintain reliability; most of the control areas are operated by the dominant investor-owned utility in the region.

Ten North American Electric Reliability Council regions have been formed within the three major national grids. The Reliability Council is a voluntary, nonprofit corporation formed by members from all segments of the industry, including utilities, power producers, power marketers, and power customers.

Beginning with passage of the Public Utility Regulatory Policies Act of 1978, transmission owners were required to allow open access to their lines by alternative energy producers, including small dams, solar, and biomass generators. The National Energy Policy Act of 1992 carried open access a step further. The vertically integrated utilities were to be "unbundled" under a plan designed to replace utility monopolies with competition.

In 1996, the FERC issued Order 888, requiring open-access transmission; and Order 889, which required establishment of electronic systems to share information about transmission capacity. Order 888 had two goals: (1) elimination of anti-competitive practices by transmission line owners, including forbidding line owner discrimination by requiring a universally applied open access transmission tariff; and (2) to enable the utilities that constructed the lines to recover what were called their *stranded costs* (also called *sunk costs*, or *transition costs*). Order 2000 issued in 1999 encouraged all public and investor-owned electric utilities to place their transmission systems under the independent control of a regional transmission organization or RTO.

The changes taking place in the electric power industry are having the greatest impact upon investor-owned utilities. Deregulation, restructuring, and competition have forced these utilities to make drastic shifts in their strategic direction. Restructuring has brought on unbundling of the industry. Former vertically integrated utilities have had to divest themselves of major components. The biggest change has been the selling off of generating plant. Most of this generation capacity has been acquired by independent power producers. The FERC is also trying to have the utilities place their transmission assets into nonprofit regional organization designed to control all transmission within a given market area. Finally, in those states where retail competition is allowed, some utilities have spun off their marketing units as separate, nonregulated meter-reading and billing businesses. The consolidation taking place in the industry has also seen some electric utilities merging with natural gas production and pipeline companies to form vertically integrated *energy* companies, which may become the predominant form of the industry in the future.

ADDITIONAL READING

Borenstein, Severin and James Bushnell (2015), *The U.S. Electricity Industry after 20 Years of Restructuring* (Energy Institute working paper). Berkeley, CA: University of California. Accessed on August 14, 2015 from ei.haas.berkeley. edu/research/papers/WP252.pdf.

Brennan, Timothy J., Karen L. Palmer and Salvador A. Martinez (2002), *Alternating Currents: Electricity Markets and Public Policy*. Washington, DC: Resources for the Future.

Brown, Matthew H. and Richard P. Sedano (2003), *A Comprehensive View of U.S. Electric Restructuring with Policy Options for the Future.* Washington, DC: National Council on Electricity Policy. Accessed on August 14, 2015 from www. ncouncil.org/restrict.pdf.

EMRF (2013), 'Evolution of the Electric Industry Structure in the U.S. and Resulting Issues.' Washington, DC: Electric Markets Research Foundation (Navigant). Accessed on August 14, 2015 from evolution_of_the_electric_indus try_for_emrf_10_8_13(2).pdf.

Fox-Penner, Peter and James E. Rogers (2014), *Smart Power (Anniversary Edition): Climate Change, the Smart Grid, and the Future of Electric Utilities*. Washington, DC: Island Press.

Lambert, Jeremiah D. (2015), *The Power Brokers: The Struggle to Shape and Control the Electric Power Industry*. Cambridge, MA: Massachusetts Institute of Technology.

5. Natural gas utilities

Unlike the electricity utility sector, the natural gas industry has largely worked its way through the minefield of structural changes that have rocked the utility sector since the 1990s. Natural gas in the United States has gone from a scarce and expensive natural resource to a widely available and relatively inexpensive energy source. This transition has brought with it a renewed interest in the environmental problems associated with the recovery process known as fracturing. Natural gas is used in homes for cooking and heating, factories, electric generation plants, and businesses. Over a ten year period from 2003, the greatest percentage increase in consumption of natural gas was for electric generation. Table 5.1 compares the consumption percent to total sales used for the four major sectors of the market.

The production and distribution of manufactured gas began in the nineteenth century, although its high price kept its use limited primarily for street and public place lighting. More extensive and varied use had to wait until competition from new electric lights and the 1876 invention of a new gas production process forced prices down. The first commercial plant was built in Baltimore, Maryland, in 1816. Other coal gas plants followed in Boston in 1822, New York in 1823, Brooklyn in 1835, and Bristol, Rhode Island, and New Orleans shortly afterward. Natural gas was first used for industrial purposes in 1870, when the Bloomfield and Rochester Natural Gas Light Company brought gas in wooden pipes to Rochester, New York. Its use continued to grow as more producing petroleum wells were drilled and new uses for natural gas were discovered.

Activities in the natural gas industry are divided into three categories: upstream, midstream, and downstream operations. Upstream operations are activities performed by exploration, drilling and production companies. These are the organizations that drill for gas and oil and pump the products out of the ground. Midstream activities include the gathering of gas, processing it into its component hydrocarbons such as butane, propane, ethane, and methane, and removing other contaminants such as water and sand. Organizations at this level also include the intrastate pipeline companies that transport gas from where it is produced to where it is either collected or processed. The final activity in the stage is the above and below ground storage of gas until it is needed by local distribution

Table 5.1 Natural Gas production and consumption by end user and percent, 2000–2014 (million cubic feet)

End Use Sector	2009	2010	2011	2012	2013	2014	%
Gas used in gas production	1,275,239	1,258,627	1,322,588	1,396,273	1,475,073	1,565,816	5.83%
Gas used in pipeline operation	670,174	674,124	687,784	730,790	861,583	884,358	3.29%
Total delivered to customers	20,964,665	22,127,046	22,467,053	23,411,423	23,794,010	24,371,224	
Residential	4,778,907	4,782,412	4,713,777	4,149,519	4,914,327	5,073,056	18.91%
Commercial	3,118,592	3,102,593	3,155,319	2,894,926	3,278,856	3,461,150	12.90%
Industrial	6,167,371	6,826,192	6,994,120	7,226,215	7413,918	7,655,058	28.54%
Vehicle fuel	27,262	28,664	29,974	29,970	33,624	32,850	0.12%
Electric generation	6,842,533	7,387,184	7,573,863	9,110,793	8,153,285	7,149,111	30.37%
Total Consumption	22,910,078	24,059,797	24,477,425	25,538,486	26,130,666	26,821,398	100%
				25,583,487			

Source: EIA (2015a).

public or private utilities. Downstream activities include the interstate pipeline companies that perform the activities necessary to safely move from regions where it is produced and processed to the communities, commercial and industrial end users of the gas. Local distribution companies (LDCs) may consist of companies owned by equity shareholders, local governments or independent nonprofit utilities. The Federal Energy Regulatory Commission (FERC) exercises control over all interstate aspects of the natural gas industry. All intrastate aspects are regulated by state and local governments. FERC's oversight of the natural gas sector includes approval of the siting and abandonment of interstate natural gas pipelines and storage facilities oversees location, construction and operation of proposed and operating liquid natural gas terminals, monitors and investigates all energy markets, and oversees environmental matters pertaining to natural gas and hydroelectric projects.

As in the electric power sector of the industry, a holding company parent often owns a number of commercial LDCs that supply gas to customers in different markets. These local gas distribution companies are regulated by the utility commissions of the states in which they operate. Holding companies may also own electricity utilities and unregulated energy marketing organizations (often called energy merchants). Holding companies are usually not liable for the debts of their wholly owned distribution utilities. Rather, they are usually required by federal and state energy regulating agencies to segregate their diverse assets to protect the creditworthiness of their regulated distribution utilities. A more or less typical diversified energy company's operations are described in Box 5.1.

NATURAL GAS PRODUCTION IN THE UNITED STATES

The United States has gone from a chronic natural gas shortage in the mid-1970s to be touted as the world's largest producer of natural gas in 2014 (EIA 2015a). A report issued from the President Gerald Ford White House in 1974 warned that the winter supply of natural gas was becoming increasingly severe, and added the situation could get even worse:

> Natural gas production peaked in 1973 at 22.5 Trillion cubic feet (Tcf) and declined significantly for the first time in 1974 to 21.2 Tcf, a decline of almost 6 percent. Last year's [1973] production decline is equivalent to over 230 million barrels of crude oil. Reserve additions failed to equal or exceed production for the seventh straight year and gas reserves in the lower 48 states are now at their lowest level since 1952. The only major reserve additions in recent years has been the Alaskan reserves of 26 Tcf added in 1970. (EIA 2015a)

BOX 5.1   COOPERATIVE INNOVATION IN A COMMUNITY OF FLORIDA NATURAL GAS DISTRIBUTORS

In 1989, a group of 25 local gas industry leaders in Florida came together to form the Florida Gas Utility (FGU), a nonprofit municipal organization with the objective of reducing the costs of purchased natural gas for its members. Three classes of members now benefit from FGU membership: natural gas distribution utilities, electric generation members, and combined natural gas distribution and electric generation members. Since then, FGU services to its members have grown to include gas scheduling and acquisition, transport and storage management, strategic planning, marketing of excess capacity, hedging strategies, capital project management, public awareness programs, operations assistance, and as a source of industry data. FGU also provides financial services for its members, including management of accounts payable and receivable, management of investments, contract administration, information technology, and credit risk management, among others.

FGU contracts for transportation of natural gas with interstate gas pipelines that are regulated by the Federal Energy Regulatory Commission (FERC). In 2014, FGU managed natural gas purchase contracts with more than 70 suppliers. Low gas prices as a result of new supplies becoming available has resulted in growth of local utilities sales to industrial and commercial customers. In addition, the State of Florida annually makes available $6 million to fund conversion of vehicles from petroleum to natural gas.

Source: Florida Gas Utility 2014 Annual Report (FGU 2014).

However, once the gas industry was deregulated and supplies of Canadian natural gas became available in the United States, the shortages of the 1970s began to fade. By the end of the 2008–2010 recession it was evident that recent drilling innovations such as fracturing in shale deposits had turned the shortage into a glut. Industry reports as early as 2005 were beginning to mention companies' decisions to curtail production in order to bring about a price increase. Since 2008, increases of U.S. production of natural gas occurred mostly in the eastern part of the country and upper Midwest. Production increased by 5 quadrillion Btu/d (13.9 billion cubic feet per day) in the five years preceding 2014 production of dry natural gas was 24.33 Tcf in 2013. The top five dry natural gas producing states in 2013 in trillions of cubic feet were:

1.   Texas—6.86 Tcf
2.   Pennsylvania—3.23 Tcf
3.   Louisiana—2.37 Tcf
4.   Oklahoma—2.00 Tcf
5.   Wyoming—1.78 Tcf

6. Also, 1.24 Tcf of dry natural gas was produced in the federal offshore waters of the Gulf of Mexico.

STRUCTURE OF THE INDUSTRY

The Natural Gas Supply Organization's website NaturalGas.org published a brief but clear description of the structure of the natural gas industry in 2013. This section is taken from that source. The industry prior to deregulation and pipeline unbundling in the 1970s consisted of four sectors: producers, processors, pipelines and distribution organizations (private companies and municipal public utilities). Before deregulation there was little competition possible in the gas production, pipeline and distribution sectors. Price controls resulted in few incentives to improve service or innovate. When severe shortages of supplies of gas occurred in the 1970s, to spur exploration and increased production the federal government deregulated wellhead prices and limited pipeline companies to transportation only. This eliminated the assured monopolies for large transportation pipelines and distribution companies.

The natural gas industry in the early twenty-first century today is much different that it was before deregulation. For one thing, it is thought to be much more open to competition and choice. Wellhead prices are no longer regulated; the price of natural gas is shaped by supply and demand interactions. Interstate pipelines no longer take ownership of the natural gas commodity; instead they offer only the transportation services and must transport any producer's gas. However, this sector is still regulated by the federal government. Distribution organizations can offer bundled products to their customers (unbundled means separate suppliers for each service) and retail unbundling in many states allows the use of their distribution network for the transportation component, and users may purchase natural gas directly from producers or distributors.

An important sector in the natural gas industry that resulted from deregulation is that of natural gas marketers. Marketers facilitate the movement of natural gas from the producer to the end user. They serve as a middleman between any two sectors, and can offer either bundled or unbundled service to customers.

The industry continued to evolve significantly since the 1990s and the reorganizing of the pipeline industry. In 2015, the industry consisted of organizations structured to perform six distinct operations, with some organizations operating in more than one type of service. At the base are the independent well owners and producers. Next in the system are the gas collectors and processors; natural gas consists of a number of gaseous (such as propane and methane) and liquid impurities and components with separate markets that must be removed before the final product can be used by residential consumers. The third major segment of the industry includes the intrastate and interstate pipeline companies that transport processed gas to major industrial users and local delivery organizations. The fourth segment of the industry are the gas marketers that buy and sell large volumes of gas to large industrial users, electricity generating firms, and some large local delivery organizations. A fifth segment of the industry includes the owners and operators of underground gas storage facilities; these operators sell gas to local distribution companies and end users. The final segment are local distribution companies (LDCs) and directly to some end users. The U.S. Department of Energy provides the following descriptions of the major sector participants.

The Producer Sector

In 2009 there were more than 8,000 producers of natural gas in the United States. These companies range from large integrated producers with worldwide operations and interests in all segments of the oil and gas industry, to small one or two person operations that may only have partial interest in a single well. The 24 largest integrated production companies ('majors') active in the United States produce most of the country's natural gas. In addition, gas is imported from Canada and Mexico.

The Processor Sector

Processing plants collect and process well-produced product before it becomes pipeline-quality gas. Their main task is to separate natural gas liquids (NGL) from natural gas. Gas processing plants often perform several other functions, including dehydration, contaminant removal, and sometimes fractionation (separating an NGL stream into its component products). Some field processing may be done at the well site to remove condensation before gas is sent to a midstream processing plant. In addition, gas producers may use gas-fired dehydration units to remove water and treat gas to remove hydrogen sulfide and carbon dioxide. In 2014 there were 517 firms with an operating capacity of 65.5 billion cubic feet per operating plants in the lower 48 states, down from more than 580 natural gas processing plants operating in the U.S. in 2009 (Figure 5.1).

The Pipeline Sector

The U.S. pipeline system is made up of a little more than 161,000 miles of hazardous liquid lines (including crude and refined petroleum); 310,000

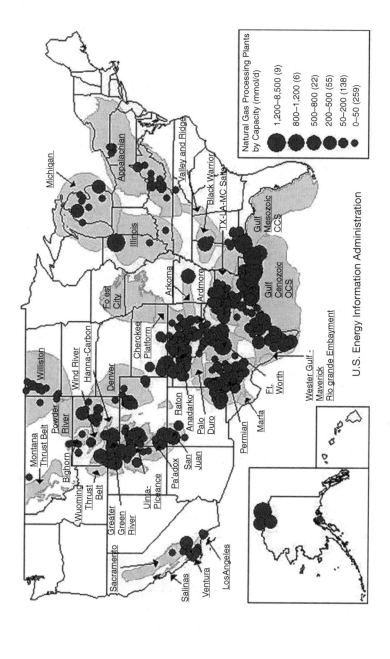

Source: EIA (2011).

Figure 5.1 Natural gas processing plants in the United States in 2010

miles of natural gas transmission lines; 1.9 million miles of natural gas distribution pipelines; and approximately 104 liquefied gas processing and storage facilities. Most of the lines are privately owned and operated. Nearly all the pipelines in the country are buried underground. In 2011, pipelines transported nearly all of the natural gas and about two-thirds of the petroleum products moved in the country. Historically, pipelines have transported most crude oil. However, in North Dakota, the existing pipeline network lacks the capacity to handle the higher production the state has seen. Railroads have been filling this gap. In recent years, as U.S. crude oil output has surged, so too have carloads of crude oil on U.S. railroads. Originated carloads of crude oil on U.S. Class I railroads (including the U.S. Class I subsidiaries of Canadian railroads) rose from 9,500 in 2008 to 493,146 in 2014 (AAR 2015).

The U.S. has approximately 160 pipeline companies that control more than 305,000 miles of pipe. Of this, 217.306 miles of line are interstate pipelines. This pipeline capacity is capable of transporting over 119 billion cubic feet (bcf) of gas per day from producing regions to consuming regions. Pipelines are permitted only to transport, not own, any of the gas they move in their pipelines. They remain closely monitored by the federal government, primarily by the Pipeline and Hazardous Materials Safety Administration (PHMS).

The interstate portion of national natural gas pipeline network represents about 71 percent of all natural gas mainline transmission mileage installed in the United States (EIA 2009). The 30 largest interstate pipeline companies own about 77 percent of all interstate natural gas pipeline mileage and about 72 percent of the total capacity available within the interstate natural gas pipeline network. The U.S. pipeline network is shown in Figure 5.2.

In April 1992, the Federal Energy Regulatory Commission (FERC) issued Order 636 and transformed the interstate natural gas transportation segment of the industry forever. Under it, interstate natural gas pipeline companies were required to restructure their operations by November 1993 and split-off any nonregulated merchant (sales) functions from their regulated transportation systems. This requirement meant that interstate natural gas pipeline companies were allowed to only transport natural gas for their customers; crude oil and other refined products could no longer be shipped by the companies. The restructuring process and subsequent operations have been supervised closely by FERC and have led to extensive changes throughout the interstate natural gas transportation segment which have impacted other segments of the industry as well.

About two thirds of the United States is dependent upon the pipeline system for natural gas. States that are at least 85 percent dependent on the interstate pipeline network are:

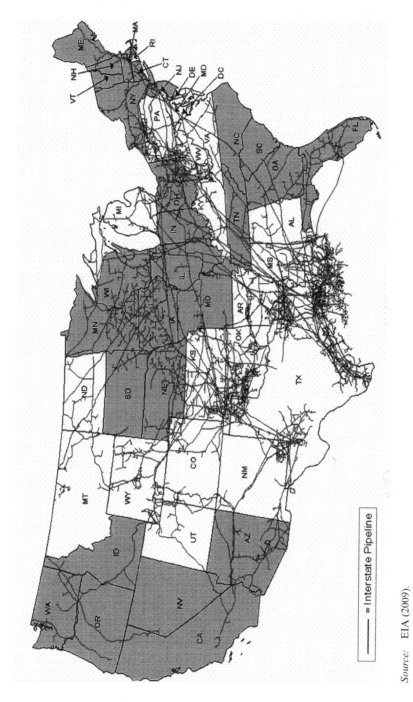

Source: EIA (2009).

Figure 5.2 U.S. 2009 interstate natural gas pipeline system

——— = Interstate Pipeline

- New England—Connecticut, Maine, Massachusetts, New Hampshire, Rhode Island, Vermont
- Southeast—Florida, Georgia, North Carolina, South Carolina, Tennessee
- Northeast—Delaware, Maryland, New Jersey, New York, District of Columbia
- Midwest—Illinois, Indiana, Minnesota, Ohio, Wisconsin
- Central—Iowa, Missouri, Nebraska, South Dakota
- West—Arizona, California, Idaho, Nevada, Oregon, Washington

The Gas Storage Sector

Cleaned and processed natural gas is often transferred from the reservoir in which it is discovered to other reservoirs, usually closer to final market areas, where it is stored until needed to meet market demand. There are about 114 natural gas storage operators in the United States. They control over 415 underground storage facilities, for a storage capacity of 4,313 billion cubic feet (bcf) of natural gas, and an average daily deliverability of 78 bcf per day.

Natural gas is most commonly held in inventory underground under pressure in three types of facilities: (1) depleted reservoirs in oil and/or gas fields, (2) aquifers, and (3) salt cavern formations (EIA 2004). Depleted production areas make up the great majority of the underground reservoirs in use, accounting for 82 percent of the total storage capacity in the United States. Aquifers make up another 15 percent, and salt caverns add another 3 percent of total capacity. Gas is also stored in above-ground tanks in close proximity to final consumers. Each storage type has its own physical characteristics and economics. Two of the most important characteristics of an underground storage reservoir are its capacity to hold natural gas for future use and the rate at which gas inventory can be withdrawn.

Most gas storage is in depleted natural gas or oil fields in areas close to where it is produced and processed. Conversion of a field from production to storage duty takes advantage of existing wells, gathering systems, and pipeline connections. According to the EIA, most salt cavern storage facilities have been developed in salt dome formations located in the Gulf Coast states, particularly in Texas and Louisiana. Salt caverns have also been leached from underground salt bed formations in Northeastern, Midwestern, and Southwestern states. Cavern storage construction is more costly than depleted field conversions when measured on the basis of dollars per thousand cubic feet of working gas capacity, but the ability to perform several withdrawal and injection cycles each year reduces the per-unit cost of each thousand cubic feet of gas injected and withdrawn.

There have been efforts to use abandoned mines to store natural gas, and use of hard-rock cavern storage has also been tried, but neither method has been financially successful. A small number of liquefied natural gas (LNG) storage facilities have been constructed and port facilities built or planned. With the 2015 surplus of natural gas produced in Canada, Mexico and the United States exporting LNG to European and Asian markets was generating great interest and plans to construct more port facilities were common.

The Gas Marketing Sector

Natural gas marketing is much like the way the movement of other commodities is facilitated in other commodity exchanges; their core purpose is to coordinate the process of bringing natural gas from the wellhead to end-users. They facilitate the sale or purchase of natural gas, and can also contract for transportation and storage. Marketers may own the natural gas being transferred, or may simply facilitate its transportation and storage. Natural gas marketers sell natural gas to resellers (other marketers and distribution companies), and to end users such as electricity generating plants and industries. On average, most natural gas can have three to four separate owners before it actually reaches the end-user. As this statement on its role as a commodity explains:

> Natural gas is sold as a commodity, much like pork bellies, corn, copper, and oil. The basic characteristic of a commodity is that it is essentially the same product no matter where it is located. Natural gas, after processing, fits this description. Commodity markets are inherently volatile, meaning the price of commodities can change often, and at times drastically. Natural gas is no exception; in fact, it is one of the most volatile commodities currently on the market. (NaturalGas. org 2013)

Marketers find buyers for natural gas, ensure secure supplies of natural gas in the market, and make it possible for natural gas to reach the end-user. They make certain that a market exists for natural gas, thus ensuring supplies are available. The task of the marketing organization includes all of the intermediate steps that a particular purchase requires, including arranging transportation, securing storage, accounting for all transactions, and stepping in when needed to take any other step required to facilitate the sale of natural gas.

The marketing element in the chain of organizations did not exist until the 1980s and 1990s, when over-supply of gas resulted in high volatility in gas prices, followed by the transformation of the pipeline industry and industry deregulation. Before deregulation of the natural gas market in the early 1990s and the open access for everyone to natural gas pipelines, natural gas marketers simply did not exist in the natural gas supply chain. The industry was relatively straightforward: "Producers sold to pipelines, who sold to local distribution companies and other large volume natural gas users. Local distribution companies sold the natural gas purchased from the pipelines to retail end users, including commercial and residential customers. Price regulation at all levels of this supply chain left no place for others to buy and sell natural gas" (NaturalGas.org 2013). The role of natural gas marketers in the twenty-first century has evolved into a complex and increasingly important activity; however, it does not fit exactly into any one spot in the natural gas supply chain. Marketers may be affiliates of producers, pipelines, or local utilities, or may be separate business entities unaffiliated with any other players in the natural gas industry. In addition to their supply function, natural gas marketers use financial instruments and commodity markets to reduce their exposure to risks and speculate in future market movements.

There are five different types of natural gas marketing organizations operating in the United States: major nationally integrated marketers, producer marketers, small geographically focused marketers, aggregators, and brokers. The nationally integrated marketers conduct the majority of the trading in natural gas. They offer a full range of services and market a basket of different products. Producer marketers are the well owners and operators who sell their own production or that of an associated natural gas production company. Smaller marketers operate in specific regional areas and/or specific gas markets; local distribution company marketers are examples. Aggregators collect product from a number of different sources, combine them and sell the larger volume for better terms than would be available to each of the smaller producers. Brokers are the only sector that does not take ownership of the gas, instead operating as facilitators of transactions between parties and paid a small commission for their services. Overall, the top gas marketers continued their multi-year decline in 2014. Natural gas amounts in billions of cubic feet per day marketed in 2013 and 2014 by the top ten marketing organizations are displayed in Table 5.2. Not included on the table were the 0.65 Bcf/d in 2013 and 0.42 Bcf/d in 2014 (a 35 percent decline) marketed by the Russian natural gas monopoly Gasprom, 23rd on the list of the top natural gas marketers.

Local Distribution Companies (LDC) Sector

In 2008, the U.S. Energy Information Administration reported there were more than 1,500 companies involved in the local distribution of natural gas.

Table 5.2   Top ten U.S. natural gas processors and estimated 2012 production

Rank	Company	Gas processing volume (billion cubic feet/day)
1	BCP Midstream	6.10
2	Enterprise Products Partners	6.05
3	Williams Companies, Inc.	4.45
4	Targa Resources	2.10
5	Mark West Energy Partners	1.68
6	Encana	1.63
7	Crosstex Energy Services	1.35
8	Western Gas Partners	1.19
9	Shell Oil Co.	1.06
10	Devon Energy	1.05

Source: Stell (2015).

By 2013, consolidation and other forces has reduced the reported number to somewhat more than 1,200 natural gas local distribution companies (LDCs) in the U.S., with ownership of over 833,000 miles of distribution pipe. While many of these companies maintain monopoly status over their distribution region, many states are currently in the process of offering consumer choice options with respect to their natural gas distribution.

According to the industry's website NaturalGas.org, some large industrial, commercial, and electric generation customers receive natural gas directly from high capacity interstate and intrastate pipelines, usually through a contract with natural gas marketing companies. Most other natural gas is received from a local gas distribution company (LDC). LDCs are regulated utilities involved in the delivery of natural gas to consumers within a geographic area. There are two basic types of natural gas utilities: those owned by investors, and public gas systems owned by local governments. The delivery of natural gas to its point of end use by a distribution utility involves moving small volumes of gas in small diameter pipes at low pressures over shorter distances to individual users.

Traditionally, rigid steel pipe was used to construct distribution networks. However, new technology is allowing the use of flexible plastic and corrugated stainless steel tubing in place of rigid steel pipe. These new types of tubing allow cost reduction, installation flexibility and easier repairs for both local distribution companies and natural gas consumers. Another innovation in the distribution of natural gas is the use of electronic meter-reading systems. The natural gas that is consumed by any one customer is measured by on-site meters, which essentially keep track of the volume of natural gas consumed at that location.

CONSUMERS OF NATURAL GAS

The total consumption of natural gas in the United States has increased in every year from the 22.91 trillion cubic feet (Tcf) in 2009, 24.33 Tcf in 2013 and 26.82 Tcf in 2014 (EIA 2015b). In 2014, gas sold for electricity production and industrial use together accounted for more than 60 percent of all gas sold to end users (Table 5.1). Residential use accounted for the third largest group with nearly 19 percent of total gas consumption, followed by commercial users with nearly 13 percent. Although increasing every year the smallest market for the use of natural gas was for powering commercial and municipal vehicles. The next section describes the current structure of the industry. The five states that consumed the most natural gas in 2013 were:

1. Texas—4.02 Tcf
2. California—2.41 Tcf
3. Louisiana—1.40 Tcf
4. New York—1.27 Tcf
5. Florida—1.22Tcf

Electric Generation Customers

The 8,149,111 million cubic feet of natural gas used for electricity production in 2013 accounted for 30.37 percent of all gas used in 2014. Natural gas can be used to generate electricity in a variety of ways. Until the widespread availability of affordable natural gas and development of new technology, the most common method was by very large steam generation units. The following section briefly describes these and other methods as published by the natural gas industry association.

Steam generation units
In steam generation units fossil fuels—predominantly coal—are burned in a boiler to heat water and produce steam that then turns a turbine to generate electricity. Natural gas is increasingly being used in new or upgraded units, although most still use coal or are nuclear generation facilities. Efficiency is fairly low; only 33 to 35 percent of the thermal energy used is converted into electrical energy.

Centralized gas turbines

In gas turbines and combustion engines hot gases from burning fossil fuels—particularly natural gas—are used to turn the turbine and generate electricity. Gas turbine and combustion engine plants have traditionally been used primarily for peak-load demands. They have been slightly less efficient than large steam-driven power plants.

Combined cycle units

Many of the new natural gas fired power plants are combined-cycle units, using both a gas turbine and a steam unit, all in one. The gas uses the hot gases released from burning natural gas to turn a turbine and generate electricity. Waste heat from the gas-turbine process is directed toward generating steam, which is then used to generate electricity. Combined-cycle plants can achieve thermal efficiencies of up to 50 to 60 percent.

Distributed generation

Technological advancements have increased the popularity of distributed generation, in which individual, smaller sized electric generation units at residential, commercial, and industrial sites used. These small scale power plants, primarily powered by natural gas, use small gas turbine or combustion engine units, or natural gas fuel cells. Distributed generation is attractive because it offers electricity that is more reliable, more efficient, and cheaper than purchasing power from a centralized utility.

Industrial natural gas fired turbines

Industrial natural gas-fired turbines operate on the same concept as the larger centralized gas turbine generators. They are located near to where the electricity being generated will be used. Industrial turbines produce electricity through the use of high temperature, high pressure gas to turn a turbine that generates a current; they are compact, lightweight, easily started, and simple to operate. Distributed generation is used by medium and large sized establishments, such as universities, hospitals, commercial buildings and industrial plants, and can achieve efficiency up to 58 percent. The heat that would normally be lost as waste energy can be used for other functions, such as powering a boiler or space heating in Combined Heat and Power (CHP) systems.

Microturbines

Microturbines are scaled down versions of industrial gas turbines. They have a relatively small electric output, capable of producing from 25 to 500 kilowatts (kW) of electricity, and are best suited for residential or small scale commercial units. Using new waste heat recovery techniques, microturbines can achieve energy efficiencies of up to 80 percent.

Natural gas-fired reciprocating engines
Natural-gas fired reciprocating engines are also used for on-site electric generation. These combustion engines convert the fossil fuel energy into mechanical energy, which rotates a piston to generate electricity. Natural-gas fired reciprocating engines typically generate from less than 5 kW, up to 7 megawatts (MW), with efficiencies ranging from 25 to 45 percent. They can also be used in CHP systems to increase energy efficiency.

Fuel cells
Fuel cells are a small but becoming an increasingly important market as a fuel for the generation of electricity. They are much like rechargeable batteries, except they use a fuel, such as natural gas, to generate electric power even when they are in use. They are often used for backup or secondary supply in industrial and commercial facilities.

Industrial Customers

Industrial customers use natural gas for space heating, heat energy in processing activities, and as a raw material in the production of such diverse products as plastics and fertilizers. Industries those are highly dependent upon natural gas included sugar production, cement production, chemical manufacture, and aluminum, among others. With a record high of 7,655,058 mcu, industrial uses accounted for nearly 29 percent of all gas end use in 2013, the second highest of all gas consumers.

Residential Gas Customers

In 2013, residential users comprised the third largest group of end users of natural gas. This was an increase from its second largest position noted in the first edition of this book. Residential consumption increased from the 4,778,907 mcu used in 2009 to 5,073,056 mcu in 2014, when it accounted for 19 percent of all sector use.

Residential customers generate the largest share of income for public utilities, although use by individual consumers is miniscule compare to power generation customers. Approximately two-thirds of residential gas is used for space heating. Other uses included in cooking stoves, clothes dryers, water heaters, and fireplace burners.

Commercial Customers

The commercial use of natural gas is the fourth largest group of gas consumers with 3,461,150 mcu used in 2014 or 12.5 percent of the total. Examples of commercial consumers include restaurants, hotels and motels, public buildings, and large office buildings. As in the residential market, more than half of all commercially consumed gas is used by climate control equipment for heating and cooling.

Other Users

Large quantities of natural gas are used in the production and processing of more natural gas. At 1,565,816 mcu, this accounted for 5.83 percent of all gas used in 2014. An additional 3.29 percent of gas consumed in 2014 was used for pipeline shipping of gas, where concentration, cooling and compression activities are involved. The smallest group of users of natural gas in 2014 was for vehicle use, with 32,850 mcu or just slightly above one tenth of one percent. However, use by this sector has increase in all but one year from 2009.

FEDERAL REGULATION OF THE NATURAL GAS INDUSTRY

Regulation of the U.S. oil and gas industries can be traced to the 1920 passage of the Federal Water Power Act that was established for licensing hydroelectric projects on land or navigable waters owned by the federal government. Ten years later, Congress established the Federal Power Commission (FPC) as an independent commission of the federal government to regulate interstate electric utilities and the natural gas industry. During the administration of President Franklin Roosevelt the FPC successfully pressured electric utilities to extend power into neglected rural areas and to lower electricity rates to increase use. The FPC was replaced by the Federal Energy Regulatory Commission in October 1977.

Direct regulation of the natural gas industry began with passage of the Natural Gas Act (NGA) in 1938. The NGA brought under government oversight firms that were engaged in the interstate sale of natural gas for resale. By determining these firms were being affected with a public interest similar to railroads, regulating the gas industry was considered justified. The FPC was then ordered to ensure that the wholesale prices for gas to be distributed to residential and business customers were, in the language of the act, *just and reasonable* (MacAvoy 2000).

The Natural Gas Policy Act

Prior to 1978, the natural gas industry was battered by chronic supply shortages. In an attempt to control prices for final consumers, the federal government set artificially low prices for gas at the wellhead. Producers could not sell gas through interstate commerce at rates higher than the government set limits. The price rules had to be removed in order to provide sufficient profit incentives to encourage further exploration. Congress passed the Natural Gas Policy Act (NGPA) in 1978. This law deregulated the wellhead price of natural gas and provided the incentives needed. No shortages occurred again until 2001. A key outcome of the NGPA was creation in the early 1980s of a competitive market, including a spot gas commodity market, the beginning of the natural gas marketer sector.

However, problems with the deregulated system soon became apparent. After arranging low-cost purchases directly from gas producers in the spot market, local distribution companies (LDCs) were often denied access by the interstate pipelines for transporting their independently procured gas. As a result, in 1985 the Federal Energy Regulatory Commission issued order 436 which required interstate pipelines to transport gas owned by the LDCs on a first-come, first-served basis or lose their licenses to operate. This did not entirely resolve the stranglehold pipelines held over the transmission of gas. Pipelines were able to negotiate long-term purchase agreements with producers at prices far below that available to the lower quantity LDCs. Pipelines soon controlled transportation, storage and other services. The government had to step in again. The FERC issued Order 636 in 1992, in which pipeline companies were required to unbundle their services. Any service a pipeline offered to utilities and other end users had to be offered and priced separately.

Once services were priced separately and offered equally to any customer, purchasers of gas were able to comparison shop for the best prices. FERC also split off the merchant function of pipelines, eliminating their ability to sell gas directly to LDCs or other consumers. Beginning in 1993, marketers and LDCs were able to negotiate directly with gas producers and storage firms for their supply of gas and to negotiate prices for each of the unbundled services offered by pipelines.

STATE REGULATION OF DISTRIBUTION UTILITIES

In most states, utility commissions have the final say on determining what should be the appropriate rate base and allowable operating expenses for distribution companies. Rates are usually set on a cost-of-service basis. In some states, however, utility commissions have allowed rates in excess of direct costs for some services and set lower rates for household customers. Distribution utilities are typically permitted to pass costs of gas and charges for transmission on interstate pipelines and storage services on to final customers. Others are allowed to do so only for certain segments of their customer base. California and New York, for example, did not allow their utilities to do so. Instead, utilities have been permitted to build rates based on the marginal costs of services plus the total costs of specific services only for a specific class of customer. Other states have offset lower costs to residential customers by higher rates for industrial customers.

FERC has also allowed residential and other small volume customers to take advantage of purchasing their own gas from competitive suppliers since the late 1990s. Customer choice programs were developed in the 1990s to increase competition in retail electricity and natural gas markets. According to the EIA, eligibility and participation in customer choice have increased substantially since 2000. The number of eligible customers has more than doubled since 2001, and is nearly 10 percent higher than it was in 2005. Participation in customer choice programs has also more than doubled, increasing from 3.3 million in 2001 to 7 million in 2013. However, at the national level, only 18 percent of residents eligible to participate in consumer choice programs chose to do so in 2013.

In 2001 state utility commissions in 20 states and the District of Columbia had implemented programs allowing residential customers to purchase the same unbundled services once available only to industrial customers. By 2013, the number of states in the select customer choice programs had grown to 24. Ohio (35 percent of national total), Georgia (20 percent), and New York (13 percent) customers make up about 69 percent of nationwide customer choice program participants. Georgia, with nearly 100 percent participation, has remained steady since 2001 as all customers of Georgia's largest utility, Atlanta Gas Light, participate in the state's choice program. New York has had participation rates greater than 20 percent since 2011.

THE FUTURE SUPPLY OF NATURAL GAS

In the first volume of this series I reported that, while the American Gas Association was convinced that the lower 48 United States contained enough gas to last until the second half of the twenty-first century, production was expected to continue at levels that fell short of annual demand for the foreseeable future. This would make access to supplemental sources of gas necessary to meet everyday demand. Supplemental sources the

---

BOX 5.2   LIQUEFIED NATURAL GAS: THE ENERGY SOURCE OF THE FUTURE?

Liquefied natural gas (LNG) is gas that has been cooled to about minus 260 degrees Fahrenheit (−162.22 Celsius). At this temperature it changes into a liquid state that can be stored in insulated tanks. LNG can then be transported from overseas ports to any nation with unloading and storage facilities. At the destination port, the gas is unloaded to special receiving terminals, where it is stored and regasified for transport to pipelines, underground storage facilities or end-user customers. The supply chain of LNG includes four necessary components: (1) gas field production and processing, (2) a cooling process for liquefication, (3) specialized tanker transportation, and (4) a receiving, storing and regasification terminal— all of which are highly capital-intensive. The U.S. has imported LNG from Trinidad and Tobago, Qatar, Algeria, Nigeria and Oman. In 2003 there were only four LNG regasification terminals in the United States, and no new ones about to be constructed. But things changed.

As of September, 2015, there were 13 LNG export/import facilities in operation in the United States and two more proposed, one in Canada and three in Mexico. The U.S. has become a major world supplier of LNG.

Source: FERC (2016).

---

industry considered would be available included pipeline deliveries of Alaskan and Canadian natural gas and overseas imports of liquefied natural gas (Shere 2004; Vital 2004). By 2005, traditional producing areas in the United States were expected to be able to provide only 75 percent of the country's gas needs. The deficit was expected to be made up by liquefied natural gas (LNG) imports and arctic gas. The state of the liquefied natural gas industry in 2015 is presented in Box 5.2.

The low probability of imported natural gas becoming a major supplier of gas needs in the U.S. were described in the 2005 edition of this book this way: It is not expected that LNG will soon alleviate the growing shortages of natural gas in North America. The few existing terminals and the very high costs of adding new facilities are likely to serve as a damper on growth in this sector for some time. Changes in gas use are displayed in Table 5.3.

What this author and industry spokesmen of that time did not consider were the technical advances that would give the U.S. a surplus of gas and the high global demand for other sources of gas that would relieve them of the dangerous dependence upon natural gas from Russia. They were right about imports, but not about exports.

Table 5.3   Ten-year change in consumption of natural gas by end-user category (percent)

End-user Sector	2003	2013
Industrial	36.2%	31.3%
Residential	23.5%	23.5%
Electric power generation	22.7%	34.1%
Commercial	14.4%	13.8%

Source: EIA (2013).

UNCONVENTIONAL GAS

Conventional sources of natural gas, while very large and growing, are surpassed by what are considered to be unconventional sources—so vast that one industry manager was confident in stating they "can supply world demand of gas indefinitely" (Mills 2008: 185). They range from what the industry considers to be extensions of conventional methods such as ultradeep, tight and contaminated gas, through currently commercially viable sources, but which are still in need of new production methods, such as coal-bed methane, to those that are still not commercially viable such as gas dissolved in vast aquifers that parallel the Texas and Louisiana Gulf coasts at depths below 800 feet, and hydrates (also called gas clathrates), which are frozen solids of a combination of water and one or more green-house gases such as methane. Hydrates are common in Arctic waters. Other unconventional sources include coal gasification and biogas. Shale gas was once considered to be an unconventional source, but the development of horizontal drilling methods and fracturing the shale with water and chemicals, has added very large sources of affordable gas to the U.S. inventory.

A very large portion of the world's natural gas reserves consists of what is known as contaminated gas. Contaminates include large quantities of incombustible nitrogen, carbon dioxide and hydrogen sulfide.

SUMMARY

Since deregulation in the 1990s and discovery of vast new supplies of shale gas in the early 2000s, natural gas distributors and consumers have benefited from lower pipeline transportation charges, unbundled supplies and increasingly lower prices. Demand for gas to fuel electricity generators and for industrial purposes has continued to expand, while residential demand has slowed. The fear the production decline of traditional North American production fields in Oklahoma, Texas and the Gulf Coast would result in short supplies and higher prices has been overturned; new methods have opened very large fields in the upper Midwest, the Northeastern states, and Canada and Mexico. Optimistic industry leaders now predict that known resources are large enough to supply world demand to the end of the century and beyond.

The U.S. natural gas industry is usually divided into three production categories: upstream activities, midstream activities, and downstream activities. Upstream activities included exploration and production by drilling companies. Midstream activities include the gathering of gas from the wellheads, cleaning and processing it into its component hydrocarbons, and storing the market-ready gas for later transmission or other use. The transmission of natural gas by intrastate and interstate pipelines is also considered a midstream function. Downstream activities include the (commodity) marketing of gas and distributing the gas to final users by local distribution companies (LDCs). In the United States, most of these distribution operations are investor-owned, although municipally owned and special-district owned gas utilities also exist.

Until deregulation, wellhead prices, that is, the price for the gas as it was taken from the well, was controlled by the federal government. When a shortage of gas occurred in the 1970s, the price was deregulated which resulted in higher prices for consumers, but in greater exploration and innovation in the production industry. Once wellhead prices were free to fluctuate, the major influence on pricing once the gas left the wellhead became the nation's major pipelines. Pipeline companies took ownership of the gas at the well, and performed merchant duties of processing and storing the gas, and transporting it to where it would be purchased by distribution companies. Pipelines charged for each of these activities in what was referred to as "bundling."

In 1985, FERC issued Order No. 436, which barred pipelines from discriminating against transportation requests based on protecting their own merchant services. The movement toward allowing pipeline customers the choice in the purchase of their natural gas and their transportation arrangements became known as *open access*. In 1992, FERC completed the process of unbundling gas supply from gas delivery by making pipeline unbundling a requirement. It provided for the complete unbundling of transportation, storage, and sales; the customer (the local gas distribution system) now chooses its gas supplier and the pipeline to transport the gas it owns.

In 1989, Congress completed deregulating the price of natural gas at the wellhead, which was begun in 1978 with the passage of the Natural Gas Policy Act, by passing the Natural Gas Wellhead Decontrol Act (NGWDA). This repealed all remaining regulated prices on wellhead sales. Distribution companies are regulated by state public utility commissions. Natural gas producers and marketers are not directly regulated by the federal government as to rates and related matters. Interstate pipeline companies are regulated regarding the rates they charge, the access they offer to their pipeline facilities, and the siting and construction of new pipelines. Similarly, local investor-owned distribution companies, but not most municipally owned public gas systems, are regulated by state commissions that oversee their rates and construction issues, and ensure that proper procedures exist for maintaining adequate supply to their customers.

Industrial users use natural gas for space heating, heat energy for production processing applications, for generating steam energy, and as a raw material for plastics and fertilizer production, among other uses. Industries that are highly dependent upon natural gas include sugar production, chemical and fertilizer manufacture, cement production, and aluminum.

ADDITIONAL READING

Hrastar, John (2014), *Liquid Natural Gas in the U.S.: A History*. Jefferson, NC: McFarland.
Kidnay, Arthur J., William R. Parrish and Daniel G. McCartney (2011), *Fundamentals of Natural Gas Processing*, Boca Raton, FL: CRC Press.
Kolb, Tobert W. (2013), *The Natural Gas Revolution: at the Pivot of the World's Energy Future*. Upper Saddle River, NJ: Pearson.
Mokhatab, Saeid, John Y. Mak, Jaleel V. Valappil, and David Atwood (2013), *Handbook of Liquefied Natural Gas*. Amsterdam: Elsevier.
Shively, Bob and John Ferrare (2011), *Understanding Today's Natural Gas Business* (6th edn). Self published.
Smil, Voclav (2015), *Natural Gas for the 21st Century*. New York: Wiley.

6.   Water and wastewater utilities

Water is one of life's absolute necessities. Without a steady supply of clean, fresh water, cities could never have been invented, let alone become the preferred living environment of a growing majority of human populations. When water supplies become polluted, disease and death follow. Contaminated water can cause many types of diarrheal diseases, including cholera, and other serious illnesses such as Guinea worm disease, typhoid, and dysentery. Water related diseases still cause 3.4 million deaths around the globe each year. The importance of clean water resulted in some of the earliest civil engineering feats, including dams and aqueducts to store and move water for human consumption and agriculture. Water and wastewater systems remain the *sine qua non* of all modern civilizations.

STRUCTURE OF THE WATER UTILITY SECTOR

In 2014 there were approximately 155,693 public water systems subject to regulations administered by the Environmental Protection Agency (EPA) in the United States. This was down from the nearly 170,000 systems reported in the 2010 census. Of these totals, there were close to 54,000 community water system in 2010 and 52,110 in 2014. Community water systems are defined as systems that provide water to at least 25 people at their primary residences, with water supplied to roughly the same population all year. Another 103,583 systems are either one of two types of non-community systems: transient non-community systems that provide water to at least 25 or more people at least 60 days a year, but not to the same people and not on a regular basis, or non-transient systems that provide water for the same 25 or more people at least six months of the year. Close to 15 percent of U.S. residents get their water from their own wells, although this number is declining as the country continues to urbanize.

The nation's public water system sector consists of two main segments: the utilities that distribute water to where it is needed and the general services segment that provides water and wastewater related services to utilities and consumers. This chapter addresses the utilities segment. The majority of systems in this segment are owned and operated by local governments or special districts, accounting for approximately 84 percent of all community water systems and 98 percent of all community wastewater systems. The utility systems are heavily regulated, both for safety and sanitation and for environmental impact.

WATER INDUSTRY SECTOR

Both the freshwater and wastewater sectors consist of a number of independent components. For freshwater, these include these seven physical elements:

- Water source: Water to be distributed to end users is acquired from groundwater or surface water, or a combination of the two. Small community water systems commonly get their water from groundwater sources, whereas large systems obtain most of their water from surface sources such as streams or lakes.
- Collection and transport: Water is transported from the source to the treatment facility via pipe or open canals. The water is moved by pump or gravity, or a combination of the two.
- Raw water storage: Untreated water is stored in reservoirs or lakes. The storage facilities may be in remote areas such as mountain ranges or facilities constructed in urban areas.
- Treatment: Raw water is either physically (filtered) or chemically treated or a combination of both to remove contaminants before being distributed to end users.
- Finished water storage: Water is often treated in a continuous operation that occurs regardless of the rate of demand. To ensure peak demand is met, treated water may be stored in large, surface or sub-surface reservoirs or in fabricated storage tanks.
- Distribution: Treated water is delivered to residential, commercial and industrial users through a network of pipes, tanks, pumps, and valves. Water flow through the system is mechanically adjusted to ensure that the proper amounts and appropriate pressure are maintained.
- Process monitoring: Continuous monitoring of the water flow at all stages in the system is conducted to ensure that contaminants do not exceed best practices standards and regulatory requirements, and to maintain proper flow and pressure. Digital Supervisory Control and Data Acquisition (SCADA) systems are often employed in process monitoring.

To carry out the many tasks involved in collecting, moving, storing, processing, decontaminating and delivering water, utilities employ their own staff or subcontract some of the activities to outside contractors. Large municipal systems often employ chemists, engineers, microbiologists, and full-time security personnel, as well as other trained specialists. Small utilities may use a small full-time staff with part-time help and special-purpose contract personnel.

Sustainable Water Supply Management

The water and wastewater sectors of the public utilities industry are facing an increasingly complex and challenging future. They must surmount these challenges and provide their publics with affordable service while meeting human health requirements. Planning for sustainability is absolutely necessary for sourcing, treatment, storage and delivery of freshwater and for the collection, treatment, and the recycling and discharge of wastewater in this exceedingly challenging environment it has never been more vital than it is today. In a review of water utility governance models prepared for the Federation of Canadian Municipalities (FCM), Dr. Karen Bakker identified a long list of obstacles to maintaining a sustainable water supply management operation facing water utilities in Canada, the U.S., and Great Britain. The list is replicated in Table 6.1.

Water Use in the U.S.

Water use statistics in the United States have been recorded and published by the U.S. Geological Survey every five years since 1950 for fresh and

Table 6.1   Water use in the United States by sector in 2010 (percent)

Water Use Sector	Percent of Total Use
Thermoelectric power generation	45%
Agriculture Irrigation	33%
Public Supply (parts, government, etc.)	12%
Industrial	4%
Aquiculture	3%
Mining	1%
General Household Use	1%
Livestock rearing and Processing	1%
Total	100%

Source: USGS *Water Use in the United States* (USGS 2015b).

saline water by eight categories of water users: public supply (domestic, commercial and municipal supplied by public and private utilities), domestic (self-supplied or by public suppliers), irrigation, livestock, aquaculture, industrial, mining and thermoelectric power generation. Water withdrawals are measured when water is removed from a source for any use and measured in gallons per day or acre feet.

The results of the 2010 survey were published in 2014. Withdrawal percentages of the estimated average daily withdrawals of surface and subsurface (ground) fresh and saline water in 2010 for each of category are shown in Table 6.1. The estimated total daily water use for all states in 2010 was 355 billion gallons per day (bgal/d)—an average of 88 gallons per person per day. While this rate of water use is significant, the important qualifier to remember is that the 2010 estimates were the lowest since 1970. Freshwater use withdrawals consisted of 306 billion gallons per day or 86 percent of the total; saline water (any water with more than 1,000 million parts per milligram of any dissolved solids) withdrawals were estimated to be 48.3 billion gallons per day (bgal/d) or 14 percent of the total. Fresh surface water withdrawals were nearly 15 percent lower than in 2005; fresh groundwater withdrawals were close to 4 percent less than 2005. Saline surface withdrawals were 24 percent below 2005; saline groundwater withdrawals were also lower, but at an undetermined rate (saline surface water is almost exclusively (97 percent of the total) used for cooling thermoelectric generator plants, although a measurable amount is also used in petroleum mining.

Thermoelectric generation and irrigation were the two largest users of water in 2010, although totals for both users were lower than the 2005 consumption rates. With public supply withdrawals in 2010 (which was 5 percent below the 2005 rate), these three users accounted for 90 percent of the total withdrawals. Electricity generation withdrawals were 20 percent below 2005 and irrigation withdrawals were 9 percent below 2005. More than 50 percent of the total withdrawals in 2010 occurred in just 12 states, led by California's 11 percent of the total withdrawals and 10 percent of the freshwater withdrawals. Texas, with 7 percent of the total withdrawals, together with Oklahoma, accounted for about 70 percent of the total saline groundwater withdrawals; most of this was used in mining. California, Arkansas, Texas and Nebraska were the four largest fresh groundwater withdrawers, together accounting for 42 percent of the national total. The largest surface water withdrawals occurred in California. An example of federal, state and local water agency cooperation in California is shown in Table 6.2.

Table 6.2   Federal, state and local water regulation hierarchy cooperation example

Environmental Concern	Federal Agency level	State Board level	Local agency level
Water Quality	U.S. Environmental Protection Agency	State Water Resources Control Board	Regional water quality control boards
Water Pollution/ Wastewater	EPA Federal Water Quality Administration	State Office of Wastewater Management	Regional intrastate water quality control boards
Air Quality	EPA	State environmental protection boards and agencies	Regional intrastate air pollution control districts
Public Health	U.S. Department of Health and Human Services; Center for Disease Control	State department of public health and agencies	Local public health enforcement agencies
Energy	Departments of Energy, Homeland Security, Interior; Federal Energy Commission	State public utility commissions (PUCs)	Regional and/or local public utility commissions

Source: California State Water Control Board (CWRCB 2016).

Managing Water and Wastewater Utilities

Public utilities are alike in many ways. They all provide a necessary public service; they are all rather heavily regulated and monitored by regulators in one or more levels of government. They are either departments of government organizations (state and local), quasi-government organizations in that they exist as independent nonprofit organizations, or they are investor-owned companies that are constantly and closely monitored at both the federal and state levels of government. They are also similar in their search for innovative solutions to all types of managerial and operation problems. A center of research on this field is the Ash Center for Democratic Governance and Innovation of Harvard University's Kennedy School of Government.

The search for innovative solutions may be the greatest challenge facing all utilities in the remaining first half of the twenty-first century. Aging infrastructure, changing weather conditions, heightened security concerns, rapidly changing technology, and the difficulty of finding and retaining qualified professional personnel all demand new and better ways of operating. In a word, this means innovation. For investor-owned utilities, innovation is spurred by the quest for maintaining and improving profits through new, creative and better ways of operating. For government and nonprofit utilities, the profit motive does not exist. Hence, public and nonprofit sector utilities depend on innovative ways of solving their daily policy and management problems. Borins (2014: 6) explained the persistence of innovation of government as a product of this underlying drive among public servants: "The urge to innovate is . . . born of a belief in government as a solution, a belief that government can find better ways to deliver services. Innovators share a conviction that creative problem solving, inspired improvisation, experimentation, and risk-taking within their organizations are possible."

The commitment to innovation continues to grow, as does the willingness to embrace open innovation through inter-organizational collaboration. It is happening in all sectors of the utility industry and all sizes of organizations. And, it is not happening just in the United States: innovation at all levels of government is now a global phenomenon. Collaboration in seeking and applying innovative solutions to problems has become increasingly the norm among organizations providing public services. Borins also found a wide shift over a 15-year period in the sources and characteristics of innovative programs among the many public service organizations applicants to the Harvard University Kennedy School's Innovations in American Government awards. The number of organizations reporting that they collaborated with external organizations increased from 28 percent of the 1990–1994 pool of applicants to 65 percent of the semifinalists in 2010. Collaboration with other government organizations similarly grew from 21 percent in the early 1990s to 58 percent of the applicants in 2010. Decreases were reported in just two of the eight categories of characteristics mentioned: process improvement, 34 percent in the early 1990s pool to 29 percent in 2010, and in citizen empowerment, from 26 percent in 1990–1994 to 16 percent in 2010 (Borins 2014).

Public service organizations, including public utilities, have been forced to change the way they operate. Political pressures and the need to fund wars in the Middle East have made it more and more difficult for governments, including utilities, to secure the funds needed to operate and repair weather damage and aging infrastructure, let alone grow to meet the mandate to serve all comers. Innovative solutions to old problems have become a necessity. Innovation begets transformational change in all types of organizations. Abramson et al. (2006: 7) described the need for greater inter-organizational cooperation in innovation this way:

> Rising public expectations for demonstrable results and enhanced responsiveness will require fundamental *transformation* of government—where roles and even continued existence of some organizations and functions will be at stake ... Government organizations need to pick up the pace to become less hierarchical, process-oriented, stovepiped [i.e., single-purpose], and inwardly focused. They will need to become more partnership-based, results-oriented, integrated and externally focused. (Abramson, Breul, and Kamensky 2006: 7)

Six broad categories of innovative solutions that utility managers must develop and adopt in response to the pressures for change they face include:

1. Changes in the rules of government, in the way public work takes place.
2. Changes in the management of government operations through implementation of performance management practices.
3. Changes from bureaucratic to market-based governance.
4. Changes that enable agencies to provide services on demand.
5. Changes from tolerating citizen participation to encouraging and re-engaging the electorate and encouraging greater volunteer involvement.
6. Changes in the structure of services delivery to include collaboration, public/private teamwork, networks, partnerships, and coalitions.

Case Study: A Small Combined District

Harsteene Island, approximately ten miles long and three miles wide, is located at the southeastern end of Puget Sound. The island is accessible by a bridge from a state highway that provides access to the area's largest city, 18 miles away. The combined Hartstene Island-Timberlakes shore county census division had a population of a little more than 7,700 at the 2010 census; of this total, the number of permanent residents on the Island was estimated to be between 1,000 and 1,500; short-term or summer visitors increase the total only slightly. There is only one small, open summer-only grocery store located at the Island's marina. Most of the Island is privately owned timberland.

The Harstene Pointe Water and Sewer District (HPWSD) serves a community of 532 home sites with single family and townhouse dwelling units at the north end of the island. Originally developed in 1970 as a lumber company employee recreational community, in the late 1960s the lots were sold to the public. In 2015, approximately half of the single-family residences and condominium units were occupied as full-time primary residences. The community employs a full time manager, office, security and maintenance staff. Seven members of the home owners' association are elected by the property owners.

When the community was first developed, the installed water and wastewater treatment systems were deeded to, maintained and managed by the county public utility department. Concerned by indication that the county's operation of the systems were not receiving government mandated upgrades and locally generated financial reserves were being used to support other small systems in the county, residents opted to take total control over the operation of both systems in 2009. The water-wastewater utility became a private nonprofit public service district, with operations monitored and audited by state and country administrations. The district obtains fresh groundwater from two wells drawing from related aquifers. The water is filtered and purified onsite and stored in a small concrete reservoir. A third reserve well and portable generators are available for emergency use. Wastewater is treated to state and federal secondary standards in an onsite treatment facility.

Both systems of the utility are owned and operated independently from the homeowners' association. The operation is governed by a board of three commissioners elected for staggered six-year terms. Although the commissioners have had extensive business operation experience, they were not operationally qualified to manage the technical complications associated with operating sustainable water or wastewater treatment systems. They recognized that they could not solve their many management problems alone. Fortunately, many solutions already had been tested by similar independent utilities and were available for others to adopt.

Cooperative innovation
The commissioners and staff embraced cooperative innovation since its formation in 2009. Examples of the district's ongoing cooperative arrangements include membership in the Washington Association of Sewer and Water Districts (WASWD), the Evergreen Rural Water of Washington (ERWoW), and the Municipal Research and Services Center (MRSC). The WASWD association's membership includes general and associate members. General members are special purpose sewer, water, or combined sewer/water districts. As of January 2014, MRSC listed a total of 2,015 water and sewer districts in the state. Associate members are individuals, companies, state or local agencies, non-district local governments, consultants or associations that are not special purpose water and/or sewer districts, but which the association board of directors have a legitimate

interest in the organization's mission. Like MRSC, the association is a source of legal, computer technology, procurement and other operations problems resolved by other member districts.

The Evergreen organization is a nonprofit organization formed in 1994 to serve the rural water districts of Washington State; it is now the Washington State affiliate of the National Rural Water Association. The official mission of Evergreen is "to provide and promote the highest level of service, technical assistance, training and advocacy for Washington State utilities." Evergreen provides training and technical assistance to districts directly to help solve operational, regulatory, administrative and financial problems faced by local water systems. Although not a state agency, its staff cooperates with the Washington State departments of health, ecology, and such federal agencies as the U.S. Department of Agriculture, Environmental Protection Agency, and local health offices and other agencies interested in solving rural water districts. ERWoW is funded by the EPA and Department of Agriculture Rural Development agency in the form of grants and contracts.

The MRSC is a nonprofit center formed in 1934 to support effective local government in Washington State. The organization continues to function as the official research and services agency for cities, towns and utility districts serving fewer than 10,000 citizens in the state. The center provides operations consultation, research, training, and collaboration to all local governments, including separate water and sewer districts. Most of MRSC's services are provided free of charge to local government employees and public officials of cities, counties, and some special purpose districts in the state. MRSC's services to utility administrators include such important management responsibilities as municipal law and finance, urban planning, public works, and public management. As a relatively independent public service organization the district particularly values the center's vetting of private water and sewer operations and equipment vendors.

Meeting water efficiency rules

Although the Pacific Northwest is known for enjoying adequate rainfall, population growth, intensive agricultural development, industrial development and federally mandated rules for maintaining salmon and other seafood populations are placing increasing demand on available water resources and wastewater treatment facilities. Responding to the problem, the Washington State legislature passed the Water Use Efficiency Requirements Act, creating what became known as the Municipal Water Law (MWL). The law was challenged by entrenched water rights holders but then upheld by the state supreme court. The MWL defines all Group

Table 6.3   Example of required water efficiency rules and compliance dates

Required Action	Deadline for completion all systems under 1,000 connections
Install water supply production meters	January 22, 2007
Collect water consumption and production data	January 1, 2008
Include efficiency program in utility planning	January 22, 2008
Set efficiency goals for the utility	January 22, 2009
Submit service meter installation schedule	July 1, 2009
Submit first annual performance report	July 1, 2009
Service meters installed for all connections	January 22, 2017
Meet at least a 10% leakage standard (based on a three-year average)	Three years after all service meters are installed

Source: Washington State Department of Health (WSDOH 2011).

A systems as community water systems with 15 or more residential connections; group A non-community systems provide water for residential use to non-residential facilities that serve 25 or more people for 60 or more days a year. Under the MWL municipal water suppliers must prove how they are using water more efficiently in order to receive water right certainty for current and future demand. In 2007, the Legislature directed the Department of Health to adopt an enforceable Water Use Efficiency (WUE) program that applied to all municipal water suppliers. All relevant water utilities are required to meet the same compliance standards; deadlines for compliance differed depending on whether the system served systems with less or more than 1,000 connections. Table 6.3 lists the requirements and the compliance dates for the Island utility.

The next section discusses operations for the fresh and wastewater sectors independently.

THE WASTEWATER SECTOR

There are between 15,000 and 16,000 publicly owned wastewater treatment systems in the United States; more than 75 percent of the U.S. population has its sanitary sewerage treated by these wastewater systems. Close to 98 percent of publicly owned treatment systems are municipally owned. According to the American Society of Civil Engineers (ASCE), in 2013 there were between 700,000 and 800,000 miles of public sewer mains in the country. Many were installed in the one or two decades after the Second World War and consequently, are approaching the end of their useful life. In its 2013 infrastructure report card, the ASCE gave the nation's wastewater system only a D+.

Wastewater is simply water that has been used—much of it many more than once. Before being treated again, it is almost always contaminated by various pollutants, depending on what it was used for. It can be classified into two major categories, by source: (1) Domestic or municipal wastewater. This comes from residential sources including toilets, sinks, bathing, and laundry. Because it can include body wastes containing intestinal disease organisms, it is treated and sanitized before the final effluent is discharged into a wetland or watercourse; (2) industrial wastewater. This is discharged by manufacturing processes and commercial enterprises. Industrial process wastewater can contain such pollutants as residual acids, plating metals, and toxic chemicals.

Wastewater is a liquid mix of suspended solids, biodegradable organic materials, pathogenic bacteria and other disease causing organisms, and nutrients such as nitrates and phosphates. Treatment and purification is needed before discharging the effluent into a watercourse. The treatment process removes the unwanted components before the effluent is discharged into a receiving body of water. Wastewater is treated by several step processes to remove pollutants, biosolids, and particulates. The purpose is to improve and purify the water, removing some or all of the contaminants, making it fit for reuse or discharge back to the environment. Discharge may be to surface water, such as a river, lake or stream, in wetland areas, or the ocean. Discharge into surface waters eventually leads to percolation into groundwater that lies beneath the land surface of the earth and which may then be retrieved for additional use downstream.

The wastewater treatment system occurs in a series of sequential processes, beginning with collection and proceeding through preliminary treatment, primary treatment, secondary treatment, disinfection, and finally, sludge treatment. In some municipal systems a third or tertiary treatment is included. The most efficient primary and secondary treatments remove from 85 to 95 percent of pollutants from the wastewater stream before the effluent is disinfected and discharged into local waterways for dispersal. In primary treatment, suspended and floating solids are removed. Screening traps solid objects, gravity sedimentation removes suspended solids, and floating objects are removed from the raw sewage. Primary treatment is referred to as a mechanical treatment, although chemicals are often added to speed up the sedimentation process. The settled solids, called primary sludge, are then removed, subjected to additional treatment and transported to landfills. The partially treated wastewater then flows to the secondary treatment system.

In the secondary treatment, what is known as the activated sludge process, remaining dissolved organic matter is removed in a biological process achieved when microbes consume the remaining organic matter, converting it into carbon dioxide, water, and energy for their own growth and reproduction. Air pumped into large aeration tanks mixes the wastewater and sludge. This stimulates the growth of oxygen-using bacteria and other organisms that are naturally present in sewage. The biological process is followed by another settling process (secondary sedimentation) to remove remaining suspended solids. Secondary treatment facilities include a basic activated sludge process, varying forms of pond and fabricated wetland systems, trickling filters and treatment forms that used additional biological activity.

Tertiary treatment is simply additional treatment of the processes employed in secondary treatment. An example of a tertiary treatment is a secondary process modified to remove more phosphorus and nitrogen. Recycled water is water that has undergone a tertiary treatment. Although considered to be very expensive, the final process can remove more than 99 percent of all the impurities from sewage.

Disinfection is the final step in the treatment process. Here, the wastewater has often been sent to a 'chlorine contact' tank where chlorine is added to kill bacteria, just as it is used in swimming pools. However, because chlorine can have harmful effects on fish and other marine organisms, other chemicals or processes such as ultraviolet radiation have been substituted.

Stormwater and Sewage Overflow Pollution

Since passage of the Clean Water Act in 1972, the EPA has administered the National Pollutant Discharge Elimination System (NPDES) permit program to control water pollution by regulating point sources that discharge pollutants into waters of the United States. The EPA statement in Box 6.1 describes its effort to stop drinking water pollution caused by sewer overflows.

Combined sewer systems are sewers that are designed to collect rainwater runoff, domestic sewage, and industrial wastewater in the same pipe. They are a major water pollution concern for the nearly 800 U.S. cities. Normally, combined sewer systems transport all of their wastewater to a sewage treatment plant, where it is treated and then discharged as effluent into nearby surface waters. In times of extreme rainfall, the wastewater treatment facilities are unable to cope with the excess flow. For this reason, combined sewer systems are designed to overflow occasionally and discharge excess wastewater directly to nearby streams, rivers, or other water bodies. Some designs utilize an overflow at the treatment plant that diverts

BOX 6.1   EPA'S PROGRAM FOR ELIMINATING SANITARY
           SEWER OVERFLOW POLLUTION

The EPA's sanitary sewer overflow control program was described in 2005 this
way:

> Properly designed, operated, and maintained sanitary sewer systems are
> meant to collect and transport all of the sewage that flows into them to a
> publicly owned treatment works (POTW). However, occasional uninten-
> tional discharges of raw sewage from municipal sanitary sewers occur in
> almost every system. These types of discharges are called sanitary sewer
> overflows (SSOs). SSOs have a variety of causes, including but not limited
> to blockages, line breaks, sewer defects that allow stormwater and ground-
> water to overload the system, lapses in sewer system operation and main-
> tenance, power failures, inadequate sewer design and vandalism. EPA
> estimates that there are at least 23,000–75,000 SSOs per year (not includ-
> ing sewage backups into buildings). The untreated sewage from these
> overflows can contaminate our waters, causing serious water quality prob-
> lems. It can also back-up into basements, causing property damage and
> threatening public health.
>
> Additionally, aging sewer line infrastructure in many communities allows
> rain and snow melt to enter sanitary sewer systems. During significant wet
> weather events it is possible for influent flows to exceed the treatment
> capacity of existing secondary treatment units. Known as "peak flows,"
> these wet weather flows are sometimes diverted around secondary treat-
> ment units and then either recombined with flows from the secondary treat-
> ment units or discharged directly into waterways from the treatment plant in
> order to prevent any damage to the treatment facility. Operators of waste-
> water treatment plants must manage these high flows to both ensure the
> continued operation of the treatment process and to prevent backups and
> overflows of raw wastewater in basements or on city streets.

Source: EPA (2015f).

the excess flow to chlorination facilities for disinfection prior to discharge.
These overflows, called combined sewer overflows (CSOs), contain not
only storm water but also untreated human and industrial waste, toxic
materials, and debris.

When this happens, storm water and partially or untreated wastewater
is discharged directly into rivers, streams or lakes, or backs up into residential streets and yards. Release of the excess flow is necessary to avoid
flooding in homes, basements, and businesses and commercial centers.
What occurred in Honolulu, Hawaii in 2014 when storm water entered the
sewage system is described in Box 6.2.

Another example was that of the aged sewage system of Indianapolis

BOX 6.2   HAWAII'S FAMOUS BEACH CLOSED BY HUGE
            SEWAGE SPILLS

An August 26, 2015 an Associated Press story highlighted one of the disastrous effects of failing infrastructure caused by sewage spills on thickly populated urban centers. Heavy rains associated with Tropical Storm Kilo caused manhole covers in Honolulu to overflow with sewage and the Honolulu Zoo to flood on Monday, prompting officials to close an area of beach including Waikiki. Sewage came out of manholes at Ala Moana Beach Park, on a street fronting a shopping mall at the edge of Waikiki where there are two pumping stations.

A day after beaches were re-opened, another spill occurred, this time releasing more treated but not disinfected water into the ocean from the Waikiki system for about five hours. Officials estimated about a million gallons of wastewater were discharged into the ocean. This caused another shutdown of the city's beaches. There are two pumping stations in the area where the spill occurred, but a key part serving one of them was missing because of construction when the storm hit.

This was not the first time Waikiki beaches were closed because of untreated sewage water released into the Pacific Ocean. In 2006, the city temporarily closed Waikiki's beaches after 48 million gallons of raw sewage poured into the Ala Wai Canal bordering the area's hotels and condominiums. That spill occurred after a sewage line ruptured following weeks of heavy rains, forcing the city to divert wastewater into the canal. Hawaii American Water, the private company that runs the treatment plant, said the incident happened Tuesday after an underground electrical cable that feeds power to their chlorination system shorted out as heavy rains fell in the area.

Sources: *New York Post*, August 26, 2015; *Huffington Post*, August 27, 2015.

that has discharged as much as 7.8 million gallons of sewage and storm water into local creeks and rivers in a single year. A major infrastructure project had long been planned to correct the problem, but had yet to take place (ASCE 2013).

Well into the twentieth century, municipalities around the globe regularly discharged the untreated or partially treated sewage and collected storm water into nearby freshwater sources or oceans. For example, the city of Seattle, Washington originally discharged its partially treated sewage into Lake Washington until algal blooms and toxic conditions led to fish die-offs. At its peak, 20 million gallons of effluent was dumped into the lake each day. Lake Washington was called "El Stinko" by local residents, whose complaints finally forced city and country administrators to remediate the problem. Conveniently, an even larger body of seawater Puget Sound was nearby. From 1963 to 1968, a massive tunnel and a new modern wastewater treatment facility were constructed that diverted Seattle's treated sewage effluent into the ocean instead of the lake. Lake

Washington recovered and became a clear lake again, its phytoplankton, zooplankton, and fish returned to their original composition. Most other similarly polluted lakes in the world cannot be restored.

NEW AND CONTINUING WATER CHALLENGES

According to the American Water Works Association (AWWA) water and wastewater utilities in the United States and around the world are facing a number of common challenges. Among the more critical of these challenges are rising costs, chronic drought conditions in large sections of the country, old and insufficient infrastructure, increasingly stringent regulatory and documentation requirements, population growth and demographic structure changes, and a changing workforce.

A list of some of the issues and challenges facing all water utilities in the twenty-first century and which need to be addressed now were published in a revised edition of the industry journal *Public Utilities*, and includes but is not limited to the following, listed here not in the order of the severity of their impact:

1. Security of supplies, distribution and records.
2. Infrastructure disintegration.
3. The impact on freshwater supplies by continued global warming and the predicted acceleration of the phenomena predicted in the near future.
4. Population growth and how it affects water supply and distribution infrastructure.
5. Settlement patterns that see migration toward warmer and drier regions of the country.
6. Changing trends in industrialization and industry's use and misuse of freshwater supplies, together with restrictions on factory location and water use.
7. National, regional and local environmental policies.
8. Drought and desertification of many parts of the country.
9. Agricultural extension and intensive water use for certain crops.
10. Impact of drought conditions on hydroelectric energy production.
11. Unequal water distribution and efforts to share resources.
12. Political pressures for use permitting, quotas, metering, reuse and recycling.

City and town dwellers' greatest needs in the first two-thirds of the nineteenth century were systems for the provision of adequate supplies of clean water, together with a means of dealing with sewage. Inadequate supply of water and wastewater control needs was a major cause of sickness and death in the crowded, unsanitary cities. Well into the 1800s, town dwellers drew their water from shallow wells and discharged their raw sewage into creeks and rivers. The number of civic water systems grew slowly but steadily between 1800 and 1900. At the beginning of the nineteenth century, there were only 16 water systems in cities with a population of 5,000 or more; smaller cities still had to make do without running water. Only one of these was municipally owned; private investors owned 15. Twenty-five years later, the total number of water systems had only doubled to 32; five were municipal systems and 27 were private systems. More rapid growth in the number of systems had to wait until after the end of the Civil War. From the 83 systems that existed in 1850, the number grew to a total of 422 in 1875 and to 3,179 systems in 1896. The shift to municipal ownership was seen in 1875, when nearly 54 percent were public systems. The proportion declined a small amount in 1896: 1,690 or 53.2 percent were public systems (Barnes 1942).

The Challenge of Finding Reliable Supplies

Large portions of the United States and many foreign countries are facing the greatest challenge of all: finding reliable sources of potable water to serve their growing populations during an age of dramatically shifting climate. The world has plenty of water; the problem is only something like 2.5 percent of all that water is freshwater. And, not all of that water is available when and where it is needed. As the USGS water school describes the world's water supply, the globe is indeed "a watery place." However, not all of it is directly available and usable for human consumption. More important, current misuse of the existing freshwater supplies is resulting in greater contamination of many sources of supply. Contamination from man-made and natural causes has made taken existing supplies unfit for human consumption. A recent example of a combination of human and natural effects groundwater is the damage done to the groundwater supplies caused by a long drought and over-pumping of wells for irrigation purposes taking place in California's rich agricultural Central Valley. Water pumped from private and municipal wells has been found to be contaminated by high levels of uranium (Box 6.3). Similar problems are surfacing in other areas of the country's western states as a result of drought conditions and over-pumping for irrigation.

Close to 96.5 percent of all Earth's water is in the world's oceans. Freshwater is stored in the air as water vapor, in rivers and lakes, in icecaps and glaciers, in the ground as soil moisture and underground

---

BOX 6.3   GROUNDWATER IN WESTERN U.S. BECOMING CONTAMINATED WITH URANIUM

Untreated water from a growing number of community and private wells in California's agricultural San Joaquin Valley has become contaminated with uranium, according to the U.S. Geological Survey (USGS). But that's not the only place the contamination is occurring. Uranium at levels above federal and state levels considered unsafe for humans is showing up in drinking water systems in other farming regions of the U.S. west. Uranium is a naturally occurring mineral found in low levels in many locations and is one of the contaminants in many water systems where it is either removed or diluted to levels not considered to be harmful. The concentration of uranium occurs as a result of intensive irrigation with groundwater, drought and over-pumping of water from underground reservoirs that concentrates the remaining aquifer supplies.

It is not uranium's naturally occurring radiation that causes the trouble, but the metal itself. If water with high concentrations of uranium is consumed over a long period, it can result in damaged kidneys and raise cancer risks. Close to two million people in the California Central Valley and other irrigated agricultural areas in the western U.S. live within a half-mile of groundwater with levels of uranium above the safety standards. Many rural municipalities have had to modify their water treatment process to remove the metal. The California farming center City of Modesto, for example, has recently spent more than $500,000 to start blending water from one contaminated well with water from a well not contaminated to dilute the uranium to safe levels.

Source: Knickmeyer and Smith (2015).

---

aquifers. These freshwater resources provide the earth's 7.3 billion people in 2015 with the water they need every day to live, and continue to do so for the estimated 11 billion inhabitants alive at the end of this century.

The combined forces of climate change, population growth, and population relocation are, as expected, making it increasingly difficult to serve customers with all the freshwater they need at a price they can afford. Desalination can generate enough water to augment demand in coastal regions, but not hundreds and thousands of miles inland. But, find new sources they must. One still controversial source that is becoming increasingly viable is recycled water. One of the country's early programs is El Paso Water Utilities (EPWU) advanced water purification system. In good water supply years, El Paso gets its water from stored surface water and groundwater wells. However, the continuing drought in the southwest has left the district's reservoirs at 10 percent of their capacity or less. The EPWU has long used reclaimed water for nonpotable reuse and for recharging the local aquifer. In 2012, the utility began a feasibility study of increasing the capacity of advanced wastewater purification for use in aquifer recharging and other potential uses.

The nation is still far from accepting the direct reuse of reclaimed wastewater into municipal freshwater delivery systems. Until a global standard for membrane technology that produces the desired water quality is accepted along with strict guidelines, the treatment and reuse of wastewater is not likely to become a sizeable quantity of new supply in the municipal water utilities of the country.

FEDERAL ASSISTANCE TO RURAL WATER AND WASTEWATER SYSTEMS

Through U.S. Department of Agriculture's Rural Utilities Service Water and Environmental Programs (WEP), rural communities are able to receive technical assistance and financing necessary to develop drinking water and waste disposal systems. WEP also provides funding for the construction of water and waste facilities in rural communities and is the only Federal program exclusively focused on rural water and waste infrastructure needs of rural communities with populations of 10,000 or less. WEP also provides funding to organizations that provide technical assistance and training to rural communities in relation to their water and waste activities. WEP is administered through National Office staff in Washington, DC, and a network of field staff in each State.

SUMMARY

Unlike the electric utility industry, where a few very large corporations dominate the industry, the water and wastewater sector has largely remained in the hands of nonprofit single-community municipal and regional district systems. However, with the inability to raise the large sums of cash necessary to provide service and replace aging infrastructure at the same time, a number of communities have privatized all or portions of these operations. Build and operate processing programs are also increasingly common. While this has provided some reductions in municipal payrolls, it has not greatly reduced the number and types of organizations or agencies in the industry. Municipal and district water treatment and service providers, agricultural water suppliers, federal and state agencies and departments, wastewater collection and processing operations have been joined by private contractors in meeting this essential need.

The nation's water and wastewater utilities are forced to deal with the effects of weather trends that are increasingly severe and damaging to existing infrastructure. Warren B. Causey reminded us in 2011 that what the United States cannot ignore is that there is just so much freshwater available in the world and supplies nearly everywhere are already under strain. Added to the supply problem is that much of the country's water and wastewater infrastructure is from one hundred to several hundred years old and buried under community streets and buildings. In the U.S., for example, many of the major mains serving cities and towns east of the Mississippi River were constructed in the nineteenth century. In Europe and Asia, many are even older. Much of that infrastructure is beginning to fail at the same time that supplies are reaching or have already reached the point where their use is no longer sustainable.

Small and rural water and combined water and wastewater sectors of the public utilities industry are operating under a cloud of a complex, restrictive and challenging future without the resources to take on all the problems they must deal with. They are stretching their available resources for meeting these challenges to the breaking point. Meeting government-mandated health, efficiency and other factor requirements add to the small systems' difficulty in maintaining their service commitments. To meet their mandate of serving their publics, managers and operators of these small and rural utilities struggle to keep up-to-date on the issues and trends that affect all aspects of their operations. They must innovate in order to survive. In this chapter we describe how a small Pacific Northwest water and wastewater utility has met recent federal and state water efficiency regulations.

Water utilities in the United States and elsewhere in the world are facing massive challenges, many of which are attributable to the climate change already under way. These changes are having an impact upon the natural weather forces that include long-term droughts and stronger intense storm conditions. There is little doubt that these adverse changes to the world's weather patterns are going to continue. Arid areas such as the western U.S. have become more arid and population growth is already taxing the limited water supplies available in many regions. In states such as Arizona and California freshwater resources are already under strain, and no end is in sight. Similar drought conditions are spreading to regions that have long enjoyed seemingly unlimited underground supplies of freshwater. Among the many challenges facing large and small water utilities today and which need to be addressed are the problem of decaying infrastructure, declining water resources, increases in water use, severe drought conditions in some areas and destructive rain storms in others, increasingly rigorous national, regional and local environmental policies and the need to protect the security and stability of supply, distribution systems, and records.

ADDITIONAL READING

Bloetscher, Fred (2011), *Utility Management for Water and Wastewater Operators.* Denver, CO: American Water Works Association.

Drinan, Joanne E. and Frank Spellman (2012), *Water and Wastewater Treatment: A Guide for the Nonengineering Professional* (2nd edn). Boca Raton, FL: CRC Press.

Hyman, Leonard S. (1998), *The Water Business: Understanding the Water Supply and Waster Industry.* Reston, VA: Public Utilities Reports.

Lohan, Tara (ed.) (2010), *Water Matters: Why We Need to Act Now to Save Our Most Critical Resource.* San Francisco, CA: AlterNet Books.

Pearce, Fred (2006), *When the Rivers Run Dry: Water—the Defining Crisis of the Twenty-first Century.* Boston: Beacon Press.

Seidenstat, Paul, Michael Nadol and Simon Hakim (2000), *America's Water and Wastewater Industries.* Washington, DC: Public Utilities Reports.

7. Solid waste collection and disposal utilities

Municipal solid waste (MSW) is waste generated by households and commercial sources that is collected and either recycled, incinerated, or disposed of in MSW landfills that are approved and monitored by the EPA and local environmental and health authorities. The EPA divides municipal waste into four broad categories: containers and packaging, yard wastes, durable goods, and nondurable goods. Examples of durable goods, which are expected to last longer than three years, include appliances, tires, batteries, and electronic equipment. Nondurable goods, which are expected to last less than three years, include newspapers, clothing, disposable tableware, office paper, wood pallets, and diapers (plastic diapers at one time were said to last for a hundred years or longer). MSW does not include dried and sanitized sludge from domestic sewage or other municipal wastewater treatment residues. Also not accepted in sanitary landfills are demolition and construction debris, agricultural and mining residues, combustion ash, and wastes from industrial processes. Although these types of waste, known collectively as industrial solid waste, are largely excluded from hazardous waste regulation; some other agency general regulations do apply. Most highly regulated are toxic and other hazardous wastes.

Rather than being directly under federal regulations specifying how solid wastes should be managed, solid-waste programs are managed by states and municipalities on the local level according to individual community needs. The EPA's waste control role is limited to setting national goals and standards, providing leadership and technical assistance, and developing and disseminating educational materials. Landfills are located and designed according to federally mandated landfill design and operating criteria to ensure the protection of groundwater and requirements for the federal purchase (recycles or reuse) of certain products recovered from the waste stream.

Public control over the collection and disposal of America's growing amounts of municipal solid waste and hazardous waste is a relatively new phenomenon in the public utility industry. For the nation's first two hundred years, solid waste management focused on answering the question, "What can be done with garbage?" (Cohen 2008). Since the

1960s and 1970s, the industry's focus has shifted from what can we do with our garbage to what can we do to reduce the amount of solid waste we generate while at the same time reduce and reuse more of what is thrown away.

SECTOR HISTORY

During the first half of the twentieth century what little government attention paid to the oversight of the waste problem was left to the task of enforcing sanitation standards by large municipalities. In practice, this meant assuring the regular collection of curbside waste; disposal was not seen as a government problem. Instead, it was typically left to private vendors. Public and industrial waste was collected and often dumped unregulated and unmonitored in nearby garbage dumps in or near America's rivers, streams and at sea with little thought to the environmental impact of such practices.

Local governments' attention to the problem of dealing with the individual and commercial waste beginning to clog their streets began with the huge wave of European migration to North and South America in the last several decades of the nineteenth and early twentieth century. By 1910, nearly 80 percent of American cities had formed offices charged with the regular collection of solid waste (NWRA 2014). Initially this meant men with horse or mule-drawn carts collecting waste. This became an important source of employment for the many immigrants and the source of largess by municipal ward healers. By the 1920s, unregulated garbage dumps had become the typical waste disposal method for much of the country's population centers. Streams, rivers, lakeshores and other wetlands were simply open sewers, filled with layers of garbage, ash and dirt.

Elsewhere, refuse tossed in unregulated dumps was burned in the open air, although a few municipalities were beginning to see refuse as a potential fuel for steam heating or electric generation. This was the state of refuse management until the beginning of the environmental protection movement in the 1960s. The American Society of Civil Engineers (ASCE) published what became the nation's first guide to sanitary landfilling. To guard against rodents and odors, ASCE recommended daily compaction of the refuse and covering it with a layer of soil. Passage of the Clean Air Act in the United States in 1970 led to the closure of many early incinerators without air pollution controls. The first federal solid waste management law, the Solid Waste Disposal Act of 1965, authorized research and provided for state grants for disposal methods and site improvements.

The early incinerators were replaced by waste-to-energy plants with pollution controls to reduce or remove particulates and greenhouse gas emissions. Since the 1970s, the solid waste industry has adopted a resource conservation and recovery philosophy that includes source reduction, recycling and reuse.

By 1975, all 50 states had adopted some level of solid waste regulation, although content varies widely from state to state. Passage of the Resource Conservation and Recovery Act in 1976 became the federal government's first significant participation in solid and hazardous waste management. The law emphasized recycling, energy and other resources conservation. The Public Utility Regulatory Policies Act of 1978 guaranteed a market for energy created by small power producers and encouraged growth of the waste-to-energy industry and methane recovery from landfills. According to the National Waste and Recycling Association (NWRA), in 2012 more than 34.5 percent of American municipal solid waste was recycled or composted.

According to the EPA, in 2013 Americans generated about 254 million tons of trash and recycled and composted about 87 million tons of this material, equivalent to a 34.3 percent recycling rate. Municipal solid waste (MSW)—more commonly known as trash or garbage—consists of everyday items that people use and then throw away. Examples include product packaging, grass clippings, furniture, clothing, bottles, food scraps, newspapers, appliances, paint, and batteries. Sources of this solid waste include residences, schools, hospitals, and businesses. On average, Americans recycled and composted 1.51 pounds of the 4.40 pounds of individual waste generated per person per day. In 2013, newspapers and other papers recovery was about 67 percent (5.4 million tons), and about 60 percent of yard trimmings were recovered from the waste stream. Paper and cardboard accounted for 27 percent and yard trimmings and food accounted for another 28 percent. Plastics comprised about 13 percent; metals made up 9 percent; and rubber, leather, and textiles accounted for 9 percent. Wood followed at around 6 percent and glass at 5 percent. Other miscellaneous wastes made up approximately 3 percent of the waste generated in 2013 (Figure 7.1).

Most of this waste is deposited in sanitary landfills, a consequence of passage of the Resource and Recovery Act of 1976 (RRA). Since the full implementation of the federal law, by 1980 landfills had been transformed from what used to be known as 'garbage dumps' to scientifically designed and operated under close supervision of the Environmental Protection Agency and state and local regulatory bodies. The largest number of landfills in operation in 2013 was located in the more sparsely populated western section of the United States, while the fewest were operating in the highly populated northeast (Table 7.1).

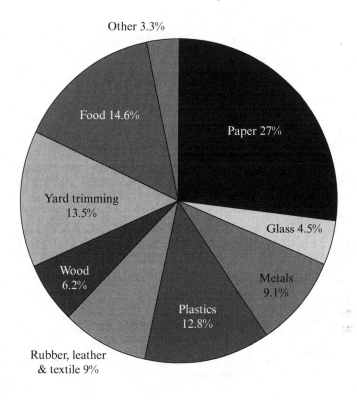

Source: EPA data (2013).

Figure 7.1   *Composition of landfill solid waste before recycling in 2013*

Table 7.1   *Regional distribution of approved landfills in the U.S. in 2013*

Region	Number
Northeast	128
South	668
Mid-West	394
Mountain and West	718
U.S. Total	1,908

Source: EPA (2015f).

Table 7.2   Number and ownership type of solid waste organizations in the U.S., 2014–2015

Governance type	2nd Quarter 2014	3rd Quarter 2014	4th Quarter 2014	1st Quarter 2015
Private Industry	26,795	26,934	27,100	27,330
Local Government	1,156	1,151	1,150	1,160
State Government	4	4	4	4
Federal Government	26	26	25	26
Totals	27,981	28,115	28,279	28,520

Source: BLS (2015a).

STRUCTURE OF THE SOLID WASTE INDUSTRY

The solid waste industry (officially, the Waste Management and Remediation, industry) consists of three main segments: waste collection, treatment and disposal, and waste problem resolution (remediation) services. The services provided by these three sections of the industry include the local collection, hauling and disposal of waste materials, materials recovery (sorting recyclable materials from the waste stream), remediation services (waste site cleanup), septic pumping and additional waste management services (BLS 2015). In 2010, approximately 478,000 workers were employed in the industry; of the total, 355,000 were employed in the private industry segment of the waste management sector. The numbers of private and public organizations in the industry in 2014 are displayed in Table 7.2; they show modest growth occurring in the private sector, from 26,795 establishments in the second quarter of 2014 to 27,330 in the first quarter of 2015.

Waste Collection

Most waste collection in the United States is regulated to some degree. Agencies with an interest in these operations include public utility commissions, energy and transportation departments, state environmental protection agencies, and departments of health. With nearly 66,000 workers, the refuse and recyclable material collection segment of the industry was by far the largest in 2014, with more than twice the number of employees (32,600) as the third largest group, hazardous materials removal workers. Employment by sector in 2014 is shown in Table 7.3.

Waste collection utilities collect solid and hazardous waste from residential, commercial, and industrial customers. The refuse can be collected

Table 7.3   *Employment in the solid waste industry by non-managerial occupation, 2014*

Occupational Category	Number Employed
Refuse and recyclable materials collectors	65,940
Truck drivers, heavy and tractor-trailer	51,240
Hazardous material removal workers	32,640
Laborers, freight and material movers	24,170
Septic tank servicers and sewer pipe cleaners	12,480
Total	186,470

Source: BLS (2015b).

from curbside trash cans or from specially provided metal containers called dumpsters at commercial and industrial locations. The collected waste is then transported to a special facility where it is transferred to landfills or other disposal facilities. At transfer stations, waste is unloaded from collection vehicles, briefly held, compacted and then reloaded onto larger long-distance transport vehicles, typically by road or rail to a disposal site. The distance from collection to disposal sites has been increasing, as landfill sites are being placed farther away from population centers. The collected and compacted waste is increasingly transported to landfills many miles away from where it is collected. Seattle, Washington and several counties on Puget Sound ship their solid waste by a dedicated or merchant train close to 320 miles to the Columbia Ridge landfill in northern Oregon State. Trucks transport the waste into Seattle to Union Pacific Railway's Argo Rail yard where it is transferred to rail cars for the journey to the landfill. Waste from counties north of Seattle is loaded on rail cars in Everett; the full cars are then moved to the Seattle Interbay Rail Yard where they are combined into a single train. Seattle's remaining garbage—the part that residents don't sort into containers for organic and recyclable waste— amounts to about 438,000 tons a year. This is trucked to a Union Pacific rail yard south of downtown Seattle. Six days a week, railcars of western Washington's non-recycled waste are shipped east in trains as long as 110 railcars.

Private and government solid waste utilities collect nonhazardous residential and commercial solid waste and recyclable materials. Nonhazardous waste includes waste from all sources. The services provided by these utilities include essential services including residential waste collection, recyclable material collection, transfer and storage facility, nonresidential waste collection; hazardous waste collection; and construction and demolition site waste. The waste handled can be anything thrown away by households, businesses and industries, including but not limited to garden clippings, glass, paper and cans, construction rubble, medical, radioactive and hazardous waste, among others.

Waste Treatment and Disposal

Treatment and disposal can take several different forms. The most common approaches taken in the United States are deposited in sanitary landfills, recycling or reuse, or used as a fuel for power generation. The EPA includes four treatments of solid waste in its solid waste management program: Source reduction or waste prevention, recycling including community composting, combustion with energy recover, and disposal in landfills. The EPA's waste management hierarchy in Figure 7.2 illustrates the solid waste disposal and treatment system from the most preferred processes to the least preferred.

Sanitary landfills are open sources typically some distance away from urban centers. All nonhazardous waste from a municipality and surrounding area is deposited, compacted, and covered at the site. Landfill management involves sorting out all the waste (waste separation), and sending only the waste that cannot be recycled and composted to the site. Modern

Waste Management Hierarchy

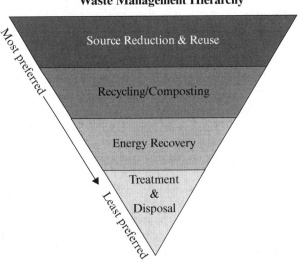

Source: U.S. EPA, Waste Hierarchy Pyramid (GSA 2016).

Figure 7.2   U.S. EPA waste hierarchy pyramid

landfills are lined at the bottom to minimize the leakage of soil pollutants and other toxins from getting into the water table. This method is almost always required by EPA landfill regulations. In many smaller or rural communities sorting is not done, and all the waste (paper, food, diapers, glass, lawn and garden trimming, construction waste, and so on) is mixed and deposited. In the EPA's integrated management hierarchy landfill disposal is the least preferred method of reducing the solid waste stream.

The size and number of approved landfills changed dramatically since the 1980s, the significant increase in the amounts of waste produced in all sources. In 1989, the EPA reported there were 7,389 landfills in use in the United States, with the lowest number, 1,754, reported in 2007. Sanitary landfills are designed to 'concentrate and contain' solid waste in means that will result in the least environmental cost (Halfman 2009). The process requires daily compaction of that day's deposit, after which it is buried under a layer of earth or construction debris, thereby serving to keep out vermin, reduce bad smells, and prevent rain water from advancing toxic liquids leaching and entering the water table. The bacterial decomposition of organic waste results in the creation of flammable gases and carbon dioxide. Modern landfills collect the methane gas produced in this way and either burn it or use it as a natural gas fuel.

Population growth, urbanization and the growing amounts of waste generated in the United States and other industrialized nations is the limited availability of affordable, conveniently located sites for operating new landfills as others are closed, either because they reach their maximum capacity or become environmentally inoperable The city of Seattle, Washington must ship its municipal waste by trainload to a site in northern Oregon. New Jersey, America's most populous state, ships more than half of its solid waste to nearby states. New York City ships much of its trash to upstate New York, Pennsylvania, Virginia and other states. Toronto, Canada has long had to ship out much of its waste to distant locations.

Remediation Service Organizations

Organizations in the mediation segment of the solid waste industry are predominantly private firms not functioning as public utilities and therefore not subject to the same regulatory restrictions that other utilities must follow. They can offer a range of services, ranging from environmental consulting, site and facility pollution remediation, waste identification and disposal, hazardous toxic waste removal, pipeline closure, facility demolition and the rehabilitation of military sites and facilities, including range and unexploded ordnance disposal. A partial list of the services a typical mediation firm might offer includes the following:

- Environmental Response, Compensation, and Liability Act contaminated site remediation
- Resource Conservation and Recovery Act contaminated site remediation
- Environmental compliance
- Waste disposal
- Environmental engineering/consulting
- Landfill design/closure plans and solid waste
- Underground Storage Tank (UST) closures/remediation
- Demolition of structures and facilities
- Regulatory site closure
- Hazardous materials handling
- Sediment remediation and dewatering
- Wetlands and stream restoration
- Remedial investigations/feasibility studies
- Baseline environmental studies
- Water quality sampling
- Beach restoration
- Groundwater sampling and analysis
- Beach restoration.

REGULATING THE SOLID WASTE SECTOR

Like all utilities, the solid waste industry is regulated by a number of federal, state and local agencies. The Resource Conservation and Recovery Act (RCRA) of 1976 was enacted to protect human health and the environment from the real and potential hazards of waste disposal, while at the same time conserve energy, reduce the amount of waste generated by all sources, and ensure that wastes are managed in a manner that is environmentally safe for all species. The waste relevant section of the RCRA is contained in Subsection D of the Act. Sections B and C deal with handling of hazardous wastes. Federal regulations of the industry include (EIR 1976):

- **Criteria for classification of solid waste disposal facilities and practices:** This section established regulatory standards to satisfy the minimum national performance criteria for sanitary landfills. Facilities that fail to meet these criteria are labeled "illegal dumps" and must either be remediated or shut down permanently.
- **Disposal standards for the receipt of conditionally exempt small quantity generator wastes at non-municipal hazardous waste sites:**

Businesses that produce small amounts of hazardous wastes are excused from special hazardous waste handling rules listed in Section C of the Act, and instead may dispose of the wastes in landfills. Section B lists requirements for receiving non-municipal nonhazardous waste receiving sites that receive these low levels of business hazardous wastes, including location restrictions and requirements for monitoring and correcting any subsequent ground-water contamination.

- **Criteria for municipal solid waste landfills:** The 1984 hazardous and solid waste amendments to RCRA contained in Subsection D establish a framework at the federal level for planning and implementing municipal solid waste landfill programs at the state and local levels.

The next major piece of legislation affecting solid and hazardous waste treatment in the United States was the Clean Air Act (CAA) of 1975. This federal law regulates air emissions from stationary and mobile sources. Among other things, this law authorized EPA to establish National Ambient Air Quality Standards (NAAQS) to protect public health and public welfare and to regulate emissions of hazardous air pollutants. Municipal solid waste combustion for waste disposal and energy production are regulated by this act.

Federal regulations also exist for disposal of construction and demolition debris only if that debris is sent to municipal solid waste landfills subject to NCRA standards. This debris is also impacted by Federal Order 1310, the federal order requiring federal acquisition, recycling and waste prevention. For example, the federal government is required to purchase carpeting and insulation made from recycled materials.

Disposal of lawn and garden composting materials is regulated under a section of the Clean Water Act (CWA) that pertains to biosolid (sewage sludge) composting, surface disposal and combustion of biosolids. Sanitized biosolid material is often used as layering material in landfills to control rodent intrusion and control odors.

State and Local Regulatory Actions

The states and local governments are also required to monitor and control solid waste collection and disposal. The example of the state of California is included here as an example of this level of regulatory activity. Private and public solid waste disposal sites in the state are regulated by the California Integrated Waste Management Board (CIWMB). This board partners with local governments in forming Local Enforcement Agencies (LEAs). Certified by the CIWMB, LEAs implement solid waste regulations in their jurisdiction, including all waste disposal sites. In addition to these agencies listed in Table 7.4, other state and local agencies with an interest in solid waste disposal sites include each country's planning, public health, and waste management departments and the state Department of Toxic Substances Control Board.

REDUCING SOLID WASTE

The three most common means employed to reduce the amounts of wastes deposited in landfills are source reduction, recycling, and composting and incineration. Source reduction—also known as waste prevention—simply means reducing the amount of materials used in production and packaging at the source; it is the practice of designing products to reduce the amount of waste that will later need to be thrown away and also to make the resulting waste less toxic. An example is the redesign of plastic milk containers that resulted in a 33 percent reduction in the amount of plastic used and thrown away. The amount of aluminum used in beer cans has also been reduced from 0.546 ounces in 1996 to 0.462 ounces, a 15 percent reduction. Recycling is the recovery of useful materials, such as paper, glass, plastic, and metals, from the trash to use to make new products, reducing the amount of raw materials needed.

Source Reduction

Reducing the amount of solid waste at the source—that is, where products are produced, the type and amount of packaging used, simplifying products to reduce the amount of resources needed to produce them, before they enter the waste stream, and similar steps are included. The types and amounts of waste in the municipal waste stream from 1960 to 2012 are shown in Table 7.5. Specific examples suggested by EPA have included designing products or packaging to reduce their toxicity, reusing existing product or packaging such as refillable bottles, renewable pallets, and reconditioned barrels and drums. Additional proposals include designing longer-lived products, such as rubber tires, so that fewer need to be produced, which in turn will mean fewer that need to be disposed of; using packaging that provides long shelf life and less damage to products; and keeping organic waste such as food, lawn trimmings and shrubbery out of landfills with onsite composting and other means of disposal. Utilities have been encouraged to provide instruction and material support for these and other source reduction activities. Table 7.5 lists historical trends of recycling in the United States in terms of the total amount of MSW generated per person.

Table 7.4 Waste products in the U.S. municipal waste stream, 1960 to 2012

	1960	1970	1980	1990	2000	2005	2008	2011	2012
Waste per person per day[1]	2.68	3.25	3.66	4.57	4.74	4.69	4.37	4.41	4.38
Product (thousand tons per year)									
Durable goods	9,920	14,660	21,800	29,810	38,870	45,060	47,060	49,560	50,030
Non-durable goods	17,330	25,060	34,420	52,170	64,010	63,650	58,690	51,610	51,340
Containers & packaging	27,370	42,560	52,670	64,530	75,840	76,330	75,750	75,320	72,230
Total product waste	54,620	82,280	108,890	146,510	178,720	185,040	181,500	176,490	173,600
Other Waste									
Food waste	12,200	12,800	13,000	23,860	30,700	32,930	34,300	36,310	36,430
Yard trimmings	20,000	23,200	27,500	35,000	30,530	32,070	32,900	33,710	33,960
Misc. organic	1,300	1,780	2,250	2,900	3,500	3,690	3,780	3,870	3,390
Total other waste	33,500	37,780	42,750	61,760	65,730	68,690	70,980	73,890	73,760
TOTAL[2]	88,120	121,060	151,640	208,270	243,450	253,730	252,480	250,380	250,890

Notes:
1 Generated before materials recovery or combustion; does not include construction or demolition debris.
2 Details presented do not add up to 100% due to unit rounding.

Source: EPA (2016a).

Table 7.5   Volume of selected scrap materials recycled, 2010 and 2013

	2010	2013
Industry annual U.S. dollar volume	$77 billion	$88 billion
Industry employment (yearly average)	107,000	137,970
Materials recycled (metric tons)		
Iron and steel	66,000,000	77,000,000
Paper	46,800,000	45,450,000
Aluminum	4,600,000	5,350,000
Copper	1,900,000	2,000,000
Lead	1,200,000	1,100,000
Zinc	160,000	240,000
Plastic (bottles)	655,000 (2009)	515,000 (2012)
Electronics	3,500,000	4,000,000 (2011)
Tires (numbers of)	90,000,000	100,000,000 (2012)

Source: ISRI (2015).

Recycling and Re-use

The recycling industry is far larger than the extra refuse container families put out on waste pick-up days. It includes the scrapping of cars, appliances, even old buildings to recycle the materials used in their fabrication of more of the same products. Construction material recyclers no longer simply bury the metal and concrete rubble they gather when taking down old bridges, sports stadiums, and cutting up old naval warships and cargo vessels; instead the materials they collect are recycled. The billions of pounds of cardboard boxes and paper sacks used by grocers and retailers, the cans and bottles in which the products we used are contained, and all the other recyclable items that contribute to the world's waste stream are also recycled. The industry recycles ferrous and nonferrous metals, paper, plastic, glass, electronic parts, textiles, used tires and motor oil, wood waste, and many other items. Much if not most of recyclable material generated in the U.S. ends its life and begins a new life at a scrap recycling facility. Table 7.6 displays the volume of selected recycled scrap materials processed in the U.S. in 2013 for most materials, and in 2011 for electronics and 2012 for plastic bottles. Utilities have been active partners in the recycling of materials by such actions as providing appropriate collection bins and information campaigns, including programs directed at the nation's school children.

Despite a history of slow but steady growth in the recycling and scrap handling industry, in 2014 and 2015 the industry was reported to be in

Table 7.6   Volume of scrap materials recycled in the U.S., 2013

Product/material	Volume in metric tons/year
Iron and steel	77,000,000
Paper	45,450,000
Aluminum	5,350,000
Copper	2,000,000
Lead	1,100,000
Zinc	240,000
Plastic bottles (2012)	515,000
Electronics (2011)	4,400,000
Tires (number of tires)	110,000,000

Source: ISRI (Institute of Scrap Recycling Industries, Inc.) 2014 Yearbook.

trouble. Most of the major firms and many municipalities were losing millions of dollars. The market for most recycled materials in the United States has matured, and the current economic stagnation in much of the world has turned the industry into what has become a "money-sucking enterprise . . . almost every [municipal recycling facility] in the country is running in the red . . . and more than 2,000 municipalities nationwide are paying to dispose of their recyclables instead of the other way around" (Davis 2015). An example of the dip in demand for recycled materials described in the *Guardian* article was that of glass. Almost of third of the glass in recycling bins is crushed and used as cover material to deter rodents and contain odors. The remaining two-thirds are essentially valueless to the recycling facilities that must pay to have the unwanted glass taken away. The EPA announced that the total amount of recycled materials declined again, to constitute no more than 34.3 percent of the municipal waste stream.

Composting and Incineration

Composting involves collecting organic waste, such as food scraps and yard trimmings, and storing it under conditions designed to help it break down naturally. The resulting compost material can then be used as a natural fertilizer. Recycling and composting together kept 87.2 million tons of material away from being disposed of in 2013, up from 15 million tons in 1980. This prevented the release of approximately 186 million metric tons of carbon dioxide equivalent into the air in 2013—equal to taking over 39 million cars off the road for a year.

Incineration is common in locations with limited landfill space. Incineration chambers can be small for domestic use, but large ones for municipal use as well. Incineration is the preferred method for dealing with contaminated waste such as from hospitals and laboratories. Hazardous waste from factories was once common, however, but the method produces too much carbon dioxide and other greenhouse gases to be common today. Modern municipal incineration processes are considered to be highly efficient and release less dioxin than home fireplaces and backyard barbecues. Incineration also has a secondary benefit: the heat is used as a means for generating electricity, which can then be used either for municipal uses or as an addition to the national electricity grid.

Incineration example: energy recovery from solid waste

In 2011 there were 86 waste-to-energy facilities in the United States, providing up to 2,700 megawatts (MW) of electricity 24-hours a day, year after year. This is enough to supply electricity to about two million homes (EIA 2012). One was the Covanta Energy Corporation's incinerator plant in Lorton, Virginia. The Covanta facility processes municipal solid waste from Alexandria and Arlington, Virginia and some parts of the District of Columbia and Maryland. Incineration-produced power generation began operating in June 1990. It is Covanta's largest facility, processing more than 3,000 tons per day of municipal solid waste for a population of more than 900,000 in the Washington, DC suburbs of Fairfax County, Virginia. The facility sells over 80 megawatts of renewable energy, enough energy to meet the needs of over 80,000 homes. It is the first Covanta facility to have a nonferrous metal recovery system in addition to the incineration of household solid waste. Covanta claims to recycle 400,000 tons of metal per year. Leftover ash is hauled off to be used as liner material in landfills.

Heat from the high-temperature incineration of waste, which company representatives term a *clean burn*, runs a generator that puts 23 megawatts of electricity back on the grid—enough to power 20,000 homes. The facility is owned and operated by one of the leaders in converting solid waste into energy, with 41 plants in North America.

In Europe there are more than 400 of these facilities, and they are particularly prevalent in states with little land available for traditional landfills. Switzerland, Japan, Denmark, France and Sweden incinerate as much as 80 percent of their municipal solid waste Another 300 facilities, many of which are in China and Japan, are located around the world, in 40 countries in total.

Although today's incinerators pollute less because of U.S. EPA's strict maximum available control technology (MACT) regulations, incineration does not eliminate the need for landfills, nor does it eliminate air pollution. Incineration can reduce the volume of waste disposed of in landfills by as much as 90 percent and the weight of refuse by 70 percent. However, burning releases CO^2, which adds to the continent's greenhouse effect. When sulfur is present in the refuse, burning released sulfur dioxide (SO_2) into the air; burning also releases nitrogen oxides into the atmosphere. Both of these gases are contributors to the acid rain problem. Burning plastics can generate chlorine gas, hydrochloric acid, and toxic and corrosive gases, as well as hydrogen cyanide. Although improvements to the incineration technology have greatly reduced these negative side effects, they have not been entirely eliminated. In 2007, EPA compared the industry's emissions performance for major pollutants between 1990 and 2005. The report found a 24 percent decrease in nitrogen oxide, an 88 percent drop in sulfur dioxide and a decrease in dioxins and mercury of 99 percent and 96 percent, respectively, over the time period.

DEALING WITH HAZARDOUS WASTE

Utilities are often required to deal with medical and other hazardous waste. EPA's regulations establish two ways of identifying solid wastes as hazardous under RCRA. A waste may be considered hazardous if it exhibits certain hazardous properties or characteristics, or if it is included on one of four lists of wastes that EPA has determined are hazardous. To be determined hazardous, the product must have been found to pose substantial "present or potential hazards to human health or the environment." EPA evaluates products on four hazardous waste characteristic properties: ignitability, corrosivity, reactivity, or toxicity. Thus, a waste product may be listed as hazardous if the waste (EPA 2016b):

- If it exhibits any of the four characteristics of ignitability, corrosivity, reactivity, or toxicity;
- If it is determined to be acutely hazardous (for example, if it is fatal to humans or animals at low doses);
- If it contains any of the toxic constituents listed in EPA documents, and
- After consideration of various factors described in current regulations, it is capable of posing a substantial present or potential hazard to human health or the environment when improperly treated, stored, transported, or disposed of, or otherwise managed.

Medical Waste

Medical waste can consist of infectious and non-infectious wastes. Hospitals are generally located within designated municipalities, and therefore, their hazardous waste may be a responsibility of local utilities. In a 2010 survey,

114 hospitals reported generating an average of 33.8 pounds of waste per day for each staffed bed. According to the American Hospital Association, there are more than 950,000 staffed hospital beds in the United States. That works out to about 5.9 million tons of garbage annually—perhaps even more, considering that the hospitals surveyed already recycle or otherwise divert at least 10 percent of their waste. According to the medical industry, the first step in medical waste management is to minimize waste and to ensure that it is properly segregated at the source. If general waste is mixed with any hazardous waste, or hazardous waste cannot be segregated, all of it must then be treated as though it is infectious or hazardous. Medical waste includes all of these waste categories; utilities and hospital personnel must develop and follow specific EPA, health department, and infectious disease control guidelines and practices. Categories include:

- Infectious waste: this is the waste stream that attracts the most attention and for which there are the most treatment requirements and options.
- Needles and other sharps: The potential for syringe needles and other sharps waste to spread HIV and hepatitis raise real concern. In some countries, rag pickers search them out and they are illegally repackaged for sale.
- Pharmaceuticals: Unused and/or expired pharmaceuticals should be either returned to the manufacturer for disposal or completely destroyed, never discarded where they can enter landfills. They should never be disposed of in the toilet where they can eventually end up in the nation's waterways.
- Radioactive materials: Many, but not all, medical facilities produce radioactive waste. However, care must be taken to ensure that when it can result from treatment (for example, radioactive tracers) or be present in diagnostic and analytical equipment it disposed of only in federally approved means.
- Pathological and anatomical waste: Human tissues, blood, placenta waste can be hard to handle and sensitive, particularly for anything recognizably human. An approved plan and means of disposal must be in place at all medical facilities where this waste is present.
- Biodegradable wastes: As much as 25 percent of the waste from a healthcare facility can be kitchen and food scraps. These can be composted or biodigested in approved treatment facilities to produce compost and biogas, a renewable fuel.
- Recyclable waste: Paper, plastic, metal and glass are the most widely recycled materials. Segregating, reusing, and recycling these wastes

can make a significant difference to the economics of the facility waste disposal operation.

2015 AWARD-WINNING PROGRAMS

The Solid Waste Association of North America (SWANA) annually recognizes outstanding solid waste programs and facilities with environmentally and economically sound solid waste management practices. Winners demonstrate effective technologies and processes in system design and operations, worker and community health and safety, and successful public education and outreach programs. Programs also must demonstrate that they are fiscally and environmentally responsible through their compliance with all applicable federal, state and local regulations. In 2015 the association honored 31 programs and facilities in 12 different categories. Categories ranged from community outreach and similar communications campaigns to the design and implementation of solid waste facilities and systems. The top winners in all but one of the categories are displayed in Box 7.1

SUMMARY

Municipal solid waste (MSW) includes residential waste from single family and apartment residences, and waste from commercial and instructional locations. More than 60 percent of the nation's solid waste utilities are operated by private enterprise organizations. The amount of refuse collected and disposed of by private and public waste utilities continues to grow, although at a much reduced rate in the United States than what had been the case up to the mid 2000s, when the growth rate became static For example, in 2007, the peak year in waste volume, the United States generated more than 256 million tons of municipal solid waste. Since that year, the amount has remained flat or declined somewhat every year. In 2011, it was 250 million tons, and MSW consists of organic material, paper, plastic, glass, metals, and other refuse collected by municipal authorities, largely from homes, offices, institutions, and commercial establishments. MSW is a subset of the larger universe of waste and typically does not include waste collected outside of formal municipal programs. Nor does it include the sewage, industrial waste, or construction and demolition waste generated by cities. And of course MSW does not include rural wastes. MSW is measured before disposal, and data on it often include collected material that is later diverted for recycling.

BOX 7.1　2015 OUTSTANDING SOLID WASTE PROGRAM
　　　　　AWARDS

Categories and highest medal winners in the annual SWANA Awards in each
category:

Award Category	Highest Medal Winner
Community Awareness Campaign	(Gold) City of Largo, Florida "Largo Recycles More"
Collection System	(Gold) City of Tacoma, Washington, "Residential Collection System"
Communication, Education and Marketing Tools	(Gold) Niagara Region "Illegal Dumping On-line Reporting Tool"
Composting System	(Gold) LaFleche Environmental, Inc. Moose Creek, Ontario "LaFleche Compost Facility"
Educational Program	(Gold) Waste Management, Inc. "Recycle Corps"
Integrated Solid Waste Management System	(Gold) Montgomery County, Maryland, DSWS
Landfill Gas and Biogas	n/a
Landfill Management	(Silver) Metro Waste Authority, Iowa "Metro Park East Landfill"
Landfill Redevelopment	(Silver) Sanford Golf Design, Florida "Trump Golf Links at Ferry Point"
Recycling System	(Gold) Dem-Con Materials recovery, Minnesota "Dem-Con Materials Recovery Facility"
Special Waste	(Gold) Arlington County Department of Environmental Services, Solid Waste Bureau, Virginia "Earth Products Recycling Yard"
Transfer Station	(Silver) Hillsborough County, Florida "Northwest Solid Waste Transfer Station"
Waste to Energy	Pasco County, Florida, Solid Waste Division of Utilities

Source:　SWANA (2015).

The Environmental Protection Agency has taken a proactive role in
reducing the amount and toxicity of the materials entering the municipal
solid waste steam. An example of the EPA's actions is the integrated waste
management program, in which four waste management strategies are

identified. These include source reduction, recycling, combustion with energy recovery, and disposal in sanitary landfills. The agency encourages greater use of the source reduction and recycling and less on combustion and landfill disposal.

In addition to its traditional message of *Reduce, Reuse, Recycle*, EPA is also encouraging producers to adopt what it terms a systematic approach that seeks to reduce materials use and associated environmental impacts over the entire life cycle of goods and services. Called Sustainable Materials Management (SMM), the concept starts with the extraction of natural resources and continues through materials processing, product design, manufacturing, product use, to the final end of the life of the product and its disposal.

ADDITIONAL READING

Buffington, Jack (2015), *The Recycling Myth: Disruptive Innovation to Improve the Environment*. Santa Barbara, CA: Praeger.

Chandrappa, Ramesha and Jeff Brown (2012), *Solid Waste Management: Principles and Practice*. Berlin: Springer.

Christensen, Thomas, H. (ed.) (2010), *Solid Waste Technology and Management* (2 volume set). New York: Wiley.

Porter, Richard C. (2002), *The Economics of Waste*. Washington, DC: Resources for the Future.

Royte, Elizabeth (2005), *Garbage Land*. New York: Little, Brown.

VanGuilder, Cliff (2011), *Hazardous Waste Management: An Introduction*. Dulles, VA: Mercer Learning and Information.

8.   Public transit utilities

Public transportation in the United States, except for ferryboats and barges, only became necessary and broadly available with the growth of cities in the mid-nineteenth century. Prior to then, work was almost always within walking distance of people. However, as municipal concentrations such as Boston and Philadelphia grew and distances increased, horse-pulled stagecoaches, patterned after the coaches common in Great Britain, were introduced. Soon, similar carriages were introduced in other growing cities. By the 1830s, carriages traveling on iron rails had been introduced in New York City. The first common carrier steam-powered railroad, the Baltimore and Ohio, began operations in 1830. Substantial growth, however, had to wait until the end of the Civil War. Street railways, elevated lines and horse-drawn carriages were soon common. The era of horse-drawn public transit was curtailed in the 1870s when an epidemic killed thousands of horses—18,000 died in New York alone. In an effort to halt the spread of the disease, as well as reduce the pollution, city fathers sought other means of public transit. One new approach, cable-hauled street railways were first installed in San Francisco in 1873. A similar system followed in hilly Seattle, Washington and many others were installed around the country. In 1882, representatives from five U.S. cities met to form the country's first Street Railway Association. By 1887, Chicago was operating 150 cable car trains daily. Urban transit was here to stay (APTA 2014a).

   Growth in public transportation began to grow at a faster pace after electrification became possible. The first electric-powered system, the Union Passenger Railway in Richmond, Virginia began operations in 1888. It was the first such system in the country. Over the next two years, the system's designer received contracts to build nearly 120 more systems. Town leaders in municipalities large and small competed with one another for immensely profitable rights to build and operate monopoly electric transit systems. Before long, private owners of the systems merged, resulting in formation of trusts. Industry growth was hurt by the 1930s Great Depression, and many of the trusts were broken by the new regulatory laws passed in the 1930s.

MODERN SYSTEMS

The systems recognizable today are based on the systems begun during boom years of urban population and infrastructure growth that shaped America's cities between the 1880s and 1940s. Possibly the most influential change was the effects on society brought about by the perfection of the internal combustion engine and the advent of affordable private automobiles. Few cities still operate electric powered trolley systems on iron rails. Even where overhead electric power lines still provide motive power, the trolleys now run on rubber tires. Gasoline and diesel powered motor buses now serve urban and rural dwellers and continue to expand their service farther and farther from the cities' cores.

As the systems have expanded geographically, so have the range and reliability of the services they offer. Many buses and other transit vehicles have increased the numbers and types of passenger amenities regularly offered to their riders (APTA 2014a). Rider security has been greatly improved by the growth in installation of onboard closed-circuitry security cameras from 13 percent of all buses in 2001 to 62 percent in 2013. Increases have also taken place in the number of vehicles with automated stop announcements, the number of exterior bicycle racks installed, and automatic vehicle location systems.

STRUCTURE OF THE PUBLIC TRANSIT SECTOR

The American Public Transportation Association reports on the status of three major classes of public transportation systems: those that serve metropolitan areas, rural area systems, and services managed by nonprofit organizations that operate demand response services exclusively, primarily for senior citizens and persons with disabilities. Not included are school bus systems. Nonprofit organizations are eligible for federal financial assistance to purchase vehicles and offer their demand services.

In 2012 there were 7,118 organizations providing public transportation in the United States. They range in numbers from the 6,511 demand response organizations to the two aerial tramways and the single cable car service still operating in San Francisco, California (Table 8.1). Demand response service (also called paratransit services) vans and small buses travel on roadways and streets, taking passengers directly from their journey origins to their destinations. Federal law requires accessible demand response service for disabled persons or those unable to use fixed route service to be provided in areas served by regular route transit service. General demand response service is not regulated by law.

Table 8.1   Number of U.S. public transportation systems by mode in 2012

Systems by Mode	Numbers of systems[a]			
	Urbanized[b]	Rural[b]	Non-profit providers[c]	Totals
Aerial tramway	2	0	0	2
Automated guideway	7	0	0	7
Bus transit	699	530	0	1,229
Bus rapid transit	4	0	0	4
Cable car	1	0	0	1
Commuter bus	72	60	0	132
Commuter rail	27	0	0	27
Demand response [b, d]	765	1,163	4,600	6,528
Ferry boat	37	6	0	43
Heavy rail	15	0	0	15
Hybrid rail	4	0	0	4
Inclined plane	4	0	0	4
Light rail	25	0	0	25
Monorail	2	0	0	2
Publico [f]	1	0	0	1
Streetcar	10	0	0	10
Transit vanpool	71	21	0	92
Trolleybus	5	0	0	5
Total [d, e]	1,751	1,780	4,600	8,131

Notes:
(a)   For systems operating during 2012; all amounts are estimates.
(b)   Some urban providers operate into surrounding rural areas and some rural providers operate into nearby urban areas.
(c)   May be either urban or rural.
(d)   Includes nonprofit providers for seniors and persons with disabilities.
(e)   Total is not sum of all modes since many providers operate more than one mode.
(f)   Publico systems are privately owned vans or small buses, regulated by a public service commission, operating on a fixed route but without fixed schedules; only systems in 2014 were in San Juan, Puerto Rico.

Source: APTA (2014a).

By far the greatest numbers of systems (1,229) operate with over-the-road buses. An increasing number of these buses run on alternative or renewable fuels such as biodiesel or natural gas, and many are now hybrid powered. More than twice as many systems operate in rural areas (1,703) compared to the 815 systems serving urbanized areas. Transit systems run from the very large to just one or a few vehicles. Large systems are usually found operating in metropolitan areas consisting of a large central city and wide semi-rural commuter regions that surround the city. The largest and most diverse of the largest systems operate within and surrounding New York City and adjoining states and counties. The nation's largest system is the MTA New York City Transit (NYCT). In 2013 NYCT had the largest number of unlinked passenger trips and passenger miles traveled, roughly 3.4 billion boardings. Table 8.2 compares the passenger trips and miles of the 20 largest systems in the United States. Unlinked passenger trips (also called boardings) are defined as the number of passengers who board public transportation vehicles; passengers are counted each time they board the vehicle, and again each time they transfer to another vehicle on their journey.

Buses traveling on roadways and heavy rail systems together make up more than 85 percent of the vehicle types in public transportation, with bus services providing more than half of all the passenger boardings (that is, passengers entering a transit vehicle) and more than 36 percent of the passenger miles traveled in 2012 (Table 8.3). Heavy rail boarding made up 35.4 percent of total passenger trips and 30.7 percent of the passenger miles traveled, These were distantly followed by commuter rail with 4.5 percent of the passenger trips and 19.6 percent of the passenger miles; light rail was next with 4.2 percent of the passenger trips and 4.1 percent of the passenger miles.

Independent public organizations have evaluated the public transit systems of the United States on such criteria as how often transit vehicles run, the distance between stops and other factors, including how supporting the community and system were for walkers and cyclists. One such organization, Walk Score, ranked systems in 316 U.S. cities and thousands of neighborhoods. Scores were scaled on a possible 100 points. Results of the top ten cities with the best transportation systems in 2014 are shown in Table 8.4. The city with the highest transit score was New York with 81.2 points. San Francisco, despite its many hills, was second with 80.5 point and Boston was third with 74.8 points.

REGULATORY OVERSIGHT

Buses, ferries, trains, and planes are all regulated by the U.S. Department of Transportation if they are used to transport people or cargo across state lines. Buses, ferries, and trains that do not cross state lines are regulated by the states in which they are registered and operate. Regardless of what authority governs a common carrier, public transportation is controlled by

*Table 8.2   Twenty largest transit agencies by trips and passenger miles,
2012 (thousands)*

Transit Agency	First City in System	Unlinked passenger Trips	Rank	Total Passenger Miles/Year	Rank
MTA/New York City Transit	New York, NY	3,381,062	1	12,189,809	1
Chicago Transit Authority	Chicago, IL	545,578	2	2,266,251	5
Los Angeles Country Metropolitan Area Transit Authority	Los Angeles, CA	464,875	3	2,269,365	4
Washington Metropolitan Area Transit Authority	Washington, DC	424,485	4	2,017,101	7
Massachusetts Bay Transportation Authority	Boston, MA	401,617	5	1,845,574	8
Southwestern Pennsylvania Transit Authority	Philadelphia, PA	363,480	6	1,632,221	10
New Jersey Transit Corporation	New York, NY	266,853	7	3,082,675	2
San Francisco Municipal Railway	San Francisco, CA	222,937	8	468,707	20
Metropolitan Atlanta Rapid Transit Authority	Atlanta, GA	134,890	9	699,257	13
MTA Bus Company	New York, NY	120,878	10	371,781	24
King Country Department of Transportation	Seattle, WA	119,952	11	576,539	16
San Francisco Bay Area Transit District	San Francisco, CA	118,675	12	1,545,718	11
Maryland Transit Administration	Baltimore, MD	112,277	13	818,308	12
Miami-Dade Transit	Miami, FL	107,340	14	613,212	14
Tri-County Metropolitan Transit District of Oregon	Portland, OR	103,219	15	471,451	19
Denver Regional Transportation District	Denver, CO	98,519	16	589,149	15
MTA Long Island Rail Road	New York, NY	96,953	17	2,083,400	6

Table 8.2   (continued)

Transit Agency	First City in System	Unlinked passenger Trips	Rank	Total Passenger Miles/Year	Rank
San Diego Metropolitan System	San Diego, CA	85,236	18	385,281	23
MTA Metro-North Commuter Railroad	New York, NY	83,357	19	2,438,202	3
Port Authority Transit-Hudson Corporation	New York, NY	81,292	20	343,380	27

Source: APTA (2014a).

Table 8.3   *Unlinked passenger trips and passenger miles by mode in 2012*

Systems by Mode	Numbers of systems[a]			
	Passenger trips (millions)	Percent of total	Passenger miles (millions)	Percent of total
Bus transit	5,301	50.1%	20,734	36.3
Bus rapid transit	16	0.2	80	0.1
Commuter bus	50	0.5	1,285	2.2
Commuter rail	471	4.5	11,181	19.5
Demand response	211	2.0	1,750	3.1
Ferry boat	79	0.7	431	0.8
Heavy rail	3,743	35.3	17,516	30.6
Hybrid rail	6	0.1	74	0.1
Light rail	449	4.2	17,516	4.1
Other rail modes	40	0.4	46	0.1
Publico	33	0.3	145	0.3
Streetcar	49	0.5	99	0.2
Transit vanpool	37	0.3	1,298	2.3
Trolleybus	66	0.9	162	0.3
Total	10,581	100%	72,317	100%

Note: (a)   Includes only transit agencies reporting to Federal Transit Administration, National Transit Data Base.

Source: APTA (2014a).

*Table 8.4   Top ten U.S. transit systems in 2014 (rated on a
           100-point scale)*

Rank	City System	Score	Comments
1	New York City	81.2	No one is ever more than a 10 or 15 minute walk to some form of public transit
2	San Francisco	80.5	BART and MINI provide superior city transit service
3	Boston	78.4	Rail and bus lines provide very convenient service; Boston is the third most walkable city in the U.S.
4	Washington, DC	70.4	Metrorail is the busiest transit rail system in the country; the city also in the midst of a 6-year rebuilding program
5	Philadelphia	67.0	SEPTA operates bus, light rail, trolley and two subway lines
6	Chicago	65.3	The city operates convenient rail systems and local bus operations
7	Seattle	57.3	Expansion of Sound Transit light rail line means the existing system will continue to be improved; the region also operates a large ferry system
8	Baltimore	56.9	Baltimore has 105 bus routes, light rail, and ferry system that provide very good commuter and local service
9	Los Angeles	49.9	This geographically very large city and county has very high bus ridership and is expanding its light rail network
10	Portland, OR	49.6	The city's bus and light rail system are rated very high

Source: Stone (2014).

extensive regulations that provide rules for the carriers and rights for the riders should an accident or injury occur.

The Americans with Disabilities Act of 1990 (ADA) mandated that no person with a disability may be denied the opportunity to use the public transportation system. Also, and where necessary or upon request, the personnel of both public and private transportation services must assist a disabled person with the use of ramps, lifts, declining entry capabilities or any other device that enable the individual to enter or exit the transit vehicle. The personnel may have to leave their seats in order to provide such assistance. Other ADA regulations require that all common wheelchairs are allowed on public and private transportation services. However, it also says they are subject to designated securement locations on the vehicle. Also, service animals must be permitted on both public and private transportation services.

The primary federal agency with standards and support responsibility for public transit utilities is the Federal Transit Administration (FTA), an agency within the United States Department of Transportation (DOT). The FTA provides financial and technical assistance to local public transit systems, including bus systems, subways, light rail, commuter rail, monorail, passenger ferry boats, trolleys, inclined railways, and people movers. The FTA is one of ten modal administrations within the DOT. Headed by an Administrator appointed by the President, the FTA carries out its functions from its Washington, DC headquarters and ten regional offices. Until 1991, it was known as the Urban Mass Transportation Administration (UMTA).

The federal government, through the FTA, provides financial assistance to develop new transit systems and improve, maintain, and operate existing systems. The FTA oversees grants to state and local transit providers, primarily through its ten regional offices. These grantees are responsible for managing their programs in accordance with federal requirements, and the FTA is responsible for ensuring that grantees do so.

Department of Labor Role

The U.S. Department of Labor plays a role in the regulatory oversight of public transit through its rules and regulations for the safety and security of transit employees. The National Transit Systems Security Act (NTSSA) includes provisions for protecting transit employees from discrimination or from retaliatory action if fired for being a whistleblower: The Act provides the following protections:

1. A public transportation agency, or a contractor or a subcontractor of such agency, or an officer or employee of such agency, shall not discharge, demote, suspend, reprimand, or in any other way discriminate against an employee for:
   A. Reporting a hazardous safety or security condition;
   B. Refusing to work when confronted by a hazardous safety or security condition related to the performance of the employee's duties, if the conditions described in paragraph (2) exist; or
   C. Refusing to authorize the use of any safety- or security-related equipment, track, or structures, if the employee is responsible for the inspection or repair of the equipment, track, or structures, when the employee believes that the equipment, track, or structures are in a hazardous safety or security condition . . . , if the conditions described in paragraph (2) of this subsection exist.

2. A refusal is protected under paragraph 1-B) and C) if:
   A. The refusal is made in good faith and no reasonable alternative to the refusal is available to the employee;
   B. A reasonable individual in the circumstances then confronting the employee would conclude that
      i. The hazardous condition presents an imminent danger of death or serious injury; and
      ii. The urgency of the situation does not allow sufficient time to eliminate the danger without such refusal; and
   C. The employee, where possible, has notified the public transportation agency of the existence of the hazardous condition and the intention not to perform further work, or not to authorize the use of the hazardous equipment, track, or structures, unless the condition is corrected immediately or the equipment, track, or structures are repaired properly or replaced. (OSHA 2015)

State Regulatory Role

All states provide some regulatory and administrative oversight for their local public transit systems. With a 2010 census population of approximately 2.07 million, New Mexico is one of the nation's most sparsely populated states. In 2010, 14 regulated bus transit systems were operating in the state, with the largest serving Santa Fe, the state capitol. The State Department of Transportation's transit and rail division provides a number of support and regulatory functions for the state's bus and rail systems. Examples of the transit and rail division's services include:

- Manages the New Mexico Park and Ride bus service.
- Provides technical and coordination assistance to public and private nonprofit transit operators.
- Administers federal transit grants used by the state's larger municipalities for Rideshare programs.
- Administers federal transit planning grants used by Metropolitan Planning Organizations.
- Administers Congestion Mitigation Air Quality and Surface Transportation Program Urban funds used for transit purposes from the Federal Highway Administration.
- Assists local governments to establish Regional Transit Districts (RTDs) and then assists the RTDs to plan, coordinate and implement service.

CHANGING RIDERSHIP TRENDS

Among the many social changes and trends contributing to the challenges facing the nation's nearly 7,200 mass transit systems are growing urban sprawl requiring more and longer services, growing auto and heavy commercial vehicle use, increased congestion in and out of urban cores, and changing travel populations of the American public. Utilities have no control over the traffic congestion that clogs most if not all the metropolitan areas where their services are most needed. The impact of these trends has grown in importance and weight since they were spelled out in a 2004 study for the American Public Transportation Association (Hemily 2004). The study also points out some of the major areas of concern that are influenced by these trends:

- Environmental degradation due to vehicular exhausts, ever-increasing demand for carbon-based fuels for transportation vehicles, the economic and safety implications of greater dependence upon automobiles.
- Health issues resulting from reduced exercise, greater automobile use, and disappearance of the environment due to development of natural areas.
- Growing need for transport assistance to meet the mobility needs of an aging population and growing numbers of immigrants in inner cities.
- The importance of public transportation to aid in the integration of all segments of society, including but not limited to the physically disadvantaged and economically disadvantaged and large immigrant population.

Millennials as Transit Riders

The Millennial Generation, transit riders born between approximately 1980 and 2000, is the largest and most diverse generation in U.S. history (APTA 2015). They are also heavy users of public transportation. In 2009, the Pew Research Center identified the following characteristics about the men and women of this generation (Keeter and Taylor 2009; Pew Research Center 2014):

- They are the most ethnically and racially diverse cohort of youth in the nation's history. On average, roughly 19 percent are Hispanic; 14 percent are black or African-American; 4 percent are Asian; 3 percent are mixed race or other; and 60 percent are white.

- They are the most politically progressive age group in modern history; about half describe themselves as political independents, although more have voted for Democrat than Republican candidates.
- They are the first generation to have used computers all their lives, and to regard behaviors like tweeting and texting, along with websites like Facebook, YouTube, Google and Wikipedia, as everyday parts of their social lives. This is one of their chief reasons for using public transit.
- They are the least religiously observant youths since survey research began charting religious behavior; about 30 percent say they do associate themselves with any religion.
- They are more inclined toward trust in institutions than were either of their two predecessor generations—Gen Xers and Baby Boomers—when they were coming of age.
- Regardless whether they live in cities or in suburbia, they maintain a strong inclination for an urban lifestyle that includes a preference for selecting the best transportation mode (bicycle, transit, driving, or walking) for the trip. The communities in which they live tend to have many transportation choices.

Millennials are inclined to use a variety of transportation systems in their typical journeys, often using several modes in the same trip (APTA 2015). Like most Americans, overall their favorite mode is privately owned or borrowed automobile. This is followed by walking; subway, light rail, streetcar or trolley; with bus and bicycle equally their least preferred mode. However, public transportation options are considered the best mode for digital socializing while traveling and 40 percent commonly work while they travel.

GROWTH OF URBAN SYSTEMS

Ridership in public transit overall continues to grow along with population growth and renewed urbanization. In 2014 alone, passengers in the U.S. took 10.8 billion trips on public transportation. This was the highest in nearly 60 years. Ridership that year had grown by nearly 40 percent since 1995. These related phenomena generate a number of challenges for both urban and rural public transportation systems. As expected, public transportation utilities and nonprofit organizations offering transit services are finding it difficult to keep pace with this growth in demand. Not the least of their problems is coming up with the funds needed for expanding and improving their services. Public transportation is a $61 billion industry in America, employing upwards of 400,000 men and women.

Despite this continued growth in ridership overall, not all systems are enjoying problem-free operations. For example, in March 2015, a *Salon* magazine article claimed that U.S. mass transit is dying. The author tied the operating problems suffered by three very large transit systems to an old and failing infrastructure which made delays and system shutdowns common during the harsh 2014–2015 northeast winter months (Grabar 2015). The systems included the New York Metropolitan Transit Authority (NYMTA), the Metrorail system of the Washington, DC Metropolitan Area Transit Authority (MATA) and Boston's Massachusetts Bay Transportation Authority (MBTA).

Success in moving people out of their automobiles and into mass rapid transit was part of New York's system's problem. In 2014, average weekday subway ridership was 5.6 million, the highest since 1949. Annual ridership was 1.751 billion, the highest since 1948. Record ridership occurred despite delays, cancellations and operations errors, partly due to old infrastructure and heavy storm damage.

The problems in Washington's system are the opposite of ridership growth; ridership in 2014 was down by 11 percent from 2009 and continues to decline. A series of equipment breakdowns and fires have occurred; smoke has driven riders out of stations on numerous different occasions. In January 2015 a third rail malfunction caused a smoke cloud that sent 84 riders to the hospital and contributed to the death of one woman.

In February 2015, *Boston Globe* writer David Scharfenberg described the Boston system's problems this way:

> Broken subway cars and rails packed in ice. A region frozen in place. And, just like that, the feisty general manager of the MBTA resigned, her boisterous defense of the agency replaced with silence. There was, no doubt, something abrupt about the crippling of the nation's fifth-largest public transit system in the face of this unprecedented run of weather. But the true story of the breakdown is not one of sudden failure. It is a decades-long tale of grand ambitions and runaway costs, of lawmakers who failed to invest amid warnings of collapse, and a system reaching for expansion even as its core deteriorated. (Scharfenberg 2015)

The system's fleet breaks down for many reasons. One is the advanced age of much of the rail cars, which it cannot afford to replace. Including interest owed, the system had a debt of $8 billion in 2012.

Designing an Optimal Urban System

Researchers in Seattle, Washington and the engineering faculty of Kumanoto University in Japan developed what they believed to be the optimal new public transit management system (Uchimura, Saitoh and Takahashi 1999). The system they described is based on three hierarchical levels of bus or rail service and a jitney or van service that would operate on the lowest level. At the highest level is the traditional regional or inter-city *trunk line* (italics in the original) bus or heavy or light rail service system. This system connects major cities and employment centers in the region served and typically runs on its own right-of-way or transit priority lanes or corridors.

At level two is the intercommunity *express* bus service. This express service connects communities with other communities with regular scheduled express buses. The system envisioned divides the region into areas of roughly one square mile each. These community centers will each have a community station. All or most express bus stops in the region are then eliminated. The traditional way of having express buses make regular stops and operating on city streets limited to high-occupancy vehicles (HOV) often results in unnecessary local congestion. Eliminating or greatly reducing these stops is expected to end or greatly reduce that congestion by providing an additional lane capacity for other traffic. Eliminating congestion on arterial streets can open lanes to other modes of transportation such as pedestrians, bicycles or even commercial freight transportation. The authors envisioned the community stations as also becoming locations for community or commercial activities, high-rise multi-use buildings, and locations for park-and-ride structures. As a consequence, they could also become a community administration's tool for growth management.

Level three is the intracommunity specialized, short-trip transit service, operated with vans, small buses, taxis or jitneys (jitneys are small buses or private automobiles or vans that may operate on a regular schedule or on an on-call basis), but only within the designated community. In this system, they are designed to eliminate regular bus stops by operating on a door-to-door, as called for basis. Pick-ups are scheduled by telephone request, preferably with some lead time. Passenger pick-ups are dispatched from a regional center. As designed, the system has a prescribed operating time of 15 minutes for service vehicles to complete each trip.

Clearly, this system is designed to reduce traffic congestion on urban residential and local commerce-related streets and roads. Potential constraints still needed to be addressed are the width of local streets, the number of lanes in each direction, whether curb-lane parking is allowed, whether the streets are one or two-way, traffic signal timing, incidence rates of accidents, and others. However, for major metropolitan areas in newly developed states, the model does hold promise.

CHALLENGES FACING URBAN SYSTEMS

Some of the issues and challenges facing urban public transportation systems in the twenty-first century have plagued cities for thousands of years. Rome, for example, suffered from urban congestion and environmental problems from waste accumulation and air pollution caused by wood fires. Others are as modern as today. However, narrow streets and the traffic congestion and environmental problems that follow are among the most pressing problems facing urban transit systems. The major problems facing urban transportation system administrators identified by Rodrique, Comtois and Slack (2013) include the following:

- *Traffic congestion.* Traffic congestion becomes a problem when cities go above about 1 million residents. In addition to the social phenomenon of more people moving back into the city and cities as magnets for recent immigrants, traffic congestion is a product of American's love affair with their automobiles. Many families have two or more automobiles. Moreover, most transportation systems in cities were designed for motor vehicles. Only a few cities have subways, and few new ones are being considered.
- *Decentralization.* Public transit systems are inefficient when used in low density and scattered urban areas such as Los Angeles and similar metropolitan areas. Office and commercial centers are developed on less expensive suburban land in ever-growing external regions of the central core. A result is longer trips on higher operating cost modes. This greater decentralization makes it harder and more expensive to justify expansion and upgrading of public transit service.
- *Public transport inadequacies* due to fixity and lack of connectivity. Rail and subway systems are fixed. As more development occurs along these fixed routes, automobile traffic increases to and from nearby residential regions. Often, urban blight grows around older fixed systems. Because of the very high cost of expanding fixed systems, expansion is extremely costly and difficult to justify. While the fixed systems are generally elements in a central core transit utility, service in the outlying areas are typically independent utilities that operate under their own schedules and limitations.
- *Competition.* Road systems were designed and continue to be constructed and expanded for motor vehicle use. Despite of growing congestion and greater difficulty in finding reasonable parking space, most commuters continue to be willing to trade time for the perceived freedom of mobility and convenience offered by the

private automobile. Public transit is often unable to compete with that promise.

- *Financing and fare structure*. Urban transit systems are almost universally unable to finance infrastructure repair and rebuilding and operating equipment purchased on income from fares alone. Hence, many systems cannot operate without subsidies from local, state or federal governments. In most cases, grants require matching funds, which are difficult to gather without increases in fares or local taxes. As a result, a number of the larger systems are heavily in debt, further reducing their ability to finance needed repairs and equipment replacement. Most urban public transit systems no longer use distance-based fares, replacing them with a flat-rate for ridership, although it is increasingly common to see a time-based fare structure in use, with higher fares applied for high demand periods. Flat-rate systems tend to discourage short trips and encourage longer-trips. Longer trips are typically more costly to provide than short trips and do not generate the income needed to supply the service.

- *Legacy costs*. Most urban and many rural systems employ unionized labor that has used the threat of strikes and service disruptions as levers to secure favorable remuneration and benefit negotiation outcomes. Other legacy costs have sometimes been engendered by using subsidies for compensation rather than to cover past debt or for performance improvements or infrastructure repair. Some public utilities find themselves forced to raise fares, defer maintenance, or break labor contracts to keep service going. Whatever the reason or outcome, the consensus of transit system analysts is that financing critical infrastructure repairs is going to become even more difficult in the future.

RURAL TRANSIT SYSTEM CHALLENGES

Rural transit issues and concerns tend to have very different characteristics as systems serving urban communities. The challenges their managers and administrators face vary depending on the service area's economic base, topography, and proximity to urban areas and popular recreational destinations. Despite this variation, they do have many challenging issues in common. The Western Rural Development Center (WRDC) is one of four regional centers receiving funds from the U.S. Department of Agriculture to help economic conditions and improve transportation systems in rural areas. A 2006 study published by the WRDC at Utah State University described some of the challenges of planning and operating transportation systems in rural areas. The key challenge facing rural transport systems is that little commonality exists in the regions to be served; few successful models exist. Hence, each system must be designed from the ground up. To enable system planners to design and operate successful rural systems, the WRDC publication presented five questions that needed to be answered when designing a rural transportation system that includes freight and human transport:

1. First, determine how transportation can be part of a plan designed to improve the rural economy. Knowing the payoffs expected to accrue from improved transportation makes it easier to justify the expenses that are sure to follow.
2. Then establish what the community believes is the appropriate balance between providing cost-effective transportation for the region and preserving the rural natural environment.
3. Then determine how rural transportation can be made accessible to the greatest number and ability of citizens in the area to be served by the system.
4. The next question is one of governance; the system cannot be expected to manage itself. So, determine how decisions on rural transportation are to be made and implemented.
5. The final and often hardest question to answer for all stakeholders in the system is how should their rural transportation system be funded?

Reliability and Security

Providing safe and reliable transit is one of the greatest challenges rural area residents face. However, a number of challenges contribute to the difficulty of designing and operating a rural area transit system that satisfactorily answers the questions included in the WRDC study. They include the following facts of rural living:

1. Generally small and disbursed population. This means fewer riders and more distant pick-ups and deliveries. This results in higher operating costs and a lower revenue base to support equipment upgrades and route expansion. For many rural residents, public transit is their only means of transportation.
2. Longer service distances: Large, sparsely populated areas such as those in western states areas lengthen response time, increase operational costs, and raise difficulties in vehicle maintenance, fuel costs and finding and keeping reliable employees.
3. Integrity of the existing road system: Something close to 40 to 50 percent of the nation's roads are located in rural areas, the proportion

of road miles to population makes for a greater responsibility, often without the financial means to repair or replace hazardous roadways.

4. Road safety: Road safety of rural residents is a continuing problem across the country. The fatality rate per million vehicle miles on rural roads is more than twice that of urban areas.
5. Limited funding: Rural transit agencies must work on tight budgets; seldom do local tax bases or fare-box fees provide all the revenues needed for innovative system improvements.
6. Aging population: More seniors remaining in their homes result in greater pressures on the on-call and demand-based transportation needs of rural systems. This has made scheduling more difficult expending limited resources.
7. Transit-dependent populations: Taxis, trains and other means of transportation are just not available for most rural residents; rural transit is often their only source of getting around. As the numbers of older citizens and dependent immigrants increase, meeting this challenge will grow even more pressing on rural transit systems.

Variability in System Design

Transit service in rural areas of the United States is as varied as are the small towns and villages that the systems serve (CTAA 2015). As a result, no two systems are alike. They vary in such areas as type and availability of funds to operate, routes to serve, schedules to maintain, governance system under which they operate, and passengers served. In addition, rural systems must also consider issues of a sparsely distributed population, long trips, aging population, higher operating costs, a lack of capital sources to develop more efficient and reliable systems, and a number of new challenges. These and other issues were addressed in a Community Transportation Association platform for a rural transportation paper:

> The role of mobility in shaping and revitalizing rural America is an evolving one . . . The traditional demand-response rural transit operation that once largely served senior citizens has been transformed in recent years to a full-service public transit system with intermodal connections with intercity operators, employer-partnered vanpools as well as providing vital medical transportation trips to dialysis, chemotherapy and to our nation's veterans and their families. These rural systems deploy state-of-the-art technology to ensure their operations are as cost effective and efficient as possible . . . New tools, such as connectivity, streamlined policies and regulations, and increased flexibility for operations will allow the next era of innovation in rural transit to move forward. Such innovation is needed more than ever to respond to the important challenges faced in rural communities, ranging from economic development and job creation to at-risk populations and health care. (CTTA 2015)

Innovation in Rural Systems

Every year the Community Transportation Association of America (CTAA) names the nation's best and most innovative urban and rural transit systems of the year. The award in 2015 went to a small rural system in Washington state, the Mason Transit Authority. Mason County is located at the southern end of Puget Sound and Hood Canal. After settlement, logging and sawmill activities became the county's chief economic activity. As the importance of forest products declined since the 1950s, the county became an important recreation destination and bedroom community to the state capital, Olympia, and Tacoma, the state's second largest city. The estimated population of the county in 2014 was 60,711, only slightly greater than the 60,699 at the 2010 census. Nearly 20 percent of the county's population in 2014 was 65 years of age or older. Shelton, the county seat, had an estimated population of 9,975 in 2014. The 2015 transportation system of the year award is described in Box 8.1.

SUMMARY

Public transportation in the United States continues to serve an increasing number of riders. However, some of the largest and most necessary systems are facing major problems. Most of these are systems that focus on rail systems, such as New York, Boston and Washington, DC. Analysts claim that the causes of the challenges can be traced to rider fees insufficient to generate the funds needed to repair and replace the aging infrastructure that for some is the root of the problems. Meanwhile, bus and other motor vehicle surface transit is having to deal with traffic congestion that has brought much urban transit to a crawl.

Despite the difficulties facing some systems, most of the country's public transit systems are making great strides in accomplishing their objective of providing mobility to urban and rural populations at risk. The American Public Transportation Association publishes an annual report of the state of the industry; the 2014 report was based on 2012 data. During that year, transportation services were provided by more than 7,100 systems, nearly all of which were public and nonprofit organizations. These ranged from very large multi-modal systems to single-vehicle, special-demand providers with a few vehicles. Data provided on 18 different transportation modes included the numbers of systems in urban areas, rural areas, and for nonprofit organizations. By far the greatest numbers of providers were the 4,600 nonprofit organizations providing demand response service primarily for senior citizens and persons with disabilities in both rural

---

BOX 8.1   MASON TRANSIT AUTHORITY NAMED RURAL TRANSIT SYSTEM OF 2015

In August 2015, less than two months after Gov. Inslee and a host of national and state legislators helped MTA celebrate the grand opening of the nation's first rural transit-community center, the agency was named the 2015 Rural Community Transportation System of the Year by the Community Transportation Association of America. It's the first time CTAA has honored a transit agency in Washington State with one of its national system of the year awards. Gov. Inslee was quick to offer his congratulations.

The opening of the transit-community center is a noteworthy milestone not just for the communities of the county it serves, but for Washington's entire network of public transportation providers. Originally a National Guard armory in downtown Shelton, the building was redesigned in a responsible, cost-effective manner by leveraging local and state commitments into much broader federal support and funding. And by repurposing the armory into the transit-community center, MTA created a new landmark that honors both Shelton's civic history and its commitment to environmental sustainability.

The innovative facility played a part in helping secure the award, to be sure, but it's far from the lone reason MTA brought home the hardware. Before handing the award over to MTA General Manager Brad Patterson, CTAA executives lauded the agency for its after-school activities bus service, volunteer driver program for seniors, partnerships with local tribal governments and its vanpool service, which transports more than 150 workers daily to the Puget Sound Naval Shipyards in Bremerton.

The award is a special source of pride, both for MTA and the communities the agency serves, said Patterson. He's also quick to point to MTA's partnership with us, saying the award has as much to do with the relationships they've built with their partners over the years as it does with anything else. According to Patterson, the people in our public transportation division http://www.wsdot.wa.gov/transit/ aren't just helpful; they're truly dedicated to MTA's success.

Source: WSDOT (2015).

---

and urbanized areas. The second largest number of transit agencies were the more than 1,700 which operate in rural areas; and 815 transit agencies provide service in urbanized areas. Although the 815 urban area transit systems are less than half the number of transit utilities in rural areas, they are much larger.

Transit agencies in urbanized areas carried more than 98 percent of all transit passenger trips in 2012; those in rural areas carried about 1.5 percent of passenger trips, and nonprofit senior citizen and persons with disabilities transit service providers carried less than one-half of one percent of all passenger trips. Many agencies headquartered in urbanized areas provide services outside of those areas and, similarly, many rural providers serve riders in areas outside their central core community. Moreover, many rural providers provide connection services with districts that serve metropolitan areas.

ADDITIONAL READING

Bruun, Eric C. (2013), *Public Transit Systems: Analyzing Investments and Performance*. New York: Routledge.

Ceccato, Vania and Andrew Newton (2015), *Safety and Security in Transit Environments: An Interdisciplinary Approach*. New York: Palgrave Macmillan.

Ceder, Avishai (2015), *Public Transit Planning and Operations: Modeling, Practice and Behavior* (2nd edn). Boca Raton, FL: CRC Press.

Rodrique, Jean-Paul, Claude Comtois and Brian Alack (2013), *The Geography of Transport Systems* (3rd edn). New York: Routledge.

Suzuki, Hiroaki and Robert Cervero (2013), *Transforming Cities with Transit: Transit and Land Use Integration for Sustainable Urban Development*. Washington, DC: World Bank.

Walker, Jarrett (2011), *Human Transit: How Clearer Thinking about Public Transit can Enrich our Communities and our Lives*. Washington, DC: Island Press.

PART III

Public utility function challenges

9. Public utility finance

The drive for deregulation and restructuring of the public utility industry has brought substantial modifications to the regulatory structure of the public utility industry. This, in turn, has resulted in a host of new challenges being added to the traditional problems of financial managers. Public utility finance officers must now focus on more than the old questions of return on investment and recovery of investments in the industry; they are becoming more involved in justifying the investment and operating decisions that must be made to meet the needs of a newly designed, unbundled industry that is characterized by financial turmoil.

Public utilities have always been heavily dependent upon outside capital. There are few if any industries that are so consistently in need of large infusions of capital. The costs for repairing and replacing these critical infrastructure repairs and improvements must be paid for in the next several decades. Payment for the new equipment and facilities that must be constructed in the next several decades will be spread over very long periods of time—in some cases, as long as fifty years or more. Repaying the huge loans that will be needed for these utility infrastructure improvements will require public utility commissions to allow utilities to subtract the debt service from operating revenues. Otherwise, reasonable rates of return will not be maintained, and investors will not provide the needed capital. Box 9.1 describes a 2012 federal grant and loan request for construction of two light rail and one dedicated rapid bus projects planned for the Maryland-Washington, DC area.

Today, one of the greatest challenges facing public utility managers is the problem of capital acquisition. Until recently, economies of scale, together with mandated reserve capacity, meant that very large utility plants represented the most economical way to add capacity. Very large plants require very large amounts of outside capital. Vertically integrated, regulated utilities were seen as sound, stable, long-term investments.

THE FINANCE FUNCTION IN PUBLIC UTILITIES

Finance deals with the processes associated with raising capital; accounting is the keeping of accounts and producing reports about the use of

---

BOX 9.1   BILLIONS NEEDED FOR FUNDING FOR TRANSIT
SYSTEM CAPITAL IMPROVEMENTS

The Maryland Transit Administration (MTA) operates a large transit system in the Baltimore-Washington metropolitan area, including more than 50 local bus lines in Baltimore and other services such as light rail, Metro subway, commuter buses, Maryland Area Regional Commuter (MARC) trains, and mobility/paratransit vehicles. MTA is coordinating the financing, construction, and future operation of three major transit projects: the Red Line and Purple Line light rail expansions and the Corridor Cities Transitway (CCT) bus rapid transit line.

1.   The Red Line is a proposed 14-mile, east–west light rail line running from Baltimore County's Woodlawn employment and commercial centers through downtown Baltimore City to the Johns Hopkins Bayview Medical Center Campus, linking the north–south light rail, metro, and MARC trains. Construction is estimated to cost $2.1 billion.
2.   The Purple Line is a proposed 16-mile light rail line extending from Bethesda in Montgomery County to New Carrollton in Prince George's County, providing a direct connection to the Metrorail, MARC, Amtrak, and regional and local bus services. The Purple Line will also provide a 4.2-mile pedestrian/bicycle trail between the Bethesda and Silver Spring central business districts. Construction is estimated to cost $1.9 billion.
3.   The CCT is a proposed 15-mile bus rapid transit line extending along a north–south corridor from the Shady Grove Metrorail station to just south of Clarksburg in Montgomery County. The CCT will operate at street level on a fully dedicated right-of-way separate from existing traffic and will connect to Metrorail, MARC, and local and regional bus networks. Construction is anticipated to cost $545 million.

The State submitted financial plans to the Federal Transportation Administration (FTA) in 2011 demonstrating it could construct all three transit lines simultaneously as part of its effort to secure federal funding. The State would be required to identify an estimated $725 million in additional revenue, either through cash, a combination of cash and debt, or alternative means, in order to construct all three transit lines simultaneously. A total of roughly $2 billion in FTA New Starts grants and loans would be needed to finish the three projects.

Source: MDLS (2012).

---

that capital. Public utility managers have at least three major objectives in mind when they plan for financial management: (1) how to maintain and increase the amount of resources available for operations, (2) how to sustain stable growth at rates high enough to fund operations (and for investor-owned utilities, to attract equity capital), and (3) how to maintain autonomy and control over resources and operations.

In utilities, the finance function requires decision-making in at least four principal areas: (1) capital structure, which refers to the ratio of debt to equity in the financing of the organization; (2) the operating expense and investment structure, which are influenced by the regulatory environment; together, these heavily influence the utility's allowed return on investment; (3) the acquisition and cost of capital, which are shaped by the financial strength of the utility; and (4) working capital requirements, as determined by the liquidity picture, which itself is influenced by the capital structure of the utility.

Traditionally, service revenues were sufficient to cover operating costs on a pay as you go basis, while capital improvements were financed through borrowing or grants. For publicly owned utilities, the traditional structure is changing, however. Fewer federal or state grants are available and loans are very hard to come by. This has placed greater pressure for rate increases to fund operations and capital improvements.

Many public utilities in the U.S. are finding it increasingly difficult to finance the repair and replacement (R&R) of aging infrastructure, much of which was installed during the last fifty years of the last century. The American Society of Civil Engineers (ASCE) has given a cumulative grade ranging between D to D+ to the nation's infrastructure since the early 2000s. These grades are based on 15 categories of infrastructure that includes nearly all public utilities: hazardous waste, inland waterways, levees, public parks and recreation, rail, streets and highways, schools, solid waste, public transit, drinking water and wastewater, aviation, bridges, dams, and electricity and natural gas energy. Very large sums are required to make these capital improvements The ASCE also estimated that to bring the existing infrastructure up to a state of good repair by 2020 would require $3.6 trillion in spending over five years. With increasing pressure and urgency to improve public infrastructure, private and public companies and agencies, and state and local governments must pay particular attention to preparing their capital improvement plans and take steps to find the funds needed to complete their improvements. This is increasingly problematic as spending by all public service agencies, governments, and private utilities are under attack.

Increasing capital improvement activity means finding and planning for financing to fund projects. Capital improvements have been financed in one or more of three ways: debt, grants, or pay-as-you-go (pay-go) financing. A fourth method of public–private partnerships is looking more and more like the way many projects will be financed in the future: financing from capital reserves. Reserves will be collected through revenue from taxes and use rate. Utilities develop capital improvement plans (CIP) to ensure the reserve funds are available when needed.

Preparing the Capital Improvement Plan

A capital improvement plan is a fiscal management tool used to coordinate the location timing and financing of capital improvements over a multi-year period that can range from four or five to as long as 20 years. Capital improvements are major non-recurring physical expenditures for such items as land, buildings, processing plants, generating and transmission equipment, dams and water mains, developing new landfills or closing old ones. Distribution centers and transit repair facilities and yards are also included, while new vehicle fleets are not. The CIP includes a description of all improvement projects, their expected useful life, ranked by their priority, an annual schedule for expected project funding needs and sources, an estimate of the costs, and the preferred funding method.

Table 9.1 shows the utility portions only of the Olathe, Kansas 2016–2020 capital improvement plan. The selected list includes most but not all the projects planned for the five-year period totals $45,744.740 out of a total planned capital expenditure over the period of $305,141,287. Not included but noted as one of several pending projects was a $10.5 million storm water project and a $807.8 million water and sewer combined project. Funding for the five-year capital improvement plan will come from a variety of sources, none of which is identified as a pay-as-you-go source. The grand total obtained from 24 identified funding sources is close to $300.8 million. A partial list of sources and the amounts is shown in Table 9.2.

The Capital Structure of Utilities

Like all enterprises, public utilities need money to pay their bills, and they often need more money to improve and grow the enterprise. Both public and investor-owned organizations borrow money to make more money (this use of borrowed money is called *leverage*). Debt can be either short- or long-term. Both investor-owned and publicly owned utilities turn to long-term debt with bond sales to finance expansion and system upgrades. Often, the city's credit rating is mirrored by the credit rating of the utility.

While equity in investor-owned utilities comes from individual investors and institutions that purchase the stock as an investment, publicly owned utilities are financed almost exclusively through debt and rate-based revenues. Eventually, retained revenues from operations may provide the organization its needed working capital, so the publicly owned utility may rely less on short-term borrowing than is the case with investor-owned utilities. Far-sighted utility managers are planning ahead for the capital improvements that must be made by setting aside reserve amounts in each annual budget cycle.

Table 9.1 Selected portion of the utilities section of a municipal capital improvement plan expenditures, 2016–2020 ($)

Utility Project	2016	2017	2018	2019	2020	Total
119th St. water transmission main improvements	0	0	0	0	957,400	957,000
Black Bob 12″ waterline replacement	261,240	0	0	0	0	261,240
Black Bob waterline upsizing	0	0	0	0	2,040,100	2,040,100
BMP cost share program	50,000	50,000	50,000	50,000	50,000	250,000
Collector well No. 5	0	0	0	5,780,750	5,593,000	11,353,750
Compressed natural gas fueling station	460,000	0	0	0	0	460,000
Covered storage for solid waste vehicles	0	0	530,000	0	0	530,000
Elevated storage tank	0	0	0	0	1,832,450	1,832,450
Indian Creek sanitary sewer master plan	0	0	0	0	519,000	519,000
Lift station replacements	752,000	703,000	1,146,000	506,000	0	3,107,000
Neighborhood sanitary sewer improvements	350,000	375,000	400,000	425,000	450,000	2,000,000
Raw water transmission main	0	0	0	10,022,100	7,691,700	17,713,800
Sanitary sewer rehabilitation	800,000	900,000	1,000,000	1,000,000	1,000,000	4,700,000
SUBTOTALS	2,673,240	2,028,000	3,126,000	17,763,850	20,133,650	45,724,740

Source: Olathe, Kansas Capital Improvement Plan 2016–1020 (2015).

179

Table 9.2 *Selected portions of a capital improvement funding source summary, 2016–2020*

Funding Source	2016	2017	2018	2019	2020	Total
10-Year GO(a) bonds, city	$0	$1,451,717	$0	$0	$0	$1,454,717
10-Year GO bonds, dev.	8,895,238	2,285,021	7,207,000	0	0	15,387,259
CARS	2,260,000	1,500,000	1,000,000	0	0	4,760,000
CIP Fund	3,110,000	3,020,000	3,230,000	3,440,000	3,650,000	16,450,000
City of Overland Park	455,000	1,825,000	0	0	0	2,280,000
Congestion Mitigation/ Air Quality	0	0	320,000	0	0	320,000
10-Year GO bonds	4,215,000	23,904,477	8,469,000	17,285,000	19,600,000	73,473,477
Johnson County Park & Recreation	122,250	122,250	0	0	0	244,000
Other funds, Federal	0	0	2,000,000	0	0	2,000,000
Other funds, state	519,000	509,000	0	0	0	1,038,000
Parks sales tax fund	3,506,394	2,586,750	3,375,000	5,115,000	3,475,000	18,458,144
Revenue bonds	13,790,140	12,543,000	3,171,000	20,605,639	22,596,305	72,706,084
Solid Waste fund	460,000	250,000	623,500	135,500	791,250	2,290,250
Stormwater fund	2,913,750	2,621,000	1,210,000	1,275,000	2,102,375	10,122,125
Surface Transportation Program: STP	368,000	3,500,000	0	0	0	3,868,000
Water and Sewer fund	1,443,510	1,467,000	594,000	1,250,400	3,374,055	8,128,965
Additional sources (not identified)	0	0	0	0	0	5004,539
Totals	42,058,282	57,585,215	31,199,500	49,106,539	55,588,985	235,538,51

Notes: (a) GO = General Obligation bonds.

Source: Olathe, Kansas Capital Improvement Plan (2015).

Capital is a key resource in all enterprises; it is particularly important in the utility industry. Organizations secure capital to finance their operations with debt or equity, or both. The proportions of debt and equity make up the financial structure of the organization. Organizations need money to start operations, and then they need more money to continue operations. *Equity* is the money an entrepreneur or investor puts up to get the enterprise going. The money received from sales of stock is *stockholder's equity*. But equity is usually not enough to enable the enterprise to grow at the desired pace. Most utilities employ a mix of long-term borrowing in the form of bonds with a relatively small proportion of bank loans in the form of a line of credit for working capital Additional financial resources may be acquired in a number of different ways, including but not limited to the following:

- Through loans from banks or other financial institutions;
- By borrowing from investors (either outright or in the form of the sale of bonds);
- By providing additional ownership to investors by selling them more stock in the company; or
- By using retained earnings or revenue.

The managing director of a large investment bank once described the relationship between three different types of utility financial structures with their associated level of risk as seen by investors. The structure with the lowest perceived risk is the traditional vertically integrated utility (VIU). The financial structure of the VIU is approximately 50 percent recourse corporate debt, 45 percent equity, and about 5 percent in preferred stock. While investor-owned utilities as a whole tend to have a high proportion of debt financing, the traditional vertically integrated utility was seen by investors as having a low level of risk because of its regulatory commission-approved "fair" level of return of investment. The availability of financing for infrastructure development is much more difficult for small and rural utilities. Box 9.2 describes how the funds for water system improvements at U.S. Department of Agriculture have dried up.

The next structure, still with a low level of perceived risk, is a nonregulated electric power generator with a long-term purchase contract in hand, as established under PURPA regulations. These power generating operations were financed with anywhere from 80 to 90 percent non-recourse corporate debt, and with a corresponding 10 to 20 percent equity. They are called Contract Power Projects (CPPs).

The capital mix structure with the highest level of risk is the merchant power-producing project (MPP), whose capital mix consisted of from

BOX 9.2   FEDERAL SUPPORT FOR SMALL WATER/
           WASTEWATER SYSTEM LOANS DISAPPEARING

The EPA and the American Water Works Association estimate that the investment needed to update or replace existing water and wastewater systems over a 20-year period is in the hundreds of billions of dollars. At the same time, events, economic conditions and policy changes have cut into the financial resources of municipally owned water and wastewater utilities and reduced or eliminated sources of public financing. The municipal bond market, once a major source of funding for large water infrastructure projects, is a viable option for large cities but can be difficult for rural communities to access. Federal grants and loans are increasingly difficult to find and there is little chance of any new water infrastructure funding coming out of Washington.

Use of private capital into rural America has been a significant priority for the past several presidential administrations. While there are existing programs supporting the concept, such as USDA loan guarantees for rural areas and communities with less than 10,000 residents, it is likely that banks will need to play a more prominent role in the future—whether alone or as part of a public–private partnership. For more than 30 years, the USDA Rural Utilities Service (RUS) has set aside funds to guarantee the repayment of loans from commercial lenders to water utilities. Loans of up to $5 million are approved at the state level, but larger amounts require additional federal approvals. Because an RUS guarantee covers up to 90 percent of the total loan value, the lender's risk is greatly reduced, making it more likely to offer attractive terms such as lower rates and longer repayment schedules Interim financing, provided in the form of a line of credit from a commercial lender, is another example of collaboration between the USDA and lenders which has seen some success but has not been used consistently.

Source: Dornbier (2015).

60 to 80 percent non-recourse project financing debt, and corresponding 40 to 20 percent equity. Many of these small generating organizations failed as a result of the power crisis that began as a result of mistakes made in California's reorganization of its electric power industry. As a result, a number of lenders found themselves owning electric power generators. Utility finance managers are still facing challenges from those problems, as the following statement indicates:

> The bank markets and the long-term fixed income markets, or institutional investors, have long memories, and their pain is still fresh. Over the last few years, they have had to watch their investments in power infrastructure become distressed, bankrupted, or reorganized . . . the undeniable fact is that investors will remember what happened in the United States, and they remember privatizations in foreign countries where they experienced similar losses. In short, investors are wary. (Napolitano 2004: 53)

Surviving Financial Crises

The public utility industry has undergone several years of financial crisis upon crisis. The first two years of the new century were marked by steep ratings downgrades and a host of other events, including the Enron scandal, high natural gas prices, and warmer than average winters. Adding to these problems is the need for capital to replace and repair infrastructure, as described in an energy utility newsletter:

> Aging utility infrastructure is creating the need for unprecedented capital investment. General upkeep and reliability upgrades are increasing in both frequency and cost. Repairs and upgrades to manage increased storm intensity are requiring massive amounts of additional capital. Adding to these capital demands is the need to address growing security concerns, specifically that the power grid is adequately protected from cyber-attacks. (Hinckley 2014)

Two of the chief concerns of utility financial managers today are looking into the future to find answers to the questions: Will investors regain their interest in utility equities? And, will enough investment capital be available for the massive investments needed in upgrading and adding capacity to the nation's utilities?

Utility managers look to an organized financial management process to help guide them through this sea of problems. Financial management in utilities consists of two major activities: (1) planning for and acquiring financial resources and (2) planning, monitoring, analyzing, and reporting how those resources are used to accomplish the organization's objectives. Among the many tasks financial managers employ in these processes are budgeting, forecasting, accounting and financial reporting, financing, auditing and related financial analysis, and development and operating financial information systems.

Financial management includes the complete process of securing capital, managing debt, and making sure the organization's debt is used efficiently. Financial management has two overarching goals: ensuring that cash flow remains positive, and ensuring that there is sufficient cash available when needed to enable the utility to grow as demand requires. Achievement of these goals is made possible by following this five step process (Rachman, Mescon, Bovée, and Thill 1993: 543):

1. Estimate month-by-month flow of income (revenue) into the utility from all sources.
2. Estimate the month-by-month flow of money out of the utility, including operating expenses and capital investments.

3. Compare income with expenses. If more cash is needed, determine the best way to acquire it. This can include reducing expenses or increasing revenues. If excess cash is generated, determine the best place to invest the excess funds.
4. Select the capital investments that must be made for continued growth; find the most cost-effective combination of inside and outside financing sources.
5. Forge a system for tracking the flow of funds and monitoring the return on investment.

To summarize, the finance challenges facing utility managers are (1) planning for and acquiring financial resources, using either debt or equity or both, as appropriate, and (2) planning, monitoring, analyzing, and reporting the use of those funds. In carrying out their responsibilities, financial managers use such tools as accounting and reporting, budgeting and forecasting, auditing and analysis, financial information systems, and custodial and resource management. This task includes facilities maintenance, personnel, inventory control, and financial services. The accounting function serves as the foundation for all financial activities that follow.

Accounting in Public Utilities

The accounting function records transactions, processes operating data, prepares financial reporting information, and collects and distributes management information. Record-keeping begins with the accumulation of information. Financial and statistical data flow into the accounting function both from within the firm and from other operations. All the transactions that take place in a utility—buying, selling, depreciating, trading, storing, and so on—must be recorded. This includes recording the movement of materials, people, and supplies from one location to another.

Utility accounting decisions and the production of financial reports are reflections of decision-making in these five management areas: (1) maintaining an historical record of all transactions, (2) designing and maintaining systems of internal controls, (3) establishing the financial basis for the regulation of rates and earnings, (4) federal, state, and local taxation, and (5) in investor-owned utilities, producing data that are used for gaining and maintaining investor confidence.

Accounting provides at least four major services in utilities: (1) it maintains an historical record of the financial transactions of the firm, (2) it makes operating information available to other people in the firm for budgeting, forecasting, and performance monitoring, (3) it provides a basis for establishing a system for controls within the organization, and

(4) it provides analysis of results and produces reports on the financial health and vigor of the utility to investors and owners who depend on the information for making investment decisions. The following information focuses on the record-keeping function of utility accounting.

Maintaining an Historical Record

Two major accounting systems are used by all sectors of the public utility industry: One, the NARUC system, is used by investor-owned utilities. The second is the GASB system, which is required for all government-owned utility organizations. Although there are more similarities in the systems than differences, each is discussed in greater detail in the following pages.

Before an accounting staff can meaningfully record and report financial transactions, a utility's assets, liabilities, equities, revenues, and expenses must be classified using a comprehensive system of accounts. The system of accounts can then serve as a basis for a logical and pertinent summary for management. Uniform systems of accounts are used to allow for proper consolidation of accounts. Most investor-owned utilities use a system of accounts recommended by their industry organization, the National Association of Regulatory Utility Commissioners (NARUC).

The need for accounting information by state utility commissions in their regulatory operations and by other interested parties is so great that the design of accounting systems used by regulated utilities is usually based on commission requirements. Privately owned and operated utilities rely on profitability as the incentive for investment. As a result, investors generally require significantly more information than may be needed in publicly owned utilities. In addition, regulatory agencies and other groups require detailed records of the revenues and expenses of utilities. The Securities and Exchange Commission (SEC) also requires a uniform set of accounts for ease of comparison.

The minimum requirements for the system of accounts used by investor-owned utilities are usually established by each individual state utility regulatory agency. In practice, however, most commission-required systems follow the NARUC system and are very nearly identical.

Key Components of the NARUC System

The NARUC system of accounts includes five chief components and several supportive components. Together, these components provide information necessary for developing and maintaining a complete record of the financial activities of the utility. The five chief components are:

1. General instructions and definitions.
2. Instructions for identifying utility plant and operating expenses.
3. A specified list of accounts into which records are maintained.
4. A definition of each account and instructions concerning the types of transactions to be recorded in each account.
5. A sequence for balance sheet and income statement items.

The first two components provide instructions that guide the utility's accountants through the system of accounts. General instructions are statements of instructions relating to approved accounting standards; new statements are issued periodically to reflect system changes and new regulations. These instructions spell out the form and content of the system of accounts that the utility's accountants must follow. Because state utility commissions must approve all expenses for inclusion in the rate base, identifying, recording, and justifying operating expenses are extremely important activities. Allowed expenses are used for developing the approved rate base and calculating the utility's rate of return.

The next three components define and delineate the number and types of accounts that must be maintained. Each of the chief summary accounts may be backed by additional supportive accounts. Two sets of primary accounts are included in the system: (1) balance sheet accounts, and (2) income accounts. A third set of accounts, the retained earnings account, is used as a means of connecting the information in the two primary accounts.

Each of these primary accounts contains two or more subsidiary accounts. For example, the two chief balance sheet accounts are (1) the assets account, and (2) the liabilities accounts. These two balance sheet accounts are further divided into 11 groups of summary accounts. In addition, many of the summary accounts are themselves supported by additional subsidiary accounts. The primary balance sheet accounts and 11 major summary accounts are displayed in Figure 9.1. Each account is assigned a numeric code for identification and consolidation; only major code categories are shown in the figure.

As noted, many of the individual summary balance sheet accounts are supported by subsidiary accounts or records. These provide additional details about specific components of the summary accounts. One such summary balance sheet account—*Utility Plant*—is supported by six functional groups of detailed subsidiary utility plant accounts under the NARUC system. Plant-in-service is the largest asset on the balance sheet of utilities. Because of this large investment, state and municipal regulations have established certain financing and cost-recovery mechanisms in some states. Identified as "capital-recovery fees," "impact fees," and "land development fees," they may require special accounting considerations.

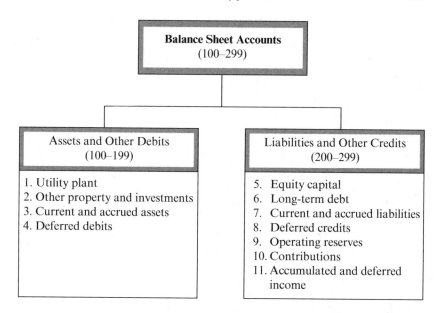

Figure 9.1   Balance sheet accounts in the NARUC system

Special uses may impact rate calculations under different cost-of-service, rate-making methods.

This detailed structure is necessary because of the importance of plant and facilities information to regulatory commissions for determining the appropriate rate base and to appropriately record depreciation. Detailed utility plant information also facilitates effective management control of plant assets. The subcategories in an example water utility plant account include the following sections: intangible plant, source-of-supply plant, pumping plant, water treatment plant, transmission and distribution plant, and general plant. Similar subsections are found in electric and gas utility balance sheets.

Income Accounts

The second set of primary balance sheet accounts is the set of income accounts. The income account is built around four major components: (1) utility operating income, (2) other income and deductions, (3) interest charges, and (4) extraordinary items. Utility operating income is computed by subtracting operating expenses from operating revenues. Only operating expenses which occur from delivering the utility's product are allowed; revenues are the income derived from normal operations of the utility.

From the point of view of public service regulatory commissions, operating income is often referred to as being *above* or *below the line*. Regulated utilities are entitled to operating revenues sufficient to cover operating expenses and provide for a "fair" rate of return. *Return* is the money that remains after operating expenses have been subtracted from operating revenues. Some of this money is used to pass dividends to investors, while some is retained and used to pay for future operating expenses, improvements, or repairs. Revenues and expenses that commissions accept in the determination of operating income are said to be above-the-line items. Expenses are above-the-line items if they are accepted as being reasonable in amount and are considered chargeable against customers for utility services provided.

Below-the-line items are not considered as operating items in calculations of rates and the determination of a fair or reasonable return. However, they are included as adjustments to operating income in arriving at the net income of the utility. Moreover, income from non-utility activities and non-utility income deductions and related income taxes are considered to be below-the-line. Interest charges are not classified as operating expenses and thus are below-the-line; they are considered in the allowable rate of return.

Other Income and Deductions

The second major category of information in the income account is other income and deductions. This account includes income that does not come from the normal business of supplying utility product. Examples include charges for installations, revenue from appliance sales or leases, interest and dividend income, and so on.

The other income deductions account includes miscellaneous amortization charges which are not included in the utility operating income and miscellaneous deductions. Examples include charitable donations, efforts to influence public opinion, elections or appointments of officials, and losses on write-downs or sales of securities, allowable taxes, and related items.

Interest Charges

Interest charges are the third component in the income accounts under the NARUC system. This account includes interest on both long-term and short-tem debt; the amortization of debt discount, debt premium, and debt-issue expense; interest on debt to associated companies; and all other interest expense.

Extraordinary Items

Extraordinary items include any unexpected gains or losses which might distort the income of the current year if they were reported as operating revenues or expenses. An example of an extraordinary gain might be proceeds from the sale of a property parcel. An example of loss in this category might be the extraordinary costs (earnest money) associated with failure to consummate the purchase of another segment of the industry, a property parcel, or similar asset.

An Example Utility Consolidated Balance Sheet

Figure 9.2 displays a five-year consolidated comparative balance sheet produced by a typical natural gas utility (the categories are real, but the values have been modified from the original). In this example, the consolidated balance sheet includes data for the utility's regulated and nonregulated, wholly-owned subsidiary businesses. This utility serves an area that extends across several states and is subject to regulation by several state commissions.

The firm's revenues come from the sale and transportation of natural gas; revenue is recognized when the gas is delivered to and received by the customer. The comparative balance sheet contains an interesting item not found in most other types of businesses: a reserve fund to be used if commission rate proceedings require refunds to utility customers in future periods. In this example, the "regulatory tax assets" sum was $48.8 million in 2003 and 48.5 million in 2002.

Retained Earnings Account

The purpose of the retained earnings account is to explain changes in a utility's retained earnings balance over a particular time period. In some cases, the category has been included in a scheduled labeled *Statement of Earnings Invested in the Business*. This group of accounts is used to explain changes in a utility's retained earnings balance over some time period, such as one year. Table 9.3 is an example of such an account for a natural gas utility.

These changes may be caused by changes in net income, distribution of retained earnings during the time period, dividend declarations or transfers to other municipal funds, or other accounting adjustments.

Comparative Consolidated Balance Sheet					
	2015	2014	2013	2012	2011
Assets:					
Utility plant	**$ 1,945,694**	1,729,722	1,584,425	1,493,321	1,303,669
Less accumulated depreciation	**627,983**	568,395	545,200	478,675	443,555
Utility plant – net	**1,317,711**	1,161,327	1,039,225	1,014,646	860,114
Non-utility property	**17,221**	14,222	9,455	8,320	7,016
Less accumulated depreciation and depletion	**3,879**	3,687	3,872	3,453	3,250
Non-utility property – net	**13,342**	10,535	5,583	4,867	3,766
Total plant and property	**1,331,053**	1,171,862	1,044,808	1,019,513	863,880
Other Investments	**19,548**	27,450	15,756	14,500	17,822
Current Assets:					
Cash and cash equivalents	**11,212**	10,455	12,586	8,459	9,275
Accounts receivable – net	**51,369**	61,258	60,457	51,227	40,789
Accrued unbilled revenue	**45,875**	59,878	54,921	48,119	41,272
Inventories of gas, materials and supplies	**61,321**	52,473	47,852	46,245	41,095
Prepayments and other current assets	**27,465**	29,527	21,545	17,982	16,532
Total current assets	**197,242**	213,591	197,361	172,032	148,963
Regulatory tax assets	**49,523**	48,588	47,300	47,895	49,525
Deferred gas costs receivable			15,745	19,256	25,421
Unrealized loss on non-trading derivatives					
Deferred debits	**83,694**	75,982	76,337	68,215	64,215
Total Assets	**$ 1,661,512**	1,510,023	1,365,806	1,307,655	1,126,583
Capitalization and liabilities:					
Capitalization:					
Common stock equity	**$ 622,116**	572,347	526,559	484,434	445,680
Redeemable preferred stock	**7,850**	7,379	6,936	6,520	6,129
Total capital stock	**629,966**	579,726	533,495	490,954	451,808
First mortgage debt	**593,750**	522,500	459,800	404,624	356,069
Unsecured debt	**5,655**	6,503	7,479	18,605	21,396
Total long-term debt	**599,405**	529,003	467,279	423,229	377,465
Total Capitalization	**1,221,521**	1,101,350	993,838	907,663	823,144
Current liabilities:					
Notes payable	**82,158**	75,996	70,296	65,024	60,147
Accounts payable	**63,899**	59,107	54,674	50,573	46,780
Long-term debt due within one year	**35,000**	32,375	29,947	27,701	25,623
Taxes accrued	**8,295**	7,673	7,097	6,565	6,073
Interest accrued	**3,120**	2,886	2,670	2,469	2,284
Other current and accrued liabilities	**28,474**	26,338	24,363	22,536	20,846
Total current liabilities	**220,946**	204,375	189,047	174,868	161,753
Deferred investment tax credits	**8,542**	7,517	8,419	7,409	8,372
Deferred income taxes	**157,695**	65,641	155,737	205,150	121,550
Fair value of non-trading derivatives		97,825			
Deferred gas costs payable	**11,278**	10,425			
Regulatory liabilities and other	**41,530**	22,890	18,765	12,565	11,763
Total capitalization and liabilities	**$ 1,661,512**	1,510,023	1,365,806	1,307,655	1,126,583

Figure 9.2   Example comparative balance sheet for a natural gas utility ($ thousands)

NARUC IN PUBLICLY OWNED UTILITIES

The NARUC system applies only to investor-owned operations; it must be modified if it is used by municipally owned utilities. Government owned organizations, including municipally owned utilities, are required to follow

Table 9.3   *Example of a private water company retained earnings account (thousands)*

Item	2012	2013	2015
Balance at beginning of the year	$118,711	$134,189	$147,950
Net income	50,224	50,187	43,792
Dividend paid			
Preferred and preference stock	(2,466)	(2,410)	(2,579)
Common stock	(31,198)	(31,307)	(32,024)
Common stock repurchase	(1,080)	(2,688)	--
Common stock expenses	(2)	(21)	(3)
Balance at end of year	$134,189	$147,950	$157,136

Source: The author.

the GASB System uniform system of accounts. The GASB system is based on recommendations of the National Association of Government Accountants (NAGA).

The government accounting system shares many of the same features with the NARUC system, but because municipal utilities are not required to earn a profit, some differences in the accounting systems exist. Differences exist in regulations on financing and cost-recovery for the physical plant, centralized support services, and accounting costs for services provided by other utilities in the same municipality. For example, water and wastewater services are often combined into one municipal utility. Costs for billing and other services must be appropriately distributed.

A municipal utility operated as a self-sustaining operation must generate revenues that are sufficient to cover all expenses, which may include taxes or payments in lieu of taxes and depreciation. It must additionally generate revenues for expansions of the system if it is required to finance expansions. Challenges arise when the municipal utility is operated to result in a break-even or a loss (subsidized) financial basis. The utility must find a way to generate enough revenue to cover future costs.

In most municipalities, a city-owned utility that operates as a separate accounting entity has important and continuing relationships with other funds for such centralized services as purchasing and transportation. For example, the utility may "rent" office space and common maintenance facilities from the city or county. Or, it may pay into a common retirement fund and be charged a proportionate share of fund overheads and participate in other centralized services. Centralized services are usually accounted for through a working-capital fund, with payment taking place by fund transfers.

There may be other important transfers between the utility and other funds of the municipality. Examples include: (1) the transfer of a portion of the utility's retained earnings to the general fund, (2) the transfer of resources from the general fund to the utility for financing purposes, or (3) pay into special revenue funds in lieu of property taxes or a return on investment. The system of accounts must be designed to record interfund transactions between municipal funds. Municipally owned utilities should be accounted for as a separate enterprise fund, not on a fund accounting basis, as are most other government operations.

The Modified GASB System

Publicly owned utility finance managers have had to learn how to implement the extensive series of changes required in the GASB system. This new system of accounts is required for government bodies, including states, cities, towns, villages, and public utilities. The new system is expected to restructure much of the information that governments must provide, with the goal of making annual reports more comprehensive and easier to understand and use.

Government organizations produce annual reports in the same way that investor-owned enterprises do. Government agency annual reports provide information about funds established by governing bodies. Such funds are used to show the planned use of resources, as well as how the agency will monitor short-term revenues and expenditures arising from their activities. Moreover, an important part of accountability is showing that the government organization is in compliance with its budget. Government agencies, including utilities, must continue to provide budgetary comparison information in their annual reports. However, they must submit the original budget to the comparison, rather than a budget that has been revised one or more times during the period in question.

Another important change is the required increased involvement of government financial managers in the annual report. For the first time, government financial managers must share their insights in a required management discussion and analysis section in the annual report—referred to as MD&A. In the MD&A, financial managers must give readers an objective and understandable analysis of the government's (that is, the utility's) performance for the year. The analysis is to give users information needed to help them assess whether the organization's financial position has improved or deteriorated as a result of the year's operations. Table 9.4 is an example of a combined income statement for a regional public utility district in the Pacific Northwest; while the schedule contains all of the information categories, it does not follow the preferred system to the letter.

Table 9.4 *Example of a combined income statement for a publicly owned utility*

	2000	1999
Total Operating Revenues	$62,381,445	$57,343,636
Operating Expenses:		
Operating Expenses	24,975,435	24,259,960
Maintenance Expenses	5,585,085	6,199,837
Depreciation Expenses	6,170,201	5,932,336
Taxes	2,259,303	2,493,404
Total Operating Expenses	38,990,024	38,885,537
Net Operating Revenues	23,391,421	18,458,099
Interest and Other Income	4,508,809	3,113,251
Gain on Early Retirement of Long-Term Debt	298,080	170,834
Non-Operating Margin – Other	46,827	147,954
Balance Available for Debt Service	28,245,137	21,890,138
Interest on Long-Term Debt	9,645,426	9,244,091
Other Debt Expense	990,159	978,381
Total interest and Other Expense	10,635,585	10,222,472
Excess of Revenues over Cost of Services	17, 609,552	11,667,666
Net Addition to Retained Earnings	17, 609,552	11,667,666
Retained Earnings, January 1	141,543,487	129,876,269
Retained Earnings, December 31	$159,153,487	141,543,935

Utilities were given a sliding time scale to follow in conforming to the new standards. Organizations and governments with total annual revenues of $100 million or more were required to apply Statement 34 by the earliest; those with revenues from $10 million to less than $100 million were given another six months to implement the statement; and those with revenues of less than $10 million had another whole year before they were required to comply.

Annual reports for publicly owned utilities contain most if not all of the same financial information found in the annual reports of investor-owned utilities. The two chief summary statements are still the balance sheet and the income statement. Balance sheets must also show assets and liabilities; income statements contain much the same four components found in investor-owned utilities: (1) utility operating income (which includes operating revenue and operating expenses), (2) other income and deductions, (3) interest charges, and (4) extraordinary items, if any.

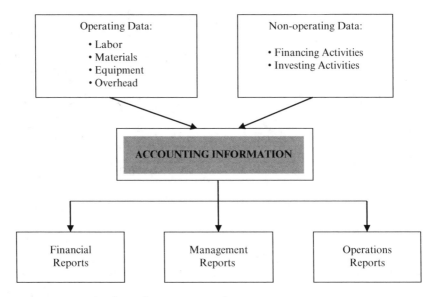

Figure 9.3   The flow of accounting information

MAKING FINANCIAL INFORMATION AVAILABLE

Information for management and operating use is an important goal of the accounting function. Metered water or electricity sales are an example of operating information. Another form of operating information is budget variance reports. Figure 9.3 illustrates the relationship between the sources of accounting information and the types of reports that use accounting data.

In this system, raw data comes from internal and external sources. Internal data includes such information as production cost figures. An external data example might be withholding tax or interest rates, inflation rates, and similar uncontrollable factors.

Controls in the NARUC System

The NARUC system of accounts emphasizes the grouping of cost data on a functional basis, such as source of supply, treatment, transmission, distribution, and marketing services. For planning and control purposes, management is interested in cost information based on a natural classification, such as labor, fuel, and rent. Therefore, within each functional group, costs are identified according to their natural classification.

Effective cost control requires that definite responsibility for costs be established. A manager should be held responsible for only those costs that he or she can control. Therefore, the system of accounts must allow for identification and presentation of costs incurred by each responsibility segment (organization unit) of the utility organization. Cost data and related operating statistics enable utility managers to set performance standards and to prepare realistic operating budgets. Comparison of actual costs and operating statistics with planned costs and performance standards grouped by unit responsibility makes it possible for the financial manager to take action to control cost and improve performance.

In addition to transaction data, procedures such as reconciliations of customer deposits, accounts receivable, and bank statements provide important internal controls for utilities. Policies and procedures are the basic guidelines and instructions to the utility and staff for the processing of these transactions. Standard operating procedures allow a consistent method of handling transactions occurring under different circumstances or process by different individuals. Consistency in reporting also allows for comparison between reporting periods and expedites management analysis and decisions.

Use of Accrual Accounting

There are two bases that can be followed in accounting: *cash* and *accrual*. In general, the accrual basis of accounting is the recommended system for both municipally owned and investor-owned water utilities. Under the cash basis, revenues are recognized as being earned when payment is received, and expenses are charged when payment is made. Under the accrual basis, revenues are recorded in the period in which service is given, although payments may be received in a prior or subsequent period. Systems may also be partly cash and partly accrual; when this happens, the systems are called either modified accrual or modified cash systems.

Under the accrual system, the amounts recorded for the delivery of a utility service (power, gas, or water) during the month of January, for example, is recorded as having been earned in January, despite the fact that payment for the service might not be received until the month of March. Accrual-basis expenses are recorded in the period in which the benefits are received, although payments may be made in a prior or subsequent period. For example, if a distribution utility buys and pays for a block of power from a generator utility in January, but does not take delivery of the power until March, the transaction is recorded as a March expense, regardless of when payment was made.

SUMMARY

An important challenge facing public utility managers today is the problem of capital acquisition. Until recently, economies of scale, together with mandated reserve capacity, meant that very large utility plants represented the most economical way to add capacity. Very large plants require very large amounts of outside capital. Vertically integrated, regulated utilities were seen as sound, stable long-term investments.

Public utility managers have three major objectives when they plan for financial management: how to increase the amount of resources available for operations, how to maintain stable growth at rates high enough to attract equity capital, and how to maintain autonomy and control over resources and operations.

In utilities, the finance function requires decision-making in at least four principal areas: (1) capital structure, (2) operating expense and investment structure, (3) acquisition and cost of capital, and (4) working capital requirements. Utility accounting decisions and the production of financial reports require decision-making in five areas: (1) maintaining an historical record of all transactions, (2) designing and maintaining systems of internal controls, (3) establishing the financial basis for the regulation of rates and earnings, (4) federal, state, and local taxation, and (5) producing data that are used for gaining and maintaining investor confidence.

Some key finance challenges facing utility managers are planning for and acquiring financial resources, using either debt or equity or both, and planning, monitoring, analyzing, and reporting the use of those funds. In carrying out their responsibilities, financial managers use such tools as accounting and reporting, budgeting and forecasting, auditing and analysis, financial information systems, and custodial and resource management (including facilities maintenance, personnel, inventory control, and financial services).

Accounting provides four services in utilities: (1) it maintains an historical record of the financial transactions of the firm, (2) it makes operating information available to other people in the firm for budgeting, forecasting, and performance monitoring, (3) it provides a basis for establishing a system for controls, and (4) it carries out analyses of results and produces reports on the financial health and vigor of the utility to managers, investors, and owners.

Two major accounting systems are used by all sectors of the public utility industry: One, the NARUC system, is used by investor-owned utilities. The second is the GASB system, which is required for all government-owned utility organizations.

ADDITIONAL READING

AWWA (2014a), *Water Utility Capital Financing*. Denver, CO: American Water Works Association.

Bui, Ann T. (2012), *Financial Management for Water Utilities: Principles of Finance, Accounting, and Management Controls*. Denver, CO: American Water Works Association.

CPUC (2012), *Trends in Utility Infrastructure Financing*. San Francisco: California Public Utilities Commission.

Griff, Neil S. (2011), *Water Finance: Public Responsibilities and Private Opportunities*. Hoboken, NJ: Wiley.

Hayne, Robert L. and Gregory E. Aliff (2014), *Accounting for Public Utilities*. Dayton, OH: LexisNexis.

Mishra, Amareshwar and R.K. Mishra (2014), *Financing Patterns for Infrastructure Projects*. New Delhi: Academic Foundation Press.

PwC (2013), *Guide to Accounting for Utilities and Power Companies*, PricewaterhouseCoopers, LLP, accessed August 13, 2015 at www.pwc.com/us/en/cfodirect/publications/accounting-guides/guide-to-accounting-for-utilities-and-power-companies-2013.jhtml.

10. Public utility pricing and rate setting

In market-based economies, prices charged for most goods and services generally are a reflection of supply and demand. When supply exceeds demand, prices fall. When demand exceeds supply, scarcity appears and prices rise. This is the *general model of pricing*. The model does not work in exactly this way when pricing the products and services of public utilities. External forces in the form of government regulations and political considerations often intervene in the price-setting process. Furthermore, federally mandated restructuring of the utility industry has introduced a new complexity into the practice of setting prices at all levels of the utility industry. The fundamentals of rate setting, price-setting practices, and such special pricing considerations as social pricing are discussed in the following paragraphs. Throughout the chapter the terms *prices* and *rates* may be used synonymously, although in the industry, *prices* are sometimes (but not always) used to describe the wholesale cost of a utility product, with *rates* used to mean the retail price of the product.

Managers in most businesses approach the rate-setting process from two interrelated positions. The first begins with the overall revenue requirements of the organization: income must meet all debt services, operating costs, and provide an appropriate return to investors. The second begins at the opposite end of the chain: determining what specific combination of prices, rate structures, and rate schedules will bring in the revenue required. This model is more complicated when the organization or business is a public utility.

Another set of conditions underlies the rate-setting decisions of utility managers and state and federal regulators, who must now devise new regulatory—including price control—systems that maintain the fundamental goals of deregulation. These goals include lowering the price of energy to consumers, while also ensuring that supply is always sufficient to meet demand, and results in prices that provide an equitable return for investors. Brennan, Palmer, and Martinez (2002: 82) identified the key questions which regulators must consider when determining rates in this new regulatory environment:

- Determining the appropriate rate levels. That is, what prices must be charged for services in order to generate the revenue needed to pay for transmission and distribution of the energy?
- Identifying the appropriate rate adjustments. That is, how and when should rates be adjusted over time to reflect actual or expected changes in the cost and profitability of transmission and distribution?
- Building the best rate structure. That is, what contribution to the rates paid by final customers should be allocated to such factors as the time and amount of energy transmitted, the distance the power is shipped, what congestion occurs in the transmission systems, the location of generating facilities, and what prices should be paid by different classes of customer (residential, commercial, or industrial)?

Ciolik, Jones, and Wilson (2003) also commented on the conditions that influence utility rate making. Other than the large amounts spent on unregulated generating facilities, much of the utility infrastructure is in serious need of repair or replacement. In addition, government sources estimated that something like $400 billion must be spent over the next twenty years in new construction to keep pace with growing energy demand. While this is taking place, many utilities have experienced significant increases in operating costs. Together, these forces have reduced the rate of return for many utilities to rates less than 10 percent.

FUNDAMENTALS OF UTILITY RATE SETTING

In practice, the process of setting prices in distribution public utilities involves four steps: (1) determining operating costs, (2) distributing costs among different customer classes, (3) considering relevant load and use factors, and (4) designing the pricing structures that reflect the influences of the first three considerations. Rate setting in regulated utilities is further complicated by the legislative and social requirement that the final rates be "just and reasonable" (fair and equitable).

Determining Operating Costs

Determining costs involves analysis of four categories of operations: customer service, operations, demand, and overhead (general expenses). Costs attributable to the customer service category include meter reading, billing, connecting and disconnecting customers to the system, collecting past-due accounts, and so on. Today, these services are often provided by a fourth segment of the utility industry, the independent marketing provider.

Regardless of who performs the service, they must still be paid for, and are included in the rate base of the utility. Moreover, whether provided in-house or contracted out to independent providers, customer services represent a relatively constant cost of operations and can generally be forecast with some accuracy.

Costs attributable to operations are more variable than customer service costs. They include personnel wages and the costs of the inputs to the system. System inputs vary by the different costs of the utility's products and services. For example, wholesale power prices vary by generation method, and by different types and sizes of generating and transmission systems. Other factors affecting price include the type of fuel used for generation, such as coal, gas, nuclear, or renewable fuels, and whether it is purchased on long-term contract or on the spot market for peak loads. The delivered price of natural gas to a utility system varies by the time and type of demand, supply contract, origin (domestic or international), and other factors, such as climate and weather. Water supply and wastewater prices vary far less than energy prices. Rates and prices for these two utility services, therefore, tend to be far more stable and less complicated to set and administer. Other operation cost factors include such factors as the maintenance and repair of the operating system, use depreciation allowances, and excise and sales taxes. Wages of operating personnel, petroleum and tires, and computer systems are also examples of operating costs.

Demand related costs for ratemaking typically constitutes the largest portion of the four categories. In the utility business, these are known by several different names, including *readiness to serve costs, capacity costs,* or *load costs.* They include the total cost of the operating system, including buildings, pipelines, power poles and lines, distribution networks, and repair facilities. Also included in this category are property taxes, depreciation expenses, capital improvements, return on the rate base, and related expenses of bringing and keeping the utility to the position where it is ready to serve any and all demand placed upon the system.

The final category of costs is overhead or general expenses. These include administrative costs, marketing and public relations expenses, supervision costs, costs of purchasing and supply, industrial relations costs, and all other costs which tend to be common or general in nature, and, therefore, difficult to place in any specific function of the utility.

Distributing Costs among Customer Classes

Once the management costs have been determined, they must be allocated among the various classes of customers served by the utility; costs are proportioned according to the share of the total cost contributed by each class of customer. In practice, each of the four categories of costs—customer, operations, demand, and overhead—are broken down and allocated according to some relevant standard. For example, customer costs are allocated according to the number of customers in the class. Each customer must have an account, each customer has a connection and, ultimately, a charge to disconnect, and each customer's meter must be read. Operations costs, on the other hand, vary with load demand. There are many different formulas for calculating prices for different use volumes, including formulas designed to produce prices that encourage or discourage additional customer use.

Demand costs are the most complex in terms of allocation between customer classes. Not only must each class have a rate schedule, each class varies in the service level demanded, the time of day, volume of use, whether peak or off-peak, and other factors. Table 10.1 illustrates some of the different rates found in a typical electric power utility's rate schedule.

Typically, prices are lowest for large users, such as factories or commercial centers, and highest for residential customers. However, prices will tend to vary more during any period for industrial and commercial users than they will for residential customers. Overhead expenses are common to the complete operation; they are usually proportionally allocated to all other costs according to some convenient accounting method. Table 10.2 is a comparison of the residential, commercial, and industrial basic rates for electricity in cents per kilowatt-hour as reported by 12 different utilities in the Western Electric Coordinating Council region (WECC).

Load and Use Factors

Electricity and natural gas utility managers and regulators typically look at four load factors when establishing rates for their services: peak load, average load, utilization, and a diversity factor. Peak load refers to the maximum capability of the system. It is measured for a particular time period such as a day, a month, or a year, and is usually referred to as *peak demand*. The utility must construct a system capable of meeting peak demand together with some level of reserve for unexpected demands on the system, to cover some breakdowns in portions of the system or temporary shutdowns for maintenance, and to meet anticipated growth in the service area.

Average load, or simply the *load factor*, is defined as the average load or use of a utility's services for a given time period. It is usually expressed as a percentage of peak demand for the period. Say, for example, that average demand for electric power in a community during August is 80 kilowatts. However, peak demand occurs during the third week of the month. The

Table 10.1 Portions of a typical rate structure for electric service

Billing code	Customer category	Type of service	Rate KWh	Daily charges	Fees and connection charges	Applicable discount rate per day
Service without guaranteed demand:						
R1	Residential[a]	Single phase	0.516	0.46/day	Permit: $35 Application: $100	Low income elderly:.46/day
R1	Unmetered temporary construction service	3-phase Single phase	0.516 0.516	0.74 0.46	Same	
R1	Metered single well service	Single phase	0.516	0.46	Same	Low income elderly:.46/day
RD	Disabled single family	Single phase	0.516	Exempt	Same	
RE	Special Exempt	Single phase	0.516	Exempt	Same	
G1	Single meter commercial[b]	Single phase 3-Phase	0.565 0.565	0.68 0.94	same	
GE	Unmetered construction dry shacks	Single phase	0.565	0.68	No transformer With transformer	$25 $50

202

Service with guaranteed demand:

21	Single metered commercial[b]	Single phase	0.0343	$1.82/day	Per billing period:
		3-phase	0.0343	0.94	$6.21
21	Metered well service	3-phase	0.0242	$1.82	
41	Fixed rate unmetered signs	1000W		0.66/Day	Pole charge for all:
		900W		0.62	0.08/day
		700W		0.55	
		600W		0.45	
		500W		0.31	
		300W		0.30	
	Outdoor lighting	100W	Unmetered	0.30	
		200W		0.45	
		400W		0.81	
		100W	Metered	0.23	
		200W		0.30	
		400W		0.44	
61	Large industrial light and power service		0.0307		Period demand rate: $5.59

Notes:

a Single family and separately metered apartment units.
b Commercial includes schools, churches, granges, community halls, public agencies.

Source: Patterned after and early Mason County PUD No. 3.report.

Table 10.2   Retail electric rate comparisons in Eastern states regions, 2016

Region and State	Average price in cents per kilowatt hour (KWh)				
	Residential	Commercial	Industrial	Transportation	All Sectors
New England	**19.68**	**15.12**	**11.78**	**8.65**	**16.31**
Connecticut	21.15	15.72	12.88	12.22	17.60
Maine	14.34	11.39	7.71	--	11.68
Massachusetts	20.64	15.56	12.96	5.94	16.93
New Hampshire	18.67	14.49	12.35	--	15.77
Rhode Island	19.43	15.13	13.44	18.28	16.58
Vermont	17.52	14.49	9.63	--	14.33
Middle Atlantic	**15.72**	**12.19**	**6.93**	**10.69**	**12.22**
New Jersey	15.52	12.02	9.66	8.14	12.93
New York	7.39	13.79	5.96	11.83	13.85
Pennsylvania	14.27	9.52	6.91	7.75	10.24
South Atlantic	**11.37**	**6.20**	**6.18**	**7.95**	**9.57**
Delaware	13.90	10.15	8.03	--	11.23
District of Columbia	13.48	11.88	9.09	9.73	12.08
Florida	11.07	9.00	7.54	8.16	9.89
Georgia	11.13	9.49	5.19	4.54	8.90
Maryland	14.37	11.01	7.91	7.84	12.14
North Carolina	11.72	8.49	5.99	7.88	9.03
South Carolina	12.77	9.78	5.77	--	9.10
Virginia	12.00	8.16	6.84	7.83	9.17
West Virginia	12.29	8.79	6.12	--	8.69

Source: EIA (2016).

utility maintains a peak capacity that is 15 percent above average load. To be able to meet peak demand, the utility will have to be physically able to supply 92 kilowatts of power (80 kW plus 15% of 80 = 80 + 12 = 92 kW)—even if it occurs just once per year.

The costs to build and maintain the necessary plant to meet average and peak demand are fixed; they are considered to be *sunk costs*. Examples of sunk costs include the cost to construct dams and nuclear generators, sink wells, build pipelines, dams and reservoirs, and wastewater collection and treatment systems. Sunk costs continue regardless of use. Therefore, it is to the utility's advantage to raise its average load factor as high as possible in order to spread these costs among as many customers as it can. In the past, increasing use has been achieved by promotional pricing, special discounts for, say, all electric kitchens, and other marketing efforts. Some vertically integrated utilities suffered from extremely high sunk costs stemming from prior investments in nuclear and/or very large coal-fired power generating facilities. Unbundling of vertically integrated utilities into separate generating, transmission, and distribution companies has caused problems in recovering the sunk costs of the integrated concern by the independent parts of the former concern; state regulatory commissions have not always allowed recovery of those sunk costs.

The third factor in load service relates to utilization of the system. It is stated as a percentage of the total system capacity represented by the highest anticipated peak load. A utility that is able to meet a peak demand while operating at 88 percent of its total capacity has a reserve capacity of 12 percent. Even if it never reaches the potential maximum demand, the utility must be capable of doing so if called upon. This contingency factor typically ranges in the area of 15 to 20 percent above the utility's normal forecast utilization factor. The excess capacity is called the utility's *reserve capacity*. Both peak demand and contingency supplies are often produced by the utility's highest cost methods, and are, therefore, priced proportionally higher than average demand. Moreover, to maintain lower rates, large users of the utility's product sign interruptible or adjustable service contracts.

The final load factor considered in utility pricing is known as the *diversity factor*. Diversity refers to the different peak loads expected from the utility's different customer classes. If the peak demands all occur at the same time, the diversity factor is one (1). If they occur at different times, the factor has a higher value. The higher the diversity value, the smaller proportion of total system capacity will be needed to serve a given customer class. Demands that occur at different times are called *noncoincidental demands*. Utilities with higher noncoincidental demands are able to meet the peak loads of all their customers with a smaller overall system than utilities with demands that occur at the same periods.

ROLE OF COMMISSIONS IN UTILITY RATES

State regulators set energy utility rates in the United States. While their names may differ—utilities commission, utility regulatory commission (URC), public utilities commission (PUC) or public service commission (PSC)—their duties and responsibilities are the same: regulate public utilities in ways that protect the public from potential harm stemming from the monopoly nature of utilities in the state. State public utility commissions, operating under their legislative mandate, set the rates that public utilities can charge final customers for their services by approving or refusing to allow proposed rate increases submitted by utilities under their jurisdiction. After establishing what they consider to be the utility's "reasonable" operating expenses, commissions then determine the rate base by calculating the value of the utility's assets. This is done in several different ways.

One valuation method is to determine the sum of the total capital invested in the property. Another way is by estimating what it would cost to replace the property at current prices. Valuation of the assets of the utility is the most problematic aspect of utility rate making.

The final approved rates for investor-owned utilities are based upon an analysis of what regulators consider to be the cost of service, as well as a determination of what constitutes a fair return for the utility. Rates established for publicly owned utilities are usually not subject to this type of regulatory oversight but, instead, are subject to local political and social forces that can have an influence as great or even greater than state utility commissions. Moreover, commissioners and other regulatory bodies are regularly called upon to approve changes in utility rates that are brought about by shifts in the utilities' operating environment, including, but not limited to, changing political, regulatory, and market conditions. These cost shifts are the decisions made by rate regulators to change the distribution of costs for rate of return decisions and rate-change requests. Box 10.1 describes the process followed by state utility commissions and departments in the rate setting procedure.

Table 10.3 is an abbreviated statement of an upper Midwest utility's requests for state utility commission approval of a multi-year rate increase request (Minnesota PUC 2010). The table also displays the utilities' authorized rate of return on equity and states how any earnings above the approved ROE will be shared with customers. The summary was included in the PUC's mandated annual report on utility earnings and rate requests to the state legislature.

Utilities must file petitions for rate relief with their state utility commissions. The commissioners hold hearings to determine that the traditional way of determining rates of return must be changed to include an allowance for the increased level of risk that exists in the utility industry. Examples of external forces affecting utilities' operating costs include mandated requirements for renewable energy supplies in elect generating operations, complying with new and changing regulatory requirements, and discounted rates for socially or economically disadvantaged citizens.

Once the value of the utility is established, commissions then develop what they consider to be a reasonable return on the fixed assets of the utility. This reasonable return is a percentage amount applied to the value of the utility investment. The result of this calculation is referred to as a fair rate of return. The total of the operating expenses and the fair rate of return on the value of the assets are independent functions that together make up the rate base. Pricing decisions for different types of service to different classes of customers are then developed as a rate schedule that will

---

BOX 10.1 EXAMPLE OF HOW THE UTILITY RATE SETTING PROCESS OCCURS

The following excerpt is from the State of Massachusetts Department of Public Utilities (DPU). Similar procedures are followed in other states where rate questions are decided by state public utility commissions:

The electric and natural gas ratemaking process is complicated. The following is an overview of the major steps included in this process:

1. Public gas and electric utilities are required to file plans for proposed rate changes with the DPU.
2. **Public notification**. The utility is required to print a legal notice about its rate plan in major newspapers in its service territory. That notice includes information about: the total amount of the proposed rate change for residential customers, the public comment period and public hearing information. The first notice must be placed 21 days before the public hearing and the second notice approximately seven days prior to the hearing. The utility also includes a notice with its monthly bill to customers. The notice must include the total dollar amount of the proposed rate change and its impact on typical residential customers. The DPU also has the authority to require additional forms of notification.
3. **Comment period**. The DPU Commission opens the public comment period and holds a public hearing. This is the opportunity for all interested parties including residents, resident advocacy groups, businesses and government officials to inform the DPU of their interests and concerns regarding rate change impacts.
4. **Adjudicatory action**. The DPU may hold an adjudicatory hearing, a proceeding involving attorneys, the AGO (as the consumer advocate), witnesses and others with legal standing in the case.
5. **DPU staff review**. DPU staff members thoroughly review all information and prepare recommendations for the DPU commissioners.
6. **Order issued**. The DPU Commission considers the staff recommendations and public hearing comments and issues its decision (order) to accept, reject or modify the utility's proposed rate change.
7. **Customer notification**. The utility is required to notify its customers of any changes in rates (usually via monthly bill mailings). The Attorney General's Office may intervene in DPU proceedings on behalf of consumers and may negotiate settlements with utilities or take additional legal action when necessary to hold down rates for customers.

Source: Commonwealth of Massachusetts (2015).

---

generate the revenue necessary to meet operating costs and provide utility investors a fair rate of return on their investments. Most of the problems associated with this process revolve around disagreements between commissions and utility managements over the value of the utility's assets.

Table 10.3   Excerpts from a utility's requested multi-year plan

Item	Description
Plan rate period	The utility agrees to increase rates at a specific dollar amount each year for the next three years
Justification of multi-year plan request	Other utilities in the state have approved or are planning multi-year plans; a number of out-of-state utilities have also initiated or completed three year plans
Multi-year rate plan structure	The utility is allowed to recover $540.8 million in year 1, $306.6 million in year 2, and $280.2 million in year 3. However, to mitigate the impact on customers, the utility agrees to levelize the increase at $420.4 million each year of the plan
Cap (limits)	Return on investment (ROI) is conditioned upon the utility reducing operation and maintenance expenses by $27 million in year 1, $20 million in year 2, and $13 million in year 3
Return on Equity (ROE)	Authorized ROE is 10.15%
Regulatory oversight	Multi-year rate cases do not limit the ability of jurisdictional regulators to call the company in at any time for a full rate review
Incentives for the first and second year	Earning Share Plan: for an ROE greater than 10.65% but less than 12.15%, the utility will share 60% of earnings with customers and retain 40%; an ROE greater than or equal to 12.15% but less than or equal to 13.13%, the utility will share 75 of earnings with customers and retain 25%; for ROE greater than 13.15%, the utility will share 90% of earnings with customers and retain 10%
Benefits of multi-year plan	The plan produces a more predictable revenue stream and certainty for the utility to make investments necessary to continue the provision of safe and reliable service. It places strong emphasis on the utility's ability to manage costs in an efficient and effective manner, provides incentives and creative measures that encourage discipline within the corporate structure, and mitigates the increases for customers

Source: MPUC (2012).

Valuation Considerations and Approaches

The first application of the valuation of a utility's assets as a basis for determining the allowable rate of return appeared in a lower court decision in 1896. In *San Diego, etc., v. Jasper* (74 Fed. 79, 83), the court ruled that it is "the actual value of the property at the time the rates are to be fixed that should form the basis upon which to compute just rates." Two years later, the principle was accepted by the U.S. Supreme Court in one of the most important cases on utility pricing ever heard: *Smyth v. Ames* (169 US 486). The majority ruled that the doctrine of fair value as it was then applied was appropriate. The court ruled that a utility rate base must supply a fair return on the value of the property used for the convenience of the public served. An earning power large enough to provide a utility this fair return is the main test of constitutionally reasonable rates (Glaeser 1957). The *Smyth v. Ames* decision ruled that in determining fair value, rate-making authorities (public utility commissions) must take into account the following factors:

- The original cost of construction; that is, the first cost of the original plant plus the cost of extensions and permanent improvements to the physical plant. This is the *historical cost* of the tangible property.
- The amount and market value of the utility's bonds and stock; that is, the aggregate par value of the capital stock actually issued and outstanding, and the market value as determined by the bonds and stock at current exchange prices. These are the capitalized value and the commercial value of the utility.
- A consideration representing the difference between the current cost of replacement construction and the original construction cost. Rate-making authorities have generally followed an approach that uses the cost of replacement at the time the rates are being set.
- *Smyth v. Ames* added to this what is known as a *factor of safety* for future courts by adding that there might be other costs to be considered in estimating the value of a utility's physical property.

In arriving at their final decisions on the rate petition, commissioners have traditionally been guided by the need to balance a number of different objectives, among which are (Costello 2014):

1. The final rate or rates must reflect the costs of an "efficient and prudently" managed utility.
2. The rates consider the different costs for serving various classes of customers, different services and different levels of service provided.
3. The rates do not overly discriminate between classes of customers.
4. The rates and levels of risks are fair among customer classes, and between investors and customers.
5. The rates are such that the utility retains a reasonable opportunity to earn sufficient revenue to attract new capital without endangered financial difficulties.

In addition to these core objectives, regulatory considerations have included: the rates do not result in political backlash, rates are stable and changes are gradual, the services provided are affordable, the rates do not result in undue curtailment of product use, rate case decisions are facilitated and not a burden, and special social goals are met.

Rate Structures

Utility managers have at least eight different ways to implement rate structures: flat charges, flat rates, fixture rates, step rates, block rates, demand rates, zone rates, and miscellaneous or combination rates. Of these, most residential customers are charged block rates, whereas commercial and industrial customers often are charged demand rates. The most common methods are flat rates, demand rates based on uniform volumes, and block rates. Classes of rate structures are described in Table 10.4.

Flat charge rates are the simplest to understand and apply. Customers pay a single flat charge for a given time period, regardless of how much or how little energy or water they consume, discharge or waste they produce. This was the system used during the early days of the development of the industry, and is still the system used for water, sewer, solid waste pick-up, and local telephone services. The problem with this system is that it tends to encourage customers to use more of the service, often wasting more than they actually use. Flat charges provide no incentives for economizing, and are no longer used in the energy sector of the public utility industry.

The flat rate system replaced the flat charge system once affordable metering devices became available. Customers pay the same amount per unit, with the unit charge remaining the same regardless of the amount used. Flat rate systems were very popular during the growth stage of the industry. The method is used by irrigation districts, and remains in use by some domestic water utilities, who charge so much per gallon, with no concern given to the amount used. It is sometimes called a straight line rate.

Fixture rates are used with either flat charge or flat rate systems. Often used by water utilities, fixture rates are based on the number of fixtures in or on the customer's premises. The fixtures may be faucets, sinks, water closets, or any other water use appliance. The more fixtures, the higher the charges or rates charged. A version of the method uses a points-system that bases the rate charged for water upon the number of water-saving (low flow) fixtures installed on the premises, the assumption being that the more fixtures that are available, the greater will be the usage.

Step rates are used by utilities that need to stimulate usage in order to decrease per unit costs of the service. They were common in the early days

Table 10.4   Types of rate structures for water utilities

Definitions:

User Classifications: Divide customers into groups such as residential, commercial, industrial, agricultural/seasonal. Some systems classify customers by meter size. Many systems have different rates for each classification of customers.

Consumption Block: A preset quantity of water at a stated price. An example follows of a rate structure with four consumption blocks.

     $x for the first 2,000 gallons used
     $x per 1,000 from 2,000 to 6,000 gallons
     $x per 1,000 from 6,001 to 10,000 gallons
     $x per 1,000 for everything over 10,000 gallons used

UNIFORM FLAT RATE

Customers pay the same amount regardless of quantity of water used. Used in unmetered systems.

Example: Each customer charged a flat rate of $x per month.

Advantages: No expense for installing, reading meters.

Disadvantages: All customers pay either too much or too little for what they use. Is not based on use. Promotes high consumption.

Not recommended.

SINGLE BLOCK RATE

Customers are charged a constant price per gallon regardless of the amount of water used. Often coupled with a minimum charge for having service available.

Example: $x minimum service or base rate (optional) plus $x per 1,000 gallons used.

Advantages: Easy to administer, may encourage water conservation. Cost to customer is in direct proportion to amount they use.

Disadvantages: May discourage high water consuming industries from locating in the service area.

DECREASING BLOCK RATE

The price of water declines as the amount used increases. Each succeeding consumption block is cheaper. This structure is based on the assumption that costs decline as consumption goes up.

Example: $14 for first 2,000 gallons used;

$2.50 per 1,000 from 2,000 to 6,000 gallons;

$2.00 per 1,000 from 6,001 to 10,000 gallons;

$1.00 per 1,000 for everything over 10,000 gallons.

INCREASING BLOCK RATE

The price of water increases as the amount used increases. Each succeeding consumption block is more expensive. Structure based on the assumption that water rates should promote water conservation.

Example: $14 minimum for first 2,000 gallons used;

$2.00 per 1,000 from 2,000 to 6,000 gallons;

$2.50 per 1,000 from 6,001 to 10,000 gallons;

$3.00 per 1,000 for everything over 10,000 gallons.

Table 10.4   (continued)

Advantages: Attractive to large volume users.

Disadvantages: Production costs may not decrease with the increase in gallons of water produced. For a limited number of customers, low volume users may be subsidizing large volume users.

Advantages: Promotes water conservation, especially important in areas of limited water supplies or high treatment costs. Less water use means less wastewater and smaller, less expensive wastewater treatment facilities. Provides a reasonable amount of water at a reasonable price and charges a premium for those using more.

Disadvantages: Higher costs for high usage may discourage industry from locating in service area.

Source: Olsen (1999 Revised Edition).

of electric and natural gas energy utilities. With step rates, the costs of providing the service is spread across a wider customer base, with everyone supposedly benefiting from the economies. With step rate pricing, charges per unit decrease as usage increases. These rates were very popular during the 1930s and 1940s, when distribution utilities were in their growth phase of operations. Electric utilities promoted usage by offering reduced rates for what they termed "all electric homes," with electricity used for lighting, heating, and cooking. Step rates are hardly ever found today; they are regressive in that low-income customers use less but are charged the higher per unit price. Moreover, step rates promote wasteful use of the resource. Solid waste utilities often base their charges on the number and/or capacity of garbage cans or refuse containers used by the customer.

The *block rate* pricing system has long been the system utilities use for residential customers. Block or tiered rate pricing is similar to step rates in that, after a minimum monthly charge, prices are set on a per-unit basis. However, in the block rate system, the first blocks of service are the lowest priced rather than the higher priced. Prices for subsequent blocks are set at higher rates. Because the earliest usage prices are the lowest charged, block rates overcome the regressive nature of step rates. Block rates also encourage conservation by making greater use of the service increasingly expensive. Block rate systems are used by many electricity, gas, and water utilities for residential customers. Since lowest rates are charged for lowest use category, they are relatively strong conservation motivators.

Demand rates are used by utilities for pricing service for commercial and industrial customers. The maximum service that might be used by the customer establishes the rate. The utility system must be designed to meet that maximum demand, and must be paid for whether the service is used or not, within given month or year time periods. Building the capacity to meet demand is sometimes referred to as the readiness to serve factor. Demand rates often follow the block rate system, with either an added load factor schedule or the demand factor incorporated into the sliding rate structure. The problem with this system is there is no incentive for conservation by the customer.

Zone rates are similar to the rates shipping companies charge their customers. They are based upon the distance the product must be moved. Zone rates are seldom seen in electricity distribution companies, but have been common in the natural gas pipeline, propane distribution services, long distance telephone, telegraph, and public transit utilities.

Rates that do not fall into any of the above categories are grouped together into a *miscellaneous rates* category. Because state utility commissions must approve almost all prices charged by utilities, a variety of miscellaneous rates are often found in published tariffs. These may include prices for such services as on-site repair or installation of appliances or fixtures, connecting and disconnecting customers, special wiring or extension of service for electricity and telephone customers, special equipment, and the like. They also include special deductions for "all electric" or "all gas" systems.

Most public utility rate schedules are constructed using combinations of two or more of these rate categories. Their rate schedules almost always include rates for different classes of customers. Many also provide rate allowances for elderly, disabled, and special groups of customers, such as those with a very low fixed income. A comparison of some of the attributes for five of the more commonly used procedures is shown in Table 10.5.

INNOVATION IN UTILITY PRICING

The following three results that have been predicted to follow widespread adoption of retail competition in the U.S. utility industry: (1) a long-term reduction in retail prices; (2) increases in the range of products and services available to consumers; and (3) improvements in the overall reliability of the delivery system. However, in the limited numbers of states that have initiated retail competition in electric energy, these payoffs have been slow in coming, if at all. A vice president of the utility firm Sempra Energy Corporation stated the following as one possible reason for the failure of the benefits to appear as expected:

Table 10.5   Comparisons of public utility rate structure types

Rate type	Description	Encourages conservation	Easy to implement	Provides equality pricing	Reliable income for provider
Flat charge	Same amount regardless of volume	No. Price never varies.	Yes. Metering not required	No. Amount same for all customers	Yes. Is independent of use
Flat rate per unit (uniform volume rate)	Same amount charged per unit	Possibly. Depends on unit price	Yes. Require metering	Possibly. Price tied to units used	No. Depends on amount used
Fixture rates	Rates based on number of fixtures	No. Rates based on number of fixtures	Yes. Metering not required	Yes. Price depends on number of fixtures	Yes. Rates based only on number of fixtures
Increasing block (step) rates	Rate increases for each additional block	Likely. Depends on size and price increase	Somewhat. Metering and step prices needed	Possibly. Price varies with use	No. Varies with amounts used
Decreasing block (step) rates	Rates drop for each additional unit	Unlikely. Price is used to stimulate demand	Somewhat. Requires metering and computation of number size and price of blocks	Possibly. Rates based on use	No. Revenue varies with amounts used

Source: Expanded and adjusted from Donnelly and Christian-Smith (2013: 13).

> [These] benefits cannot be achieved without the addition of an essential element of a competitive market: presenting price signals through the use of hourly [retail] prices reflecting wholesale price fluctuations in the broader regional commodity markets for electricity. The hourly pricing of electricity at the retail level should induce many customers to reduce on-peak consumption, bringing pressure on suppliers to drop prices. Furthermore, exposing peak prices to customer choice can also spur the development and introduction of smart services and alternative products.
> (Reed 2003: 30–31)

The technology for real-time metering of utility product use is currently available, and is in use for large industrial and commercial users of the products. The widespread use of real-time metering systems was made possible by installation of fiber-optic communication systems. In some utilities, contracts have been negotiated with large users of the product that enable the utility to either reduce a customer's current load, or to send signals to customers about a forthcoming steep increase in peak load prices.

The ability to install such demand-control systems for residential customers is as yet not economically feasible, although many utilities have prepared for its expected occurrence by installing fiber-optic systems within their delivery areas. Until it is possible, retail customers are generally unaware of how volatility in wholesale markets can affect utility operations. Retail customers continue to receive monthly bills determined by a weighted average supply price. Price averaging tends to smooth out and hide daily— sometimes hourly—price fluctuations, including extreme prices.

Examples of what are referred to as "hidden" extreme wholesale prices are often found in systems where rates for commercial customers are set very high to subsidize the rates charged for residential customers. A customer paying energy rates of 14 cents or less per kilowatt hour might be using power that the utility was forced to pay at a much higher price per kilowatt hour. The true cost of the power is not included in the rate setting for community relations reasons.

One of the greatest disadvantages of the current weighted average retail pricing system is that consumers come to look at electricity as an undifferentiated product. This is not the case in the real world, however. The electricity used at 9:30 in the morning is not the same product as electricity purchased at 11:00 at night. Equally, electricity purchased at 3:00 in the afternoon of a mild spring day is not the same as electricity purchased at 3:00pm on a peak summer day. If customers pay the same price for the product regardless of the time of day or time of year, they are unable to see any difference in the product and, therefore, are unlikely to alter their consumption patterns without substantial incentives.

SOCIAL PRICING CONSIDERATIONS

Public utility managers face social cost considerations that are not found in most other types of businesses: the need to factor in the regulatory requirement to provide reliable, affordable service to all customers, some of whom are simply unable to pay all or part of the cost of the service. These concerns are particularly important among investor-owned electric utilities, where they are often referred to as *public purpose programs* (Brennan, Palmer, and Martinez 2002). The programs result in benefits that extend beyond the normal supply of power. They include offering rebates or discounts to customers who install weather stripping and insulation, and energy efficient (double paned) windows and appliances. Other programs provide price breaks for the use of renewable (green) fuels, funding research, and subsidizing low income, disabled, and elderly customers.

An example of social pricing consideration can be seen in the public utility district partial rate structure reproduced earlier in this chapter. The utility does not charge low-income elderly customers the daily charge of $0.46 for home power use that other residential customers must pay. The $0.46 daily charge for water well power is also waived for this customer class. The utility rate schedule also includes a discounted rate for disabled persons and a special rate for a category of residential customers who qualify for an exemption of the daily power charge.

Another special service not available to the customers of many public utilities is the option to specifically purchase blocks of energy that has been generated by renewable fuel and/or environmentally friendly facilities. These *green power* options include biomass generation, wind power, and geothermal production. A typical rate for blocks of green power is the $2.00 charge for a 100-kW-hour-block charged by the PUD. All utilities, whether consumer-owned or investor-owned, employ similar rate adjustments for one or more groups of customers.

Consumer Price Protection

One of the traditional responsibilities of state utility commissions—and one of the rationales for their establishment in the first place—is the setting and monitoring provisions for consumer protection. Commissions establish consumer protection rules that apply to all investor-owned utilities (IOUs) within their jurisdiction, while local governing boards do so for consumer-owned utilities (COUs). As a result, there tends to be more uniformity among protection policies for IOUs and greater diversity among COUs. Consumer protection rules exist for such services as credit policies, collecting past due amounts, metering, billing and adjustments, and for handling customer complaints.

Consumers' Perceptions of Utility Prices

Box 10.2 is abstracted from a research study funded by the Utility Regulatory Commissions' primary research organization at Ohio State University (Costello and Burns 2003). The study was conducted to provide commissions with benchmark data for use in their evaluations of regulated utility requests for rate relief. The study design involved a nationwide telephone survey of the attitudes of residential consumers of electric power, natural gas, and other utility services.

BOX 10.2   CONSUMER PERCEPTIONS OF UTILITY RATES

In August 2003, the National Regulatory Research Institute published a bench-mark survey of more than 18,000 customers' opinions of the prices they paid for electricity and natural gas. The data were collected between January 9 and February 3, 2003. Not surprisingly, most respondents reported that the price they paid for electric and natural gas services was "high." Nearly 66 percent said their electricity rates were "high" and 64.5 percent said that their gas prices were "high." Nearly 36 percent said they felt that all utility prices were "fair," while just 1 percent of all respondents said that the price of electricity and natural gas was low. Overall, female respondents were more likely than male respondents to see utility prices as high. On the other hand, younger customers were slightly more likely to con-sider prices to be "low" or "fair" than were older customers.

Other than for respondents claiming East Indian or Hispanic ancestry, there were few differences in the way that members of different ethnic groups responded to the survey; 53 percent of Hispanics and 76 percent of East Indians reported they believed the price of natural gas to be "fair." All other groups reported they believed the prices to be high.

The researchers were not surprised that consumers believed that prices were high. Natural gas and electricity have low elasticities. Because these services are considered to be "non-optional necessities," consumers are seldom willing to lower demand in the face of moderately higher prices for utility service.

Source: Costello and Burns (2003).

THE IMPACT OF DEREGULATION ON UTILITY PRICING

In both the natural gas and electricity utilities, the production segments of the industries have been almost entirely deregulated; wholesale prices for natural gas and electricity are now established by market forces, rather than through the previous method that involved utilities making rate-change requests, holding public hearings to validate rate-change rationales, and utility rate-of-return decisions based on valuations approved or con-tested by commissions.

Deregulation has also been introduced into the power transmission segment, although not as completely as for the producer segment. For example, the gas pipeline (transmission) segment is still controlled by the Federal Energy Regulatory Commission (FERC). Pipeline companies are required by law to permit open access to their lines and are forbidden to exercise price discrimination. Their prices are based on the scope of the services they provide and the distances they carry a customer's gas. Pipeline firms may provide such ancillary activities as gas collection from production fields, processing and cleaning natural gas, and underground and surface storage. Customers may be independent gas distribution utilities or large commercial or industrial gas users.

A similar process occurs in the transmission segment of the electricity industry. The Federal Energy Regulatory Commission (FERC) has for some time controlled wholesale transmission prices. Prices are based on type of demand, volume, and distance from the generator. Different prices exist for long-term, short-term or spot, peak or off-peak demand load. The FERC has introduced two different types of independent operating organizations to provide transmission services. The first is the independent service operator (ISO); the second is the regional transmission organization (RTO). Vertically integrated utilities are required to turn their transmission lines over to independent operators, which are then required to provide universal access and non-discriminatory prices.

Traditionally, state public utility commissions controlled prices for vertically integrated utilities by adding up all the costs of generating, transmitting, and distributing electricity during peak and off-peak times, then calculating an average cost per kilowatt-hour produced, and approving a price that guaranteed the utility an approved rate of return. Utilities developed schedules of prices for various customer classes for commission approval. Restructuring—unbundling of the utility industry—has changed this system. The FERC and state utility commissions now require separate regulatory structures for transmission and distribution. Transmission operators are subject to interstate commerce regulation and regulatory control of the FERC. Distribution utilities, on the other hand, are considered to be intrastate and, as a result, come under the supervision of state public utility commissions (PUCs).

SUMMARY

An entire new set of conditions underlies the rate-setting decisions of utility regulators today. Some of the questions regulators must consider when determining rates in this new regulatory environment include: (1) The appropriate rate *levels*—how much revenue should be raised by prices charged for services; (2) The appropriate rate *adjustments*—how and when should rates be adjusted over time to reflect actual or expected changes; (3) the best rate *structure*—what contribution to the rates paid by customers should be allocated to various services.

The process of setting rates in distribution public utilities involves four steps: (1) determining operating costs, (2) distributing costs among different customer classes, (3) considering relevant load and use factors, and

(4) designing the pricing structures that reflect the influences of the first three considerations. Determining costs involves analysis of four categories of operations: customer service, operations, demand, and overhead (general expenses). Once the management costs have been determined, they must be allocated among the various classes of customers served by the utility. Each of the four categories of costs—customer, operations, demand, and overhead—are broken down and allocated according to some relevant standard.

Utility managers and regulators look at four factors when establishing rates for their services: peak load, average load, utilization, and a diversity factor. Peak load refers to the maximum capability of the system; it is measured for a particular time period such as a day, a month, or a year, and is usually referred to as *peak demand*. Average load, or simply the *load factor*, is the average load or use of a utility's services for a given time period. The third factor in load service relates to utilization of the system. It is stated as a percentage of the total system capacity represented by the highest anticipated peak load. The final load factor considered in utility pricing is known as the *diversity factor*. Diversity refers to the different peak loads expected from the utility's different customer classes.

Utility managers have at least eight different ways to implement rate structures: flat charges, flat rates, fixture rates, step rates, block rates, demand rates, zone rates, and miscellaneous or combination rates. Of these, most residential customers are charged block rates, whereas commercial and industrial customers often are charged demand rates. State public utility commissions, operating under their legislative mandate, set the rates that public utilities can charge final customers for their services by approving rate proposals submitted by utilities under their jurisdiction.

In both the natural gas and electricity utility segments, the production components of the industry have been almost entirely deregulated; wholesale prices for natural gas and electricity are established by market forces. Deregulation has also been introduced into the transmission segments, although not as completely as for the producer segment.

Public utility managers face a social cost that is not found in most other types of businesses: the need to factor in the regulatory requirement to provide reliable, affordable service to all customers, some of whom are simply unable to pay all or part of the cost of the service.

ADDITIONAL READING

AWWA (2014a), *Water Utility Capital Financing*. Denver, CO: American Water Works Association.

CPUC (2012), 'Trends in utility infrastructure financing,' San Francisco: California Public Utilities Commission.

Donnelly, Kristina and Juliet Christian-Smith (2013), *An Overview of the "New Normal" and Water Rate Basics* (Pacific Institute White Paper). Oakland, CA: Pacific Institute.

Griff, Neil S. (2011), *Water Finance: Public Responsibilities and Private Opportunities*. Hoboken, NJ: Wiley.

Hempling, Scott (2015), *Regulating Public Utility Performance: The Law of Market Structure, Pricing and Jurisdiction*. Chicago: American Bar Association.

Mishra, Amareshwar and R.K. Mishra (2014), *Financing Patterns for Infrastructure Projects*. New Delhi: Academic Foundation Press.

11. Public utility marketing

For most of the history of the public utility industry, marketing was an uncomplicated, straightforward process. Most integrated utility providers were interested in increasing overall demand for their product. Generating facilities and source supplies were large in order to benefit from economies of scale, often resulting in an oversupply of product. Rates were controlled by state government agencies; because utilities were considered to be "natural" monopolies price competition did not exist. Most customers were charged a flat rate for the product or service, regardless of the amount used. Marketing consisted of encouraging existing customers to use more of the product, or of expanding by moving into new market territories or in the power business, by buying up other suppliers. State laws required utilities to serve all customers; growth from normal population and economic growth taking place in the existing service area was generally slow enough for utilities to meet and exceed all requirements for service.

The utility business was considered to be a slow, steady, safe, and undramatic business. Assuming that you knew what you were doing and did it reasonably well, profits were "guaranteed" by law in the form of state-approved "fair" rates of return on investments. In the few spots where integrated utilities still exist, this level of marketing still functions. It is, however, rapidly dying out, and *utility marketing* now includes activities related to *risk management*.

Beginning in the 1970s, the nature of the utility industry's marketing environment changed. A series of petroleum-based energy shocks spread throughout the industry. Government reacted by passing laws to conserve and search for more and new sources of energy. The term "demarketing" came into vogue to describe the efforts introduced to control or restrict demand. Many utilities began programs to market conservation ideas and products. Federal legislation was passed requiring utilities to seek or develop alternative sources of supply. Marketing funds were directed toward research and development. At about the same time, environmental protection and conservation laws were passed. These required utilities to design marketing programs to help eliminate air, water, and soil pollution.

By the 1980s, portions of the utility industry were partially deregulated, with competition introduced to the wholesale segment of the supply chain.

The industry developed a futures market to enable producers and distributors to manage the risk associated with deregulated wholesale prices.

Marketing means many things to different people. For some, the mention of the word brings to mind the practice of *advertising* and other persuasive communications to influence demand. For others, it means *sales* or *selling*—often with the adjective "high-pressure" attached. In parts of the utility business, marketing has come to mean wholesale sales of electricity or natural gas, most often in a futures market. Therefore, some definitions are in order before proceeding with this description of some of the marketing challenges facing utilities. This chapter discusses some of the challenges that have emerged in utility marketing over the last several decades.

THE EVOLVING ROLE OF MARKETING

Marketing as a business function has changed over the past fifty years. Emphasis has shifted from gaining market share and growing larger in order to reap the benefits of economies of scale, to what is increasingly seen as an emphasis on developing relationships with customers. Developing and maintaining mutually beneficial relationships with customers, not market share, is seen as the key to sustaining profitability. In the utility business, large size was the preferred norm. Scale economies resulted in construction of ever larger physical plant. As plant size increased, more customers or greater volume of use was needed to lower unit costs.

Beginning in the 1960s and 1970s, a number of important social and economic phenomena occurred to bring about changes in the way the utility industry markets its products and services. They also brought about a redesign of the organization, structure, and operations of the utility industry. Several energy crises exacerbated the growth problems faced by energy utilities in the 1960s and 1970s. The public suffered through rapidly increasing energy prices, long lines at the gasoline pump, and shortages of natural gas. The price of producing utility products paralleled increases in the price of fuel. A quadrupling of the price of oil and gas was a painful reminder of our growing dependence upon foreign supplies for energy. These events brought to light the dangers faced by the nation as a result of shortages of supply and reliance upon foreign sources of energy.

Another phenomenon taking place throughout the 1960s and 1970s was a great wave of environmental concern that made consumer protection, conservation, and clean-up a national priority. Among other concerns for the environment, the public's attention was focused on widespread pollution of the nation's water supplies. Along with the conservation movement came a public demand for protecting natural resources and a widespread disenchantment with the use of nuclear power for generating electricity. By the end of the 1970s, consumer activism had effectively halted all construction of nuclear generators in the United States. In response to public pressure, the idea of demarketing—reducing instead of stimulating demand—emerged in the 1970s. With flat- or average-rate pricing and the absence of non-conformance penalties, however, conservation programs had little long-term effect on consumption patterns.

As a result of the baby boom of the 1940s and 1950s, by the 1970s, growth in demand was outpacing the ability of the utilities to meet their service mandates. Power shortages resulted in electricity blackouts and natural gas shortages. High prices resulted from federally regulated wholesale price caps at the wellhead source. Health problems surfaced from impurities in drinking water, and other system failures came to plague utility management. Moreover, air, ground, visual, and water pollution was rampant. The nation's utilities needed help. Eventually, the nation's leaders and the public in general came to recognize that the utility industry played a critical role in the economic well-being of the nation. Stiff government regulation was not alleviating these problems. Deregulation was proposed as one solution to the industry's ills.

To deal with these and similar problems, the federal government adopted a major public policy initiative designed to achieve energy self-sufficiency. Federal grants were awarded for the development of innovative ways to meet the demand for energy. The introduction of wind and solar power, biomass, cogeneration, and thermal generation methods, production of synthetic natural gas and methods of handling and shipping liquefied natural gas, among others, came from these federal programs.

A consequence of these radical changes in the operating environment of public utilities was greater involvement of the marketing function in utility operations. Also increasing the importance of marketing was the international trend toward deregulation, which resulted in the reorganization of many essential public services, including transportation, telecommunications, natural gas, and most recently, electrical energy.

Deregulation includes two important economic and political elements: unbundling of the industry and the preemption of state utility regulatory powers by the federal government. Unbundling of the traditional vertically integrated utility business was proposed as a way of lowering prices and increasing the reliability of supply for all participants in the utility industry. It would do this by introducing market *competition* at the production, transmission, and in some states, the retail distribution levels of the utility industry. Competition at all levels of the industry meant that each organization had to learn the techniques of marketing in the management of its value chain, including demand analysis, advertising, public relations, selling, and other marketing techniques.

As markets throughout North America, Europe, and parts of Asia matured in the 1980s and the 1990s, the lifetime value of a customer (CLV) became a central marketing issue in utilities. This concept emphasizes the need to build relationships and to keep customers over time to recapture the "back loading" of revenue (Johnson and Seines 2004).

UNDERSTANDING UTILITY DEMAND FACTORS

To understand the marketing function in public utilities, it is necessary to examine the nature of demand for utility products or services (Ilic 2001). At the retail level, utilities typically divide their customers into three broad classes: residential, commercial, and industrial. The average of the service demands by all customers in each of three classes of customers over a given period of time is the utility's average or *base service* load. The utility must be prepared to meet all average load requirements; it must also maintain a reserve for contingencies—that is, for meeting *peak* demand. Extenuating circumstances often result in a load factor that exceeds both base and peak demand. Utilities have several choices when this happens. They can purchase product (gas or electric power) from other utilities or from private, nonregulated producers, on what is called the *spot* market. Or, they can curtail delivery. In 2000 and 2001, the State of California was forced to follow the second path when purchasing power on the spot market became too expensive, and producers refused to sell power to distribution firms that were teetering on the brink of insolvency; it instituted a series of "rolling blackouts," in which power was cut for brief periods of time in different parts of the state (Brennan, Palmer, and Martinez 2002).

Within a utility's service load, each customer group has a different load pattern and a different elasticity of demand. Elasticity refers to the willingness and/or ability of a customer to shift consumption in response to price signals. Residential customers exhibit relatively low elasticity; raising or lowering the price of a utility product usually has little effect upon consumption. When the wholesale price of energy or water increases, customers do not take fewer morning showers, brew fewer pots of coffee, or wash fewer dishes. Utility costs represent only a small portion of most residential customers' budgets. Equally, lower utility costs do not result in greater consumption. This is the rationale given for the prevalence of flat- or average-rate billing for residential customers.

Commercial and industrial customers, on the other hand, have greater price elasticity. Utility costs make up a far larger proportion of their operating costs than is the case for residential customers. Owners of office buildings, factories, and the like are far more likely to change their utility consumption patterns when faced with significant price increases or decreases. The rates these customers pay may fluctuate with the type of demand provided. For example, the price of non-peak period supply is typically lower that for peak-demand period. Therefore, commercial and industrial customers are encouraged to either shift their load use to non-peak periods, or to cut back on their use in peak-demand times. For example, on days when the outside temperature exceeds 85 or 90 degrees, most workers are just as comfortable when air conditioning cools the inside air to between 68 and 74 degrees Fahrenheit. Thus, getting these customers to raise their thermostats to the higher end of the range can greatly reduce the amount of power needed for air conditioning.

THE ROLE OF MARKETS

Markets have been defined in as groups of potential customers with similar needs who are willing to exchange something of value with sellers offering goods and/or services (ways of satisfying those needs). Potential customers for utility products and services include households, commercial and industrial firms, government agencies, and not-for-profit organizations. Each of the categories of customers may be considered a *market*. Moreover, each market includes smaller groups or *segments* of a larger market. For example, included in the industrial and government categories are other utilities who purchase utility products for resale to other groups of wholesale and/or retail customers.

Customers of a market do not have to all be in the same location; many markets for goods and services are global. Nor do they have to be limited to one or a few suppliers. The *energy market*, for example, refers to all the possible suppliers and buyers of electricity, coal, natural gas, and petroleum. There are markets for each of these energy components. The market may be national, regional, or local. The duration of the market may be stated for time periods as long as a century, a decade, a year, or even a day or shorter period. A description of a market for a specific utility's products generally describes demand in a specific area for a specific period of time.

Two Levels of Marketing

Marketing—the exchange of utility products or services for payment—takes place at two levels in the utility supply chain: wholesale and retail. Utility wholesaling is the sale of the electricity, gas, or water in bulk to a down-channel organization that will then resell the product on to another channel member or to final customers. The objective of wholesale marketing is to facilitate the transactions between segments. Utility retail marketing, on the other hand, refers to the activities involved in the sale of utility products and services to customers who actually use the product. In product segments of the utility industry—electricity, natural gas, water, and wastewater—both investor-owned and publicly owned utilities must perform this function. In the services sector of the industry—solid and hazard waste disposal and public transit—utilities provide a service for which a fee is levied.

Utility Wholesale Markets

The term *market* also refers to the demand for products at different levels of the supply chain. Wholesale markets are customers who purchase the product in order to resell it to another firm in the supply chain. In the electricity industry, independent generators sell the power they produce to either transmission or distribution firms, or both. In the natural gas industry, production companies sell gas to pipeline companies and/or local distribution utilities. In the water industry, a few large government-owned water agencies sell water at wholesale to local and regional distributors. For all utilities, wholesale and retail markets sometimes include overlap, For example, a local retail market may also include large industrial or government customers who buy direct from producers or distributors, but at what are close-to-wholesale prices. For example, Tacoma (Washington) Public Utilities sells a mix of utility products at wholesale rates to two local military bases, the U.S. Army's Ft. Lewis and McCord Air Force Base, now operating as Joint Base Lewis-McCord.

At the wholesale level, utility products are sold in three different markets: the *unregulated market*, the *regulated market*, and the *spot market* (Brennan, Palmer, and Martinez 2002; Twenty-first Century Power Partnership 2013; Yoshimura 2013). The unregulated market consists of sales by either generating or distributing companies to large industrial users under both short and long-term contracts. The contract prices generally reflect market conditions at the time the contract was negotiated. The price may remain constant throughout the life of the contract or include provisions for adjustments through escalation clauses. If changes are made, they usually do not fluctuate widely. Other producers often compete for these contracts.

The regulated market consists of sales to distribution utilities for resale to any type of customers. Electricity and gas utility distribution companies like long-term contracts because they are assured of a stable source of supply at predictable, reasonably stable prices. Producers like long-term contracts because they are assured of a stable source of revenue to service their often very large debt. However, long-term contracts usually only cover a predicted load (demand) level that does not cover all possible demand.

Wholesale sales in the unregulated market typically occur as a result of long-term contracts between suppliers and either transmission or distribution organizations. Often, they take the form of *take-or-pay* contracts. These contracts assure the producer an income stream which can be used for debt service as well as for investor dividends. The unregulated market includes independent generators of electricity and natural gas producers. The "green power" market—that is, wind, solar, geothermal, biomass, and other renewable fuel energy producers—are often included in the unregulated segment.

When demand exceeds the normal or average load, regulated utilities face what is called peak load or peak demand, and they must find other sources of supply to comply with their license to serve. Utilities look to the third type of wholesale market: the spot market. The spot market differs from the contract market because the sales/purchases are made essentially at the very moment the product is delivered. Buyers must pay the going price at that moment. Contract purchases are made in advance of delivery of the product. Contract sales are sold (that is, traded) in futures markets.

The process of buying and selling future contracts in energy products is similar to futures trading activities in agricultural commodity exchanges. Futures exchanges make it possible for organizations in an industry to transfer the risks from price changes to other parties willing to accept those risks. They are willing to accept the risk because they gain the potential of earning large profits from buying and selling futures contracts. A futures contract binds the parties to the sale/purchase of an amount of utility product for delivery at some time in the future. The contract also typically spells out a way for the parties to be relieved of their contract responsibility, such as a seller refusing to deliver a product and giving the buyer his money back with no penalty. Box 11.1 briefly describes how Dominion Resources, Inc., a large, vertically integrated natural gas and electricity utility located in Richmond, Virginia, participates in market trading.

In an unregulated market, prices for alternative supplies to meet *peak load* can be very high. Distribution utilities have several ways to reduce their reliance on the spot market for meeting load spikes. One of these is by installing real-time metering at the facilities of large users. Real-time metering gives users time to decide to accept delivery of the utility product at a much higher price or whether to shut down or shift usage to off-peak time periods. Experience has shown that when customers are charged

BOX 11.1   TRADING ACTIVITIES OF INVESTOR- AND
           PUBLICLY OWNED UTILITIES

Investor-owned utilities
As part of its strategy to market energy and to manage related risk, Dominion Resources, an investor-owned utility, manages a portfolio of commodity-based derivative instruments held for trading purposes. These contracts are sensitive to changes in the prices of energy commodities, primarily natural gas and electricity. Dominion uses established policies and procedures to manage the risks associated with these price fluctuations. Dominion also uses various derivative instruments, such as futures, swaps, and options, to mitigate risk by creating offsetting market positions. In addition, Dominion seeks to use its generation capacity, when not needed to serve customers in its service territory, to satisfy commitments to sell energy.

Publicly owned utilities
Publicly owned utilities, although subject to many of the same risks, typically do not engage in the same degree of trading common to at investor-owned utilities. The following exert from an explanatory document by the Riverside (California) Public Utility (RPU) helps describe how large public utilities engage in risk-management activities:

> Although RPU does not engage in risk-taking activities typical to a private-sector organization, management recognizes that certain risks are incidental to normal power supply operations and hedging activities. RPU's Policy is to manage risk inherent with serving load, including the risks associated with normal cost-hedging activities, those associated with participation in wholesale markets in general and the California Independent System Operator ("CAISO") in particular. RPU's supply portfolio is exposed to several risks, including but not limited to: (i) load variability; (ii) cost variability (including applicable CAISO resource sufficiency and associated price caps, congestion costs, energy costs and energy losses); (iii) Counterparty Risk; (iv) energy commodity price volatility; and (v) regulatory/legislative risk. From the perspective of risk mitigation, RPU's primary objective is to manage the cost of serving its customers. Taking unnecessary risk in order to arbitrage market opportunities, or risks unrelated to RPU's normal power supply business activities, is considered inappropriate. (Dominion Resources 2002: 54 and City of Riverside Public Utilities 2014: 2)

real-time prices, peak-demand for the product is reduced. This, in turn, allows the utility to enjoy a reduction in its required generating capacity (Stoft 2002). As a way of avoiding peak demand price spikes, a large number of electricity distribution companies have purchased relatively small gas turbine generators that they use only for meeting peak demand, thus enabling them to avoid very high peak-load spot purchases. In one sense, this may be seen as a step backward in the move toward unbundling of the vertically integrated industry.

Marketing in the Retail Sector

The process of providing electricity, gas, or water to ultimate consumers is what is known in the industry as retail marketing or retail sales. It is usually but not always a part of the distribution segment of the industry. Before deregulation and reorganization of the industry, this was the only place where marketing activities were employed. However, unbundling of the industry into separate production–transmission–distribution components has resulted in an entirely new role for the marketing function. As a result of retail competition, marketing today is often a separate function.

Competition will not result in the construction of duplicate distribution systems in a market area. Therefore, distribution systems will continue to function as regulated utilities. To meet their required supply requirements, they will also require substantial investments in permanent physical plants. Marketing activities, on the other hand, usually do not require huge investments. This has resulted in the retail sales/billing/customer service functions of marketing being opened to competition as a nonregulated business. Utility holding companies are permitted to establish and operate nonregulated marketing operations separate from their regulated utility distribution companies. In some locations, marketing services are outsourced to completely independent specialist firms.

Classes of retail customers

There are three main classes of retail customers: households, commercial customers, and industrial customers. Households include single-family homes and apartments, Commercial buyers include offices, retail stores, schools, and government facilities. Industrial customers include manufacturing, processing, and construction firms. Farms may be either residential or commercial buyers, or both.

Several types of utility wholesalers exist. They can be investor or publicly owned producing organizations, such as electricity generators, natural gas producers, or water storage organizations. They can also be electric power transmission-grid managing organizations, or natural gas pipeline companies, or operators of water aqueducts or pumping facilities. Any of these organizations may sell to firms who will then resell the product. The 2013 and 2014 volumes handled by the top ten natural gas marketers in the U.S. are shown in Table 11.1. The top two were firms headquartered outside of the United States: BP (formerly British Petroleum) and Shell Energy (a branch of the former Royal Dutch/Shell oil company).

Table 11.1   Sales of top ten North American natural gas marketers, 2013 and 1014 (in billion cubic feet per day)

Rank	Company	2013	2014	Percent change
1	BP	22.70	23.70	4.0%
2	Shell Energy NA	11.70	11.30	−3.0%
3	ConocoPhillips	11.76	9.80	−17.0%
4	Macquarie Energy[1]	9.38	9.68	3.0%
5	Tenaska	6.80	6.90	1.0%
6	EDF Trading NA	7.12	6.58	−8.0%
7	Sequent	5.73	6.32	10.0%
8	J. Aron & Co.[2]	4.28	5.50	29.0%
9	Chevron	5.77	4.31	−25.0%
10	ExxonMobil	3.90	3.71	−5.0%

Notes:
1   Includes company's Canada transaction.
2   The commodity trading subsidiary of Goldman Sachs.

Source: Data from consolidated table as reported to *Natural Gas Intelligence* (NGI 2015).

The retail organizations that sell utility products to the three classes of customers can be classified into five different types: (1) investor-owned utilities; (2) consumer-owned utilities, including public power districts, utility districts, and state authorities such as the California Water Board; (3) rural cooperatives, including farm-group owned and rural municipality-owned cooperatives; (4) federally owned utilities, such as TVA and Bonneville Power; and (5) independent producers and/or transmission (shipping) organizations, such as pipelines and independent power-grid operators, who also serve customers in a particular area, often near the utility's source of supply.

MARKETING MANAGEMENT

The process of marketing management consists of three key activities: Developing a plan with specific objectives, implementing the plan, and monitoring progress in achieving planned objectives. Developing the marketing plan and managing implementation of the program are the two chief tasks of marketing management. The planning activity includes setting realistic objectives for all the marketing program activities. The product of planning is the *strategic marketing plan*, which specifies both short- and long-term objectives. The marketing plan spells out the tasks that are to be carried out in order to accomplish the marketing objectives. As the basis for the marketing planning activity, marketing managers use the data they gathered during the analysis of the utility's external and external environments for the overall strategic plan.

The second major task of marketing management is to direct the *implementation* of the plan. This involves allocating people, money, and other resources to the tasks where they can do the most good. The third activity is *controlling* the implementation of the plans. Two of the chief ways that controlling takes place is through effective budget control and *Managing for Results* programs, using such tools as balanced score-cards and the like.

Marketing managers are also required to plan, implement, and monitor programs designed to encourage customers to modify their patterns of use. This may mean using less electricity, natural gas, or water; changing the time it is used; or even investing in load reduction technologies. Collectively, these activities are referred to as demand-side management (DSM), and refer only to demand modifications that take place in response to utility-managed programs. DSM activities include the entire range of actions to achieve load modification objectives, including strategic conservation, load management, and strategic load-growth management.

The American Water Works Association—although warning that marketing should not take the place of serious public participation programs—reported that all utilities can benefit from the judicious use of marketing: "Marketing and branding have become the latest buzzwords for water utilities seeking to improve their communication effectiveness. The marketing paradigm has many advantages and can—in many respects—apply just as easily to a water utility as to consumer products" (Katz 2002: 32).

Katz went on to suggest that typical goals for a marketing program might include raising public awareness, creating a brand identity, and gaining acceptance through persuasion. Goals for a public participation program, on the other hand, could be sharing decision-making with the public, learning more about community values and priorities, and gaining acceptance through consensus.

An increasingly important tool used in marketing plan implementation in the age of wholesale and retail competition in the utility industry is customer relationship managementr(CRM). CRM is both a management activity and a software program that enables management to gather, collect, and make available all relevant information about customers, their needs, and their preferences. The fundamental processes of a CRM system is the merger into one comprehensive database all the customer information from all sources in the company, with access available to all relevant company users. The goal of the CRM program is to make long-term partners out of customers. On the negative side, the costs of converting customers to even closer relationships also increase (Johnson and Seines 2004).

MARKETING IN ACTION

The marketing function in all segments of the utility industry, including investor-owned and publicly owned operations, involves application of the following four major activities: (1) defining, measuring, and forecasting demand; (2) analyzing and interpreting the relevant controllable and uncontrollable environmental forces which positively or negatively influence the short- and long-term financial strength of the utility; (3) planning, designing and implementing persuasive tools to increase, change, or reduce demand; and (4) the designing, implementing, and managing of related activities to help achieve the operational and growth objectives of the organization. Box 11.2 describes the marketing role in diversified gas company.

BOX 11.2   MARKETING IN A DIVERSIFIED GAS COMPANY

WGL Holdings, Inc. is a public utility holding company doing business in Washington, DC, Maryland, and Virginia. Its regulated gas distribution company, Washington Gas Light Company, distributes natural gas to roughly 940,000 residential, commercial, and industrial customers. Marketing to the regulated segment includes customer service, meter-reading and billing, and conservation education programs.

The firm's unregulated affiliates sell gas and electricity in competitive markets, and provide heating, ventilating, and air conditioning products and services (HVAC). The company's retail energy-marketing subsidiary, WGEServices, sells natural gas on an unregulated, competitive basis directly to residential, commercial and industrial customers. Natural gas marketers compete mainly on price, resulting in relative small gross margins. In 2001, WGEServices also began selling electricity in competition with regulated power utilities in its market area. By 2002, the unregulated segment had 155,000 natural gas customers and 66,000 electricity customers. Its two HVAC affiliates, ACI and WGESystems, market installation and related services to commercial and governmental customers. Marketing programs are used to acquire and keep these customers in the unregulated segment.

The nonregulated arm of the firm enters into long-term delivery contracts for retail gas and electricity. As a result, it is exposed to market risk from changes in wholesale gas and electricity prices and from demand fluctuations from periods of higher or lower temperatures (weather risk).

Source: WGL Holdings (2002).

Forecasting demand is an art as much as it is a science. Utility managers used a number of different forecasting tools when undertaking this process. The most commonly used method is based on historical information; that is, it uses the record of past load as the basis for projecting future demand. An historical percentage rate of growth or decline is calculated and used with past data to project future levels. The process is called *time series analysis*, and can be carried out with simple, readily available spreadsheet software, such as Microsoft® Excel™. This software also permits manipulating the number used for percentage rate of growth to develop optimistic and pessimistic projections.

The demand for energy is often described in terms of a load-duration curve that displays the time period in a year that the total load (demand) is at or above some specified "typical" or "average" demand level for that period (Stoft 2002). Because water and wastewater demand growth rates tend to be less volatile than natural gas and electricity, they are typically forecast from historical patterns. Extraordinary events—such as opening or closing of a major water user, or the effects of a protracted drought—are superimposed as positive or negative "states of nature" contributions to the calculated historical rate of growth. As such, their effects are often "smoothed" from the time series projection.

Environmental analysis for marketing planning is patterned after the same type of situational analysis used for strategic planning. External, non-controllable factors are evaluated for potential threats and opportunities; internal, controllable factors are examined for highlighting the organizational strengths and weaknesses which affect the utility's ability to accomplish its objectives. Competitive analysis is becoming increasingly important in certain segments of the industry; this process, together with analysis for strengths and weaknesses, helps management identify what are called *strategic gaps* in the market. These are potential areas of business growth in which the organization has the potential for gaining a competitive advantage. Care must be taken, however, that the utility's management follows strategies that keep the utility competitive in its core business.

Environmental Concerns

For the early decades of the twenty-first century, a number of conflicting factors beyond the direct control of public utility managers converged upon the industry. Utilities facing these challenges turned to human resources programs to help resolve the conflicting forces. In some cases, the forces have sent conflicting messages to utility marketing personnel. Within investor-owned utilities, these eternal pressures and challenges include:

- Balancing the need for revenue growth with requirements to encourage conservation by customers.
- Balancing the need for shareholder returns with the need to maintain inexpensive, reliable service.
- Managing diversified (regulated and nonregulated) businesses with competitive problems that are different than those facing the core utility business.

Management responses have included programs that improve the organization's customer focus, reducing operating costs, and maintaining functional and product quality. Human resource's role in these programs include building two-way goal setting, increased customer feedback, and expanded emphasis on the utility's mission and senior management vision.

Two-way goal setting has been most problematic. For example, in one northeastern U.S. electric utility, marketing representatives were confused over the mixed messages they were receiving from management. Marketing staff were told to secure more customers, while at the same time, push for greater conservation. They did not know whether to continue to push the benefits of all-electric homes to housing developers, or to work with existing customers to find ways to use less power, or even to accept the utility's new interruptible service.

Marketing Includes Buyers and Sellers

At its most basic, marketing involves buying and selling, regardless of whether the utility functions in the regulated or unregulated sector of the industry. A utility marketer must determine the needs of one or more customer groups, and then design a profitable mix of marketing activities that provide the customers the greatest possible satisfaction with what they pay for a product or service. In a competitive situation, the marketer must design a marketing mix that provides an advantage over the offering of other sellers wanting to meet customer demand. When a firm operates in a monopoly, government regulators often substitute price controls for that of the competitive market.

Every market contains buyers and sellers. Often, more than one level of buyers and sellers are needed to get products or services to market. As the utility industry developed over the past 100 or so years, considerable consolidation and vertical integration took place. In many cases, large investor-owned utilities evolved to produce, ship, distribute, and deliver the product to final customers. These individual firms did all the buying, transporting, selling, billing and other related marketing activities based on their analyses of how the marketing function operates in the then-current natural gas market.

MAINTAINING QUALITY AND RELIABILITY

Maintaining service quality and reliability is a big part of the responsibility often assigned to marketing units. In the utility industry, a number of organizations play a role in this effort. Foremost of these in the energy field is the *North American Electric Reliability Council* (NERC). This organization was established in 1968 after a disastrous blackout on November 9, 1965, cut off power in the northeastern United States and Ontario, Canada. The mission of the NERC is to promote the reliability of the electricity supply for all of North America. NERC is a nonprofit organization controlled by nine regional councils: East Central Area Reliability Coordination Agreement (ECAR), Electric Reliability of Texas (ERCOT), Mid-Atlantic Area Council (MAAC), Mid-America Interconnected Network (MAIN), Mid-Continent Area Power Pool (MAPP), Northeast Power Coordinating Council (NPCC), Southeastern Electric Reliability Council (SERC), Southwest Power Pool (SPP), Western Systems Coordinating Council (WSCC); the Alaska Systems Coordinating Council (ASCC) is an affiliate member. In 2015, energy customers in the U.S. rated energy supply utilities in Florida and Washington states as the best in the nation at meeting the needs of their customers on reliability and customer communications (Box 11. 3).

The Environmental Protection Agency (EPA) is the agency with greatest control over water quality in the United States. EPA's authority extends to monitoring and controlling the treatment and discharge of all recycled wastewater into the environment. The EPA establishes standards on particulate matter, bacteria, and various toxic chemicals found in water. The utility must monitor and correct, if necessary, any discrepancies they find in their water supply.

SUMMARY

For most of the history of the public utility industry, marketing was an uncomplicated, straightforward process. Marketing objectives were achieved by encouraging existing customers to use more of the product or by expanding service into new market territories. State laws required utilities to serve all customers in their service areas; growth from population and economic growth in the existing service area was generally slow enough for utilities to meet and exceed all requirements for service.

**BOX 11.3   FLORIDA AND WASHINGTON UTILITIES RATED
HIGHEST IN CUSTOMER SATISFACTION**

Every year, E Source, an energy consulting firm, conducts a survey of utilities'
largest business customers to determine how well electricity and natural gas
energy providers are meeting the needs of their large customers. The company
then ranks the customers' overall satisfaction with both their utility and utility
account representative. In 2014 more than 1,000 large business customers of 25
North American utilities were surveyed, revealing the top utilities in business customer satisfaction as well as the top attribute that leads to high satisfaction. This
year, respondents named reliability as the attribute that large business customers
consider most important for utilities. Customers also place high importance on
effective communications, especially during energy emergencies. Three service
items are consistently rated by customers as most important for utilities to deliver:
reliable energy, low prices, and emergency communications.

Florida Power & Light (FPL) and Tacoma (Washington) Public Utilities earned
top honors in large business customer satisfaction:

> FPL earned top marks among large utilities in a number of areas, including
> satisfaction with the utility itself as well as with the utility's account manage-
> ment team. Among small and midsize utilities, Tacoma Public Utilities was
> rated highest for utility satisfaction thanks to superior marks for the utility's
> account management team. Tacoma Public Utilities' large business cus-
> tomers were particularly pleased with their account representatives' effec-
> tive communication skills and customer service.

Source: ELP (2010).

The utility business was considered to be a slow, steady, safe, and
undramatic business to be in and a safe place to invest your money.
Assuming that you knew what you were doing and did it reasonably well,
profits were "guaranteed" by law in the form of state-approved "fair"
rates of return on investments. Beginning in the 1970s, the nature of
the utility industry's marketing environment began to change. A series
of petroleum-based energy shocks spread throughout the industry.
Government reacted by passing laws to conserve and search for more
and new sources of energy. The term "demarketing" came into vogue to
describe the efforts introduced to control or restrict demand. Many utilities began programs to market conservation ideas and products. Federal
legislation was passed requiring utilities to seek or develop alternative
sources of supply. By the 1980s, portions of the utility industry were partially deregulated, with competition introduced to the wholesale segment
of the supply chain. The industry developed a futures market to enable

producers and distributors to manage the risk associated with deregulated wholesale prices.

Marketing has changed over the past fifty years. Emphasis has shifted from gaining market share and growing larger to what is increasingly seen as an emphasis on developing relationships with customers.

As markets throughout North America, Europe, and parts of Asia matured in the 1980s and the 1990s, the lifetime value of a customer (CLV) became a central marketing issue in utilities. This concept emphasizes the need to build relationships and to keep customers over time to recapture the "back loading" of revenue.

To understand the marketing function in public utilities, it is necessary to examine the nature of demand for utility products or services. At the retail level, utilities divide their customers into three classes: residential, commercial, and industrial. Within a utility's service load, each group has a different *load pattern*, and different elasticity of demand. Elasticity refers to the willingness and/or ability of a customer to shift consumption in response to price signals. Residential customers exhibit relatively low elasticity; raising or lowering the price of a product has little effect upon consumption.

At the wholesale level, utility products are sold in three different markets: the *unregulated market*, the *regulated market*, and the *spot market*. The process of providing electricity, gas, or water to ultimate consumers is what is known in the industry as *retail marketing* or *retail sales*. It is usually but not always a part of the distribution segment of the industry. Before deregulation and reorganization of the industry, this was the only place where marketing activities were employed. However, unbundling of the industry into separate production–transmission–distribution components has resulted in an entirely new role for the marketing function. As a result of retail competition, marketing today is often a separate function.

Maintaining product quality and reliability is a big part of the responsibility often assigned to marketing units. In the utility industry, a number of organizations play a role in this effort. Foremost of these in the energy field is the *North American Electric Reliability Council* (NERC). The Environmental Protection Agency (EPA) has greatest control over water quality in the United States. EPA also monitors and controls the treatment and discharge of all recycled wastewater.

ADDITIONAL READING

Bradley Jr., Robert L. (2011), *Edison to Enron: Energy Markets and Political Strategies*. Salem, MA: Scrivener.

Brennan, Timothy L., Karen L. Palmer and Salvador A. Martinez (2002), *Alternating Currents*: *Electricity Markets and Public Policy*. Washington, DC: Resources for the Future.

Drummond, Jim and Fred Hanna (2006), *Selling Power*: *Marketing Energy Under Deregulation*. Victoria, Canada: Trafford.

Goetz, Melanie (2014), *Communicating Water's Value: Talking Points, Tips and Strategies*. Denver: American Water Works Association.

Hill, Peter J. (ed.) (1997), *Water Marketing*: *The Next Generation*. Lanham, MD: Rowman and Littlefield.

Lovelock, Christopher H. and Jochen Wertz (2014), *Services Marketing*: *People, Technology, Strategy* (7th edn). New York: Prentice Hall.

McLean-Conner, P. (2004), *Customer Service: Utility Style*. Tulsa, OK: PennWell.

12. Public utility information systems

In the modern public utility industry, skill in information technology has become a central management requirement. One of the chief academic analysts of the utilities industry during the last half of the twentieth century, University of Wisconsin Professor of Economics and Commerce Martin G. Glaeser, never mentioned information technology in his 1957 encyclopedic review of the industry, *Public Utilities in American Capitalism*. Sixteen years later, the concept was still missing from a later overview of the industry by Martin Farris and Roy Sampson (1973). By the 1980, 1990s and early twenty-first century, however, hardly any public utility text or business journal is published without a discussion of some aspect of information technology (IT), information technology management (ITM), or simply information management (IM).

A typical utility's IT infrastructure is built around three central IT functions: operational systems, organizational or enterprise information systems, and subscribed systems (also called publish-subscribed systems). Operational systems integrate supervisory control and data acquisition (SCADA), process and other critical technologies employed for the control, movement and monitoring of product (electricity gas, water, waste, transit vehicles) and customer services. Organizational information systems include the core product operating system, applications systems, and business systems. Information systems technology in the water and wastewater sector, for example, includes the information technology (IT) as it relates to facilities and process management for water acquisition, treatment and distribution, and wastewater treatment and discharge facilities; it also covers the associated methodologies, technologies, and best management practices.

Subscribed systems are the managed systems outside of the utility but which are regularly or intermittently accessed by utilities. They include Internet service providers, hosted networks, data storage and cloud services and many others. There are two general categories of publish-subscribe systems, subject-based or content-based. In *subject-based systems*, a message belongs to one of a fixed set of what are variously referred to as groups, channels, or topics. Subscription targets a group, channel, or topic, and the user receives all events that are associated with that group. *Content-based systems*, on the other hand, are not constrained to the notion that a message must belong to a particular group in order to access or otherwise participate in the system. Instead, the decision is made on a message-by-message basis based on a query or predicate issued by a subscriber.

As these information systems came to be almost universally applied during the last twenty years of the twentieth century, information technology has come to be a powerful, indispensable function in the management of utilities, whether they are large or small, publicly or investor-owned, for-profit or not-for-profit. Computers and complex telecommunications systems are now a critical component in the strategies of all electrical, natural gas, and water and wastewater systems. IT has taken on a critical and strategic role in numerous organizations; these firms have become so dependent upon IT to support many core activities that the failure of these systems would critically impair operations (Kearns and Lederer 2003).

KEY CONCEPTS IN INFORMATION MANAGEMENT

Public utility information management is enabled through application of information systems, information management, information technology management, and computer-based information systems. *Information systems* are the information technology tools used by organization managers; they include the firm's computing and communications systems, and involve both hardware and software. *Information management* refers to the control mechanisms pertaining to business-related information and communications standards, policies, and procedures within the firm. *Information technology management* refers to the planning and management of all IT resources, including people, the infrastructure, standards, and operations of the IT system in the utility. Some authors group the various components of the information system under the activity known as *computer-based information system* (CBIS). Whatever name is used, the parts and purposes of information technology are more or less the same.

The key point to remember about all information technology is that it is dependent upon computers. Computers are used to collect, process, generate, manage, store, and retrieve data, which is the raw material of IT. The product of the IT system is *information*. Information is what managers and workers need to become more creative and effective than they would be without the technology. The purpose of information technology is to help people solve problems. These can be management problems, marketing problems, production problems, quality problems, and many, many more. Some of the many different problem-solving applications of IT in utilities include accounting information systems, supervisory control and data acquisition systems, geographic information systems, energy management systems, customer information systems, maintenance management systems, marketing management systems, laboratory information systems, various production models (such as water quality models and power generation models), and distribution and transmission network models, among others.

Many different claims have been made about the benefits that accrue from the use of information technology. For example, IT has been described as the major facilitator of business activities in the world, and as a *catalyst of changes in the structure, operations, and management of organizations* (Turban, McLean and Weatherbe 2015). Information systems affect how managers decide, plan, and often determine what products and services are produced or provided and how they are to be distributed. Information systems play a major role in the life of these organizations. The next section describes some of the ways IT is applied in public utilities.

IT APPLICATIONS

The introduction of IT in utility management that has taken place over the last several decades has produced performance gains that Heller, Von Sacken, and Gerstberger (2001) traced to the continual improvement in four IT applications: (1) *information system technology* (IST), (2) *utility communications architecture* (UCA), (3) *utility business architecture* (UBA), and (4) what may be described as *industrial* or *business ecology* (BE). At the beginning of this century, chief information officers of several large public utilities were asked what their IT needs were. Their answers are summarized in Box 12.1; those needs have not change markedly over the succeeding years.

Information System Technology

In the broadest sense, information system technology in public utilities refers to the application of computers and software to provide essential information to managers and anyone else needing the information. Utility communications architecture (UCA) is that part of the system that allows full exchange of data within and outside of the utility; the UCA links sections and units, administration, customers, vendors, and other utilities electronically, using *Internet*, *extranet*, and *intranet* architecture. Utility business architecture, on the other hand, refers to the methods and tools used to model operations in terms of the utility's organization, processes, and resources. And finally, industrial (or business) ecology (BE) refers to

---

BOX 12.1   UTILITY CHIEF INFORMATION OFFICERS
DISCUSS PLANS AND PROBLEMS

Early in the new century, the editors of *Utility Business* asked the chief information officers of three U.S. utilities about their insights on the information needs of their firms, their IT spending plans, and internal IT issues they then faced. Interviewed were Jim Kenesok of Avista Corp., Spokane, Washington; Willard Evans of People's Energy in Chicago, Illinois; and Bryan Kearney of the Idaho Power Co., Boise, Idaho. Kenesok described Avista's objectives for information technology: "Improve earnings, customer management, community relations and employee focus through integrated business, financial, and operations applications and data; accommodate existing legacy systems while introducing strategic applications."

Willard Evans, CIO of People's Energy, described his firm's IT experiences: "Recently, we've reorganized human resources, IT, and other support services to form a shared services organization. . . . Our challenge is to shift the paradigm of our customers from thinking of IT as a cost center, or in some cases a free service, to leveraging IT as a strategic business enabler." When asked what the *digital utility concept* meant to him, Evans replied:

> The digital utility extends beyond the e-biz hype. The digital utility employs technology to all aspects of its business processes. For example, it involves the digitalization of facilities, commodity loads and acquisitions, automated metering, and service notifications and dispatching, automatic e-billing and e-payment, smart appliance and smart house integration and customer service self-provisioning. The digital utility provides a seamless automated integration of products and services to customer.

Idaho Power provides electric power in Idaho, Oregon, and Nevada. The firm generates most of its own power in 17 hydroelectric and three coal-fired plants. Bryan Kearney, the firm's CIO, described his information technology objectives: "[To] leverage technology to improve customer service, operational efficiencies, reliability and safety, physical and cyber security." He identified several of his chief challenges as: "Managing the convergence of new and sometimes competing technologies, managing the increasing physical hardware inventory effectively, [and] staying current on all software fixes and patches."

Source: Anonymous. *Utility Business*. June 2002, pp. 55–59.

---

the integration of operational, environmental, and economic systems; the BE process involves a drive toward alternative production and consumption of utility products and services to minimize waste and control the use of natural resources. These concepts are discussed in greater detail in the following pages.

Use of information systems by public service organizations management, including public utilities, has involved the five chief components of all information systems technology. These include: (1) input systems, (2) information processors, (3) data storage, (4) management controls, and (5) information output systems. *Inputs* are the raw data collected for the system. For utilities, these data may include information about demographics, financial data, tax rates, and the rate and period of product use for various classes of customers. Other data of concern include stream flows, snow pack quantity, power production capacities, interest rates, wages, benefits, and a host of other production, operations, and management data.

Processing refers to the ability of the system and its operators to manipulate, organize, sort, and perform statistical processes on the data. Processing has two key objectives. The first is to convert raw data into information that can be used by managers. The second is to organize data and information into meaningful collections of relevant tools for decision-making. Processed data is not always needed when processing is completed. The data must be held for the time that it is needed. This action takes place in the data storage function of the information system. Proper data storage and database maintenance are important to all of the five functions. Data must be retrievable and up-to-date to be of value. Closely associated with the storage function is the control of information system data. Control systems exist to ensure that the information delivered meets time, quality, completeness, and relevance requirements of system users.

Output in information systems refers to the many different types of reports and other information produced by the information system. A problem in the past was that the information supplied by the system was often what the information system managers felt that users should have or only what the earliest software could provide, not what the users needed or asked for. Output was often unsuited for the task of improving decision-making by utility managers and system operators. Today, however, this problem has been largely resolved. Now, information management planning begins with identifying user needs. Once needs are established, teams work together to integrate the reports that provide the needed information in a timely and efficient manner with the specific needs of managers and other organization users. The integration process is illustrated in Box 12.2.

Web-Based Utility Communications Architecture

The many components of information technology, including the Internet, are at the heart of the new way of carrying out the activities of public and private organizations referred to as e-government. In the private sector, it is electronic commerce, or simply e-commerce. Both e-government and e-commerce employ telecommunications as a key part of the organization's

---

BOX 12.2   INTEGRATING COMMUNICATIONS SYSTEMS ARCHITECTURE

An integrated utility information management model includes a network of systems and subsystems, many of which have different hardware. Utilities information systems and subsystems must be able to supply information communication with each other in order to support intersystem applications. Integrated systems under a common database structure allow units to share data.

To achieve integration, a utility must adopt the following interrelated system development principles:

- Multiple function integration—as many functions as reasonable should be built into the same system.
- Modular design—design hardware as discrete modules.
- Distributed intelligence—locate information storage, processing, retrieval, and decision-making as close to the operation as possible.
- Expandability—incorporates extra capacity into the system, its components, and interconnections.
- Open architecture—standardize component interfaces, software specifications, and protocols.

Source: Heller, Von Sacken, and Gerstberger (2001: 282).

---

value creation and value delivery processes. The public utility sector of the economy—which includes both publicly and investor-owned electricity, gas, water and wastewater utilities—involves both e-government and e-commerce.

E-government is the "use of information technology, in particular the Internet, to deliver public services in a much more convenient, customer-oriented, cost-effective, and altogether different and better way," or simply the adoption of any information and communication technology by government (Hughes 2003: 182). The information technologies included in this definition include video conferencing, touch-tone phone entry, CD-ROMs, the Internet and private intranets. New technologies such as interactive television and mobile telephone and personal digital notebook access to the Internet may also be included. One observer has reported that information technology and e-government are now critical components in all other sectors of government. Riggins and Rhee (1998: 89) defined e-commerce as "the sharing of business information, maintaining business relationships, and conducting business transactions by means of telecommunications networks." For public utilities, e-commerce represents more than just buying and selling their services electronically. It includes using network communications technology to conduct a variety of business activities up and down the entire system, both in and out of the organization. A more comprehensive definition provided by Business Dictionary. com (2015a) defined e-commerce as business activities:

> Conducted through the use of computers, telephones, fax machines, barcode readers, credit cards, automated teller machines (ATMs) or other electronic appliances (whether or not using the Internet) without the exchange of paper-based documents. It includes activities such as procurement order entry, transaction processing, payment, authentication and non-repudiation, inventory control, order fulfillment, and customer support. When a buyer pays with a bank card swiped through a magnetic-stripe-reader, he or she is participating in e-commerce.

E-commerce applications include customer-to-utility and utility-to-customer, utility to and from external suppliers, utility-to-oversight agencies, communications within the organization, and similar uses. These applications take place via four or more telecommunications architectures. The most common are the Internet, intranets and extranets. The Internet is the global communications medium generally available to everyone. One of the primary uses of the Internet by utilities is for communicating with customers. Intranets are internal private information networks. They are used by utilities as cooperative networks that use Internet technology to link with suppliers, regulators, and other organizations in their supply chain. A fourth network is has been referred to as a *supranet*. A supranet is a semi-open, organization-to-organization consortium-sponsored network of organizations in a supply chain or with a common interest. Examples of firms in a natural gas supply chain include wellhead producers of natural gas, pipeline companies, storage firms, distribution organizations, and possibly one or more large gas user, such as an industrial firm. Similar connections of organizations exist in the electric power industry. Water, wastewater, solid waste, and transit utility supply chains are similar. In addition to the primary organizations in the supranet, a number of service and equipment vendors might also belong to the consortium network.

The modern, integrated information systems now in use by public utilities incorporate knowledge management systems with supply chain management systems, customer information and relationship management systems.

Utility Business Architecture

Among the many types of system applications that became available with the explosion in the availability and use of the personal computer and the four basic computerized information systems were computerized management information systems. These were followed by transaction processing systems, decision support systems, and expert systems. Utilities now use independent *business applications programs* and *applications servers* (an applications server is a computer that only runs specific application programs) to perform specific functions, such as billing, calculating payroll, and so on. While generally better and more efficient than earlier hand-calculated systems, they were not without their shortcomings. The following statement points out the perils of sticking with systems that have been developed independently:

> Information systems designed and implemented in isolation only serve the needs of other utility divisions by coincidence. The ability to share data must be designed into systems . . . . Otherwise, a utility will not be able to use existing data to the extent necessary to be truly competitive or will be forced to duplicate the data, often by manual reentry, in numerous internal systems. The result is increased costs, data discrepancies, unwieldy database management, and confusion. (Heller, Von Sacken, and Gerstberger 2001: 280–281)

Although each component in the system was designed to perform specific functions, a great deal of overlap was seen in the information needs of managers. Therefore, it became apparent that the systems needed to be coordinated and meshed somehow. Coordinating systems resulted in avoiding duplication while also making needed information available when, where, and to whom it is needed. Modern information technology management ties all these individual systems together. Information systems are built around telecommunication systems that make use of the Internet, extranets, and intranet technology. The process of tying together all systems in the organization and to the Internet is called *enterprise application integration*.

UTILITY BUSINESS SYSTEMS

For years, the heart of all information technology in utilities was the *management information system* (MIS); this application is discussed here as an application of business ecology. The MIS was the first attempt at integrating production and consumption data to improve the management of the complete value-generating and delivery system. MIS-based systems are still used by many small utilities who have not yet upgraded to modern, integrated systems. They are, therefore, briefly discussed here. The following is a definition of the MIS:

> A management information system (MIS) is a computer-based system that makes information available to users with similar needs. The users typically

comprise a formal organizational entity—the firm or a subsidiary subunit. The information describes the firm or one of its major systems in terms of what has happened in the past, what is happening now, and what is likely to happen in the future. The information is made available in the form of periodic reports, special reports, and outputs of mathematical simulations. The information output is used by both managers and supervisors as they make decisions to solve the firm's problems. (McLeod and Schell 2006: 239–240)

Older MIS-based systems are referred to as *legacy systems* because of the way they developed piece by piece around the MIS over the years and were passed down to later management with little or no modification. Newer IT applications added to the firm usually had to mesh with the basic management system. Other applications supported and added to the management system. Moreover, these newer applications had to reflect the basic values and beliefs of utility management. Some of the chief components that evolved to augment the basic MIS include transaction processing systems, decision support systems, and expert systems. The fundamental purpose of the MIS is to collect, organize, and distribute the data that managers and other personnel need to perform their particular tasks in the organization. Managers use MIS-produced data to follow the status of their programs, projects, personnel, revenues, expenses, and similar activities.

Transaction processing systems (TPS) were among the first applications of computers in utility operations. The TPS systems that emerged during the 1960s were introduced to reduce clerical costs and time by standardizing and computerizing day-to-day transactions. Examples included meter reading interpretations and utility billing and payment. Today, TPS systems still perform the routine, recurring transactions of many small utilities, although modern comprehensive systems have absorbed many of their functions.

Decision support systems (DSS) are another product of computerized information systems. DSS systems were developed to aid public service managers solve both unstructured and semi structured problems that most early TPS and MIS systems were unable to handle. DSS systems enable the utility to collect and recover, process, and make available the information a manager needs to make a specific decision. Capital project planning and management are typical applications of DSS systems.

The term *artificial intelligence* (AI) is used to describe a variety of computer applications designed to mimic human behavior. This includes learning from experience, understanding written and spoken language, and making inferences from evidence. *Expert systems* are a version of AI. These systems use the collected knowledge of human experts to enable the computer to infer that situations with similar characteristics are likely to have similar summaries. Example applications relevant to utility operations include zoning law problems, construction regulations, rate-making procedures, and similar regulatory issues.

IT Upgrades

Many utilities are upgrading their IT systems. For example, the combined electricity–water–rail utility of Tacoma, Washington, began major improvements to its IT systems with contracts for a total enterprise system with SAP, the German software company, and TUI Consulting, a global consulting firm. The Tacoma Utility implemented a *Business System Improvement Project* to improve customer service, enhance work efficiency, and give managers more and better tools for evaluation and analysis. The utility redesigned work flows and implemented new customer billing, financial management, and work management systems. When completed, the utility's four major computer systems—customer information, financial management, work management, and human resources—were completely integrated. They shared a single database, thus improving service to customers and employees. The customer information system is an example of IT adopted by utilities of all types and sizes.

Maine Public Service Co. (MPS) is a small rural power provider with business in Northern Maine and New Brunswick, Canada. Until 1947, the firm was a wholly owned subsidiary of Consolidated Electric & Gas Company. In 1999, the regulated, fully integrated utility chose to reorganize as a holding company, and filed for a name change to Maine & Maritimes Corporation. Operating company subsidiaries including Energy Atlantic and Maine & New Brunswick Electric Power Company remained regulated utilities. Increased investment in information technology was an important part of the company's reorganization plan. Box 12.3 is a report on the company's growth since its acquisition.

The shift from legacy systems to fully integrated, web-based IT systems and data warehouses in these utilities is not without its problems, however. For example, not everyone agrees on the advisability of placing all of the organization's data into one integrated repository with open access for all users. Some of the dangers associated with this development are highlighted in Box 12.4. The discussion also includes a number of safeguards which are recommended for use by database system designers.

The merchant power generating firm *Cinergy* represents another example of how utility firms are expanding their investment in IT. According to Bennett Gaines, Cinergy chief technology officer, the firm is making major investments in IT applications, including its customer management, billing, and financial systems. The firm is also consolidating its various databases into one combined set called a *data warehouse*, with

---

BOX 12.3   INVESTMENT INFORMATION TECHNOLOGY IN A SMALL INVESTOR-OWNED UTILITY

With its change in management and governance, MPS made an increased commitment to information technologies, which included a major policy change. The new policy is based on the belief that computer literacy must be a mandate for all employees, regardless of the position they hold in the company. Therefore, every employee is provided access to computer education. The goal of the program is to increase the computer application-skills of all employees.

A first step in the new emphasis on information technologies was to employ a nationally recognized consulting firm to conduct a comprehensive audit of the computer use and information needs of the firm. That benchmarking study resulted in a plan to upgrade all information technologies in the firm, including an evaluation of the use of mobile computing for line crews. Additional steps included an increased emphasis on the use of the geographic information system (GIS), and evaluation of a new finance system to facilitate a planned move to activity-based accounting.

The utility's continued growth has been eased by management's early commitment to remaining current in information technology. Bangor Hydro Electric Co. was acquired by Halifax-based Emera in 2002. Emera then acquired Maine Public Service Co. in 2010. The two companies became Emera Electric in 2014.

Source: Maine Public Service Company (2002).

---

common terminologies and an indexing system with the same meaning for everyone. It is focusing on linking financial and operational data so that they can be used in different operational environments. The ultimate goal for the integrated system is for everyone in the corporation to have access to the data they need to do their job.

The Utility CIS and CRM

The Customer Information System (CIS) has become an important contributor to improvements in public utility effectiveness and profitability. Its two chief benefits are that it can help the utility build revenues, while at the same time promote greater customer loyalty (Burkhart 2004).

Much of the MIS is now part of the modern information system. Customer information systems are a major component in the new integrated information technology systems that are replacing old legacy systems in utilities. The CIS is a spoke in the wheel of technology-enabled relationship management; it is a part of the broader concept of customer relationship management, or CRM (Smart Insights). Other terms used to describe the same activity include technology-enabled customer

---

**BOX 12.4   DATA WAREHOUSE PROBLEMS AND
SAFEGUARDS**

Data warehousing is a hot topic. However, it has the potential to "burn a company," according to *Public Utilities Fortnightly* editor Jennifer Alvey. A recent survey found that 41 percent of all data warehousing programs fail.

Data warehousing is the consolidation of all company data and information into a single database, regardless of the application that generated the data. Information technology managers know that not all parts of the integrated system will fit well together; as a result, they often turn to outside consultants for assistance in developing the system.

The following six safeguards are recommended for any utility planning to develop a data warehouse project:

- Make absolutely sure you are extracting, transforming, and loading the data right the first time; this is critical if the warehouse is to work.
- Have a clear idea of the utility problems to be solved with use of a data warehouse.
- Do not add more and more features to the project as development moves along.
- Plan any additions before beginning.
- Take special care to avoid "scope creep"—expanding the scope almost guarantees missing implementation deadlines.
- Gain end-user participation and acceptance during all phases of the project, but particularly during the planning and development periods.
- Plan to spend more money to maintain the warehouse once it is up and operating.

Source: Alvey (2003: 25).

---

relationship management (TCRM) and electronic customer relationship management (ECRM).

Every utility has a distinct group of customers; CRM uses the Internet to gather detailed information about those customers, including preferences, needs, and buying patterns. These data are then used to set prices, shift demand to off-peak periods, negotiate terms, tailor promotions, add features and services, and other customer-related actions.

Developing a comprehensive customer database that includes need-satisfaction information about each class of customers is the initial step in what is called customer portfolio management. The principal process of a customer relationship program is merging the once-isolated parts of customer relationship information into a single comprehensive database. No information can be considered to be "owned" by any unit or person in the utility. Rather, all vital information must be available through the firm's intranet to everyone who needs it. Moreover, it is also important that the system not remain static; it must change to reflect changes in the operating environment of the utility. An example of the changes taking place in customer relationship management is the evolution of cloud data storage and advanced data analysis techniques associated with what is called "big data analysis" (Burr 2013).

As an example of the dynamic nature of the CIS, the IT consulting firm *Wipro Technologies* was called on to redesign a CIS system they had developed earlier for a utility in the Pacific Northwest. The primary users of the customer information system in the utility are customer call centers, business centers, engineering and operations departments, field crews, and management at all levels of the utility. For reasons beyond control of the utility, the old system was found to be failing to meet the needs of these users. The system needed to be brought up to date.

The needed changes to the CIS were brought on by passage of state legislation introducing choice and competition in the market area of the power utility. That legislation required (1) unbundling of services the company provided to its customers, (2) increased customer choice, and (3) introduction of competition in the non-residential energy services market. These changes then resulted in widespread revisions to the regulatory environment of the utility. Changes were needed in each of the following seven functions of the integrated CIS:

1. Electricity service supplier management.
2. Retail customer management.
3. Franchise license taxes.
4. Product offerings management.
5. Retail customer settlement payments and collections.
6. Retail customer billing, and
7. Electricity service supplier billing.

IT IN PUBLICLY OWNED UTILITIES

Publicly owned utilities are also making major investments in information technology infrastructure. Recent legislation gave wholesale telecommunications authority to public utility districts. This has resulted in public utilities making large investments into fiber-optic communications systems. For example, the Chelan County Public Utility District is developing an open-access, public fiber network for delivery of broadband communications services to its private and public customers. Mason County PUD No. 3 has developed a fiber-optic telecommunications system between its

10 distribution substations and has installed a Supervisory Control and Data Acquisition (SCADA) system for control of operations. The next step in their program is to connect business and industrial customers to the network.

The network-expansion experience of Chelan County PUD, a combined electricity, water, and wastewater integrated utility, illustrates how utilities are taking advantage of this new business opportunity. The PUD spent more than $12.5 million in 2001 and 2002 to install a more than 60-mile system of fiber-optic cable and related equipment to its dams, substations, and headquarters. The objective of the network was to improve the control and communications systems of the utility. Over the past several years, the utility has expanded the network into outlying communities in order to link all school districts, hospitals, and community facilities in the country. Businesses and private citizens will also be given access to the network.

The Tacoma, Washington, municipal utility has developed an even more ambitious goal for its fiber-optic network. In its primary mission, the network is considered to be the central tool for automated controls throughout the utility electrical distribution system. The system has enabled the utility to reduce the length, frequency, and scope of power outages. Tacoma Power has also tested a project that combines available meters, cable modems, computers and software with fiber-optic telecommunications. The goal of this project is to enable more accurate and timely reading of specialized industrial meters for eventual real-time metering of power use in peak-load conditions.

What may possibly be the most far reaching application of IT in the Tacoma utility has been the development of an integrated fiber-optic cable network that serves customers in the city and two neighboring communities. The system, named *Click!* includes cable television, business telecommunications, and Internet access. Special metering connected to the Click! network will soon give customers the ability to read their energy-use patterns, thus controlling heating, cooling, and air conditioning use. Moreover, Tacoma Power will be able to conduct such normal utility operations as connecting and disconnecting service, and detecting meter tampering, electronically.

An example of how IT systems have evolved was the development and installation of an integrated IT system designed for a multi-product, vertically integrated metropolitan utility. The system was constructed to replace an old system of diverse, independent applications and batch information system that was no longer able to meet operational needs. The old *legacy system* was not only inflexible, it was also difficult to maintain and use. The legacy system employed sequential batch processing using tapes. Daily updating of the Information System Master File was carried out from different locations including order entry, cash, meter reading, bill calculation, revenue, rate system, audit system, and other subsystems. The legacy system could not produce on-demand reports needed by management.

The event that triggered replacement of the antiquated legacy system was construction of a new nuclear generating plant. The utility had to raise rates to pay for the new nuclear plant. This, together with increases in demand, made the new system necessary. Management wanted to offset higher rates by providing better customer service. The old IBM mainframe-based system and hodge-podge of additional systems added over time was replaced with a *Lean Management Information System* (LMIS) that could meet current and expected future growth.

The new LMIS uses a mid-range central server with magnetic disk carousel storage, an Oracle database system, and a user-friendly interface. Online processing has replaced batch processing. Users have access to information on user-friendly screens and can submit reports and other results via the Internet. The LMIS also meets current IT requirements, including: (1) a new method of storing information; (2) a new system for collecting customer information; (3) a new system for handling service orders; (4) an effective process to create statistical reports on customer service orders; and (5) user-friendly entry panels. The LMIS has three chief components: (1) Customer Application Maintenance System (CAMS), (2) Service Order Entry System (SOES), and (3) Reporting System (RS). The Customer Information System (CIS) is also part of the LMIS. CID data are stored on the magnetic disk carousel, which allows random access to the data by any utility user. The database includes such information as customer name, account number, work request history, payment history, and meter reading history.

The CAMS System

The CAMS system is used primarily by marketing and energy service representatives to gather customer information. CAMS is used to gather, analyze, monitor, and store information based on new customer accounts, account delinquency, account changes and closures.

The SOES System

The SOES system is used by customer account analysts to enter and schedule work requests and collect and retrieve information about current accounts, work request history, and new data entries. The concept originated in electronic securities trading as the Small Order Execution System computer network that automatically executed trades in market securities.

SOES allows individual investors to execute trades in fast moving markets and gave them the same access to orders and execution as larger traders. It was implemented after the 1987 stock market crash. The acronym is also found in electric grid security as the Security of Energy System.

The RS System

The RS produces standardized reports such as the number of service orders issued daily, and all service work not completed within 30 days. Managers are also able to produce customized reports, selecting the RS tables they want and add other information. State and federal regulatory and health agencies require a very large number of reports from all types of utilities; RS systems are particularly helpful to small utilities in their struggle to meet the increasing number and complexity of these required reports.

The CIS and CRM Systems

Customer information systems collect, store and manage information about utility customers' use of the product or service, billing, payment history and other relevant data regarding the customer and sales transaction. Customer relationship management systems collect, store and analyze aspects of interactions a utility has with its customers; the data may be sales or service-related. CRM systems also manage business to business (B2B) relationships, including Information on contacts, clients, contract wins and sales leads and more. Relationship data are analyzed for developing and administering marketing programs and customer relations.

SUMMARY

Since it began to be widely applied in the 1960s and 1970s, information technology has come to be a powerful, indispensable function in the management of large and small, publicly or investor-owned, for-profit and not-for-profit, public utilities. Computers and telecommunications technologies are now a critical component in the strategies of all electrical, natural gas, and water and wastewater systems. The introduction of IT in utility management has produced performance gains that may be traced to the introduction of four applications models: information technology, utility communications architecture (UCA), utility business architecture (UBA), and what has been described as industrial ecology.

Information technology is the descriptive term used to describe the management and application of information in organizations. IT incorporates the utility computing and communications systems and includes both hardware and software. Information management refers to the control mechanisms pertaining to business-related information and communications standards, policies, and procedures within the firm. Information technology management is used to cover the planning and management of all IT resources, including people, the infrastructure, standards, and operations of the IT system in the utility.

All information technology is computer based. Computers are used to collect, process, generate, manage, store, and retrieve data. The product of the IT system is information that can be used by managers and employees. Information is what managers and workers need to become more creative and effective than they would be without the technology. The purpose of information technology is to help people solve management problems, marketing problems, production problems, quality problems, and other problems in organizations.

The five chief components of all information systems are: (1) inputs; (2) processing; (3) storage; (4) control; and (5) output. *Inputs* are the raw data collected for the system. Processing refers to the ability of the system and its operators to manipulate, organize, sort, and perform statistical processes on the data. The data is held in the data storage part of the information system. Control systems exist to ensure that the information delivered meets time, quality, completeness, and relevance requirements of system users. Output refers to the many different types of reports and other information produced by the information system.

Four basic types of computerized systems comprise the information found in many small public utilities: management information systems, transaction processing systems, decision support systems, and expert systems (artificial intelligence). The core of these systems was the management information system (MIS). Other applications must support and add to the management system.

The many components of information technology, including the Internet, are at the heart of the new way of carrying out the activities of public and private organizations. In the public sector, this new way of operating is referred to as e-government. In the private sector, it is called electronic commerce or simply e-commerce. Both e-government and e-commerce employ telecommunications as a key part of the organization's value creation and value delivery processes. The public utility sector of the economy—which includes both publicly and investor-owned electricity, gas, water and wastewater utilities—involves both e-government and e-commerce. The modern, integrated information systems that are now being implemented in public utilities incorporate knowledge management systems with supply chain management systems, customer information and relationship management systems.

The Customer Information System (CIS) and Customer Relationship Management (CRM) have become important contributors to improvements in public utility effectiveness and profitability. The two chief benefits of this approach are (1) it can help the utility build revenues, and (2) at the same time promote greater customer loyalty.

Publicly owned utilities are also making major investments in the installation of information technology infrastructure. Recent legislation gave wholesale telecommunications authority to public utility districts. These utilities are providing fiber-optic telecommunications service and Internet access to businesses and community agencies in their service areas.

ADDITIONAL READING

Hill, Trevor and Graham Symonds (2013), *The Smart Grid For Water: How Data Will Save Our Water and Your Utility*. Charleston, SC: Advantage.

Lutchman, Roopchan (2003), *Computerized Work Systems for Utility and Plant Operations*. Lancaster, PA: DESTech Publications.

Marchewka, Jack T. (2014), *Information Technology Project Management: Providing Measurable Organizational Value* (5th edn). New York: Wiley.

Otenyo, Eric E. and Nancy S. Lind (2011), *E-Government: The Use of Information and Communication Technologies in Administration*. New York: Teneo Press.

Turban, Efraim, Linda Volonino and Gregory R. Wood (2015), *Information Technology Management: Digital Strategies for Insight, Action, and Sustainable Performance* (10th edn). New York: Wiley.

PART IV

Public utility management and operations challenges

13. Public utility governance

As happened during the fight in the mid-1930s between advocates of private power versus the supporters of government ownership of power, the question of public utility governance again became a major issue in public utility management in the first decade of the twenty-first century. In the 1930s the fight centered on President Franklin Roosevelt's plan for creating the Tennessee Valley Authority (TVA) and its power generation and land reclamation proposals. A new wave of stockholder activism emerged, driven by large institutional shareholders who charged that large corporations had not gone far enough in their efforts to ensure good governance. The utility industry, as much or more than other industries, had to endure the same scandals that surfaced in the late 1990s, including improprieties in accounting, market manipulation, and executive corruption. In addition, demands for improvements in corporate governance have also been made by state public utility commissions. Some state public utility commissions proposed regulatory changes that directly hit at governance policies and actions (Genieser 2004; Finon, Johnsen, and Midttun 2004).

Governance has been defined as "the processes and institutions, both formal and informal, that guide and restrain the collective activities of a group" (Keohane and Nye 2002: 12). Water governance has been defined by a United Nations-affiliated organization as, "Water governance refers to the political, social, economic and administrative systems in place that influence water's use and management. Essentially, who gets what water, when and how, and who has the right to water and related services, and their benefits" (WCF 2016). These definitions refer to the internal and external exercise of direction, control, management, and policy shaping of all sectors of the public and investor-owned utility industry. However, governance is not, and never has been, a static principle. Demands for change and more or less control over utility governance have been aired over three major waves of activism. These demands first appeared during the Progressive Era and reached their peak during the early 1900s with the trust-busting activity of President Teddy Roosevelt's Administration. At that time the issue was at the top of proposed reforms of the American economic system. The drive for better governance saw passage in 1887 of the Act that established the Interstate Commerce Commission and near unanimous passage of the Sherman Antitrust Act of 1890 (Bruchey 1990). The second coincided with the Great Depression of the 1930s. The Stock Market Crash of 1929 brought about the failure of many firms—including a number of large public utility holding companies. Demands for better governance resulted in passage of the Securities Exchange Act in 1934 and the Public Utilities Holding Company Act in 1935.

The third wave in governance reform began during the 1980s with restructuring of the industry. It reached its apex with the California deregulation failures in 2000 and 2001 and the collapse of Enron, once the largest energy trading company in the world. Until the first few years of the twentieth century, the trend in public utility governance was leading away from government ownership and control toward deregulation and privatization of government-owned systems. Since then, restructuring and its controversial offspring—deregulation—are definitely on hold. They may remain so for the foreseeable future.

Governance of public utilities in the United States may be the most complex of all industries. To begin with, ownership in the electricity and natural gas sectors is shared by two very different enterprise forms. In rural areas, utilities are more often than not owned by consumer cooperatives, of which the public utility district (PUD) is the most popular model. PUD utilities serve about 25 percent of the U.S. population. Cooperatives own and maintain 43 percent of the distribution lines in the United States. Because they serve rural areas predominantly, cooperatives cover something like three-fourths of the land area, serving customers in eight out of every ten counties. Their customer density is naturally small, with less than seven consumers per mile of line, compared with 34 customers per mile of line for investor-owned utilities. In total, less than 12 percent of the country's electricity customers receive their power from cooperatives.

In urban areas, governance in the public utility industry is most often exercised through state and local regulatory authorities controlling the operations of private or investor-owned utilities (IOUs). IOUs serve about 75 percent of the population. Ownership of water and wastewater utilities has, until recently, generally followed a municipal or mutual society-owned model. Today, however, many of these systems have been sold or leased to private operators, while in others a number of traditional utility services are now contracted out to the private sector—the practice of *outsourcing*.

Governance also defines the process of managing the operations of organizations and their relationships with their internal and external stakeholders. In most industries strategy is decided by directors and senior officers, while the responsibility for carrying out operations is delegated to managers and supervisors. These operators are generally free to run the organization without fear of excessive external interference from government. The picture is different in the utility industry, however. This industry is made up of a variety of public and private participants. Investors, voters, individual citizens, and government enterprises also play a role in privately owned utility governance. In addition to the private and public delivery organizations, a multi-organizational variety of federal, state, and local government agencies regulate and oversee operations. These agencies have the power to monitor and approve or deny the investment decisions of investor-owned utilities to set rates; they must also approve what returns on investments are allowed and can force utilities to install environmental protection equipment.

In the electricity and natural gas industries, the majority of organizations are private enterprises that are collectively known as investor-owned utilities (IOUs). Most private utilities are organized as corporations. In corporations, owners of common stock have the right to elect their representatives to the corporation's board of directors. Board members are responsible for monitoring, directing, and appointing the firm's top managers. In this way, shareholders are able to set the direction for the corporation, evaluate the performance of managers, and control the distribution of the corporation's profits. The board has the right—and the obligation—to remove poorly performing managers (Lashgari 2004). An increasing number of water services are also becoming commercial enterprises, although ownership of the water itself is usually retained in the hands of a public body, with only distribution and billing given over to the IOUs. Nearly all waste collection operations are independent commercial operations, while ownership of landfills generally are almost all retained in public ownership. Except for a few heavy rail commuter systems in the northeast and local taxi services, in the United States public transport systems are almost exclusively government operations.

CONSOLIDATION SHAPING GOVERNANCE

Utilities have traditionally been among the nation's most capital-intensive industries. Until recently, very large facilities were constructed so as to benefit from perceived economies of scale and provide the mandated excess capacity to cover future growth and potential spikes in demand. Only public agencies and large public service corporations are able to acquire the large amounts of capital needed for the large projects. In the early history of the industry, mergers and acquisitions brought together the many small, competing utilities that once characterized the industry into very large, connected "natural monopolies." This early integration of the private utility industry was nearly completed by 1910 (Glaeser 1957).

Eventually, these consolidated monopolies grew into very large, often national, monopolies. The next step in industry consolidation involved widespread expansion of the utility holding company concept.

Holding companies are corporations that are organized to own the stock of other companies or corporations. Holding companies are not operating companies, although a holding company can own the common stock and other securities of one or more operating companies. In this way, holding companies are able to control the operating company's policies and operations. Box 13.1 describes a typical modern utility holding company and its subsidiaries.

To gain control, the holding company need only control a simple majority of the voting stock of the subsidiary. Control can also be gained by minority owners through the use of the proxy system. Therefore, the "capital" of a holding company is not any actual physical property, patents, or other similar assets, but is instead the stocks and bonds of other companies or corporations.

BOX 13.1   A TYPICAL UTILITY HOLDING COMPANY

South Jersey Industries, Inc. (SJI), of Folsom, New Jersey, is an energy services holding company with four wholly owned energy subsidiaries and one joint venture. South Jersey Gas Company, a regulated natural gas operating company, is the core operation in SJI's business. This subsidiary delivers natural gas to nearly 300,000 residential, commercial, and industrial customers in the seven southern counties of New Jersey. Through its Gas Supply and Off-System operations, South Jersey Gas also sells natural gas to wholesale customers in the interstate market and manages the subsidiary's pipeline and storage facilities. A separate operation provides repair to household and commercial appliances on a competitive basis.

South Jersey Energy Company (SJE), the second subsidiary, acquires and markets natural gas to retail end users and provides energy management services to commercial and industrial customers. SJE has one subsidiary, SH EnerTrade, which provides energy services to the Atlantic City casino industry and markets an air quality monitoring system. The third subsidiary is South Jersey Resources Group. This business markets wholesale gas storage and transportation in the mid-Atlantic and southern states. The Resources Group also conducts price-risk management activities.

Marina Energy, SJI's fourth subsidiary, develops and operates energy-related projects in southern New Jersey. A recent project of this firm was development of a cooling, heating, and hot water facility for an Atlantic City resort. Finally, SJI is a joint-venture partner with Conectiv Solutions (the electricity provider) in Millennium Account Services, a contract meter reading company that serves both partners throughout southern New Jersey.

Source: South Jersey Industries (2002).

The growth of holding companies was the chief contributor to the giant wave of mergers that hit American industry from 1895 to 1904. Holding companies were involved in 86 percent of all the mergers during that brief period. Individual firms that are absorbed into the holding companies retain their own name and focus of operations. The holding company's chief source of earnings is the dividends paid by the controlled operating company. During the peak of their popularity before the Great Depression, some holding companies were also able to use their captive ownership relationship to charge their subsidiaries excessive fees for services such as engineering, management, and financial support. In 1934, the Securities and Exchange Commission was given the responsibility to monitor and control the abuses that existed in the system. In 1935, holding companies were limited to ownership of just four levels of subsidiaries (Bruchey 1990).

The holding company model has again become an important participant in the utility industry. On August 8, 2005, the Energy Policy Act passed both houses of Congress and was signed into law, replacing Public Utility Holding Company Act of 1935 (PUHCA). The PUHCA made it necessary to gain approval of the U.S. Securities and Exchange Commission (SEC) before any holding company acquisitions could take place. SEC approval was also required for issuing new stock and other financial transactions (Genieser 2004).

GOVERNMENTS' ROLE IN UTILITY GOVERNANCE

Governments' involvement in and oversight of utility governance functions on three levels: federal, state, and local. The federal government owns and operates the nation's largest power generating plants and conducts most investigations of private company operations and alleged fraud. It also regulates the issuance of securities, controls and issues permits to build hydroelectric facilities on navigable streams, and is responsible for the locating and construction of nuclear generators. State governments exercise most direct rate regulatory authority.

Only a few state governments actively participate in one or more sectors of the delivery of utility services. The New York State Power Authority (NYSPA) was created in 1931, primarily to handle power produced from the St. Lawrence River Project developed with Canada. The NYSPA also produces power from the Niagara River. A similar Authority was formed by South Carolina in 1934 to handle power from the Santee-Cooper Project. Both Texas and Oklahoma established public agencies in the 1930s to build and operate hydroelectric plants. The greatest commitment to public power is found in Nebraska, where public ownership of all electric utilities exists. Nebraska created a Consumers Public Power District in 1939, and then set out to acquire existing private facilities. By 1946, all power distribution in the state was under public ownership.

Municipal governments still own many utility systems, mostly in the distribution segment of the industry. Few municipalities produce their own power, purchasing it instead from either public or private producers. They do, however, own and operate much of their water and wastewater systems, although wastewater systems are more likely to be regional in scope today. Municipalities also issue franchises and permits to private companies and non-municipal public utilities for the use of the public rights-of-way. In the 1920s, some 3,000 municipal systems operated in the U.S.; their numbers declined from then on, although a renewed interest in municipal ownership of utilities, and particularly electric power utilities, appeared for a period during the 1930s. In addition to the collapse of the holding company pyramids, several other factors contributed to this renewed interest:

- The development of diesel engines made it possible for municipalities to install relatively inexpensive, small generating plants, several of which could be strategically placed throughout the community.
- Low-priced federal power became available in much of the country. Federal power also includes preference clauses that favor public purchasers. This greatly stimulated the growth of public utility districts throughout much of the Pacific Northwest.
- The 1929 stock crash resulted in the collapse of many of the pyramided utility holding companies. This caused many small stockholders to lose all their savings. As a result, there was a strong reaction against the abuses of holding company executives.

In 2010, only some 2,000 municipalities operated community-owned electricity utilities—close to 1,000 fewer than the number of city-owned systems that existed during the 1920s peak. Their numbers have continued to decline. Most water and wastewater systems remained under municipal ownership, however.

The American Public Power Association regularly carries out a survey of its members to identify the governance system followed in their community. In April 2010 the American Public Power Association (APPA) released results of its eighth Governance Survey. The survey is taken to determine the type of governance systems are followed in publicly owned electric utilities. Questionnaires were mailed to almost 1,900 local publicly owned electric systems in the U.S., and 658 completed survey forms were returned. Not included in the survey are public power systems that sell

Table 13.1   Number of primary government bodies by type

Class of utility	Number	Independent Utility Board		City Council
		Appointed	Elected	
Less than 5,000 customers	408	5%	23%	72%
5,000 to 20,000 customers	161	20%	40%	40%
20,000 to 50,000 customers	55	33%	34%	33%
More than 50,000 customers	34	34%	44%	32%
Total	658			

Source: APPA (2010).

power at wholesale. As shown in Table 13.1, 86 percent of utilities responding serve less than 20,000 customers; the two largest customer size classes account for the remaining 14 percent of respondents.

Ninety-three percent of respondents were municipally owned utilities. The other 7 percent are state-owned utilities or political subdivisions, such as county-wide utilities, public power districts or public utility districts in Washington, Oregon and Nebraska, and irrigation or utility districts in Arizona and California. The majority of respondents (59 percent) were governed by a city council, while the remaining 41 percent are governed by an independent utility board. (The term "city council" includes similar entities such as a county council, town council, borough council or board of selectmen.) Appointed independent utility boards were more than twice as common as elected utility boards. However, all public utility districts and public power districts are governed by elected utility boards. Eighty-five percent of utilities with independent utility boards have either residency or service territory requirements for board members, requiring board members to be a resident of the city or to be a customer of the utility.

EVOLUTION OF UTILITY GOVERNANCE

The complex governance system of federal, state, and local governments exercising some level of control over both public and investor-owned utilities has evolved over six different periods (Dimock 1935). The first was the granting of charters by colonies and later by individual states. This period, which lasted until after the Civil War, was characterized by corruption and misuse of rights granted by those charters. Municipalities had little or no control over the companies receiving the charters. Eventually, widespread dissatisfaction with this system led to demands for home rule and municipal ownership.

The second phase lasted through the decade after the Civil War, and featured passage of state laws that set minimum standards with which charter recipients had to comply. In the third phase, which began around 1875, home rule charters were finally granted to larger municipalities; cities could now develop and operate their own utility systems. During this period, public ownership advocates based their arguments on two chief premises: First, public ownership would provide essential public services to everyone without enriching any particular individual or group at the expense of others. Second, with public service as the driving force in place of profits, service would be made available to everyone, not just to a select few.

Passage of the Act establishing the Interstate Commerce Commission in 1887 ushered in the fourth phase. At the close of the 1800s, there were few investors willing to make the investment needed to finance the great expense of building generating facilities, stringing power lines, building dams, and installing water lines. As a result, gas lights and electric power were available almost exclusively in larger cities, where business and industries could benefit from its use, and a small number of wealthy, private citizens could afford the cost. This period saw more states establishing regulations to control specific public services, beginning with the railroads. When the U.S. Supreme Court upheld the first test case in Illinois, *Munn vs. Illinois*, 1887, government's involvement in the governance of all public utilities took a big step forward. In deciding the case in favor of Illinois, the Court referenced a 1676 study by the Lord Chief Justice of England. The British Justice found that if a privately owned wharf was one that all persons used for loading and unloading, it thus became "affected with the public interest," and just and reasonable rates had to be charged for its use. The U.S. Court found the privately owned grain elevators in the Illinois case to be affected with a similar public interest; the grain elevator was, in effect, a public warehouse (Glaeser 1957).

The fifth step in the evolution of government involvement in utility governance began in the first decades of the twentieth century. By that time many states had established formal public utility commissions and set about establishing standards they hoped would control any potential misdeeds by private firms. The federal government's participation in the ownership and governance of electric power facilities and the private utility sector really took off during the administration of President Theodore Roosevelt. From 1873 to 1888, the U.S. Supreme Court heard only 70 cases relating to the government and public utilities; but from 1888 to 1918, a period roughly corresponding to the Progressive era, the Court heard 725 such cases (Warren 1928). The seeds of the disaster that ultimately led to their collapse sprouted in earnest after the end of the First World War.

The 1920s were a period of relative affluence for the urban populations of the United States. Both private and public power utilities expanded their generating and distribution facilities as quickly as they found the money to do so. Municipal water and sewer utilities were also driven to expand as more of the rural population moved into the nation's cities. Despite their frenzied efforts, utilities were hard pressed to keep up with the growing demand for power and water. Partly to secure the investment funds they needed for expansion and partly to consolidate their financial gains, many of the investor-owned power companies joined together to form giant, many layered holding companies. Many municipal systems, which were often "pathetically antiquated and inefficient," also needed investment. However, some political leaders, tired of the responsibility of meeting the never-ending demands for power, water, and wastewater treatment facilities, sold out to private firms. Thus, the 1920s experienced a net decline in public ownership (Sparks 1964; McNabb 1968).

The sixth stage began with the economic upheaval that began with the stock market crash in 1929. This stage saw the direct government involvement in all sectors of the industry. Under the New Deal programs of President Franklin Roosevelt, the federal government constructed the Tennessee Valley Authority project, went ahead with Hoover Dam on the Colorado River, and built the dams on the Columbia River that became the heart of the Bonneville Power Administration. Included in these and other federal developments were extensive land reclamation projects and irrigation systems that distributed the water stored behind the huge new dams. More importantly to a large segment of the population at the time was establishment of the rural electrification program, which eventually brought electric power to farmers all across the country.

The major New Deal legislation firmly establishing federal control over the utility industry was the Public Utility Holding Company Act of 1935 (Koontz, 1941). Prior to this, federal control had only been marginal at best. It was based on provisions in the Water Power Act of 1920, which was concerned primarily with conservation and control of hydroelectric plant locating and construction. The 1920 Act created the Federal Power Commission (FPC), which remained in effect until it was replaced in 1935.

Publicly owned utilities serve something like 25 percent of the electricity market. These include municipal operations, cooperatives, and a few mutual operations. Most of these operations are small; less than half produce their own power. Instead, they still purchase federally produced power for resale. Recent changes in the federal government's preference clause system have opened up this market to investor-owned utilities as well. This is cause for considerable concern to publicly owned utilities who initiated lawsuits to reverse the decision.

MODELS OF UTILITY GOVERNANCE

Birchall (2002), a critic of utility restructuring and privatization, identified six separate utility governance models prevalent in the early twenty-first century, four of which lie between what he termed "the extremes" of private ownership on one hand, and public ownership on the other. In between these poles are the following four governance variations: (1) a nonprofit trust or company, (2) a public interest company, (3) a consumer mutual society, and (4) a public authority (such as the New York Water Authority).

Nonprofit trusts function in much the same manner as for-profit organizations. They have the same ability to turn to the bond market to raise long-term capital. They can also borrow from banks for short-term funding. Often, prices charged by nonprofit trusts for services are the same or somewhat less than prices charged by investor-owned firms for the same or similar services. Like all businesses, nonprofit trust organizations must retain some surpluses for future expenses. However, because low earnings are necessary to keep their federally granted nonprofit status, a key objective of these organizations is to avoid earning greater than minimally needed profits. Finally, a nonprofit trust can issue membership shares. Therefore, its governance can become widely community based. As more shares are issued in the community, the more this model comes to resemble a mutual society.

Public interest companies are designed to reap the social benefits of public service with the economic benefits of entrepreneurship. Like a non-profit, the public interest company has public benefit goals permanently etched into its charter. However, this type of organization is also able to distribute surplus earnings to investors or entrepreneurs. The public interest company is a model that is sometimes used for governing water and wastewater utilities.

The mutual society form of utility governance is a form of the basic consumer cooperative (co-op). The co-op model has its roots in associations of farmers and ranchers in the western United States for building irrigation projects. Many farm cooperatives still provide an important function in the supply and distribution of agricultural products and for the marketing of farm products. The co-op model adopted by nearly all early rural utility organizations in the United States is similar to a model that was common across Europe before the wave of privatization programs that have been seen in the past 25 years or so. The governance of rural electricity co-ops is shaped by these seven principles of the cooperative movement (Basin Electric Power Cooperative 2004):

1. Voluntary and open membership.
2. Democratic member control.
3. Member economic participation (members contribute equally to the cooperative capital).
4. Autonomy and independence.
5. Education, training, information for managers and employees.
6. Cooperation among cooperatives.
7. Concern for the (sustainable development) of the communities they serve.

Box 13.2 describes the operations of Basin Electric, a consumer-owned regional cooperative that produces power for 124 other co-ops, manufactures natural gas from coal, and is also involved in the competitive retail distribution of electricity.

Mutual societies are similar to consumer cooperatives. Mutual societies are registered as businesses, but only for specific purposes. Mutual societies are owned by their customers. Each customer has an equal voting right, thus making it difficult for any single individual or group to gain control of the operation. Directors are elected by the membership. Earnings surpluses are distributed to members as annual dividends or percentage discounts on future purchases. Dividend amounts received by utility customers are based upon the amount of business done with the society, not on ownership. This governance model is very popular in the United States, where there are nearly 1,000 electricity co-ops and more than 700 telecommunications co-ops. Although almost all of these co-ops operate in rural areas, suburban sprawl and the move of industry to rural sites have seen some of their service areas become more urban than rural.

Public authority utilities are quasi-governmental institutions established specifically to provide one or more public service to customers within a specific—often regional—taxing area. Authorities have the same power to tax property in their service areas as do other levels of government. However, they function independently of all other government jurisdictions in their service area. Authorities also have the power to issue government bonds and to borrow on the value of the property in their service area. This model has become a popular substitute for the privatized utility model initially proposed in the 1980s in Great Britain. Until 1996, most water and wastewater services in the United Kingdom were the responsibility of municipal or other local governments. When the national

---

BOX 13.2   GOVERNANCE IN A LARGE REGIONAL POWER
COOPERATIVE

Some observers believe that the days of the traditional utility co-op are limited
(Burr 2004). Most power co-ops are small, local organizations, unable to enjoy any
economies of scale. All decisions are made by elected board members. This local
control has been one of the strengths of the cooperative system. However, local
control may now be limiting the co-op's ability to achieve its primary mission, that
of providing its customers reliable power at the lowest possible price. Some are
arguing that co-ops are wasting their customer-owners' money by not consolidating and economizing administrative costs. Critics of the system point to Basin
Electric Power Cooperative (BEPC) in Bismarck, North Dakota, as an example of
the new collaborative model emerging in the co-op governance picture.

BEPC is a cooperative of cooperatives. The co-op operates coal-fired electricity
generating plants with a total capacity of 3,373 megawatts, providing power to 124
rural electric cooperatives which in turn serve 1.8 million consumers in nine states
from North Dakota to New Mexico. Much like an investor-owned holding company,
DEPC controls five subsidiaries: Dakota Gasification Co., which produces natural
gas by a coal gasification process to produce chemicals and fertilizers; Dakota
Coal Co., which purchases coal for its power plants and owns a lime processing
plant; Basin Telecommunications, Ind., which provides customized Internet
service through *BTInet*; Basic Cooperative Services, which owns and manages
properties in North Dakota and Wyoming, including reclamation maintenance of a
former mine; and Granite Peak Energy, Inc., a for-profit subsidiary for marketing
electricity in Montana under that state's 1997 customer choice program.

Consolidation is definitely the wave of the future for cooperatives. According to
Michael Burr, 2004, "The world is changing around electric cooperatives, and in
time they will be forced to adapt to these new environments." BEPC is involved in
two examples of changes underway in this sector: DEPC has joined with three
other utilities—two municipals and one investor-owned—to conduct a transmission study to help establish the best location for a new 600 megawatt coal-fired
power plant and a 100 megawatt wind farm. DEPC also joined a group of 550 U.S.
cooperatives in 1998 to form a nationwide alliance, *Touchstone Energy*, which
provides a retail-marketing resource for co-ops expecting to face retail competition.

Source: Burr (2004).

---

government decided to restructure the water utility industry, some water
services were sold to private firms, while others adopted alternative ownership models. In Scotland, for example, municipal water utilities were transferred to three regional public water and sewer authorities. These were later
merged into a single national public water authority that provides water
and wastewater services to all of Scotland.

Public Ownership Evolution

The public ownership of utilities has a long and controversial history. For most of recorded history, only governments had the power and ability to muster, direct, and control the resources needed to build and maintain large-scale public services. Government control of utilities may have begun with the need for collective action for the erection of public monuments, such as the pyramids, and for public works, such as harbors, bridges, roads, grain storage, and irrigation systems. Government participation in these early infrastructure projects was common in Mesopotamia, India, Egypt, Greece and Rome, and early nation states. They were commonplace in colonial and revolutionary North America, as well, where collective action was needed to build the first roads, waterways, and a few municipal water systems. When public expenditure began to supplant private development of public utilities, however, controversy erupted. The battle to halt public participation in the industry turned to the courts (Bruchey 1990; Farris and Sampson 1973).

Public ownership advocates prevailed, when in 1892 the U.S. Supreme Court upheld a municipality's right to establish its own coal gas lighting utility over the protest of a privately owned firm that had been supplying the city's gas needs for many years. The next important case occurred in 1903, when the court upheld the right of a municipality to maintain and operate its own electric utility. The following year saw a similar decision in a water utility case. Shortly afterward, court decisions upheld the rights of cities to maintain and operate public fuel yards. In 1934, the court upheld the right of a city-owned utility to operate without making a profit, even though it was competing with a privately owned utility that paid taxes to the city. The rights of individual states to establish regulatory commissions quickly followed.

Federal ownership of utilities did not become an important issue until the 1930s, when it was determined that the federal government is no more constitutionally limited than were state and local governments. In determining the constitutionality of the federal government's Tennessee Valley Authority (TVA) program, the Court found that the Constitution neither specifically says that federal ownership of a utility is permitted or forbidden. As a result, there was no constitutional basis for halting development of the project. The right of a federal agency to issue municipal revenue bonds to finance electricity plants and distribution systems was also upheld.

The federal government's development of power projects and the sale of power can be traced to the Reclamation Act of 1906. The Act states that whenever developing a power source is needed for irrigation, or when power generation is developed in association with a reclamation project, the Secretary of the Interior may sell any excess power. In such cases, municipalities always have preferred rights to purchase any of this "excess" power. The federal government did not become involved in power production on any large scale until 1928, when passage of the Boulder Canyon Project Act of 1928 authorized construction of Hoover Dam on the Colorado River. Water stored behind the dam was to be used for irrigation, domestic water supplies, and electric power generation. When TVA was organized as a government corporation in 1933, it included strong elements of regional development, improvements in land use, reforestation, and creation of employment. It also included flood control and navigation improvement as goals. The Bonneville Power Administration Act of 1937 was charged with encouraging the widest possible use of all electric energy that could be generated and marketed from dams on the Columbia River. In sum, the chief reasons that supporters put forth for public ownership of public utilities include the following:

- Public ownership permits lower prices to consumers.
- Publicly owned utilities generally have a lower rate base upon which to calculate rates (they do not include federal dams for water storage and power generation in their calculations).
- Public ownership has lower executive salaries.
- Public ownership has lower financing costs.
- Public ownership has lower advertising and public relations expenses.
- Public ownership has no costs for regulation.
- Public ownership has no need to distribute profits.
- Some also say that public ownership often has better labor-management relations.

Advocates of investor-owned utilities counter the lower cost arguments of public power supporters by contending that private ownership contributes to the economic health of a community or region though taxes and wages. As a result, private ownership should not be compared with publicly owned utilities. Moreover, investor-owned utilities are required to pay both income and property taxes and, in some cases, franchise fees as well. Publicly owned utilities pay some fees, but little or no income or property taxes. In addition, low financing cost may be more of a detriment than an advantage because it can lead to uneconomic overexpansion and resource misallocation. Money borrowed for utility expansion limits the amount that the municipality can borrow for other needed programs. This argument is often used to support the privatization and outsourcing movements that now characterize the utility industry.

Private ownership advocates also contend that advertising promotes better utilization of facilities and sends messages encouraging conservation; and, that there is no proof that labor-management relations are better under public ownership. Because investor-owned utilities must answer to state public utility commissions and publicly owned utilities do not, they contend that dissatisfied consumers have more recourse to redress complaints under private ownership than they would under public ownership. Although this argument is not as prevalent today as it has been in the past, private ownership advocates also contended that public ownership often led to political rather than economic decisions. For example, inefficient workers may be retained by publicly owned utilities to avoid a political fight rather than be dismissed. No such inefficiencies would be tolerated in an investor-owned utility.

NEW GOVERNANCE MODELS

Seldom can any government organization function without interacting with and gaining the cooperation of other organizations. In the past, this interaction was sometimes coercive—compliance was dictated by law or by the power of the purse. In the long run, however, this governance model has been shown to be less effective than a collaborative approach. Organizational cooperation can be attained in several different ways: by competition, collusion, overlapping fields of operations, and dependence on the expertise available only in other organizations' specialization (Lusk and Birks 2014).

The evolution in the way that various levels of government are approaching their operational and regulatory oversight of public utilities suggests that a major governance paradigm shift is underway in all levels of government (Agranoff and McGuire 2001). Utility managers are now struggling to find their way through what is becoming this new competitive environment. For example, investor-owned utilities that still operate in the regulated environment often face a more authoritative and bureaucratic operating environment than the publicly owned utilities that are outsourcing their traditional activities to private-sector contractors.

Traditionally, management of public service has operated under a top-down or donor–recipient governance model. Both of the models emphasize superior level control over subordinate's actions. These models emphasized the enforcement of laws, regulations, standards, and guidelines. The top-down model mirrors a national governance model, in which the federal government manages its policies and programs through state and local governments. Federal laws such as the Public Utility Holding

Company Act of 1935 ensured that utility operations at the customer delivery interface would forever be controlled by elected or appointed state public utility commissioners. Equally, local administrators were given the responsibility to ensure that rules, regulations, and standards were followed. Congress passed laws which established policy; the FERC, EPA, and SEC interpreted the policy and set operating policies; state legislators developed specific rules from those standards; and utility commissions approved industry-suggested ways of implementing the rules.

The donor–recipient management model addressed some of the pitfalls inherent in an authoritative top-down management approach. This model presupposes the existence of a mutually dependent relationship among the various intergovernmental and private enterprise actors functioning cooperatively, but still working toward accomplishing the objectives of the superior organization. This model is exemplified in the way lower level agencies have organized their activities to comply with standards established by grant disseminating, higher level agencies. It is an implied "Do it our way or no way" model.

Today, however, two new governance models seem to be replacing the traditional management approaches. These are a *network model* and a *jurisdiction-based* model. Both are more collaborative than are the top-down or donor–recipient models. Utility industry restructuring and deregulation are reflections of this major paradigm shift in utility governance.

The Network Model

The network model is characterized by multiple, independent government and nongovernment organizations pursuing similar goals. The model is applicable in situations where a group of different participants, none of whom has the power to shape the strategies of others in the group, form a loose network to accomplish some specific goal. Under this scenario, the boundaries between public and private utility operations are often blurred. For example, the EPA and local water utilities share a common goal of providing only clean, safe drinking water to the public. The EPA has issued a large number of standards and regulations that require utilities to test for and remove toxic chemicals and other pollutants.

A growing number of cities are negotiating with EPA to modify the workload and cost burden placed upon them by federal water quality rules. EPA requires even very small water utilities to regularly test for and remove a long list of toxic chemicals, minerals, and other pollutants from their drinking water. In some locations, however, it is highly unlikely that certain pollutants on the list will appear in the local water supply. These community utilities have proposed to the EPA that they develop their own water quality standards, with their own priorities for removal. EPA has approved the proposals.

In sum, the network of municipal utilities and EPA has resulted in a model that is based on the assumption that "not everybody will comply and not everybody will defy" (Agranoff and McGuire 2001: 674). It is far more efficient for EPA to focus their efforts on those who do not comply, simply receiving periodic reports from others in the network. Clearly, this governance approach allows far greater flexibility than the top-down and donor–recipient models. The network model is based on the interdependencies of the participating organizations, agencies, or individuals. Interdependence means that all participants will benefit in some way because of their mutual interest in some program or activity. It also implies that a problem cannot be solved unless all participants freely collaborate.

The Jurisdiction-Based Model

The jurisdiction-based governance model is found most often in highly complex situations where significant intergovernmental and interorganizational cooperation is required. This model is seen in situations where one government jurisdiction requests and incorporates contributions of other public- and private-participant organizations. The plan developed by the initial jurisdiction includes the contributions and adjustments proposed by other jurisdictions. An example of a jurisdiction-based governance model can be seen in the utility extension plan of the rural community of Shelton, Washington. The utility department of this small city is the lead agency in a multi-jurisdictional plan to extend water and sewer service to other jurisdictions outside of the city boundaries.

In an effort to coordinate current and be able to meet future needs service, the City of Shelton, Washington entered into an interim intergovernmental agreement in partnership with the local Port of Shelton, the State Department of Corrections and its nearby Correction Center, the State Patrol's Training Academy, Mason County, and Public Utility District No. 1, which provides power to part of the area to be served. Other organizations such as local Native American Tribes, the EPA, and state and federal fish and wildlife agencies are also tangentially involved in the outcome of the project. The agreement addresses extending city sewer and water lines, enlarging the city's sewage treatment plant, sinking new wells, and installing new water treatment facilities. The Port operates a former U.S. Navy auxiliary airport and industrial park outside of the City; both the State Patrol Training Academy and State Corrections Center are also outside of the City. All of the facilities lie in the State-approved Urban

Development Area plan (required of all communities for controlling urban sprawl and planning for future growth).

As lead agency in the more than \$42 million proposal, the City of Shelton is responsible for recordkeeping and recording. The City has set up two special business funds to account for the regional project, with each fund having four "customers": the City, Port, Training Academy, and Corrections Center. Environmental analyses and construction planning are being conducted by outside consulting engineers and designers. Planning sessions took place in the City's new Civic Center Building, a recently remodeled former retail facility. The project was financed through a mix of grants and loans. Each of the four chief partners is to pay its proportionate share of the construction costs and normal usage rates. Construction was expected to begin in 2004 or 2005. After what was described in the local press as a series of costly delays, in early 2004 the group employed the retired county director of utilities on a six-months' contract to monitor internal and external project progress.

This example of a jurisdiction-based activity follows the model described by Agranoff and McGuire, who described jurisdiction-based management as providing significant benefits for all project participants:

> Jurisdiction-based activity emphasizes local managers taking strategic action with multiple actors and agencies from various governments and sectors . . . Bargaining and negotiation are important instruments of jurisdiction-based management. Bargaining by local managers within programs of vertical (state or federal government) or horizontal (metropolitan, regional, or intersectional) origin provide alternatives to unilateral concession, resulting in a 'mutually beneficial solution.' (Agranoff and McGuire 2001: 675)

Although in a classic multi-organizational agreement no one unit is deemed to be superior or subordinate to others and no central participant provides guidance or control. In the Shelton interorganizational agreement, the City has assumed the role of lead agency. Whether this was by default or by plan, the delays and cost escalation experienced clearly show the need for someone to be in charge. The Shelton agreement may thus be said to incorporate parts of both the network and jurisdictional governance models. This may be a portent of the nature of other such cooperative and collaborative utility ventures, regardless of the formal ownership or governance model of any or all of the participants.

EXAMPLES OF EVOLVING UTILITY GOVERNANCE

The mixed nature of public utilities oversight between federal, state, and local agencies has resulted in a variety of different models of governance. Governance models for municipally-owned utilities (MOUs) in two municipalities are Austin, Texas and Colorado Springs, Colorado.

MOU Governance in Texas

There are three basic governance models of municipally-owned public utilities (MOUs) in Texas. These are (1) city council governance by elected officials; (2) a board of trustees with not more than five members, one of which must be the mayor (Section 1502.070 of the Texas Government Code-Appendix J); and (3) a board of trustees where the City Council may prescribe the number of members for appointment to the board. In addition, the Council may delegate to the board virtually all of its powers including the power to establish rates, the power of eminent domain, and to issue obligations.

The City of Austin is an example of the first type. Austin has a City Manager form of governance. The City Council governs the electric utility department, Austin Energy (AE). A citizens' advisory committee, Electric Utility Commission (EUC), has seven members that serve three year staggered terms and are appointed by Council members. The Commission has members from outside the City limits. The EUC responsibilities include reviewing and analyzing all policies and procedures of AE, rate structure, fuel costs and charges, new generation facilities, budget, the general fund transfer, and strategic planning. Austin Energy has approximately 417,000 customers (City of Austin 2012).

Utility Governance in Colorado

Colorado Springs Utilities has evolved from being a small department of the City of Colorado Springs, governed solely by City Council, to being a large multi-service utility governed partially by a Utilities Board and partially by City Council. Colorado Springs Utilities became an enterprise of the Municipal Government in 1993. Under the current structure, City Council has three main roles with respect to Colorado Springs Utilities: (1) sitting as the Board of Directors (comprised of all City Council members) to establish policies and operational direction for the organization and monitor performance; (2) meeting as City Council to approve the budget, act in a legislative capacity to establish ordinances regarding utility services via the City Code and to issue bonds; and (3) meeting in a regulatory role similar to the Public Utilities Commission, to establish tariffs, rates, extension policies, and other items as needed. Through policy governance, all management responsibilities reside with the Chief Executive Officer. The CEO is bound by executive limitations, developed by the board, that establish specific limits on his or her authority.

On July 1, 1925, The City of Colorado Springs Light & Power Department was established. That same year, the City took over operation of the hydro plant, opened a new steam power plant, completed construction of a hydro plant, and acquired and began operating the electric and natural gas distribution systems, thus launching four-service municipal ownership. Colorado Springs Utilities provides electricity, natural gas, water and wastewater service to an approximately 500-square-mile service area and employs more than 1,800 men and women.

In April 2011 Colorado Springs Utilities governance again shifted to a full time mayor who works with a City Council comprised of a majority of new members, each with a variety of roles and responsibilities. Alternative governance structures for Colorado Springs Utilities examined included: governance by a new fully independent board of directors, separate service units owned by the city, transfer to a new metropolitan utility district (state authorized for water and wastewater but not for electric power service), creation of a special district that would fit the Colorado Springs Utilities four-service model (new legislation required), a new organization formed from a merger with other communities (Colorado Springs Utilities 2011; *Colorado Springs Independent* 2014). Included in the original charge for the study was the possible sale of the electric utility, plagued with declining revenues and increasing operating costs. A second look at possibly adopting a new governance model—this time without considering sale of the electric utility—was initiated in late 2014; no changes to the system have yet been announced.

SUMMARY

The question of governance models has again become an issue in public utility management. Restructuring, unbundling, deregulation, privatization, wholesale and retail competition, and outsourcing: these and other trends are having an impact on the already complex governance system that exists in this industry.

Governance of public utilities in the U.S. may be the most complex of all industries. Ownership in the electricity and natural gas sectors is shared by two very different enterprise forms. In rural areas, utilities are more often than not owned by consumer cooperatives. In urban areas, governance takes place through state and local regulatory authorities controlling the operations of private or investor-owned utilities (IOUs). IOUs serve about 75 percent of the population. Ownership of water and wastewater utilities has, until recently, generally followed a municipal or mutual society-owned model.

Most private utilities are organized as corporations. In corporations, owners of common stock have the right to elect their representatives to the corporation's board of directors. Board members are responsible for monitoring, directing, and appointing the firm's top managers.

In the early history of the industry, mergers and acquisitions brought together the many small, competing utilities into very large, connected "natural monopolies." Eventually, these consolidated monopolies grew into very large, often national, monopolies. Progressive Era reforms attempted to control these large enterprises.

Government's involvement in utility governance functions on three levels: federal, state, and local. The federal government owns and operates the nation's largest power generating plants and conducts most investigations of private company operations and alleged fraud. It also regulates the issuance of securities, controls and issues permits to build hydroelectric facilities on navigable streams, and is responsible for the locating and construction of new nuclear power generators. State governments exercise most direct rate regulatory authority. Municipal governments still own many utility systems, mostly in the distribution segment of the industry. Few municipalities produce their own power, purchasing it from either public or private producers. They own and operate much of their water and wastewater systems, although wastewater systems are more likely to be regional in scope today.

Six separate utility governance models exist today, four of which lie between the extremes of private ownership and public ownership. Between these poles are four ownership variations: (1) nonprofit trust or company, (2) public interest company, (3) consumer mutual society, and (4) public authority.

Two new governance models seem to be replacing the traditional *top-down* or *donor–recipient* management approaches. These are a *network model* and a *jurisdiction-based* model. Both are more collaborative than are the top-down or donor–recipient models. The network model is characterized by multiple independent governments and nongovernment organizations pursuing similar goals; it is applicable in situations where a group of different participants, none of whom has the power to shape the strategies of others in the group, form a loose network to accomplish some specific goal. The jurisdiction-based governance model is found most often in highly complex contexts such as those situations where significant intergovernmental and interorganizational cooperation is required. This model is seen in situations where one government jurisdiction requests and incorporates contributions of other public and private participant organizations. Meanwhile, the governance of public utilities continues to evolve.

ADDITIONAL READING

Bakker, Karen (2010), *Privatizing Water: Governance Failure and the World's Urban Water Crisis*. Ithaca, NY: Cornell University Press.
Berry, Kate and Eric Mollard (2009), *Social Participation in Water Governance and Management: Critical and Global Perspectives*. London: Routledge.
Gunawansa, Asanga and Lovleen Bhullar (eds) (2013), *Water Governance: An Evaluation of Alternative Architectures*. Cheltenham, UK and Northampton, MA, USA: Edward Elgar Publishing.
Kettl, Donald F. (2002), *The Transformation of Governance*. Baltimore, MD: Johns Hopkins University Press.
McNabb, David E. (2009), *The New Face of Government: How Public Managers Are Forging a New Approach to Governance*. Boca Raton, FL: CRC Press.
Mullin, Megan (2009), *Governing the Tap: Special District Governance and the New Local Politics of Water*. Boston: MIT Press.

14. Public utility management

Skilled, knowledgeable management may be the most important asset and scarcest resource that any utility has; it must be used wisely and revitalized regularly. Existing management must provide the environment and conditions under which future good management will be available when it is needed. This chapter is a brief introduction to some of the more important principles of management that utility operators, supervisors, and commission members need to understand and apply in public service management. It focuses on the open innovation model as appropriate for the public utility operating environment within which managers guide the utility's activities. It includes an overview of the key constraints and universal principles that guide managers in carrying out their tasks

There is no single best path to follow and no one best way of recruiting future utility managers. However, two paths to senior management are followed. One is the engineering side of the enterprise; the other is the professional public service management path. Engineers benefit from additional education in management; business management professionals often need additional education in the technical aspects of the utility. Managers benefit from greater knowledge of the technical aspects of the utility. Innovation is critical for success in both sides of the organization. All utilities—large and small, energy, water, or sanitation—have need for both types of managers. Equally, there is no one best way of developing future utility managers. One school of thought suggests that potential future managers should be allowed and encouraged to extend themselves as much as possible, even at the risk of failure. Stellar performers must not be held back by organizational inertia or seniority rules.

The term management is used to mean several different things. For some individuals in and out of management positions, management is closely associated with the concept of leadership and innovation. Others see it as just a different word for administration. Still others use the word to mean supervision; that is, management is supervising people who do the work of the organization. Here, the term *management* is used to mean *the set of guiding activities taken by human actors to help others accomplish the many objectives of an organization*. Public utility managers apply these activities to accomplish objectives in organizations engaged in providing a public service, including managing all actions relating to the organization's franchise granted by some public body.

Management in public utility organizations includes elements of government management, public administration, and management in unregulated business (Bozeman and Straussman 1991). Public management is management under political authority; it is subject to public accountability, shared power, and attention to political influence. Public authority is based in the laws affecting industry operations, the political philosophies of elected public officials, and the attitudes and opinions of public managers who are appointed to administer rules and regulations.

FAILURE OF THE OLD MANAGEMENT MODEL

Public utility administration has long thought to function best under the old bureaucratic management model. The bureaucratic model of government proposed by Max Weber in Germany and Woodrow Wilson in the United States was built upon the following characteristics:

- Control within the organization was centralized and hierarchical.
- Manager and worker performance was guided by rules and administrative regulations that tended to be fairly stable and exhaustive—a place for everything and everything in its place.
- Services to the public were standardized and impersonal; everyone received the same treatment.
- Internal staff handled all operations; no outside contractors or private providers existed.
- Staff members were chosen by competitive examination, not subjective criteria.

This bureaucratic model of organizational management is no longer appropriate; technology and nature has rendered the model obsolete. Change occurs too rapidly for stable, exhaustive rules to limit manager's thinking; public services must gain and maintain support of all their publics; without continuing education and training, internal staff cannot keep up with the changes in demand, oversight, and distribution taking place in their fields; professional staff are becoming harder and harder to recruit. Although all enterprises are subject to legal constraints such as taxation, anti-trust legislation, prohibition of false advertising, avoidance of price discrimination, and similar generic legislation, the services industries are also subject to close political authority; they cannot arbitrarily change prices, quality of services, or distribution methods. Provided they comply with the laws that apply to all businesses in their industry, managers of public utilities are subject to direct governmental regulation at the federal, state and local levels.

THE MANAGER'S OPERATING ENVIRONMENT

The operating environment of public utilities includes portions of both private and public management. Managers in utility organizations use management practices that are similar to, if not identical with, the fundamental management principles that are used in all organizations. It is important to remember that many differences do exist, however, and have been recognized for many years. Osborne and Plastrik identified a number of these differences in their *Banishing Bureaucracy*, the 1992 follow-up volume to their landmark *Reinventing Government*:

> [Perhaps] the most profound difference is that private organizations exist within larger systems, or markets, that are generally fairly functional. Most private, for-profit organizations have clear missions, know how to measure their bottom-line performance, face competition, experience very real consequences for their performance, and are accountable to their customers ... In government, most organizations exist within fairly dysfunctional systems. Many organizations have multiple (sometimes conflicting) missions; few face direct competition; few experience consequences for their performance; few have clear bottom lines (few even measure their performance); and very few are accountable to their customers. (Osborne and Plastrik 1992: 12)

The bleak picture of public organizations painted by Osborne and Plastrik in the early 1990s no longer accurately describes the complex public utility industry, if it ever did. Restructuring and reorganization have interposed market competition upon the once monopolistic utility-industry structure (Stucki 2009). However, managing utilities has always required an absolute need to gain, monitor, and attempt to influence political authority to operate. Much of the industry still functions under conditions of monopoly and does so by franchise granted by some governmental body. The implication is that franchises, once granted, can also be rescinded.

UNIVERSAL MANAGEMENT FUNCTIONS

Management of public utilities differs from the administrative management that once characterized most government bureaucracies, government regulated utilities, and nonprofit organizations. Public utility management today can be said to incorporate a mix of traditional dedication to public service that is being increasingly tempered by the entrepreneurial, market-oriented managerialism.

In terms of ownership or *governance*, the public utility industry is a diverse mix of public, private, and cooperative ownership. Utility management includes elements of managing in both the public and private sectors. Organizations in the utility supply chain often find themselves operating in both profit and not-for-profit economic environments. As a result, discussion of the functions and processes that make up utility management is often more theoretical rather than descriptive. In discussing management, in the past more emphasis has been placed upon "what ought to be" or "what could be" than upon "what is." In this book, the focus is the reverse; greater emphasis is upon "what is" in the industry.

Utility managers operate within a dynamic environment that is loosely anchored in the shifting policy sands of the political, economic, environmental, and social environments of the time. Policy shifts have tended to be cyclical, occurring something like every ten to thirty years. In addition, every generation of managers discovers and applies new tools to guide them in the conduct of their managerial tasks. Fortunately, many of the fundamental principles of management appear to have always been applicable, and are as useful today as they were when they were first introduced. At the beginning of the twenty-first century, utility management has seen adoption of performance-based management procedures, privatization, contract services, and market-based competition, among others. Among the universal management principles are these basic functions performed by all managers: analyzing, planning, organizing, directing (leading), and controlling the decisions made to enable the utility to accomplish its objectives.

Analyzing for Management Decisions

Management analysis is the ability to locate, examine, evaluate, and interpret meaningful data for the purpose of making a management decision. The first step in any planning process, for example, is conducting a comprehensive analysis of the factors contributing to the present situation. Before any objective for future operations can be formed, planners must have a thorough picture of the existing state of affairs. In performance measurement, this process is sometimes referred to as benchmarking, and includes comparisons with best example operations.

Analysis is both a skill and an art; it requires knowledge and creativity. Managers need to have an understanding of the greater economic system, the social and cultural trends that shape the industry, and the structure and scope of the utility industry. They also need to know when and how to use management principles and tools. This requires knowledge of economic theory, quantitative and qualitative analysis techniques, principles of business administration, and the use of analytic and forecasting computer software. Interpreting theory and data, however, is a matter of judgment, which is where the art of analysis comes to play and which is best learned by following the example of one or more effective leaders.

The Art of Forecasting

One of the chief products of meaningful analysis in utilities management is the ability to make valid *forecasts*. Utility forecasting is the process of determining, with some acceptable degree of reliability, some future state of affairs relating to the organization. Although no individual forecast can be completely accurate, the ability to make good forecasts is critical for all future utility operations (Farris and Sampson 1973; Sun and Lynch 2008).

The legal and economic constraints of public utilities make reliable forecasting and good planning more important for public service organizations than it does for other businesses. Utilities are legally required to meet all demands for their products or services whenever it is needed. As a result, most utilities invest in some excess capacity, or they must resort to making spot purchases of high-priced supplies at periods of peak demand. Utilities use demand forecasts to avoid problems of under-supply or excess capacity.

Skill in analysis is what makes it possible for a utility manager to construct a five- or ten-year forecast of future investment requirements from a series of predicted growth patterns in the service area, economic conditions, climatic changes, employment projections, and other, related economic and social data.

Utility managers often use simulations as a tool for analyzing the organization. One such simulation consisted of a financial performance simulation to first evaluate profitability of a new gas-fired, combined-cycle electric generator unit, and then to apply those performance results as a benchmark used in a wider prediction, using the simulation as a way to gauge the health of the generation segment of the entire electricity sector.

The Critical Role of Planning

Managers who formulate strategy in investor-owned utilities usually are corporate directors and/or principal executives, all of whom are responsible to stockholders. In publicly owned utilities, strategy is typically formed by elected or legislatively appointed officials, municipal or district administrative commissions, senior-level civil servants, top administrators, or professional public service managers. At the strategy formation level, management's functions are, first, to establish overall goals or objectives of the organization, and second, to establish general policies designed to meet these goals.

At the administrative or tactical level, managers employ four processes: (1) they forecast future resource needs of the organization, (2) make plans to meet those needs that are based on forecasted customer demands, (3) acquire and organize the necessary financial, human, and physical resources necessary to carry out the plans, and (4) develop and apply appropriate performance measurement and control procedures. The actual use or supervision of these resources requires constant checking to assure that the best possible use is being made of existing resources, while continuing to study possibilities for obtaining even better performance by varying the mix of resources.

The Organizing Function

Organizing is the process of bringing all the needed resources of the utility—money, people, facilities—together when and where they are needed to ensure accomplishment of the utility's objectives. Managers use both short- and long-range forecasts for this purpose. The important thing to remember about organizing is that it is a team activity involving representation from all chief functions of the organization. A change in any one of the chief resource elements has a direct impact on the others.

Closely related to the organizing function are *reorganization* and *restructuring*. Reorganization refers to current changes made in the allocation or distribution of resources. Reorganization involves operational and structural changes in the organization. For example, changing economic conditions may require a utility to revise its growth projections upward or downward. Differences in demand forecasts resulting from changing economic conditions often requires organizational changes which more accurately reflect the state of reality, such as adding or reducing staff, mothballing or building new generating plants, or locating additional sources of water or natural gas.

Restructuring, on the other hand, refers to broadly based, long-term changes in either an industry or an organization. Restructuring often involves changes in the mission or grand strategy of the utility. For example, in response to lower than expected revenues, higher than expected costs, and critical shifts in the economic environment of its international electricity operations, the AES Corporation of Arlington, Virginia, set up a Restructuring Office in 2002 to focus on improving the operating and financial performance of the firm. The office was given responsibility to evaluate prospects for its underperforming businesses, make changes where deemed appropriate, and sell or abandon others.

A similar reorganization was recently carried out by CH Energy Group, a utility holding company that controls the regulated Central Hudson Gas & Electric Corporation. Central Hudson provides public utility electric and gas services to an area with a population of approximately 662,700 living along the central Hudson River north of New York City. The purpose of the reorganization was to streamline administration and improve management effectiveness in nonregulated, competitive portions of its business. The program involved merging some businesses into others, selling others, and other organizational actions.

The utility industry overall is undergoing restructuring as a result of government regulatory changes. Restructuring in this case involves "unbundling" the components of the old vertically integrated, regulated utility industry into separate generation/production entities, transmission organizations, and independent local distributors of utility services. Restructuring of the industry in this way is referred to as deregulation. The goal of deregulation is to replace existing government regulation with market controls in order to lower the price consumers pay for utility services. Restructuring has worked well in the natural gas industry, not as well in the electricity industry, and as yet, has not been tried to any degree in the water, wastewater, or sanitation industries. While the water, wastewater and sanitation industries remain largely municipally owned, a growing number of cities have elected to privatize some or all of their utility operations. The city maintains ownership, but contracts with outside suppliers for the operation of those systems.

The Directing Function

Directing the operations of an organization is another of the fundamental activities of management. Managers manage people. The chief function of management is to assure that the organization is able to perform its basic functions—the supply of desired goods or services to customers at reasonable prices—while also protecting the various interests of its employees, investors, and affiliated groups. Responsible management must plan for and deal with the individuals, teams, and groups which together make the organization what it is. For managers to be able to make this happen, organizations must maintain a dependable system of policies, procedures, conditions, motivations, and rewards. The tasks necessary to achieve the goals and objectives of an organization are shaped by the organization's formal and informal policies and procedures. Organization effectiveness depends on the way that leaders, managers, supervisors, and workers are motivated to subsume their own objectives to those of the organization.

In his volume on leadership and organizational renewal, Nanus (1996:

4–5) defined a leader as "a person who marshals the resources of an organization—the people, capital, and technologies—to move it in the right direction." By *right direction*, Nanus meant operations that ensure future success, growth, and viability of the organization. The leader functions as a change agent, influencing or making choices about investments, personnel, markets, if and with whom to arrange partnerships, and which new directions or businesses to enter. Finally, he describes a leader as "the chief coach and mentor," the manager who "creates hope and high expectations, acts as a teacher, learner, facilitator, role model, and friend to those who do the actual work of the organization."

Leadership skills are needed for success in dealing with people. Leading means guiding and motivating managers, supervisors, and employees in actions to achieve organizational objectives (Spillane and Joullié 2015). The four key laws of leadership are: know the task, know the situation, know the group, and know yourself. The laws and questions to ask yourself as you develop leadership skill are presented in Box 14.1.

The Controlling Function

Controlling is the management function that (1) establishes standards of performance, (2) facilitates monitoring and evaluating performance, (3) weighs actual performance against planned standards or targets, and (4) institutes changes where needed and reinforcement where performance meets or exceeds targets.

As they guide organization's operations, managers are concerned with two groups of questions (Pearce and Robinson 2014). The first set deals with strategy; the second set is concerned with performance. By analyzing the operating environment and performance of the organization, managers ask such questions as:

- Is the utility moving in the right direction?
- Are the critical success factors present?
- If the utility operates in a competitive environment, does it have a maintainable competitive advantage?
- Are management's assumptions about major trends and changes upon which utility strategy is constructed correct?
- Is management doing the critical things that need to be done, when they need to be done?
- Should the strategy be changed, fine-tuned, or dropped entirely?

Performance questions involve measuring performance against established, measurable objectives. Examples include the following: checking to

---

BOX 14.1   HODGKINSON'S FOUR LAWS OF LEADERSHIP

Know the Task.
1. What is the mission of the organization?
2. What are the factors that contribute to the mission?
3. How are they expressed?
4. How are they coordinated in the organization?
5. What is my role in accomplishing the mission?

Know the Situation.
6. What significant and most prominent features of the environment are threatening to keep the organization from accomplishing its tasks?
7. Which of these need special attention?
8. Which can be ignored?
9. How is my contribution affected by the situation?

Know the Group.
10. What do I need to know about the group? (You can never know too much!)
11. In principle, there is no upper limit to human accomplishment.
12. What, then, stands between superior achievement and minimal achievement?

Know Yourself.
13. What, if any, are the boundaries of my obligation to the organization?
14. Do I have the requisite capabilities to achieve my maximum potential?
15. What is my capacity for dealing with uncertainty?
16. Above all, what are my weaknesses, and how can I turn them into strengths?
17. Am I able to cope with adverse emotion—*anger, frustration, fear, hatred, envy, resentment, greed*—in ways that serve as examples to others in the organization?

Source: Hodgkinson (1983: 211).

---

see that schedules are being met, and determining whether financial objectives for revenues, earnings, cash flows, debt servicing, and other financial targets are being met.

MANAGEMENT CONSTRAINTS

A manager's freedom of movement to initiate change is limited by certain constraints or limitations. Two broad classes of constraints limit management action: external and internal constraints. It is essential that managers at all levels identify and understand these environmental limitations; doing so is one of the first steps in the utility's strategic planning and management processes.

Perhaps the five most important external environmental constraints on public utility management are, in order of importance, profits, regulatory laws, general laws, public opinion, and social factors. Internal constraints tend to be resource related, although organizational culture may also have a limiting effect upon management's actions.

Profit Constraints

Profits are a major goal and motive for privately owned utilities, whether regulated or nonregulated. Profits are a major constraint because no privately owned business can indefinitely maintain or attract the capital resources necessary to continue its services, or to expand or improve its services without profits. Profits are used to pay dividends to the utility's owners (investors) and to gather the retained earnings that pay for future expansion and for funding contingency actions.

Economic reality demands that a privately owned business be profitable in the long term if it is to survive. A nonregulated business can build up reserves, but a regulated utility may not be able to do so. Therefore, regulated utilities are often highly leveraged. They turn to bonds and securities markets to fund capital improvements. In such cases, cash flow must be sufficient to fund current operations and service. Public utility commissions have not always been receptive to the idea of including plant-expansion debt service in rate revisions.

Regulatory Constraints

The utility industry has for many years been one of the most tightly regulated industries in the country. Utilities provide services that are deemed to be critical for modern life. When the large electric light and power holding companies collapsed after the Stock Market Crash of 1929, many citizens and legislators felt that the companies took advantage of their monopoly positions, and therefore needed to be brought under strict federal regulation. The Democratic Party platform for the election of 1932 singled out the electric power and light industry as the target for the proposed regulation.

Prior to the 1920s, most public utilities were operated locally and if regulated at all, were regulated at the local level. Congress established the Federal Power Commission in 1920, but at the time its power was limited to conducting investigations. In 1928, a Federal Trade Commission investigation of the public utility industry found that something like 75 percent of the industry was controlled by a few holding companies. In 1935, Congress enacted the Wheeler-Rayburn Act, more commonly known as the Public Utility Holding Company Act. The Act limited the number of separate company levels that could be owned by a holding company. It also required public utility holding companies to register with the Securities and Exchange Commission, established rules for issuing utility company securities, and established regulations for asset acquisitions, intercompany transactions, and service contracts between operating and parent holding companies (Clough and Marburg 1968).

Regulation at the state level generally preceded federal level regulation. State regulation took the form of the establishment of public utility commissions. Commissioners, operating under state legislative guidance, issued operating certificates, granted licenses and issued franchises, set territorial limitations to utility service areas, restricted the number of businesses a utility company could acquire, established rules for rate determinations, set common accounting standards, and set allowable rates of return on investments for operating utilities.

Today, utilities are a mix of regulated and unregulated businesses. While some regulatory constraints have been lifted, others have appeared to take their place. The federal government has mandated restructuring of the industry, subjected certain segments to market competition, and forced other utilities to divest portions of their vertically integrated operations. The most heavily regulated segment of the industry at the beginning of the twenty-first century is the local distribution companies. Deregulation seems to be creating as many or more new regulations as it is eliminating others.

Legal Constraints

All businesses must comply with general laws of society in which they operate. Utility businesses operate in a more restrictive environment than do most other businesses, such as many special regulatory limitations or requirements on such matters as profits, pricing, operating rights, service performance, financing, and the like. Many of these laws conflict with one another.

Examples of the types of legal actions and constraints faced by public utilities can be seen in the list of legal proceedings discussed in the Maine Public Service Company's (MPSC) 2002 Annual Report (MPSC is a utility holding company that owns all of the common stock of Maine and New Brunswick Electrical Power Company and other subsidiaries). A sample of the proceedings includes (1) a complaint by a competitor alleging that actions of MPSC employees resulted in the firm's competitive electricity provider (CEP) receiving a competitive advantage over competitors by Maine Public Utility Commission (MPUC) decisions; (2) disagreements regarding including possible changes to the annual charges of $12.5 million for recovery of stranded costs (stranded costs result from unbundling of vertically integrated utility systems); (3) an investigation by the MPUC regarding the design of transmission and distribution rates; (4) request for approval by the MPUC of the firm's request to reorganize the company into a holding company structure; (5) a request to the MPUC for approval of an alternative rate plan; and (6) an MPUC inquiry into the status of the competitive market for electricity supply in Northern Maine.

Public Opinion Constraints

Utility managers are by necessity very sensitive to public opinion. Managers have long considered maintaining a good public image an important success factor, particularly in the regulatory environment in which most utilities must operate. Negative public opinion can have a direct impact on bottom line results by failure to secure needed rate increases. As a result, decision-makers generally are careful to avoid making decisions or actions that adversely affect the reputation of the organization. Managers in investor-owned utilities must be aware of the potential threats of public ownership, public competition, loss or cancellation of franchises, enactment of more stringent regulatory legislation, or more stringent enforcement of existing legislation.

On the other hand, yielding to the pressures of public opinion can be quite costly and conflicts with the need to maintain adequate profits. Examples include yielding to demands for less visual pollution. Clearly the free-wheeling days of almost unlimited entrepreneurial or managerial freedom and flexibility are only a historical memory.

Social Constraints

Utility managers long ago learned that their organizations do not exist exclusively for the benefit of government administrators, owners, managers, employees, financiers, or suppliers. Certainly all these groups and others have legitimate economic, legal, or moral interests in a business, but these interests are subservient to overall customer and social interests.

A major course of social constraint today is pressure upon operations brought about for reasons related to the environment. Social environmental constraints, both legal and extralegal, affect the amount, rate, and direction of growth. They affect the siting of power generating facilities, as well as transmission lines and gas pipelines. They have forced removal of dams on rivers and streams, and severely restricted the development of wastewater treatment facilities and solid waste earth fills. The high capital cost of construction of nuclear generation plants is largely due to excessive environmental concerns. This high cost, concern over plant safety and disposal of spent nuclear fuel has all but eliminated construction of new nuclear power generating plants—despite the fact that nuclear generators are still the lowest cost producers of electricity.

UTILITY ASSOCIATION ASSISTANCE

In May 2007, six water and wastewater trade associations and the U.S. Environmental Protection Agency joined in a program to aid public utilities gain effective management techniques and processes. The associations included the Association of Metropolitan Water Agencies, American Public Works Association, American Water Works Association, National Association of Clean Water Agencies, National Association of Water Companies, and the Water Environment Federation. The chief product of that collaboration was the June 2008 *Effective Utility Management* primer for water and wastewater utilities. That document includes three focal points: (1) agreement on the ten most important attributes of effectively managed water and wastewater utilities, (2) keys of successful assessment and implementation of the management attributes, and (3) an individual utility-focused self-assessment tool to help utility managers determine where to begin their improvement efforts.

Management Attributes

The management attributes were intended to serve as a set of "reference points" on which to plan and implement a management improvement program and to help utility managers keep a balanced focus on all of the operational issues. Table 14.1 lists the ten key management areas and includes brief descriptions of each area.

The payoff expected to be gained from following the approach was that by making improvements in any of the management areas at whatever pace was appropriate for a utility would result in real, if incremental, improvements in total operations achievement and effectiveness.

Where to Begin

The authors of the primer were quick to point out that the guide was not to be considered a universal solution to all utility management challenges and

Table 14.1   Sustainable rural and small water utility management issues and descriptions

Management issue	Descriptions
Product quality	System complies with permit requirements and regulatory or reliability requirements, meets expectations for potable water and/or treated effluent and public health and ecology demands
Customer satisfaction	System is informed about what customers expect in service, water quality and rates, provides reliable, responsive and affordable services; receives and requests customer feedback
Employee and leadership development	System receives and retains a competent, motivated and safe working workforce. Opportunities exist for employee skill development and career enhancement. Training programs are in place or are available. Job descriptions are clearly established as is a code of conduct for all employees
Operational optimization	System ensures ongoing, timely, cost-effective, reliable, and sustainable performance in key aspects of its operations; pressure, flow, and quality are documented and monitored
Financial viability	System operates and maintains a balance between long-term debt, asset values, operations and maintenance expenditures and operational revenues. Rates charged are adequate to pay its bills, save some for future capital expenditures and unanticipated issues; system maintains, repairs and replaces equipment and infrastructure as needed, discusses rate requirements with its customers and other key stakeholders
Infrastructure stability	System understands conditions and costs of its critical infrastructure assets; has inventoried system components, conditions and costs and has a plan to repair and replace them as needed
Operational resiliency	System ensures leadership and staff work together to anticipate and avoid problems; proactively identifies legal, financial, non-compliance, environmental, safety, security, and natural threats to the system, and has conducted a vulnerability assessment for safety, natural disasters and other environmental threats and has prepared an emergency plan for these hazards
Community sustainability	System is active in its community and is aware of the impacts that its decisions have on current and long-term future community health and welfare; supports overall watershed, source water protection and community economic goals

Table 14.1 (continued)

Management issue	Descriptions
Water source adequacy	System ensures that water availability is consistent with current and future customer needs, understands its role in water availability, and manages its operations to provide for long-term aquifer and surface water sustainability and replenishment; has performed a long-term water supply and demand analysis and is able to meet water and sanitation needs of its customers now and for the reasonable future
Stakeholder understanding and support	System actively seeks understanding and support from decision-making bodies, community members, and regulatory bodies related to service levels, operating budgets, capital improvement programs and risk management decisions; works with stakeholders to build support for its performance goals, resources, and the value of the service it provides, promotes the value of clean, safe water and the services the utility provides, consistent with available resources

Source: USDA and EPA (2016).

that not all utilities are the same. Each utility was advised to determine for itself and its own distinctive service community what is the most important issue for its operations, what should be its own long-term objectives and priorities. To guide utility managers through the process of establishing its own relevant starting point, this five-step process was recommended: (1) assess current conditions and constraints; (2) rank the importance of each attribute for its own utility; (3) using a numerical importance rating scale, chart the results of the analysis; (4) prioritize the attributes on which to focus and schedule achievement dates in an improvements plan; and (5) determine and plan for the actions needed to achieve improvement objectives.

Measuring Performance: A Self-assessment

Noting that management improvement depends on performance measurement, the primer then described an internal performance approach for utilities. Again reminding readers that performance measures are best when they are utility organization specific, the primer identified ten guidelines that can help managers identify and apply useful measures for their own organization. Abbreviated, the list includes the following processes:

1. Select measures that support the utility's strategic objectives and 10 attributes.
2. Select the right number, level and type of measures for your utility.
3. Allocate adequate resources to start and continue the process.
4. Develop clear, consistent, definitions for each measure.
5. Engage all levels of the utility in developing, tracking and reporting measures.
6. Set targets rationally, based on appropriate criteria.
7. Select and use measures in a positive way to foster improvements.
8. When selecting measures, consider how they relate to one another.
9. Develop a means to evaluate and respond to results.
10. Incorporate the "plan-do-check-act" cycle into evaluating specific measures and the system as a whole. Regularly review the performance measurement system for opportunities to improve.

IMPROVING UTILITY MANAGEMENT

In 2013 the U.S. Department of Agriculture and the Environmental Protection Agency collaborated on a nation-wide study to disseminate key management areas of sustainability managed organizations for managers and operators of rural and small public utilities (USDA and EPA 2016). These management points were first introduced for all water and wastewater utilities in 2007 and re-issued in 2016. Three objectives projected from use of the management recommendations were: (1) high achievement of operational goals, (2) increasing long-term sustainability and effectiveness, and (3) improve the ability of managers and operators of small and rural systems to address the ongoing challenges they face.

A combined task force collected data from a wide range of rural and small water system operators, specialists, and managers. They also held a series of workshops with system operators. Out of those activities the task force arrived at what they determined to be ten key management areas or topics appropriate for rural and small systems operators. Through self analysis, managers and operators were coached in a process of identifying strong and weak point status along with system priorities, the product of which can become strategic objectives for sustainable management (Table 14.1).

The management system suggests that utility managers evaluate their performance on each of the management area, determine what it means and what it takes to accomplish high achievement in each area and what will be needed to change the system to reach that level. The next step is to develop an implementation plan. A particularly valuable recommendation is that utilities develop relationships with nearby systems to share their experiences and strengths, collaborate where feasible, and to share training resources.

SUMMARY

Utility management consists of the set of guiding activities taken by human actors to help others accomplish the many objectives of an organization. Public utility managers apply these activities to accomplish objectives in organizations engaged in providing a public service, including managing all actions relating to the organization's franchise.

Management in public utility organizations includes elements of government management, public administration, and management in unregulated business. Public management is management under political authority; it is subject to public accountability, shared power, and attention to political influence. Public administration is bureaucratic management. The bureaucratic model of government proposed by Max Weber in Germany and Woodrow Wilson in the United States was built upon the following characteristics: centralized and hierarchical control, performance guided by rules and regulations, standardized services, internal staff performing all activities, and objective selection of staff. Business management is the opposite of public management. Although all businesses are subject to many legal constraints, private businesses are subject to little direct governmental regulation. Managers in utilities use practices that are similar to the fundamental management principles that are used in all organizations.

Two key factors which distinguish the majority of the utility industry from other economic endeavors are: (1) elements of the utility industry operate under socially-sanctioned conditions of monopoly competition, and (2) one or more element of the organizations' operations or supply chain are regulated by one or more levels of government.

Management of public utilities differs from the administrative management that once characterized most government bureaucracies, government regulated utilities, and nonprofit organizations. Public utility management today incorporates a mix of traditional dedication to public service tempered by an entrepreneurial, market-oriented managerialism. Among the universal management principles are these basic functions performed by all managers: analyzing, planning, organizing, directing (leading), and controlling the decisions made to enable the utility to accomplish its objectives. A manager's freedom to initiate change is limited by certain constraints or limitations. The two broad classes of constraints are *external* and *internal* constraints. Five important external constraints are profits, regulatory laws, general laws, public opinion, and social factors. Internal constraints are resource related, although organizational culture may also have a limiting effect upon management's actions.

Recent disasters have made innovation and crisis planning and management a major concern of utilities managers. Crisis planning is programming the combined tools of analysis, forecasting, and planning in order to be prepared to deal with unexpected crises and disasters. Crisis management is the system that exists for prompt and effective handling of unusual, unanticipated, and serious problems that all utilities face.

ADDITIONAL READING

Afullo, Augustine (2014), *Integrated Solid Waste Management Handbook: For Engineers, Planners, Environmentalists, Students and Policy Makers*. Nairobi, Kenya: I. Wamra Technoprises.

Alauer, William C. (ed.) (2001), *Excellence in Action: Water Utility Management in the 21st Century*. Denver: American Water Works Association.

Bakker, Karen J. (2010), *Privatizing Water: Governance Failure and the World's Urban Water Crisis*. Ithaca, NY: Cornell University.

Chesbrough, Henry W. (2011), *Open Services Innovation*. San Francisco: Jossey-Bass.

Starling, Grover (2010), *Managing the Public Sector* (9th edn). Fort Worth, TX: Harcourt Brace.

Sun, Jinping and Thomas D. Lynch (2008), *Government Budget Forecasting: Theory and Practice*. Boca Raton, FL: Taylor & Francis.

15. Public utility operations, maintenance and planning

The obstacles confronting effective public utilities operations and planning are similar to what managers of other public services organizations face every day. Operations management (OM) is essential for the smooth and efficient running of all types of organizations. As a fundamental function of management, OM controls the processes and procedures needed for producing all the products and services provided by public utilities. Utility products differ from other goods and services purchased by consumers and industrial users in that they tend to be highly homogeneous in quality, consumed at generally predictable quantities and little affected by readily attainable substitutes, whereas products manufactured are typically differentiated by brand, quality level, and price.

OMM IN PUBLIC UTILITIES

Operation and maintenance management (OMM) in utilities consists of a number of asset management activities related to the collection, processing, transmission and distribution of the organization's resources, products and services and residual product processing and disposal. These activities are generally grouped into three broad systems: operations, maintenance, and planning. The application of the operation function is facilitated through such subsystems as:

- Equipment operations systems
- Crisis and emergency response operations
- Heating and cooling systems
- Compressed air and chemical storage, use and disposal systems
- Product processing and treatment systems
- Transportation and distribution systems
- Route scheduling and equipment maintenance systems
- Safety and security systems
- Collection, transportation, segregation, management and disposal of solid residues.

Operations Management

Operations management is the design, implementation and administration of the actions by which managers guide the development, production or acquisition of goods and services provided the public by all public utilities. The function's core activities are planning, organizing, coordinating and controlling of all the resources involved in making utility products available to consumers and industrial users. The skills needed in operations management include people management; knowledge of the function and purpose of the equipment and technology necessary for acquiring and/or producing the product or service; management of information collection, storage and distribution; storage and distribution of products to consumers; and all other human, technical and financial resources needed for the supply of utility products and services. Operations management can also be considered the management function that guides and oversees the activities and decisions of the organization that are involved in making sure that what the utility produces and provides is what its customers want and need (CSCMP and Sanders 2014).

Equipment and Systems Maintenance

The maintenance portion of operations falls into two broad classes: routine and non-routine maintenance. Typical routine and non-routine maintenance is further divided into three types of maintenance tasks: preventative, corrective, and emergency maintenance. Preventive maintenance includes regularly scheduled tasks such as changing oil and checking bearing temperature in motors and generator turbines. Corrective maintenance such as replacing a worn belt before it breaks or rebuilding a chemical feed, effluent or cooling water pumps twice each year. Emergency maintenance involves such actions as repairing a broken water main or replacing an electric line after heavy snows caused a tree to fall across the line. In a small utility, preventive and corrective maintenance may be grouped with routine operations tasks and are collectively called preventive maintenance. Utility managers agree that the most effective means of managing these operation and maintenance tasks is through a maintenance management system. A primary portion of this system is focused on identifying and scheduling operations tasks, preventive, and corrective maintenance.

Table 15.1   Operational differences between manufacturing, service and utility providers

Manufacturers	Service Organizations	Public Utilities
Provide a tangible produce	Provide intangible products	Provide both tangible and intangible products
Product can be stored	Products cannot be stored	Some products can be stored; others cannot
Little direct consumer contact	High customer contact	Little direct customer contact
Long response time	Short response time	General short or immediate customer response
Capital intensive	Labor intensive	Capital intensive
Product purchase can be delayed	Product purchase is usually not delayed	Product purchase generally indispensable
Selective regulatory oversight	Lower regulatory oversight	High regulatory oversight

Source: Adapted from CSCMP and Sanders (2014).

OMM SYSTEM ORGANIZATIONAL STRUCTURES

In their basic structure, public and private organizations can be considered to be either producers or suppliers of goods or services, although many organizations provide both. Public utilities belong in this combined category. Table 15.1 displays the different organizational characteristics of the different organizations. The differences between operations management in manufacturing organizations and service providers are clear; operations management in utilities, however, includes elements of both sectors. For example, manufacturers design, produce and market tangible products such as refrigerators, telephones, and steel pipes. Service firms provide such intangible products as fire insurance, financial and investment guidance, and first-aid services to injured workers. Utilities as a group provide elements of both tangible and intangible products. They meet the needs of consumers for water—a tangible product—and the intangible products of the collection and disposal of wastewater. Others utilities provide mass transportation—an intangible product. Still others provide the intangible services of collection and disposal of solid and hazardous waste. Electrical and natural gas utilities provide products that are tangible and intangible. Electrical energy is generally considered to be an intangible product that is used to produce heat or light. The heaters and electric lighting fixtures are tangible products. However, in 2009, the State of Illinois passed a bill that taxes electricity as a tangible personal product for including the cost of its production in computing the Corporate Income and Replacement Tax. Natural gas is produced, transmitted, stored, and distributed as energy—an intangible product. However, the basic ingredients of natural gas are also tangible components for the manufacture of such products as plastic, fertilizer, anti-freeze and synthetic fabrics.

The utility production manager's primary objective in wastewater collection and treatment, for example, is to ensure that no faults occur in the provision of the service. Customers cannot be encouraged to use more of the service and are generally uninterested in using less. Production managers of water utilities must concentrate providing a single high quality product that meets all the requirements of regulatory agencies, and doing so at an affordable price. Electricity and natural gas operations also focus on supplying a single product when needed, safely, and reliably. Another difference is that the products of utilities are not "manufactured" In the traditional product sense; instead, they are considered services. Selected elements of a municipal water and wastewater utility are included in Box 15.1.

Operations Planning

Operations management in public utilities involves the same core managerial activities found in all public and private commercial and services enterprises. Traditionally, these have been identified as analyzing, planning, directing, and controlling. Analyzing provides the background and current status of the operation from which plans are developed. Analyzing has been made significantly more efficient with the development of information systems. Planning is building on the data established during the analyzing phase for preparing the utility to meet the ongoing and emergency operating activities at various periods in the future.

Current operations are closely aligned with budgeting, while planning for future operations centers on the chosen strategy to follow to achieve the organization's long-term objectives. Operations' planning is the responsibility of department heads; it specifies what resources are needed for the utility to function on a day-to-day, month-to-month basis; the operations plan is the first year of the strategic plan. Strategic planning is the function of the chief administrator, with the contribution and advice of chief department heads; it is planning for operations for three, five or more years ahead. Strategic planning is the path to be taken to achieve the vision of what the senior administrators envisions the utility is to be five, ten or twenty years in the future.

BOX 15.1 ELEMENTS OF A JOB DESCRIPTION OF A TYPICAL MUNICIPAL UTILITY OPERATIONS MANAGER

Under the general direction of the Director of Environmental & Engineering Services plans, the operations manager (OM) develops, organizes and directs operations and maintenance activities of the City's water, wastewater and reclaimed water systems, reviews and supervises the work of subordinate personnel involved in water, wastewater and reuse treatment, collection, transmission, and distribution systems.

The OM is responsible for the effective, efficient and safe operation of plant and equipment serving a moderately large number of residential and commercial users. Technical expertise is essential as error in technical judgment could result in extensive damage to the environment, facilities or both. Administrative activities include policy formulation, budget development, and personnel management. The OM exercises a high degree of independent judgment in selection of work methods and procedures, subject to executive directive and review by the director, and local, state and federal requirements pertaining to water, wastewater and reuse operations. Work is reviewed through conferences, reports and observation of the operational success of the systems and achievement of objectives.

The OM ensures that water, wastewater and reclaimed water systems are functioning in compliance with the Environmental Protection Agency, state Department of Environmental Protection, Department of Health, County Department of Natural Resource Protection and various other regulatory entities. The OM coordinates the daily operations of the Water and Wastewater/Reuse divisions; establishes operational and administrative policies, relays instructions and procedural revisions to the management staff and keeps staff informed on matters that pertain to their operations.

Both types of planning are necessary for smooth functioning at both the short and long term time periods. In this chapter the focus is on long-term or strategic planning. Strategic planning is a complex, critical function required of all types and sizes of public utility sectors, regulatory levels, and individual enterprises. At the regulatory level it is carried on at three or more separate levels: federal, state, and regional and/or local. It also occurs at three separate but related levels within individual organizations or enterprises, and is done for many different purposes. All types of plans are necessary for achieving organization objectives.

Planning at the Policy Level

Planning at the federal level is most complex and is typically carried out for long period of time that extend for periods up to and including 50 years or longer periods in the future. Planning at this level is done in order for relevant government agencies in keeping with the public policies promoted at the highest political levels.

Planning at the Enterprise Level

The most comprehensive level of enterprise planning is *strategic planning*. The purpose of strategic planning is to provide the organization long-term direction for achieving its fundamental objectives. The second, but typically more specific level is operational planning. The purpose of operational planning is to effectively and efficiently allocate scarce resources for carrying out the work of the organization. Strategic plans usually extend over several years—typically from three to five years. Organizational plans usually cover a one-year period. Upper-level management is responsible for strategic planning—usually under the direction of the chief executive officer and other top officers. Managers and supervisors are responsible for operational planning, sometimes assisted by professional planning staff. The third and most specific level of planning is planning and programming for individual units, functions or process. Planning at this level entails elements of all three levels.

Strategic planning has three main purposes: The first purpose is to establish the specific markets and environments in which the organization will compete. The second purpose of the strategic plan is establishing the position that the firm wants to hold at some time in the future—its long-term objectives. The third purpose is to identify how the firm proposes to reach its long-term objectives. The *how* purpose is expressed as the strategies the organization will follow. For example, strategic options that a public utility might take include choosing to either do its own meter-reading, billing, and customer service, or to outsource these and other ancillary services. In another strategic choice, the utility might elect to focus on the delivery of electric power purchased from independent generators at the best possible long-term contract price it can negotiate, depending upon market purchases for day-ahead or peak power needs at competitive market prices. Or, it might decide to purchase its own gas-fired turbine generator for reserve or peak power supplies.

Strategic objectives and policy formulation are developed after comprehensive analyses of both the external and internal environments of the utility. External analysis surveys the economic, legal and political, social, and technological environments in which the utility operates. Internal analysis examines the resources that are available for tactical implementation. From the results of these two comprehensive analyses of the utility's situation, managers determine which of the external environmental forces have greatest threat potential and which may result in business opportunities.

Managers then determine what opportunities to follow and determine what internal resources are available, which can be acquired, and which are unavailable for planned operations. From these analyses, management then prepares a forecast of probable business levels for the current and subsequent years, taking threats, opportunities, resource strengths and weaknesses into account. The strategic and operational plans specify what actions management elects to take in its operational capacity.

Planning at the Operations Level

Operational planning focuses on the production, equipment, personnel, inventory and processes of all types of public utilities. In practice, the operational plan links the organization's strategic goals and objectives to tactical goals and objectives. Describing what actions are anticipated for from one to three years in advance, they describe key milestones, conditions for success and explain how, or what portion of, a strategic plan are affected by their completion and what portion of the long-range strategic plan will be put into operation during the designated operational period. Operational plans are generally made by frontline supervisors or low-level managers who are responsible for specific procedures and processes that occur within the operating levels of the utility. These supervisors or lower-level managers typically have more knowledge of core operations and better understanding of the day-to-day needed organizational operation resources. Collected and assigned to annual budgets, the sections become the annual operations plan. These plans include the following sections:

- A statement of the existing state of the utility's operations; the starting point of the plan.
- A statement of where the utility is expected or desired to be at some designated future point, usually from five to ten years in the future.
- An estimate of the resources needed to maintain sustainability during ongoing operations during the planning period.
- Estimated determination of what specific decisions will have to be made and operational activities taken during the planning period to get to the expected or desired point.
- An estimate of the resources needed to carry out the actions necessary to achieve the short-range position objective.
- The quantitative and qualitative measurements that will be used to measure progress during the planning period.

FORECASTING OPERATIONAL NEEDS

Forecasts of future growth are often included in utilities' annual reports. However, the Private Securities Litigation Reform Act of 1995 requires utility managements to qualify those "forward-looking" statements as being only their "best guesses" of future events. Forward-looking statements are identified by the use of such words as *estimates, expects, anticipates, intends, believes, plans,* and conditional verbs such as *should, would,* and *could.* Management is not restricted in the use of such words, but must also include any qualifying statements regarding such forecasts. WGL Holdings, the Washington, DC, natural gas holding company, identified the following events or circumstances that could cause actual future results to differ materially from forward-looking statements included in the firm's annual report. The list could service as a good guide for all conducting external analyses in all utilities regardless of the degree to which they are regulated.

- Changes in capital and energy commodity market conditions.
- Changes in credit market conditions and creditworthiness of customers and suppliers.
- Changes in economic, competitive, political and regulatory statements or developments.
- Changes in relevant laws and regulations, including tax, environmental and employment laws and regulations.
- Legislative, regulatory, and judicial mandates and decisions.
- Other uncertainties.
- Technological improvements.
- Terrorist activities.
- The pace of deregulation efforts and the availability of other competitive alternatives.
- Timing and success of business and product development efforts.
- Weather conditions.

The reason for utility managers' concern with their legal and political environments—often called operational constraints—is based on their need to regularly deal with the regulatory actions of governments. Although deregulation has been partially successful in some segments of the industry, such as telecommunications and natural gas, in other segments deregulation still has far to go to achieve its goals. Deregulation, or *restructuring,* as it is euphemistically called, of the electric power industry has been put on hold as a result of the California experience and collapse of the energy trading industry. Very little deregulation has been tried in the water and sanitation industries thus far. Public utility commissions are as active today as they were before the deregulation movement began in the 1970s. Utilities have long been one of the most highly leveraged industries in the United States. Economic conditions affect interest rates and the ability of utilities to sell long-term bonds. Regulation policy has a major impact upon the operations of a utility.

When the strategic plan is developed for new or restructured organization, it is often referred to as a *strategic business plan*. When Tampa Bay Water—a wholesale-only water collection and transmission public utility—adopted its first strategic business plan in 1999, the situation analysis portion of the planning process included assessments and strategies for implementation in these major aspects of operations (Rogoff et al. 2002):

- Predictive and preventive maintenance of operating equipment needs, processes, and schedules.
- Energy use optimization and management.
- Automation in the workplace.
- Management information systems for report-standardization and improved documentation.
- Activity-based accounting systems for monitoring project costs.
- Centralized purchasing, standardized equipment and materials, and materials management systems.
- Records management, including document management and improved drawing access.
- Opportunities to expand services and enhance the revenue base.
- Outsourcing of non-core business functions.
- Enhance workforce flexibility by greater cross-training and changes in shift configurations, among other steps.

A Foundation for the Strategic Plan

Utility managers must construct a strong foundation upon which to build their strategic plans. The key activity in this phase of the planning process is establishing the specific mission for the organization. A mission statement is a written statement that explains the way the utility wants to be perceived by its stakeholders. The statement also defines the utility's scope of operations, its goals, and the strategies it will take to accomplish those goals. The scope of operations specifies the sector or sectors of the industry the utility wishes to serve. It also presents a clear description of the organization's belief systems, including the moral standards it follows (Boone and Kurtz 2015).

A major purpose of the mission statement is to guide workers in the way they carry out the work of the utility. Therefore, the best mission statements are developed in a democratic process, from the bottom up. The senior manager has the responsibility for setting forth a vision for the organization's future, but all managers and staff should be involved in the development of the mission statement. One way to accomplish this task is to form cross-functional teams of managers, supervisors and staff personnel in task groups set up just for this purpose. Once the mission is established and integrated into the organization, it frames the ultimate organizational culture. Developing an organization profile is a descriptive activity; it describes for all stakeholders the shape and scope of the organization as it exists at the time of preparing the strategic plan.

Constructing a Mission Statement

Virginia-based AES Corporation (AES) is a large, independent power company with 36,000 employees and assets in excess of $33 billion in 30 countries on five continents. The company operates 160 facilities capable of generating more than 55 gigawatts of power. AES also operates 20 electric distribution companies that deliver electricity to something like 16 million end-use customers.

Before it was acquired in 2009 by the Calgary-Canada based TransAlta Corporation, Canadian Hydro Developers, Inc. (Canadian Hydro) owned and operated 12 low-impact, run-of-river water and wind electric power generating plants, biofuel generating and natural gas fueled generating plants in British Columbia, Alberta, and Ontario, Canada, with several additional plants at various stages of development. The company's mission was spelled out in these six guiding principles:

- We strive to meet or surpass all legislative, regulatory and other adopted requirements;
- We fully integrate health, safety and environmental considerations into corporate planning exercises and operational activities;
- We strive to continually improve our performance through achieving and advancing health, safety and environmental objectives and targets, including pollution prevention;
- We undertake all our activities in a manner that identifies, assesses and manages all health, safety and environmental risks;
- We engage communities, governments and other stakeholders in meaningful dialogue to address health, safety and environmental concerns; and
- We advance our ideals through implementation of an effective and efficient health, safety and environmental management system.

BOX 15.2   EXAMPLE OF AN ENERGY UTILITY PROFILE
INCLUDED IN ITS ANNUAL REPORT

This is an example of how a company described itself to customers and investors:
"Westar Energy [is] committed to operating a safe, reliable, open and innovative electric utility with uncompromising integrity. We will provide first-class service to our customers, and, given the choice, they will not hesitate to choose us. We will be a friendly, caring neighbor and business partner worthy of trust. Westar Energy will be a thriving, positive environment where employees are proud to work, diversity is celebrated and all are treated with respect. Talent and leadership of all employees will set industry standards of excellence that foster job security. We will be a premier utility investment opportunity. Our financially balanced organization will deliver consistent returns to our investors. By partnering with our communities, Westar Energy will be an outstanding model of civic leadership and environmental stewardship. All of us working together will make Kansas a better place to live!"

Source: Westar Energy (2002).

Westar Energy of Topeka operates the largest electric utility in Kansas—Kansas City Gas and Electric—and several other unregulated businesses, including Protection One and Protection One Europe, among others. The mission statement was included in the firm's 2002 Annual Report and is shown in Box 15.2.

Artesian Resources Corporation is one of the relatively few investor-owned water utility holding companies in the United States. The company serves approximately 68,000 metered customers in a population base of about 226,000, which represents nearly 27 percent of the population of the State of Delaware. Artesian Resources provided the following company profile in its annual report (Box 15.3).

Mason County, Washington, PUD No. 3 is an example of a profile of a publicly owned utility organization. The profile published in one of its reports is shown in Box 15.4. PUD No. 3 is one of two such publicly owned utilities in the county.

The Strategic Planning Process

The strategic planning process begins with an analysis of both the external and internal environments of the utility. The external environment is the source of threats and opportunities. The internal environment contains both strengths and weaknesses.

BOX 15.3   2002 COMPANY PROFILE OF ARTESIAN
RESOURCES CORPORATION

Artesian Resources Corporation is a non-operating holding company, whose
income is derived from the earnings of our four wholly owned subsidiary companies and a one-third interest in AquaStructure, a Limited Liability Corporation
whose primary activity is marketing wastewater services. Artesian Water Company,
Inc., our principal subsidiary, is the oldest and largest public water utility in the
State of Delaware and has been providing water service within the state since
1905. We distribute and sell water to residential, commercial, industrial, governmental, municipal and utility customers . . . .. We provide services to other water
utilities, including operations and billing functions . . . [and] have contract operation
agreements with thirteen private and municipal water providers. In 2002, approximately 99.1% of our net income applicable to common stock was attributable to
Artesian Water's service to customers . . .. Upon recognition from the
Pennsylvania Public Utility Commission as a regulated utility, our other water utility
subsidiary . . . began operations in 2002, providing water service to a residential
community . . . in Chester County. Other subsidiaries . . . provide wastewater
services in Delaware, and ownership of an eleven-acre parcel of land.

Source: Artesian Resources Corporation (2002).

BOX 15.4   PROFILE OF A PUBLIC UTILITY DISTRICT (PUD)

This is an example of how a publicly owned utility describes itself to its customers:
"Mason County PUD No. 3 was established by vote in 1934 and began operations
in 1939 under the direction of three elected commissioners. The district's headquarters are in Shelton, Washington, approximately 22 miles northwest of
Olympia, the capital of Washington State. The district's service area encompasses
567 square miles, most of which is in Mason County. Electric service is provided
to 5 square miles in southern Kitsap County, 18 square miles in eastern Grays
Harbor County, and 0.00156 square miles in southwestern Pierce County. The
district owns and operates 26.69 miles of 115KV transmission lines. During 2002
a project to provide 5.2 MW of generating capacity was completed with the
Olympic View Generating Station being put on-line. The district is now a full
requirements customer of the Bonneville Power Administration (BPA), taking
delivery of power at ten substations. It has 1,593.4 miles of primary (distribution)
lines. As of December 31, 2002, the value of the district's net plant totaled
$95 million [and] served 28,678 customers. Gross utility sales and service reve-
nues for 2002 were $37,698,736."

Source: Mason County Public Utility District No. 3 (n.d.) Annual Report.

Assessing the external environment

A number of external factors may have some degree of impact upon the operations of a utility. Among the most important are (1) economic conditions, (2) political trends and the legal constraints that follow political actions, (3) shifts in social trends, (4) changes in the physical environment, and (5) technological innovation.

Not all of these environmental factors exercise the same degree of influence over utilities' operations. However, the social environment is one of the major problems faced by utility managers today. Managers are expected to operate their utility in such a way that conflicts between various stakeholder interests are minimized. Conflicts occur primarily because of changes in public policy toward utilities. Often, changes have been mandated at the federal level, but were not thought out sufficiently before utilities had to adopt the changes. A particularly painful example of these conflicts occurred as a result of well-meaning changes introduced during the last decade of the twentieth century into the electric utility industry. The power industry was unbundled; competition was introduced in the generating and distribution segments, but not in the distribution industry, where regulation and prior approval on rate changes were required. Distributors were not allowed to change their prices to cover the steep increases in the prices they paid for energy. As distributors found themselves forced to seek bankruptcy protection, the State of California was forced to purchase very high-priced power to ensure that customer demand was met. An imbalance was artificially created in the market; utilities' carefully crafted strategic planning went out the window. State regulators soon realized that a balance must be reached between the need to protect the interests of all those concerned in any way with the organization (its stakeholders), with the need to not sacrifice the fundamental economic or social activity of the organizations that make up the industry.

Environmental pressures constitute an ongoing threat to utility operations. Emissions, water pollution, visual pollution, species extinction, site clean-up requirements, and similar concerns affect operation of existing facilities and have a major limiting impact upon future production facility locating decisions. An example of the way electric energy production impacts the environment was explained in this 2015 report by the EPA:

All forms of electricity generation have an environmental impact on our air, water and land, but it varies. Of the total energy consumed in the United States, about 40% is used to generate electricity, making electricity use an important part of each person's environmental footprint. Producing and using electricity more efficiently reduces both the amount of fuel needed to generate electricity and the amount of greenhouse gases and other air pollution emitted as a result. Electricity from renewable resources such as solar, geothermal, and wind generally does not contribute to climate change or local air pollution since no fuels are combusted. (EPA 2015h)

Analyzing the Company's Resources

A utility's chief resources are people, money, and facilities—all of which are limited in both public and private utilities. Determining the best use of these resources is a management function. Managers must also develop priorities for their use and provide a system for dealing with the competitive conflicts that often occur during the operational planning phase of developing the organization's strategy.

Another important resource consists of the critical skills that are needed to safely, effectively, and efficiently carry out utility services. Electricity and gas are dangerous to handle and often require detailed engineering knowledge for proper design and implementation of service. Managers at many utilities report that they are having difficulty recruiting young engineers. All utilities are required to prepare secure contingency plans in place to protect continuity of service in the event of a crisis. As utilities' skilled operators retire in growing numbers, a problem that virtually all will have to contend with in their emergency planning is a shortage of personnel with the needed expertise in technical skills. Although outsourcing may be good for the bottom line in the short-term, it will leave most utilities that make the decision to outsource with only the barest resources for devising and developing plans for business survival.

Selecting long-term objectives and grand strategies

Identification of an overall strategy for the utility occurs during the analysis phase of the strategic planning process. Desired objectives and projections of required service levels are compared with the outcomes of current operations. The gap between the two measurements constitutes the workloads that need to be planned for. The process of reviewing the gap for opportunities and threats is called *gap analysis*. The best mix of activities and priorities for carrying out the workloads are determined by the strategies that are to be followed.

Pinnacle West Capital Corporation is a Phoenix, Arizona-based diversified utility company with combined assets of approximately $8.4 billion and consolidated annual earnings of more than $2.6 billion. Pinnacle West subsidiaries generate, sell, and deliver electricity; in addition, they sell energy-related products and services to retail and wholesale customers in the Western United States. In addition, the firm develops residential, commercial, and industrial real estate projects. On its web page the company defines its strategic direction as it focuses on one constant common goal:

creating value for customers and shareholders. Value for customers, shareholders, employees, and communities served is created, producing and delivering safe, reliable energy. In order to achieve that goal, Pinnacle West has established seven core strategic objectives:

1. Focus on superior long-term total returns for shareholders.
2. Provide Arizona electricity customers with reliable energy at stable prices.
3. Capture growth opportunities in electricity markets.
4. Actively manage costs and business risks.
5. Maximize the long-term value of assets.
6. Maintain a disciplined focus on long-term goals while remaining agile.
7. Build generation portfolio consistent with our native load, cash flow, and market conditions.

Pinnacle West's operations are guided by these strategic objectives as management develops detailed long- and short-range plans for the coming year and longer planning horizons used by the company. Operational level managers identify the best mix of resources that will be used to accomplish the objectives, submit their proposals for approval, and implement the approved programs.

To accomplish the fundamental strategic objective of meeting all the service demands of its electricity consumers, Pinnacle West's regulated subsidiary, Arizona Public Service (APS), implemented a growth strategy by adding new state-of-the art, gas-fired, combined-cycle power generating plants. To meet its objective of continuing to improve the value it provides its customers, Pinnacle West continued its series of electricity price reductions even as it added the new generating capacity.

STRATEGIC OPERATIONS MANAGEMENT

To put the planning process into the necessary operational frame, the strategic planning process is sometimes referred to as long-range planning. Strategic management includes the set of decisions and actions that result in the formulation and implementation of plans designed to achieve a company's objectives (Pearce and Robinson 1994). Broadly, the process involves identifying preferred objectives for the organization, developing strategies for meeting those objectives, and selecting a mix of resources to use in a system of related tasks (tactics). The first two tasks are closely related: the first says what the company does; the second says what the organization is.

The organization's objectives are typically spelled out in its *mission statement*. Mission statements include broad statements about the firm's purpose, philosophy, and goals. The mission statement is a written description of the company's philosophy. It may include the products or services offered by the organization, what market it serves, information about the belief system or position on ethical behaviors, and its treatment of employees. A primary purpose of the mission statement is to inform and guide organization employees, but it can also inform customers and stakeholders of its operating philosophy.

The last task is developing an organization profile that identifies its internal conditions and capabilities. Strategic management refers to this task as an analysis of the organization's *strengths and weaknesses*. A brief summary statement of the organization profile appears in every investor-owned utility's Form 10-K annual financial report required by the U.S. Securities and Exchange Commission Act of 1934.

A number of important differences have long existed between strategic management carried out in publicly owned utilities and investor-owned utilities, although changes underway now in public management are narrowing these differences. The budget process still drives much public agency planning; whereas, plans and objectives drive budgeting in investor-owned utilities. Eadie made note of this difference in the following statement:

> Formal long-range planning in the public sector has little in common with strategic planning. Rather than looking outward and focusing on organizational change, long-range planning has tended to be an extension of the annual operational planning process. This is to say that it starts on the inside and focuses on the projection of current activities into the future, usually for some arbitrary period, say, five years. (Eadie 1983: 447)

The experience of Public Utility District No. 1 of Chelan County, Washington, is an example of the long-range planning process in a publicly owned, diversified utility organization. The utility carries out electricity generation, transmission, and distribution operations, and water and wastewater operations. Rates charged for water and wastewater services were not bringing in sufficient revenue to cover operating costs. Because it is publicly owned, the utility is exempt from state public utility commission regulations on rates. However, it elected to hold a series of public hearings before initiating rate changes. The utility raised water and wastewater rates an average of 15 percent in 2001. The rate increase was part of a long-range plan developed after the series of public meetings.

Annual Objectives, Short-Term Strategies, and Budgets

In the past—other than responding to disasters—little if anything took place quickly in utilities. Downed power lines, broken water mains, overloaded sanitary treatment facilities, and similar disaster scenarios required rapid responses. On the other hand, most production and transmission components of utility systems take several years or longer to construct. Changes and upgrades made to installed distribution systems are long-term projects. It can often take months if not years for regulated segments of the industry to bring about changes in their pricing structure, proposed acquisitions, mergers, and other restructuring moves. As a result, preparing annual functional plans and budgets for utilities is often a multi-year process rather than one year at a time. An example of the complexity of converting long-range plans into annual tactical plans can be seen in the federal requirement for energy utilities to develop integrated resource planning.

A large portion of utility demand is cyclical and weather sensitive. Cash requirements for purchasing additional product supplies reflect these cyclical variations in demand. As a result, short-term, tactical plans and subsequent budgets for utilities take these seasonal variations into consideration. For example, in fiscal year 2002, nearly three-fourths of total annual consumer demand for gas from WGL Holdings, the Washington, DC natural gas distributor, occurred in the first and second quarters. To meet this demand, the firm's cash requirements peak in the fall and winter months, when accounts receivable, revenues, and storage gas inventories are at their highest peaks. After the winter heating season, many of those assets are converted to cash, which the company uses to pay down short-term debt and acquire storage gas for the next heating season. Gas is purchased from separate gas producers and stored in facilities owned by interstate pipelines. Managing supply purchase and demand distribution requires quarterly plans and budgets, in addition to the annual business plan and long-term strategic plan.

Implementing the Strategic Choices

Implementing planned activities may be the most difficult of all tasks in the strategic management process. Implementing requires the participation of the entire management team, not just a few senior managers (Thompson and Strickland 2003). Each manager must develop answers to such questions as: What needs to be done in my department or unit to implement the strategic plan? What do we need to do to make sure that our objectives are accomplished? In what ways must I coordinate our activities with those of other departments or units? What parts of my unit's activities are open to regular accomplishment measurement? What new measurement tools do we need to devise? What contingency actions should we take if we exceed or fail to reach performance targets? What needs to be done now, and what can be done later? How much of the supervisory role can be delegated?

For execution of the unit's planned tasks to proceed in an effective and efficient manner, managers should look upon program implementation as a *systematic process*. Thomas and Strickland identified eight key implementation tasks that must be completed by management regardless of the type or size of organization. The eight steps include:

1. Begin by making sure the organization is capable of carrying out the tasks necessary to meet the strategic objectives.
2. Build an activity-based budget that ensures the resources needed to carry out those tasks are available when and where they are needed.
3. Establish appropriate operational policies and procedures.
4. Include provisions for continuous improvement.
5. Install the support systems necessary to ensure that operational personnel are able to carry out their daily tasks.
6. Develop a reward and incentive system tied to performance.
7. Build and reinforce a supportive work environment and organizational culture.
8. Display the leadership needed to keep the work team moving unwaveringly toward accomplishment of corporate, group, and individual objectives, while continuing to support and improve operational procedures.

Controlling the Strategic Management Process

The goal of the control process is to make sure that operational progress meets or exceeds projected goals. There are two parts to this portion of the strategic process: establishing targets and monitoring progress. Managers establish targets during the objectives stage of the planning process. Monitoring progress is done in many ways. However, today a number of organizations are using formal evaluation procedures for this purpose. Evaluation has been defined as the "systematic assessment of the operation and/or outcomes of a program or policy, compared to a set of explicit or implicit standards, as a means of contributing to the improvement of the program or policy" (Weiss 1998: 4).

Evaluating the success of a program, policy, or activity involves measuring the *outcomes* resulting from implementation. The evaluator must measure the end results of the program in terms of its contribution to achieving goals and objectives. Other terms for results include *contribution, effects, impacts, net results,* and so on. During the evaluation the manager must ask such questions as: What are the results of our unit's program or activity? Are our operational programs achieving the objectives that we planned to accomplish? Did any wanted or unwanted side effects occur because of our work, and if so, what impact did they have on other parts of the organization as a whole? In terms of the overall strategic direction of the organization, what are the short- and/or long-term outcomes of our contribution?

Integrated Resource Planning (IRP)

The Energy Policy Act of 1992 (EPAct) introduced a requirement for all electric utilities to begin a planning process for integrating new generating capacity, power purchases, energy conservation and efficiency, cogeneration and service area heating and cooling applications, and renewable energy resources. The process is called *Integrated Resource Planning* (IRP); the law became effective on May 1, 2000. In many ways, this new IRP planning process mirrored many of the features of traditional strategic planning.

The goal of the IRP planning process is to ensure that adequate and reliable service is provided to the utilities' customers at the lowest system cost. This comprehensive planning process forces the utilities to consider necessary features as diversity, reliability, dispatch ability, and other risk factors that might affect system operation. Furthermore, utilities must take into account their ability to verify energy savings that they can gain through energy conservation and efficiency, together with the projected durability of the savings over time. According to the Western Energy Services five-state transmission grid organization, the IRP process treats demand and supply resources on a consistent and integrated process.

Integrated resource planning is the government's attempt at introducing common planning processes and procedures into the operations of long-term, firm power customers of the grid. Power customers are distributors of electricity to residential, commercial, and industrial customers. IRPs must consider electrical energy resource needs and may consider, as an option, water, natural gas, and other energy resources as well. All purchasers of power supplied by the grid must satisfy the following EPAct requirements in their IRP plans:

- Provide an identification and comparison of all practical energy efficiency and energy supply resource options.
- Develop an action plan (a tactical plan) covering a minimum period of five years, describing specific actions the firm will take to implement its IRP.

- Designate least-cost options available to the customer firm.
- Describe the efforts taken to minimize adverse environmental effects of new resource acquisitions.
- Schedule public hearings to provide the opportunity for public participation in the preparation and development of the IRP.
- Conduct and include in the plan load forecasts.
- Come up with methods for measuring and validating predicted performance to determine whether objectives are being met.

Integrated Resource Action Plans and Measurements

Every IRP must include a comprehensive body of action plans and an annual progress report. Action plans are the short-term, tactical plans discussed in the section of strategic planning. Action plans include the time period covered by the plan. When the time period expires, the IRP must be revised and resubmitted. The action plan must include: (1) the actions the customer proposes to take to accomplish the goals it includes in the IRP; (2) periodic measurement dates (milestones) for evaluating actions as they are implemented; and (3) the estimated energy and capacity benefits expected to accrue from each action planned.

Related to action plan milestones is the requirement for identifying and briefly describing the customer's proposed measurement strategies. Progress in implementing the resource options adopted by the customers must be measured regularly to determine whether the objectives of IRP are being met.

EXAMPLES OF UTILITY STRATEGIC PLANS

The City of Riverside, California provides water, wastewater, solid waste and electric power services to its slightly more than 300,000 residents. Riverside is situated approximately 60 miles east of Los Angeles and is included as part of the greater Los Angeles Metropolitan statistical area. The utility department posted an abridged version of its strategic plan in 2015. The abridgment follows the traditional strategic planning structure. As spelled out in the strategic plan, the department's mission, vision and core values were:

Mission: The City of Riverside Public Utilities Department is committed to the highest quality water and electric services at the lowest possible rates to benefit the community.

Our Ten-Year Vision: Our customers will recognize Riverside Public Utilities as a unique community asset with a global reputation for innovation, sustainability and an enhanced quality of life.

Core Values: The department's plan listed these core values: Safety, Honesty and Integrity, Teamwork, Professionalism, Quality Service, Creativity and Innovation, Inclusiveness and Mutual Respect, Community Involvement, and Environmental Stewardship.

Department Goals and Objectives

The plan identified operational and managerial goals and objectives for three periods: short-term (three years), medium-term (10 years), and long-term (strategic goals for period beyond ten years):

Three-Year Goals: Short-term goals are:

- Contribute to the City of Riverside's economic development while preserving RPU's financial strength.
- Maximize the use of technology to improve utility operations.
- Impact positively legislation and regulations at all levels of government.
- Develop and implement electric and water resource plans.
- Create and implement a workforce development plan.

Ten-Year Goals: Long-term goals are:

- Employ state-of-the-art technology to maximize reliability and customer service.
- Foster economic development and job growth in the City of Riverside.
- Communicate effectively the accomplishments, challenges and opportunities for the full utilization of our electric and water resources.
- Develop fully our low-cost, sustainable, reliable electric and water resources.
- Enhance the effective and efficient operation of all areas of the utility.

Specific Area Long-Range Plans to Implement Mission Statement: Long-range plans are:

- Workforce Development Plan
- Long Range Space Plan
- Renewable Portfolio Standard Power Implementation Plan
- Integrated Power Resources Plan
- Riverside Transmission Reliability Project
- Electric Distribution System Master Plan & Infrastructure Roadmap
- Water Infrastructure Replacement Plan & Infrastructure Roadmap

- Recycled Water Plan
- Integrated Water Management Plan
- Conservation/Efficiency Plan
- Strategic Technology Plan
- Ten Year Financial Pro-forma.

Lee's Summit, Missouri Water Department Strategic Plan

Lee's Summit, a town of 91,000 on the western border of Missouri, issued its strategic plan for the water utilities department in 2011. The planning process was initiated as a consequence of the utility's difficulties in responding to the region's changing economic climate, and a perception that the utility's values did not reflect those of its customers. The utility engaged a citizens' advisory group and professional consultants to work with the staff in developing the plan. The process began with a survey that covered 60 separate measurements. The assessment revealed that the utility's highest priorities for improvements were for financial responsibility and infrastructure renewal. Other priorities included a need for better customer relations and understanding of the challenges faced by the utility, and a need to take steps to assure the sustainability of the utility.

Harstene Pointe Water and Sewer District Capital Improvement Plan

Harstene Pointe Water and Sewer District (HPWSD) is an independent water and wastewater district that provides services in a gated community with both weekend and holiday recreational visitors and permanent residents. Most of the permanent residents are retirees. Established in 1968, the community is on an island in Puget Sound and is approximately 60 miles from Seattle, the largest city in the State of Washington and about 35 miles from Tacoma, the state's third largest city. The water and wastewater treatment operation was managed by the county's utility department until 2009. Community residents took control of the facility when it was determined the county's devotion to operations managing and scheduling necessary repairs and upgrades were not receiving the attention they needed. Under the county operation, the rate for combined water and sewer services were too low to meet repairs and replacement of aging infrastructure. The small utility provides service to 498 residential connections and the community club house.

The district employs one full-time professional manager, a part-time office manager and a part-time certified wastewater treatment facility operator. A three-person board of commissioners of residents each elected for a staggered six-year term provides operations oversight. As part of the annual budgeting process, the commission and manager upgrade a

BOX 15.5 SMALL WATER AND SEWER DISTRICT SIX-YEAR CAPITAL IMPROVEMENT PLAN, 2015–2021

No.	Item	Amount	Status
	2015 Projects		
1.	WWTP Jet pumps refurbished	$13,053.72	Completed
2.	DW filtration upgrade	$25,000.00	Financed
3.	WWTP sludge pump upgrade Two new pumps $69,000 Engineering the upgrade $32,000	$101,000.00	In progress
4.	Replace gaseous Cl2 system System and installation $7,000 Engineering $5,000	$12,000.00	In progress
5.	Inflow and infiltration abatement	$14,000.00	In progress
	2015 Total (cash)	**$140,053.72**	
	2015 Total (including work financed)	**$165,053.72**	
	2016 Projects		
1.	DW filtration upgrade Completes project, closes out loan	$570,000.00	Financed
2.	Phase 3 WWT SCADA/ Lift telemetry upgrade Coincides with DW telemetry and SCADA	$20,000.00	
3.	DW reservoir mixer	$13,000.00	
4.	DW reservoir Cathodic protection	$10,000.00	
5.	Booster pump generator (installation)	$30,000.00	
6.	Well 2 inspection, pump test; possible rehabilitation	$25,000.00	
7.	Well 3 inspection and pump test	$10,000.00	
8.	Inflow and infiltration abatement	$16,000.00	
	2016 Total (cash)	**$124,000.00**	
	2016 Total (including work financed)	**$694,000.00**	
	2017 Projects		

1.	Well 1 replacement planning and DOH approvals	$10,000.00
2.	Inflow and infiltration abatement Capital Improvement budget contribution	$18,000.00
3.	Paint and repair reservoir	$150,000.00
	2017 Total (cash)	**$178,000.00**
	2018 Projects	
1.	Well 1 replacement start (carry through 2019)	$100,000.00
2.	Inflow and infiltration abatement Capital Improvement budget contribution	$20,000.00
	2018 Total (cash)	**$120,000.00**
	2019 Projects	
1.	Well 1 replacement (continued)	$150,000.00
2.	Inflow and infiltration abatement Capital Improvement budget contribution	$22,000.00
	2019 Total (cash)	**$172,000.00**
	2020 Projects	
1.	Inflow and infiltration abatement Capital Improvement budget contribution	$24,000.00
	2020 Total (cash)	**$24,000.00**
	2021 Projects	
	Inflow and infiltration abatement Capital Improvement budget contribution	$26,000.00
	2020 Total (cash)	**$26,000.00**

Notes: WWTP: Waste Water Treatment Plant.
DW: Drinking Water.
DOH: Department of Health.
SCADA: Supervisory Control and Data Acquisition system.

new strategic plan that includes a six-year capital improvement plan. The 2015–2021 plan is included in Box 15.5.

SUMMARY

Planning in public utilities is carried on at two separate but related levels and for different purposes. The highest level of planning is *strategic planning*. The second major type of planning is referred to either as *operational* or *tactical planning*. The strategic plan is typically the responsibility of senior management; tactical plans are developed and implemented at the operational level.

The strategic planning process involves identifying objectives for the organization, developing strategies for meeting those objectives, and selecting a mix of resources to use in a system of related tasks (tactics). The first two tasks are closely related: the first says what the company does; the second says what the organization is. The organization's objectives are typically spelled out in its *mission statement*. Mission statements include broad statements about the firm's purpose, philosophy, and goals. The mission statement is a written description of the company's philosophy.

The organization profile identifies its internal conditions and capabilities. Strategic management refers to this task as an analysis of the organization's *strengths and weaknesses*. A brief summary statement of the organization profile appears in every investor-owned utility's Form 10-K annual financial report required by the U.S. Securities and Exchange Commission Act of 1934.

A number of important differences have long existed between strategic management carried out in publicly owned utilities and investor-owned utilities, although changes underway now in public management are narrowing these differences. The budget process still drives much public agency planning; whereas, plans and objectives drive budgeting in investor-owned utilities.

A number of external factors impact the operations of a utility. Among the most important are (1) economic conditions, (2) political trends and the legal constraints that follow political actions, (3) shifts in social trends, (4) changes in the physical environment, and (5) technological innovation.

A utility's chief resources are people, money, and facilities—all of which are limited in both public and private utilities. Determining the best use of these resources is a management function. Managers must also develop priorities for their use, and provide a system for dealing with the competitive conflicts that often occur during the operational planning phase of developing the organization's strategy. Another important resource consists of the critical skills that are needed to safely, effectively, and efficiently carry out utility services.

Identification of an overall strategy for the utility occurs during the analysis phase of the strategic planning process. Implementing planned activities is possibly the most difficult of all tasks in the strategic management process. Implementing requires the participation of the entire management team, not just a few senior managers.

The control process is designed to make sure that operational progress meets or exceeds projected goals. There are two parts to this process: establishing targets and monitoring progress. Managers establish targets during the objectives stage of the planning process. Monitoring progress is done in many ways. However, today a number of organizations are using formal evaluation procedures for this purpose.

The Energy Policy Act of 1992 (EPAct) introduced a requirement for utilities to begin planning for integrating new generating capacity, power purchases, energy conservation and efficiency, cogeneration and service area heating and cooling applications, and renewable energy resources. The process is called *Integrated Resource Planning* (IRP); the law became effective on May 1, 2000. Every IRP must include action plans, environmental impact evaluations, and progress measurement schemes.

ADDITIONAL READING

Balzer, Berd and Christian Schorn (2015), *Asset Management for Infrastructure Systems: Energy and Water*. New York: Springer.

Bryson, John M. (2011), *Strategic Planning for Public and Nonprofit Organizations* (4th edn). New York: Wiley.

Levitt, Joel D. (2013), *Facilities Management: Managing Maintenance for Buildings and Facilities*. NEW York: Momentum Press.

Mullen, Samuel (2011), *Emergency Planning for Utilities* (2nd edn). Boca Raton, FL: CRC Press.

Sioshansi, Fereidoon P. (ed.) (2014), *Distributed Generation and its Implications for the Utility Industry*. Oxford, UK: Academic Press.

Uddin, Waheed, W. Ronald Hudson and Ralph Haass (2013), *Public Infrastructure Asset Management* (2nd edn). New York: McGraw-Hill.

16. Managing the public utility workforce

Utility industry leaders are nearly unanimous in agreeing that a number of external forces are becoming increasingly pressing as managers and administers work to shape the public utility workforce. These old problems, in turn, are only going to become more pressing over the next decade or longer. The consensus is that it will be a long time before the human resources management problem is resolved. The fundamental problem is the difficulty of simply finding enough workers with the necessary skills to replace the many aging "baby boom" workers entering retirement. In addition, there is no doubt that the United States workforce is changing from a majority of white males—the traditional utility workforce—to becoming a majority of minority males and females of all ethnic persuasions. Utility industry observers have referred to this trend as a "mega trend" in the utility industry, and a time when utilities will soon be unable to acquire workers with the technical skills needed just to maintain the technology that has already been installed (Kitterman and Dugan 2006).

The nature of the industry itself adds to the difficulty of identifying and employing the best and the brightest of today's college and university graduates. Deregulation, reorganization, privatization, bankruptcy, and system failure are some operational forces affecting the industry that bring prospective employees to question whether they should commit to a utility career. In addition, many utilities find themselves forced to deal with infrastructure that is aging and, in some cases, crumbling. Other forces that are re-shaping the industry include federal mandates to make expensive investments in environmental protection. Scandal and unethical behavior are additional themes seen today in many descriptions of the utility industry. This chapter will look at some of these themes in the context of their impact on human resources management in investor-owned and publicly owned gas, electricity, and water utilities.

As early as the late 1990s the editors of *Public Utilities Fortnightly* asked five human resources vice presidents to discuss a variety of concerns that were expected to have a major impact on utility operations during the first decades of the new century. The five companies ranged in size from less than 5,000 workers to more than 32,000 employees. All of the organizations had recently undergone downsizing that had reduced employment by as much as 20 percent. Topics discussed included retraining, going global, hiring specialists, tough positions to fill, elastic rosters, worker safety, union shops, the hiring boom and hiring bust, and what lies ahead for utilities?

Although surveyed individually, the responses of the HR managers were remarkably similar. All were finding it difficult to fill staff needs in two areas: information systems and trading and risk management. Because the firms were facing stiff competition, the companies found themselves forced to train employees in ways to function in a competitive environment rather than the former, regulated monopoly way of doing business. Some utilities established training programs to enhance worker skills in both sectors of the business: regulated and competitive. Almost all of the HR managers acknowledged the continuing role of labor unions in their future employee mix.

The activities of the human resources department of the Kissimmee, Florida, electric utility (KEU) is an example of the human resources function in small municipally owned utilities. KEU, with 58,000 customers in Kissimmee and surrounding areas, is the sixth largest utility in Florida. The HR department manages the recruiting, staffing, safety, and communications activities. The department manages pensions, healthcare, and unemployment compensation programs, and is responsible for all insurance claims against the utility. Until recently, the risk management function was also housed in the HR department, but has subsequently been transferred to the finance office (Gent 2004).

EMPLOYMENT IN THE UTILITIES INDUSTRIES

The U.S. Labor Department's bureau of labor Statistics publishes annual upgrades of employment characteristics of the North American Industry Classification System (NAICS), with a census taken every five years. Statistics of the electric and natural gas industries and the water industries are group into a single group, the utilities services sector. Solid and hazardous waste employment statistics are included in a single category; public transit and rail transportation are separate subsectors of a large transportation and warehousing group. Table 16.1 displays employment trend data for employment in all major sectors of the U.S. economy. Data for all occupations in the utilities sector for 2004, 2014 and projections for 2024 are included. Data for employment in the state and local government sector is also included for comparison purposes. The salient point to discern from these data is that employment in the sector is expected to

Table 16.1   *Employment in the utilities and government sectors 2004–2024 (thousands)*

Sector	2004	2014	2014	2004–2014 Change	2014–2024 Change
Utilities sector	563.8	555.0	505.1	−10.8	−47.9
State and local government	18,891.3	19,134.0	19,890.1	242.7	756.1

Source: Bureau of Labor Statistics (BLS 2015).

decline substantially during the periods while employment in state and local government is projected to increase over the same period.

In the North American Industry Classification System (NAICS), data on employment in the utilities sector are compiled and published in three sections: (1) utilities services, (2) waste removal and mitigation, and (3) public transportation. Under the utility services category, utility data are included for electric power, natural gas, steam supply, water supply, and sewage removal. Specific activities in the utility services provided vary by utility: electric power includes generation, transmission, and distribution; natural gas includes distribution; steam supply includes provision and/or distribution; water supply includes treatment and distribution; and sewage removal includes collection, treatment, and disposal of waste through sewer systems and sewage treatment facilities. Data for major employment categories for each of the three sectors are shown in Tables 16.2, 16.3 and 16.4.

Total employment for the utilities and government sectors in 2015 is shown in Table 16.1, and for the utilities services sector in Table 16.2. The labor union representation of the workforce in the electric, natural gas, water and wastewater utility segments as group has declined each year from the 26.9 percent of the total sector workforce in 2012 to 22.3 percent of the workforce in 2015. The percentages of total number of workers in the sector being represented by labor unions has also declined each year, from 25.7 percent of the workforce in 2011 to 23.7 percent in 2014. Since 2000, the peak for union membership was 28.4 percent in 2004 and 2007. Peak shares of the workforce represented by unions were 30.1 percent in 2004 and 30.3 percent in 2010.

Solid and hazardous waste utilities are included in the Waste Management and Remediation sector (NAICS subsector 562). Industries in this group include public and private establishments engaged in the collection, treatment, and disposal of waste materials. This includes establishments

Table 16.2   Employment in the utility services sector by selected occupation

Occupation	Workers employed in 2015
All employees in the sector	569,000
Control and valve installers, repairers	16,550
Electrical engineers	18,740
Power line installers and repairers	58,840
First-line supervisors and managers	15,640
Meter readers	13,820

Source: BLS (2015).

Table 16.3   Employment in the solid waste sector by selected occupation

Occupation	Workers employed in 2015
All employees in the sector	403,400
Hazardous materials removal workers	32,640
Laborers and freight, stock, material movers	24,170
Refuse and recyclable material collectors	65,940
Sewer pipe cleaners and septic tank servicers	13,480
Truck drivers, heavy and tractor-trailer	51,240

Source: BLS (2015).

engaged in local hauling of waste materials; operating materials recovery facilities (that is, those that sort recyclable materials from the trash stream); providing remediation services. Remediation services include workers engaged in the cleanup of contaminated buildings, mine sites, soil, or ground water. The sector also includes septic pumping and other miscellaneous waste management services. There are three industry groups within the subsector that separate these activities into waste collection, waste treatment and disposal, and remediation and other waste management. The number of workers employed in the surface and rail transportation groups are shown in Table 16.4.

Public transit employment statistics are included in the transportation and warehousing sector (NAICS 48–49). This sector includes industries providing transportation of passengers and cargo, warehousing and storage for goods, scenic and sightseeing transportation, and support activities related to modes of transportation. Establishments in these

Table 16.4   *Employment in road transportation and rail sectors by selected occupations*

Sector and Occupation	Workers employed in 2014
Road Transportation	
All occupations in category	471,100
Mechanics and diesel engine specialists	12,510
Transit and intercity bus drivers	196,520
Dispatchers and related	17,620
Taxi drivers and chauffeurs	78,910
Rail Transportation (passenger and freight)	
All occupations in category	235,500
Locomotive engineers	37,230
Rail car repairers	12,150
Signal and switch operators	19,210
Conductors and yard workers	39,460

Source: BLS (2015).

industries use transportation equipment or transportation related facilities as a productive asset. The type of equipment depends on the mode of transportation. The modes of transportation are air, rail, water, road, and pipeline. Public transit and ground transportation data are included in sector 485, transit and ground passenger transportation subsector; rail transportation data are included in the rail transportation subsector (NAICS 482), and includes workers in the rail transportation of passengers and/or cargo using railroad rolling stock.

The railroads in this subsector primarily either operate on networks, with physical facilities, labor force, and equipment spread over an extensive geographic area, or operate over a short distance on a local rail line. Organizations in this subsector include a variety of passenger transportation activities, such as urban transit systems; chartered bus, school bus, and interurban bus transportation; and taxis. Industries in the rail transportation subsector provide rail transportation of passengers and/or cargo using railroad rolling stock. The bulk of this section is freight carried by the 106 private sector railroads and just two state-owned lines. Because some railroads carry large numbers of commuters, employment statistics for the sector are included in the table.

REPLACING THE SHRINKING WORKFORCE

In 2008, the American Water Works Association Research Foundation and the U.S. Environmental Protection Agency published results of a contractor-produced 228-page booklet on workforce planning for water utilities, in which they described what they called "a perfect storm in today's utility workforce" and outlined a series of recommendations for aiding utilities in resolving their workforce problems They then went on to explain the extent of the workforce problem facing utilities:

> In addition to the mass exodus of utility employees that is anticipated due to retirement in the next 10 [to 15] years, there is increasing diversity in the current workforce, fewer United States college graduates earning science or engineering degrees and values differences in younger generations of employees entering the labor market. Utilities are caught in the center of the storm. A shift in approach to operations is required. Utilities must move away from the 'lean operations' mentality that has been forced upon them in recent years—at least in terms of not filling vacancies—and develop a strategic approach to ensure the skills needed to complete the work of the organization are on board. (AWWA and EPA 2008: xix)

Nearly half of the utilities participating in a study by the American Public Power Association (APPA) reported that from 15 to 50 percent of their workforce will become eligible for retirement during the first and second decades of the twenty-first century. Shortages were expected to occur in a wide range of key positions, but the greatest challenge would be in finding replacements for management, administration, and technical positions. Moreover, fewer engineering graduates are preparing themselves to enter the utility industry. The number of college and university degrees in power engineering awarded each year has declined from the more than 2,000 annually in the 1980s to less than 500 per year now.

The loss of critical knowledge will be most painful for utilities. Staff reductions and eliminating training during cost-cutting initiatives are also contributing to the "brain drain" faced by many utilities. Cost-containment and shrinking workforce programs in the 1990s have exacerbated the problems expected from the many technical and managerial workers retiring in the near future. A big part of cost containment was reductions in or, in some cases, the elimination of working training and management development programs.

The following programs designed to deal with the expected worker shortages were recommended by the APPA:

● Track workforce statistics (mean age, age group distribution, years of service, etc.).

- Project retirements and identify likely talent shortages.
- Plan the utility's future workforce, in light of changing organization, market, and technical needs.
- Inform internal and external company stakeholders about the issue and potential impact.
- Collect and record existing staff knowledge and facilitate knowledge transfer from older employees to their replacements.
- Recruit, develop, and retain younger workers; enhance leadership and critical skill-development programs.
- Where appropriate, rehire selected retirees.
- Slow the departure of older workers.
- Develop and maintain a workplace culture that promotes mutual respect among all workers.

The experience of Chelan County PUD in Wenatchee, Washington, is representative of the human resources challenges faced by public utilities. The district estimated that over most of the first decade of the twenty-first century it would lose more than 10 percent of its workforce every year. Moreover, it expected to have difficulty in finding replacements for retiring skilled crafts and management personnel. In order to deal with the missing management challenge, the utility developed a formal succession program it calls "Leadership from within." The program was designed and is administered by the organizational development manager and the human resources management unit.

The district identified four strategic factors which it considers critical to its future success: customer service, operational excellence, environmental stewardship, and community responsiveness. The succession program covers developing eight basic competencies associated with the four success factors. It includes a compensation program that rewards individuals for what it terms value-added skills, leadership ability, and job performance. Programs function at four organization levels: the bargaining unit, the professional/technical unit, supervisors, and directors.

The High Cost of Retirements

Human resource departments are responsible for managing a variety of employee benefit plans. Among the most costly of these benefit programs is the retirement fund. Retirement plans for investor-owned utilities are often more complex than plans managed for employees in publicly owned utilities. This is because investor-owned utilities typically include stock purchase options in the mix of retirement benefits. Retirement benefits for employees in publicly owned utilities are often included in the larger pool of worker benefits for municipal, county, or state employees. Two investor-owned plans are discussed below: Calpine Corporation of San Jose, California, and Artesian Resources Corporation of Newark, Delaware. The retirement plan system of the Tacoma, Washington, municipally owned utility is also described.

The retirement benefits plan of the international mixed-product utility firm *Calpine Corporation* is typical of programs found in large utilities. Three investment plans were described in their annual report: a contribution savings plan, an employee stock purchase plan, and a stock incentive plan. The contribution savings plan, which is based on Section 401 (a) and 501 (a) of the Internal Revenue Code, includes deferred salary deductions, after-tax employee contributions, and profit sharing contributions of up to 4 percent of employees' salaries. Employees qualify for participation immediately after being hired. Profit sharing contributions totaled more than $11.6 million annually.

The employee stock purchase plan allows eligible employees to purchase common stock at semi-annual intervals through periodic payroll deductions. Purchases of up to $25,000 per year may be made. The purchase price of the stock is 85 percent of the fair market value of the stock at either the date of the employee's entry date into the offering period, or the fair market value on the semi-annual purchase date. Calpine's stock incentive provides options to purchase stock at specified prices. Options to purchase stock are vested after four years with the firm and expire after ten years.

Artesian Resources Corporation is a non-operating holding company with four wholly-owned subsidiary companies and a one-third interest in a wastewater services marketing company. Its most important subsidiary is Artesian Water, the largest public water utility in Delaware. The regulated firm serves something like 68,000 metered customers. The human resources department manages three employee retirement benefit plans: a 401(k) salary reduction plan, a postretirement benefit plan, and a supplemental pension plan. The 401(k) plan covers all employees. Artesian Resources contributes 2 percent of eligible salaries and wages and matches employee contributions up to 6 percent of gross pay at a rate of 50 percent. The company's annual report noted that additional contributions of up to 3 percent of eligible salaries and wages may be made when circumstances permit.

Artesian Resources' postretirement benefit plan provides medical and life insurance benefits to some retired employees. Accounting standards (No. 106) require the firm to accrue the expected cost of providing the benefit while the workers are employed. Artesian's supplemental pension plan provides additional retirement benefits to full-time employees hired before April 1994. The plan was established to help employees save for future retiree medical costs. Artesian Water contributes from 2 percent to 6 percent of the employee's salaries and wages, based on years of service. A second version of the plan was developed for employees over the age of 50 when the plan began in 1994.

The city of Tacoma, Washington, operates a public utilities department with three separate components: Tacoma Power, Tacoma Water, and Tacoma Rail. Employees of the power and water utilities are covered by the Tacoma Employees' Retirement System, which is a system funded and managed by the city for all employees. Covered employees are required to contribute 6.44 percent of their gross wages to the system, with the utility employer contributing an additional 7.56 percent, for a total of 14 percent of gross wages. The combined sums are invested in equity securities, fixed income securities, real estate, and short-term investments. Tacoma Utilities contributed $11.6 million to the plan, with employees contributing $9.8 million.

CHANGES IN HUMAN RESOURCES MANAGEMENT

The human resources activities of many publicly owned utilities operate under civil service system, or merit system, rules. However, a number of state and municipal utilities have participated in a broadly based movement for reform of the traditional merit system. If they continue, these reforms are most likely to fall into one of three different categories: (1) reforms designed to reduce the size and scope of the civil service by making it easier for government agencies to terminate workers, while also doing away with certain entitlement aspects of civil service; (2) reforms that promise to establish greater flexibility within the existing civil service system by delegating authority for some personnel functions to agencies and managers, cutting personnel regulations, and setting incentives for greater performance—while not doing away with core merit system principles; and (3) reforms that abolish civil service entirely. The underlying goal of these reforms is establishing a plan for improving government performance by modernizing human resources management practices and initiating innovative personnel techniques.

The changes taking place in government employment—including employment in publicly owned utilities—are resulting in an entirely new way of performing the personnel services that have evolved over the last hundred years. The authors of a four-year, national study described the changes in human relations systems that were underway or being considered early in the new century as if a paradigm shift was taking place.

Governments appeared to be replacing the bureaucratic paradigm that once dominated personnel decisions with a new approach that emphasized service, front-line workers, efficiency, and results. As work on this edition was underway little new information about the change was available.

Some of the major changes in human resources management that have occurred in publicly owned utilities are (1) the adoption of workforce planning, (2) decentralized selection processes, and (3) simplified and more flexible worker classification systems. Changing the classification system includes reducing the numbers of job classifications (a process called *broad banding*) and new approaches to performance evaluation. The new performance evaluation systems require employees and managers to collaborate on setting performance targets which are direct reflections of agency objectives.

The two chief tasks in the labor relations process are administering existing contracts and negotiating new contracts. The administration of ongoing contracts, including the handling of grievance procedures, is typically a responsibility of the human resource department. In small utilities, contract provisions may be negotiated by the managing director, a member of the legal staff, or some other management staff person. In larger utilities, new-contract negotiations and renegotiations of old contracts are often led by a vice president in charge of industrial relations. However, both small and large utilities may hire special consultants to carry out the collective bargaining task, thus refraining from creating unnecessary animosities as a result of negotiation breakdowns. Negotiators for the union may be either the business agent of the local union or a negotiator provided by the union's national headquarters.

Negotiating labor contracts in most municipal utilities takes place in the systematic collective bargaining process. The intent of the bargaining process has always been the amicable resolution of differences in the needs and desires of both sides. Resolution of the conflict is based upon an assessment of what will provide the greatest gain for all parties with a stake in the health and welfare of the utility. However, labor negotiations are not always held in an atmosphere of cordiality and mutual respect. Contract negotiations have often become acrimonious and counterproductive. Meetings may last 12 to 15 hours, and calm discussion may give way to acrimonious insults.

Few Problems in Utility Negotiations

Importantly for the health of the utility industry, adversarial contract negotiations appear to be the exception rather than the norm. A consensus is evolving that it is to everyone's advantage to reach an agreement before negotiations break down, and without such costly actions as strikes, lockouts, slowdowns, picketing, boycotting, and similar legal, but often-destructive, behaviors. The experience of WGL Holdings, Inc. is an example of how all stakeholders—employees, management, stockholders, and customers—benefit from non-confrontational contract negotiations.

WGL Holdings is a public utility holding company serving customers in the District of Columbia, Maryland, and Virginia. As of September 30, 2013, WGL had 1,416 employees comprising 1,297 utility and 119 non-utility employees (WGL 2013 Annual Report). Its regulated natural gas distribution subsidiary serves nearly 960,000 customers. The firm's unregulated affiliates sell natural gas, electricity, and energy-related products and services in competitive markets. WGL described the success as a product of the enterprise and efforts of its employees. Bonus opportunities related to customer service performance and safety standards are included in the labor contracts. Performance standards are also integrated with the incentive rate plans in each jurisdiction.

The Collective Bargaining Challenge

Many employees of public utilities are employed under union contracts. As a result, union–management relations are an important part of the utility management process, and one of the most problematic challenges facing utilities managers. Public utilities, whether regulated or unregulated, investor- or publicly owned, are expected to provide their products and services at reasonable rates.

The rate-making process may take place in open hearings, where every aspect of utility costs is open for inspection and subject to public question. At the same time, utilities are required to provide continuous service and to meet all reasonable demand for their product. If utility workers choose to engage in a prolonged strike, the ability of the utility to meet these legal requirements is severely curtailed. On the other hand, utility management may decide it is in the best interest of the utility and its customers to increase wages and benefits substantially in order to avoid a strike. Because of the monopolistic nature of the industry, utility rates of return must be maintained. Therefore, the rates customers pay for the service must be raised to pay for the labor cost increase—resulting in customer objections and resistance from regulatory commissions. Publicly owned utilities may not have to gain acquiescence of a regulatory agency, but must justify rate increases to their owner/customers, or management may find itself trying to avoid a voter revolt that includes but is not limited to, the recall of directors.

EMPLOYEES AND PRIVATIZATION

A major challenge facing human resource managers in municipal public utilities has been brought on by the current trend in shifting from municipal ownership and operation to privatization through partnerships with private firms. Nationally, more than 85 percent of all water utilities and 95 percent of all wastewater utilities are municipally owned. A growing number of these municipalities are privatizing their utility operations. Partnering with a private contractor may allow a municipality to reduce its costs and improve the quality of service. They are doing so because they cannot afford to fund needed expansion to meet demand growth and to pay for the improvements required by new regulatory laws demanding cleaner systems. The water utility industry has estimated that needed rebuilding and repair of water and wastewater systems in the U.S. will cost in excess of $300 billion.

Employees at many municipal utilities are government employees and enjoy all the protections and benefits, including the medical and retirement programs, of their fellow municipal workers. Many are members of strong, municipal-employee labor unions. What happens to these employees when operation of the system is given over to a private firm has been a major concern, both to the employees and their labor unions. An example is the City of Perth Amboy, New Jersey, which entered into a 20-year contract with Middlesex Water, a British utility management firm, to manage the city's water services. Ownership models of water systems in New Jersey are often varied, resulting in a the need for a wide variety of labor-management negation models. The complex system is described in the following report:

> Public community water supply (PCWS) systems may be owned by the municipality, a municipal utility authority, a regional agency or an investor-owned company such as NJ American Water or United Water New Jersey. Where either a municipality or municipal utilities authority owns the PCWS system, they may in turn contract out operations and maintenance of the system to a private firm. The distribution system may be owned by a different entity than the water supply source or water treatment plant. The source of the water may be controlled by the local PCWS system (e.g. Newark, Jersey City, Camden), or it may be in turn provided by a separate entity by contract. Regarding CSO municipalities, the two major sources of bulk water by contract are North Jersey District Water Supply Commission (NJDWSC; treated water) and New Jersey Water Supply Authority (NJWSA; untreated water), both of which were established by special State legislation and cannot by law operate distribution systems. (New Jersey Future 2015)

THE CHANGING ROLE OF HR

In both investor-owned and publicly owned utilities, the human resources function has undergone a dramatic shift of role and function. Changes in human resources management (HRM) in businesses and all levels of government have been shown to be equally effective and entirely applicable to all levels of the public utility industry. HRM is experiencing a near revolution in its operating practices. One of the reasons for this is the aging of the workforce. Task-oriented techniques implemented during the growth years after the Second World War are being abandoned, replaced by new, person-oriented approaches to the HRM function which is taking hold within the personnel profession. Persuasive control has had to give way to a more consultative role for in the HR office. It has become an important contributor to achieving the organization's strategic objectives, guided by organizational values, mission, and vision of the organization.

HR Changes in a Pennsylvania Utility

The vice president of PECO Energy, Inc., William Kaschub, used similar concepts to describe the redesign of the HR function then taking place at the Pennsylvania investor-owned electric utility. PECO Energy is part of the Exelon Corporation, which was formed in 2000 through the merger of PECO Energy of Philadelphia, and Unicom, the Chicago parent company of Commonwealth Edison, which serves the northern Illinois energy market. PECO remains an energy services company with 1.5 million electricity and 430,000 natural gas customers in southeastern Pennsylvania. Ten years earlier, PECO Energy's six business units were restructured in response to deregulation of the power industry, with mandated competition.

The HR unit, which alone remained unchanged, was determined to be in need of better, more cost-effective ways of meeting the needs of the reengineered divisions. The department was considered to be overstaffed and bogged down with myriad transactions for individual employees, who relied on the HR staff for services they could easily perform themselves with modern Information Technology. At the time, the HR department included a staff of 230 people, or one HR staff person for every 35 employees. In addition, the outdated grievance process required job supervisors to acquire HR approval before sanctioning employees, and the hiring process was badly in need of change.

The utility began a comprehensive, four-phase, employee-centered reorganization program that was designed to change the transactional focus to become a discussion group strategic senior consultants who coach and guide, but do not manage. The four phases include (1) visioning, (2) process design, (3) organizational design, and (4) implementation and planning. Rotating groups of 200 employees, representing every level of the firm, participated at each meeting. Eventually, nearly 800 employees were involved in the final shaping of the PECO human resources mission, vision, process, and organizational culture.

The transactional process was replaced with a computerized call center, which was expected to meet 80 percent of employees' information needs, which center on benefits updates, retirement plan information, and policy guidelines. The HR staff has been freed to serve strategically as consultants when great needs arise.

THE FUTURE OF THE HR FUNCTION

In a 1998 survey of 295 members of the International Personnel and Labor Relations Association (IPMA) and the section on personnel and labor relations (SPALR) of the American Society for Public Administration, respondents were asked to rate the importance of 80 personnel techniques and activities. They were then asked to project how important they believed those same activities would be in the future. Respondents reported little or no difference in the predicted importance of such activities as staffing, responding to agency and department heads, benefits administration, pay administration, and developing human resources management (HRM) policy. Activities that were considered to be of little importance in both periods included responding to requests from elected officials, processing grievances, engaging in collective bargaining, and administering labor contracts—an indication that labor union influence will continue its decades-long decline.

KBC Advanced Technologies, Inc. is an independent process engineering group serving utilities from offices in the United Kingdom, the United States, Singapore, Japan, and the Netherlands. Box 16.1 displays the company's enlightened approach to human resources management as spelled out in its annual report.

SUMMARY

The public utility industry consists of an eclectic mix of private and publicly owned, regulated and unregulated, very small and very large, local and global, competitive and monopolistic organizations serving different supply chain operators in different segments of a complex industry. Utility

---

BOX 16.1 THE HUMAN RESOURCES POLICIES OF KBC ADVANCED TECHNOLOGIES

The Group continues to place a high emphasis on attracting, retaining and developing employees to achieve the Group's business plan objectives. The Group pursues an active policy of employee involvement and development, including communication through staff meetings, written communications to all staff, internal newsletters and use of the Group's intranet. Employees are provided with information on matters affecting them as employees, on developments within the business and on the various factors affecting the Group's performance. Group policies and practices are continually reviewed and improved to meet the needs of employees and the firm.

The Group is committed to providing equality of opportunity for all employees and in particular ensures that fair selection and development procedures apply. The aim of the Group's policy is to ensure that no job applicant or employee receives less favorable treatment than any other on the grounds of age, sex, sexual orientation, disability, marital status, color, religion, race or ethnic origin.

The Group encourages the involvement of employees in the Group's success through a share option scheme, as well as a bonus scheme which emphasizes performance and delivery of business plan objectives. There is a formal reward and recognition program to encourage and reward outstanding employee and team performance on a quarterly basis. The program provides cash awards, which are separate and distinct from salary, and formally recognizes employees who make a specific, extraordinary and measurable contribution to the profitability, productivity or efficiency of the Group.

Source: KBC Advance Technologies (2002: 18).

---

workers run the gamut from ditch-diggers and custodial staff to nuclear engineers and highly paid chief executives. Some workers are under union contract; others are not. It is no wonder that little common ground can be found for establishing a best-practices model for human resources that can be applied across all utility operations. Human resources management involves a number of different tasks and roles. Among the most common of the tasks carried out by HR staff are: (1) locating, hiring and, when necessary, firing appropriate personnel; (2), developing and conducting management development and worker training programs; (3) constructing fair compensation plans; (4) determining appropriate motivational activities; and (5) counseling workers in times of crisis.

External forces are continuing to change the shape of the public utility workforce. This, in turn, is presenting a number of important challenges to the practice of human resources management. The United States workforce is changing from a majority of white males to a majority of minority males and white females—a change that one utility industry observer has referred to as the "biggest mega trend" in the utility industry, and a time when utilities will soon be unable to acquire workers with the technical skills needed just to maintain the technology that has already been installed. More important is the retirement of key personnel and the inability to find trained replacement staff.

Deregulation, reorganization, privatization, bankruptcy, and system failure are some operational forces affecting the industry that bring prospective employees to question whether they should commit to a utility career. Many utilities find themselves forced to deal with infrastructure that is aging and, in some cases, crumbling. Other forces re-shaping the industry include (1) federal mandates to invest in environmental protection, (2) corporate scandal, and (3) unethical behavior by senior and mid-level managers.

Five human resources vice presidents identified the following concerns that were expected to have a major impact on utility operations during the first decades of the new century: retraining, going global, hiring specialists, tough positions to fill, elastic rosters, worker protections, union shops, the hiring boom and hiring bust, and what lies ahead for utilities. The HR managers were finding it difficult to fill staff needs in two areas: information systems and trading and risk management. Because the firms were facing stiff competition, the companies also found themselves forced to train employees in ways to function in a competitive environment. Some utilities established training programs to enhance worker skills in both sectors of the business: regulated and competitive. Almost all of the HR managers acknowledged the continuing role of labor unions in their future employee mix.

Utilities participating in a 2003 study by the APPA reported that from 15 to 50 percent of their workforce will become eligible for retirement by 2006. Shortages will occur in a wide range of key positions, but the greatest challenge will occur in finding replacements for management, administration, and technical positions. Moreover, a smaller number of engineering graduates are preparing themselves to enter the utility industry.

Retirement plans for investor-owned utilities are often more complex than plans managed for employees in publicly owned utilities. This is because investor-owned utilities typically include stock purchase options in the mix of retirement benefits. Retirement benefits for employees in publicly owned utilities are often included in the larger pool of worker benefits for municipal, county, or state employees.

The human resources activities of many publicly owned utilities operate under civil service system, or merit system, rules. However, over the past decade, a number of state and municipal utilities have been wrapped up in a broadly based movement for reform of the traditional merit system.

Some of the major changes taking place in government owned utilities are the adoption of workforce planning, decentralized selection processes, and simplified and more flexible worker classification systems, including reductions in the numbers of job classifications, and new approaches to performance evaluation.

Many employees of public utilities are employed under union contracts. As a result, union–management relations are an important part of the utility management process, and one of the most problematic challenges facing utilities managers. The two chief tasks in the labor relations process are administering existing contracts and negotiating new contracts. The administration of ongoing contracts, including the handling of grievance procedures, is typically a responsibility of the human resource department.

Negotiating labor contracts takes place in the systematic process of *collective bargaining*. The intent of the bargaining process is, or should be, the amicable resolution of differences in the needs and desires of both sides. The collective-bargaining process takes place in a well-proven series of steps in which both sides participate. The process occurs in four distinct stages: (1) pre-planning, or preparing to meet, (2) meetings of both sides to present their demands, (3) reaching an agreement, and (4) voting and ratification of the contract.

ADDITIONAL READING

Ballaglio, Randy P. (2014), *Public Human Resource Management*. Thousand Oaks, CA: CQ Press.

Berman, Evan M., James S. Bowman, Jonathan P. West and Montgomery R. Van Wart (2012), *Human Resources in Public Service: Paradoxes, Processes, and Problems* (4th edn). Thousand Oaks, CA: Sage.

Gomez-Mejia, Louis R., David B. Balkin and Robert L. Cardy (2011), *Managing Human Resources* 7th edn). Upper Saddle River, NJ: Prentice Hall.

Lauer, William C. (ed.) (2001), *Excellence in Action: Water Utility Management in the 21st Century*. Denver, CO: American Water Works Association.

Pynes, Joan (2013), *Human Resources Management for Public and Nonprofit Organizations* (4th edn). San Francisco, CA: Jossey-Bass.

17. Public utility management ethics

Researchers investigating possible unethical activities of traders at the bankrupt energy trading company Enron, found a number of incriminating statements in the more than 2,600 hours of recorded conversations taped during the 2000 and 2001 energy crisis. The recordings indicated that company traders regularly over-priced customers during the power crisis in California and other Western states. Enron regularly recorded their traders' discussions to have a record of the rapid-paced "wheeling and dealing" for evidence in case of trade disputes. The tapes included records of traders, who boasted of creating artificial congestion on transmission lines, shipping power away from areas where it was needed, lying about power shortages and competition for power in order to drive up spot prices, and joking about profiting from high prices for power as stealing money from "those poor grandmothers in California." This evidence of greed and market manipulation is indicative of a major failure in the moral standards of a large part of the public utility industry. The greed exhibited on the grand scale of Enron in the state of California is not the type of ethics breech that most public utility managers and administrations must contend with. Compared to the millions of dollars stolen in the Enron example and the $1.1 million taken by the water utility in Seattle, Washington or the little more than $244,000 embezzled by a middle-aged bookkeeper from a utility serving a North Dakota Indian Reservation might sound like small change. But it was a large amount to both utilities. The Seattle case is described in Box 17.1 and the North Dakota case in Box 17.2.

Following the disclosure of these and similar ethical breakdowns, both public and private organizations have been increasingly subjected to regulatory oversight and control. The drive for deregulation and privatization has been put on hold in much of the country—an outcome with significant impact on the entire industry. And this crisis in the ethical standards of utility industry managers is just one of a number of forces shaping the industry for good and bad. In addition, utility managers everywhere are also being battered by uncontrollable forces emanating from the global economic, political, environmental, and social environments.

Government agency administrators and managers in investor-owned utilities are regularly faced with demands for ethical reform emanating

---

BOX 17.1　FORMER CITY EMPLOYEE ARRESTED IN $1 MILLION THEFT FROM SEATTLE PUBLIC UTILITIES

A former Seattle Public Utilities (SPU) project engineer was arrested in March of 2012 for reportedly stealing more than $1.1 million over five years by diverting money for water-main extensions into a private bank account. The employee met with developers and customers to estimate the cost of extending or installing city water mains and meters. He collected deposits and payments for the work, usually as checks made out to the City of Seattle. Instead of turning the checks into the city, he deposited them in a bank account in his name. Before being caught, he purchased a rental house, an automobile, other property and paid off credit cards with some of the money. Police were able to seize $220,000 from the bank account, but reported close to $500,000 was unaccounted for. He was described by a cousin, who with the engineer's wife, denied having any knowledge of the thefts, as a very loving father and a good husband.

The charges were made after a year of audits of the utility's financial controls led to the firing of five employees, including the engineer, for improperly accessing and in some cases crediting their own utility accounts. The Seattle City Auditor regularly performed audits on five other utility sectors, including water, wastewater, drainage, solid waste transfer stations, and commercial solid waste operations, but had never examined the activities of the utility engineers.

SPU was formed in 1997 by merging the city's separate water, garbage and wastewater utilities.

Source: Thompson (2012).

---

from the popular press, the general public, and a growing number of crusading social scientists. Legislators are urged to enact more and more stringent ethics laws and codes. All types of organizations are required or strongly urged to design and adopt comprehensive programs of development education and training in ethical behavior for managers and staff. Calls for ethics reform have been directed at every level of government, from the Office of the President of the United States to the smallest local special service district.

Ethical problems in public and private organizations run the gamut from sexual harassment to misappropriation or outright embezzlement of millions and billions of dollars. Ethics breakdowns are loudly pointed out by the press as examples of the poor quality of public servants in general. Examples include newspaper stories of the alleged sale of presidential pardons and diplomatic passports (*New York Times*, June 17, 2001: A1), charges that a town mayor and nine others in Illinois misappropriated $10 million in taxpayer money; and the conviction of a former New Jersey mayor on charges of laundering drug money and accepting bribes from

BOX 17.2   FORMER PUBLIC UTILITIES EMPLOYEE PLEADS
            GUILTY TO THEFT

The following May 5, 2010 FBI press release describes the arrest of a 23-year
employee of a North Dakota public utilities commission for theft of more than
$244,000 from a local Native American reservation:

Acting United States Attorney Lynn Jordheim announced that on May 4, 2010,
Betty Fargo*, 55, of Dunseith, North Dakota, pleaded guilty before United States
District Court Judge Daniel L. Hovland to a charge of theft from an Indian tribal
organization. Fargo was employed with the Belcourt Public Utilities Commission
(BPUC), an entity of the Turtle Mountain Band of Chippewa. As the secretary and
bookkeeper, Fargo was responsible for all finances for BPUC. When management
officials became suspicious about missing money, a forensic audit was conducted,
which revealed a shortage of deposits totaling $244,618.85. Fargo admitted to
allowing other employees to write personal checks and take money from BPUC,
with the intent to pay the money back before the checks were deposited.
Eventually, Fargo stopped depositing the checks and the money was never paid
back. Fargo also admitted that she wrote personal checks to BPUC, received
money, and then never deposited her checks in a BPUC account and never paid
back the money. Fargo was employed with BPUC for 23 years before her termina-
tion.

The charge of theft from an Indian tribal organization carries a statutory
maximum penalty of five years in prison and a $250,000 fine. The case was inves-
tigated by the Federal Bureau of Investigation and Minot Police Department.
*Name changed

Source: FBI (2010).

racketeers (*San Francisco Chronicle*, June 16, 2001: A2 and A5, respectively).
Public utilities and other businesses that serve the utility industry are not
immune to allegations of ethical misconduct, as the example of Enron
attests. A number of energy companies associated with Enron were being
investigated for fraudulent dealings in the California energy crisis.

Sherron Watkins, the former vice-president at Enron, has been credited
with warning senior managers at the bankrupt energy trading company
about what she has called "an elaborate accounting hoax," and "what I
thought was the worst accounting fraud I'd ever seen." After the company
collapsed in 2001, U.S. Congressional investigators found her warnings
buried in boxes of documents and brought her to Washington to testify
before the United States Senate. Enron's chief financial officer was accused
of becoming general partner in an investment partnership, LJM, while
employed at Enron. He raised $600 million in limited-partnership funds
and then proceeded to conduct business activities that maximized returns
for the limited partners, not Enron's stockholders. The conflict of interest

was that LJM's sole reason for existing was to do business exclusively with Enron. Nearly all of the transactions had no economic substance, but paper profits were recorded. Addressing the Academy of Management on August 3, 2003, Watkins described Enron's accounting practices this way:

> Enron's accounting moved from creative, to aggressive, to fraudulent, like the pot of water moving from cool to lukewarm to boiling; those involved with the creative transactions soon found themselves working on the aggressive transactions and were finally in the uncomfortable situation of working on fraudulent deals . . .. It is now clear that there were problems in the executive suite at Enron and in the other companies accused of fraudulent behavior, but what happened to all the watchdog groups in business to protect investors? That whole system failed at Enron. Enron's outside auditors failed. The legal counsel Enron received is suspect. The investment bankers and traditional bankers seem to have been 'in on it.' (Watkins 2003: 122)

THE WHISTLEBLOWER PROCESS

The airing of misconduct typically begins with a whistleblower airing allegations of employer or fellow employee misconduct; newspaper headlines pick up on the story and question the sincerity of administrators who deny the claims and the denials of government watchdogs whose responsibility it is to monitor utility operations. Congress begins to hold legislative oversight hearings on misconduct by the utility and/or regulatory agencies. In the past, other than more bad press for everyone involved, little concrete change took place, and often the utility or organization in question continues operations with little change. Some states have adopted new laws to prevent the old "slap-on-the-wrist" manner of dealing with ethical infractions. In Washington State, for example, the legislature passed a law that took effect in January 2003 that gave the State Department of Licensing disciplinary power for enforcing its regulations, including the right to issue cease-and-desist orders (Lewis 2003). A Texas-based, third-party company that collects utility bills on behalf of landlords and property managers was ordered to stop operating without a collection agency license.

Those were not isolated, seldom seen instances, nor is the problem a new one. The problem of unethical behavior by utility and related industry managers became a particularly important political issue for Congress in 2001 with the plight of the California electric power industry and allegations of gross over-charging and staged shortages to drive wholesale energy prices up. The series of scandals that followed the California energy crisis and Enron collapse resulted in demands by regulators and investors that utilities demonstrate that they are "squeaky-clean, inside and out."

Many large energy utilities have instituted programs for renewing their commitment to ethics and good governance.

Legislators are often slow to investigate and monitor the management practices of public utility administrators and managers when they receive allegations of misconduct from constituents. In fulfilling their oversight responsibilities, Congress has the power to authorize inquiries and hold hearings on issues of (1) allegations of over-charging for public utilities, (2) the qualifications of the state utility commissions responsible for setting and monitoring utility rates, and (3) the organizational policies which guide and influence such processes. Congress conducts these oversight activities in three ways: by directly communicating with responsible agency personnel, by holding hearings, or by initiating investigative reports by appropriate regulatory and watch-dog agencies and organizations. Public interest in business and government ethics increased significantly during the Enron crisis. That interest resulted in greater in-service training, publication of many management ethics articles, and professional conferences devoted to ethics problems in public and investor-owned public utilities, industry regulators, and other arms of government.

MANAGEMENT ETHICS IN PRACTICE

Ethics, a branch of philosophy, is the study of the *moral* behavior of humans as individuals and within society. It has been further defined as the set of principles that govern the conduct of an individual or a group of persons, and briefly as the study of morality or moral behavior (Velasquez 2011). *Morality* refers to the standards that people have about what is right, what is wrong, what is good, or what is evil; these standards are the behavior norms of a society. *Moral behavior* is acting in ways that follow the moral standards that exist in society. Collectively, the behaviors of individuals and groups in a society, as well as their dispositions to behave in particular ways, are referred to as the *ethos* of the group. *Moral standards* are the rules by which a society functions. Examples of moral standards include the commandments: *Do not kill, Do not steal, Do not lie*, and so on. Standards are about what behavior is acceptable, what is 'right' and what is 'good' in society, and their opposites, of course. While moral standards often differ from time to time, they remain relatively constant for at least a generation or more. When they do change, they tend to do so very slowly.

Unethical behavior in public utility management refers to the broader concept of misconduct in all public service. Misconduct, in the words of Fox and Braxton (1994: 374), "encompasses acts of deception—alteration of data or materials, false representation of authorship or originality, and misrepresentation to advance oneself or to hurt the career or position of another." A charge of misconduct in the utilities department of New York is an example of unethical behavior in a public utility:

> The [New York] Inspector General determined that from 2002 to 2010 several employees in the New York State Department of Public Service, Office of Electric, Gas, and Water, Safety—Electric, Gas, and Steam Section improperly received gifts totaling more than $7,000 in the form of meals and games of golf from regulated entities. The Inspector General's investigation further determined that two Department of Public Service (DPS) employees violated DPS policy by sharing confidential information, which included drafts of documents to be submitted to the New York State Public Service Commission. The New York State Public Service Commission ("Commission") regulates the manufacture, sale, distribution, and transportation of electric, gas, steam, telecommunications, and water by utility companies that operate within New York State. (New York State Inspector General 2012a)

As a consequence of the charge, the New York Department of Public Service now requires annual ethics training for its employees. The agency announced that it was planning to inform all public utilities under its oversight jurisdiction review and submit to the agency their own plan for ethics training. The utility company that provided the gifts agreed to pay a fine of nearly $1.7 million.

Opinions about what constitutes unethical behavior and what moral standards to follow vary from society to society, and often from organization to organization within the same society. There are few absolutes in ethics, and the dichotomies are exacerbated when conflicting ethos exist to provide similar services, as they do in public versus investor-owned public utilities. Still, the fundamental standards of behavior tend to be quite similar throughout the industrialized nations of the world. This is so because, if standards were wildly different, nations would have a difficult time cooperating in such value-laden areas as international relations, commerce, and other global activities.

What distinguishes moral standards from standards that are not moral? Five characteristics of moral behavior that make this distinction are shown in Figure 17.1. First, moral standards are concerned with matters that people think can seriously injure or benefit human beings. Second, most people absorb their initial moral standards as children. People will often typically revise these moral positions as they mature; some of that revision occurs in response to the organizational culture they find as they move through their careers.

Although it is not impossible, it is difficult for a person's moral standards to be completely reshaped by the decisions of authoritative bodies; ethical behavior can seldom be successfully legislated, as America's failed

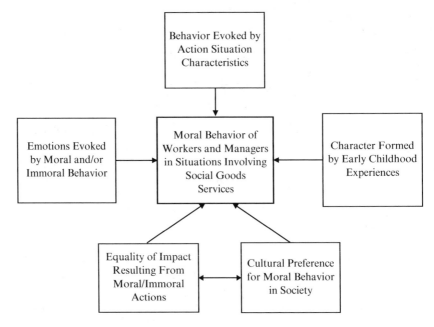

Figure 17.1   Factors influencing moral behavior by workers and managers
in public utilities

experience with Prohibition and the sale and consumption of illegal drugs today will attest. Third, by their very nature as fundamental norms of behavior in a society, moral standards are preferred over other values, including self-interest. Fourth, moral standards are based on impartial considerations; they apply equally to all persons in society. Finally, moral standards evoke special emotions, including guilt and shame, and are associated with a special vocabulary; words such as good and bad, honesty, greed, justice, and injustice are examples. Western moral standards have evolved from a number of different philosophical traditions, some of which are as old as recorded time.

Sources of Managers' Moral Standards

Today, a number of different ways to approach an ethical situation have evolved from these earliest guidelines for the moral behavior of workers in public service. The model in Figure 17.1 illustrates how different antecedents might shape and direct a manager's moral behavior. The most popular approaches include the teleological approach known as utilitarian ethics and the deontological theory of ethics based on universal rules. Others include rights theories, the ethics of justice, caring ethics, and virtue ethics (Velasquez 2011). In the past, business ethicists have generally agreed with this summary of the various theories: "No single theory has emerged that is fully capable of providing guidance about the gamut of challenging business ethics matters that fill business ethics casebooks and confront practicing businesspeople" (Donaldson and Dunfee 1999: 12). As a result, traditional ethics theories are used when describing problems of professional ethics. Several of these major traditional theories are discussed in the following pages, beginning with *utilitarianism*.

Utilitarian ethics

Utilitarian ethics is based on the view that the 'right' action or policy is the one that will result in the greatest benefit (or the lowest costs) to society. Thus, decisions on actions and policies must be evaluated according to their net benefits and costs. It is concerned with the *consequences* of an action, not the means to achieve the results. Today's cost–benefit analysis is based on this principle. Because it supports the value of efficiency, utilitarianism is often used in the resolution of political dilemmas. A key characteristic of utilitarianism is that the benefits need not be equally distributed; some people may not benefit at all, while others may even be negatively impacted—they will lose more than they gain. What counts in the final analysis is the *greatest good for all concerned*. The great moral dilemma with utilitarianism is determining who is to decide what is meant by 'good'. A costly example of not making the right decision and not immediately taking the right corrective action cost the top two managers of an eastern Oregon electric utility their jobs, one a prison sentence, and the utility itself $1.3 million in damages in a 2012 sexual harassment case (see Box 17.3).

Categorical imperatives (rule ethics)

The basis for rule ethics comes from the writings of philosopher Emanuel Kant (1724–1804). Kant believed that all human beings possess some rights and duties, and that these exist regardless of any utilitarian benefit they might have for or against others in a society. Kant proposed moral principles he called *categorical imperatives* to make this point. Kant's first categorical imperative states that an action is morally right if—and only if—the reason for doing it is one that the person would be willing for everyone to act upon in a similar situation.

There are two parts to Kant's categorical imperative concept; the concept of *universalizability*—that is, the principle must apply to everyone, and *reversibility*—people must be willing to have all others use the same concept in the same way that the first actor treats other persons. Kant's second imperative holds that an action is morally right if—and only

---

BOX 17.3   UTILITY PAYS $1.3 MILLION IN SEXUAL HARASSMENT CHARGE—WITH MORE TO COME

Sexual harassment should never be allowed in any office. When it does happen, management must act on the charge immediately or face strict penalties. This is what happened in an Oregon public utility. When two female employees reported unwanted physical advances to the general manager of an Oregon power utility, the charge was ignored and allowed the two female victims to be shunted aside and ignored; that cost the perpetrator, the power manager who was the second in command of the utility, and the general manager their jobs—and the utility $1.3 million in payments to the victims. The story was published in Portland, *Oregonian*.

The power manager had squeezed one woman's breast and grabbed another woman's buttocks in two separate incidents in March 2011. But the response by the manager the then general-manager in the months afterward convinced the two women they needed to stand up for themselves, they said, even at the cost of their jobs. Not only did the manager's harassment continue, they also found themselves transferred to other positions. Their responsibilities taken from them; they were isolated from other employees; and were eventually forced out of their jobs.

One year after filing their lawsuits the women agreed to a $1.3 million settlement from the utility to settle their claims of sexual harassment, discrimination and retaliation. Although the utility admitted no wrongdoing, both the manager and general manager retired from the utility. Even with the two lawsuits settled, litigation is far from over for the utility, which still faces lawsuits from four other former employees on sexual harassment or retaliation claims in connection with both men. The power manager was sentenced to three years of probation for the misdemeanors; the general manager retired.

Source: Jung (2014).

---

if—when performing the action, a person does not use others as a means for improving his or her own interests. Thus, when making an ethical decision, administrators must respect the right of others to choose freely for themselves. This concept was clearly breached when Enron energy traders chose to reap huge profits at the expense of energy industry participants and consumers. Earning a profit in the Western economic system is clearly morally permissible; using others who are unable to defend themselves as a means for reaping excessive personal profits is not.

Rights ethics

A *right* is often defined as a person's entitlement to something. Because of its focus on the individual, it differs from the utilitarian approach, where the focus is on the greater good of a society. Rights have been classified in several different ways. In one classification system, two types of rights are included in ethics, *legal* rights and *human* rights. Legal rights are based upon laws; consumer protection and contract rights are examples. Human rights, on the other hand, are culturally based; they provide people with a way of justifying their actions; they are also associated with *duties*.

A second way to classify rights is by determining whether they are first generation or second-generation rights (Joseph, Schultz, and Castan 2000: 3–4). First generation rights include civil rights and political rights. Civil rights are rights that apply to citizen's physical integrity, the procedural right of due process, and non-discrimination rights. Political rights enable citizens to participate in the political life of their society. They include such rights as freedom of expression, assembly and association, and the right to vote. Civil and political rights are called first generation rights because they are a large part of the content of the Bills of Rights that were written in the eighteenth and nineteenth centuries. Collectively, they are considered as rights to be free from government influence.

Second generation rights embrace economic, social, and cultural rights. Among these are rights to an adequate standard of living, right to an education, and the right to good health. Collectively, second generation rights are considered to be rights that require positive government action. Of the two sets of rights, second generation rights tend to be less developed than first generation civil and political rights.

Several key concepts in political science are founded upon Kantian rule-based rights theories. Among others, these include the idea that all people have positive rights to work, clothing, housing, and medical care; that everyone has a negative right to freedom from injury or fraud; and, that humans have the right to enter into contracts.

Justice ethics

Moral standards based on the idea of justice include the concept of *fairness*. Together, these ideas contribute to three fundamental bases for moral behavior: *Distributive justice, retributive justice,* and *compensatory justice. Distributive justice* is concerned with the 'fair' distribution of society's benefits—and burdens. The idea of a just distribution based on a person's contribution to society is the value behind the *capitalist* system, whereas distributive justice based on needs and abilities underlies *socialism,* and justice, as freedom to do as he or she chooses, is the idea behind *libertarianism*.

Retributive justice is concerned with the providing of punishments and penalties that are 'just.' Thus, a person should not be considered to be morally responsible under conditions of ignorance or inability. This principle is the idea behind the standard of enlightened consent for participation in research studies. *Compensatory justice* supports the idea of compensating people for what they lose when they are wronged by other individuals or by society (including government). Requiring the energy trading companies convicted of illegally manipulating the wholesale energy market in 2000 and 2001 to compensate the victims is an example of compensatory justice.

Caring ethics

The ethics of caring means making a decision in the face of an ethical dilemma based upon a genuine caring for the best interests of another individual. Key virtues of the caring administrator include friendship, kindness, concern, and love for fellow human beings. As might be expected, these ethical standards are often employed in describing decisions made in social welfare agencies and activities.

The care ethic emphasizes two moral demands. First, because we all live in our own web of relationships, we should preserve and nurture the valuable relationships we have with others. Second, we must care for those with whom we are related by attending to their particular needs, values, desires and concrete well-being as seen from their perspective. This also means responding to the needs, values, desires, and well-being of those who are vulnerable and dependent on our care. Three different types of care ethics come into play in social situations: caring *about* something, caring *after* someone, and caring *for* someone. In the political world, the applicable ethic is caring for someone. It focuses on people and their well-being, not on things.

Virtue ethics

Based upon the writings of Aristotle and others, virtue ethics refers to the idea of using society's virtues as the basis for making ethical decisions. Aristotle identified four 'pivotal' virtues: courage, temperance, justice, and prudence. St. Thomas Aquinas added the following 'Christian' virtues: *faith, hope,* and *charity*. In today's society, the virtues considered most important include *honesty, courage, temperance, integrity, compassion,* and *self-control*—terms often used to describe the 'ideal' public servant. Vices are the opposite of virtues; they include such examples of 'bad' behavior as dishonesty, ruthlessness, greed, lack of integrity, and cowardice. These are considered to be undesirable because of the way they can destroy human relationships. Velasquez described the thinking that shapes decision-making in virtue theory in the following way: *An action is morally right if in carrying out the action the agent exercises, exhibits, or develops a morally virtuous character, and is morally wrong to the extent that by carrying out the action the agent exercises, exhibits, or develops a morally vicious character* (Velasquez 2011).

WHICH THEORY SHOULD GUIDE UTILTIY OPERATIONS?

Which, if any, of these ethical principles should guide administrative behavior for workers in the public utilities? For many, the question is moot; no choice is necessary, let alone possible. Public service ethics is "eclectic, eccentric, and undisciplined," and is, therefore, "interwoven into a single moral complex" (Garofalo and Geuras, 1999: 45 and 97; Geuras and Garofalo 2010). Out of these diverse underlying principles that characterize public service ethics have emerged many of the laws (rules) that define specifically what utility managers and administrators can and cannot do. Laws forbidding discrimination and sexual harassment, regulatory rules and procedures for setting rates, and even what customers can and cannot be served, are examples. However, it is not enough to simply do what is legal; public utility administrators have a moral responsibility that goes far beyond adhering to the letter of the law. An example is the moral question of whether to cut off electricity service to the poor or aged in the dead of winter for failure to pay a utility bill on time, or to halt water service to a family with small children for the same reason.

Ethical Dilemmas Facing Utility Managers

The principal ethical question facing public utility managers often comes down to one of how to balance the need for greater good of the utility system and the promises given to shareholders for investing their savings, against the rights to the fundamental services required for life to all citizens in a civil society. Because there is no one comprehensive moral theory that is capable of stating exactly when a *utilitarian* consideration should take precedence over a *right*, a standard of justice, or the need for caring, the public utility administrator or manager is forced to follow his or her conscience when faced with these types of ethical dilemmas. The dilemmas that cause most difficulty for public utilities are not those associated with what has been described as outright knavery; in other words, lying, bad faith, intentional misrepresentation for payment, or the deliberate breach of the terms of the contract on which the agreement was reached. These are practical problems of a legal nature rather than problems of ethics. Instead, the problems may be those associated with conflicts between the long-term good of the organization versus the principles of the public good. Who in any society is to decide what the best good is for the most people, and what level of pain should be allowed to make the good happen. This is the ethical dilemma of public utility management. Looking further at the ethos of public service may help the reader to a point of self-accepted closure over the issues involved.

THE ETHOS OF PUBLIC SERVICE

Most professionals like to think that their profession is in some way unique, that it has an ethics or a morality of its own, and that their ethics takes precedence over the ethics of ordinary people. It is logical to assume that administrators, managers, and staff workers feel the same about their profession. Thus, like all professions, the public utility/public service industry is hurt by misconduct or allegations of avarice and other impropriety by persons in whom the public has placed its trust.

In the long run, every person who works in the public service industry is subject to social, economic, and political control (Fox and Braxton 1994). This contention was supported by research reported by Goss in 1996. Goss compared the attitudes of 100 elected state officials with those of 378 public administrators and a random sample of 250 voting citizens. Attitudes were measured across 12 dimensions arranged in two scales of six items each. One set of items referred to the service or democratic ethos; the second set of items covered the professional or bureaucratic ethos. Public administrators valued *Professional Competence* above all other eleven value characteristics, and rated *Being an Advocate of the Public Interest* as the least important characteristic. Clearly, practicing administrators were more concerned with their professional skills than they were in service to the public.

Both the elected legislator and general public samples rated *Trustworthiness* as the most important behavioral characteristic for public servants. If Goss' one-state case study is valid, that is, if his results can be considered to be representative of administrators everywhere, it appears that many politicians may be out of touch with the publics they serve.

Appointed administrators apply their skills to the job at hand in ways that are different than the public and elected legislators would have them do. From his findings, Goss found that appointed administrators are less sensitive to the public interest and individual rights than the general public, directly or through their elected representatives, would prefer them to be.

The term *ethos* refers to the characteristics, thoughts, and behaviors that distinguish a particular person or group. Ethics in public service exists on two dominant levels or *ethos*: the professional or bureaucratic ethos and the service or democratic ethos (Garofalo and Geuras 1999; Geuras and Garofalo 2010; Woller and Patterson 1997). This two-part ethos is illustrated in Figure 17.2.

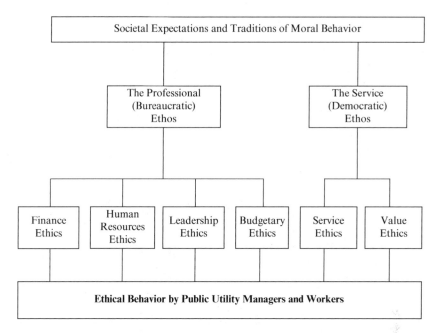

Figure 17.2   Functional ethics classes in public service

In this model, workers in public service organizations must first deal with a professional or *bureaucratic* ethos. This influences the ways that people perform their jobs. Administrators in both private and investor-owned utilities are faced with this professional service ethos which is based on hierarchical control and obedience to political (party) superiors. In some ways, the ethics of publicly owned utilities are not much different than the ethics of any private enterprise, profession, or public office or agency; the major distinguishing characteristic is the lack of a profit factor that motivates behavior in the private sector.

The second standard shaping manager's moral behavior is the underlying belief and commitment to public service. This is the *democratic ethos* (possibly an unfortunate selection of names since it can exist in non-democratic societies as well; a better choice might have been a *service ethos*). These ideas deal with such values as liberty, justice, human rights, and equality. It is important to remember that moral standards differ from agency to agency and firm to firm, and that what works in one organization may not be the right approach for others (Donaldson and Dunfee 1999).

Public service workers in government organizations face ethical questions in both of these areas of morality. For example, while maintaining

a sense of fiscal responsibility and professional competence in their principal areas of administrative activity, administrators are also expected to
live up to several distinctive service ethos characteristics in order to retain
the public's trust. These additional characteristics include: (1) avoiding
conflicts of interest, (2) maintaining impartiality toward the public and
stakeholders with conflicting interests, (3) avoiding any appearance of
impropriety, and (4) regularly submitting to public disclosure in most every
detail of their existence (Petrick and Quinn 1997).

SUMMARY

The potential for unethical behavior is a universal problem; it equally affects
private sector businesses and public agencies at the federal, state, and
local levels and non-government, not-for-profit organizations. Politicians,
elected officials, public administrators, private citizens, society watchdog
agencies, and the popular press have all called for moral reform, passage of
ethics laws and codes, and greater education and training in ethical behavior for everyone involved in public service.

Managers and workers in public utilities have a moral obligation to do
the right thing. Society has given them the authority to provide a public
service. Regardless of the class of service, whether publicly or investor
owned, the obligation is the same. The health and safety of the men,
women and children they serve is in the hands of those who provide this
service. The morality they share as workers in public utilities is above and
beyond what might be expected in other sectors. The moral behavior they
exhibit is shaped by the standards that are a fundamental part of the *ethos
of public service*. That moral behavior may be products of any one or more
of the five different philosophical traditions discussed in this chapter.
When faced with an ethical dilemma, men and women in public service
draw upon the ethical foundations they learned at an earlier age; no one
tradition is more correct than any of the others. When it comes down to
making a decision in such situations, they can know they have done the
right thing by following the ethos of public service.

In the long run, everyone who works in the public service industry is
subject to social, economic, and political control. In a study that compared
the attitudes of 100 elected state officials with those of 378 public administrators and a random sample of 250 voting citizens, attitudes were measured across 12 dimensions arranged in two scales of six items each. One set
referred to the service or democratic ethos; the second set covered the professional or bureaucratic ethos. Public administrators valued *Professional
Competence* above all other eleven value characteristics, and rated '*Being*

an Advocate of the Public Interest' as the least important characteristic. Elected legislators and the general public rated *Trustworthiness* as the most important behavioral characteristic for public service workers.

Appointed administrators apply their skills to the job at hand in ways that are different than the public and elected legislators would have them do. Goss found that appointed administrators are less sensitive to the public interest and individual rights than the general public or their elected representatives would prefer them to be.

ADDITIONAL READING

Cooper, Terry L. (1998), *The Responsible Administrator: An Approach to Ethics for the Administrative Role* (4th edn). San Francisco: Jossey-Bass.

Denhardt, Janet V. and Robert B. Denhardt (2011), *The New Public Service* (3rd edn). New York: Taylor & Francis.

Geuras, Dean and Charles Garofalo (2010), *Public Ethics in Administration* (3rd edn). Vienna, VA: Management Concepts.

Menzel, Donald C. (2012), *Ethics Management for Public Administration* (2nd edn). New York: Taylor & Francis.

Rohr, John A. (1998), *Public Service, Ethics & Constitutional Practice*. Lawrence: University Press of Kansas.

PART V

Public utilities: new challenges

18. Public utility environmental challenges

Throughout the previous chapters it has been apparent that public utilities faced a wide variety of problems in the past—and they face an even greater number of challenges in the years ahead. Problems or challenges, the pressures on managers are similar: they frame the operations world within which utilities must plan and function. Problems are managerial difficulties that managers must deal with when developing operational plans; they function as constraints that limit the time and money options available to utility managers. Challenges are broader in scope; they are the structure within which utilities as organisms had to adapt to survive. They often take years to overcome or adjust to. Problems are generally solvable in the short term; managers must adjust their operations in ways that solutions are available and achievable. Aging infrastructure is a problem when it fails. When it continues to function economically and efficiently, it is a challenge, but not necessarily a problem.

An environmental problem has been defined as a "known process (such as resource consumption) that has negative effects on the sustainability of the environmental quality necessary for the well-being of the organisms living in it" (Businessdictionary.com 2015b). Utility operators and managers know how to deal with environmental problems; they have been doing so successfully since the 1970s and even earlier. Innovation focuses on finding solutions to problems.

Challenges are conditions that establish the scope of operational opportunities. Environmental regulations are challenges. Health, safety and employment rules and regulations are challenges. Sustainable operations under dramatic climate change are a challenge. Maintaining sustainable delivery of services in the face of population growth and demographic changes is a challenge. This chapter reviews how utilities are developing the means and willpower to survive and thrive in the face of a host of challenges based in our natural environment.

An environmental challenge is a given barrier that utility managers must learn not to live with, but to surmount. Coping with increasingly restrictive environmental regulations is an example of an ongoing challenge to the sustainability of public utilities large and small. These regulations dictate the range of options available to the utility manager, and most often, do not allow any leeway in operations. Environmental problems are surmountable dictates that utilities must follow as a matter of course. Sanitary landfills, for example, have known requirements for operation. Increasing rates of recycling, on the other hand, is a challenge for which there are no easy solutions or quick fixes.

ENVIRONMENT CHALLENGES IN THE ENERGY SECTOR

Although electric power generation is generally evaluated as being closely related to, but not an actual member of the public utility family, environmental problems that the generation and transmission sectors face do have a real and extensive effect on distribution utilities, state utility commissions, and eventual consumers of electric power. As a result, effects of the federal proposal to enforce CO_2 emissions restrictions in the 2015 Clean Power Plan effects on generators must be included in the operating plans of all electric utilities. The plan will require coal-fired steam generating plants to either invest in major emission control equipment or to shift to natural gas and renewable fuels.

On August 3, 2015, President Obama and EPA announced the final version of the country's Clean Power Plan, a program for reducing carbon pollution from all sources, but particularly from fossil-fueled electric power plants. The final plan was designed to support and strengthen the trend toward the use of cleaner and lower-polluting fuels in the country. When fully implemented, it is expected to reduce carbon dioxide emissions in 2030 by 32 percent below CO_2 emissions levels in 2005 (when first introduced in 2014, the targeted reduction was 30 percent). The rule establishes a target emissions rate or for the amount of carbon dioxide that could be emitted per megawatt-hour of power produced for each state. Targeted emissions rate reductions range from 7 percent in Connecticut to 47 percent in Montana. The percentages represent how much states must reduce their power fleet emissions rates below 2012 levels. States are permitted to choose how they will reduce emissions from methods that include upgrading existing facilities, greater use of renewable energy sources, higher electricity efficiency improvements, and others. EPA set the state CO_2 emission rate limits based on analyses of emission reduction opportunities in each state. States submitted final carbon-cutting plans or initial plans by September 6, 2016, and were to begin working toward interim emissions goals by 2022, and meet final goals by 2030. The states' options included these four "building blocks" or goals:

- Block 1: Heat rate improvements at coal units;
- Block 2: Increased use of existing natural gas combined cycle (NGCC) units;
- Block 3: Increases in renewables and nuclear energy; and
- Block 4: Increases in end-use energy efficiency.

Close to 21 percent of the world's coal-fired power generation capacity is located in the United States, second only to the 37 percent that exists in China. Coal-fired power plants are the largest source of carbon pollution in the United States, accounting for approximately a third of all domestic greenhouse gas emissions. Reduction in additional emissions by eliminating coal as a fuel were expected to include an estimated 72 percent reduction on nitrogen oxides and more than 25 percent reduction in soot and smog. Changes to the electric power generation sector are expected to remove 870 million tons of CO_2 from the air, the estimated equivalent of annual emissions by 166 million automobiles. The EPA announced in 2014 that the plan would lead to climate and health benefits worth an estimated $55 billion to $93 billion in 2030, including cutting 2,700 to 6,600 premature deaths and 140,000 to 150,000 asthma attacks in children (EPA 2015d).

A consequence of EPA requirements for removing coal ash from the air and storing it in ponds where the particulates can settle out and then be deposited in sanitary landfills was pointed out in a 2014 infrastructure failure. A broken storm water pipe polluted regional watercourses and cost a North Carolina electric utility $21.1 million in state environmental control fines. The failure also brought to light a five-year history of malfeasance in collecting and storing coal ash from electricity generation facilities by the firm (Box 18.1).

ENVIRONMENT CHALLENGES IN THE WATER SECTOR

U.S. public utilities in the water industry face several major environmental challenges, the impacts of which are beginning to be felt across both the water and wastewater segments of the industry. Among the most pressing are increasing water scarcity, aging infrastructure, climate volatility, maintaining sustainable water quality, and rising water-related energy risks. To address these challenges effectively, the water and wastewater sectors must focus on the underlying structural and financial problems that hamper the adoption of system innovation and implementing advanced water and wastewater sustainability strategies such as generating the public's

Public utilities, second edition

BOX 18.1   NORTH CAROLINA ELECTRIC ENERGY UTILITY FINED $21.1 MILLION FOR WATER POLLUTION

In February 2014, nearly 40,000 tons of coal ash and wastewater were released into North Carolina's Dan River after a storm-water pipe burst at Duke Energy's Dan River power station. North Carolina officials fined Duke Energy the largest-ever penalty for environmental damages, fining the utility $25.1 million for ground-water contamination caused by the spill of the water-laced with coal ash. The North Carolina Department of Environment and Natural Resources (NCDENR) fined the utility after determining the environmental damage resulted from unsafe levels of such contaminants as boron, thallium, selenium and arsenic in the stored and released wastewater. The pollution had apparently been collected and stored at the utility's power generation plants. Toxic pollution in the ash ponds at one the utility's plants had been stored for nearly five years. The fine followed violations cited by the state environmental agency at the Duke facility in August 2014.

   The report of the fine explained that the coal ash contained in settlement ponds is a byproduct of coal-fired electric power generation. Coal-fired electric power generation reportedly produces one of the nation's largest refuse streams at 36 million tons a year. Coal ash released into the environment has fouled drinking water supplies, "endangered public health and threatened communities across the country. The U.S. Environmental Protection Agency itself has recognized as many as 160 'damage' cases in which coal ash from ponds, landfills and other dumpsites have contaminated nearby aquifers, streams, rivers and lakes or tainted the air, including in North Carolina."

Source: Lombardi (2015).

---

acceptance of otherwise wasted alternative water as a sustainable potable water resource. Major demographic and socioeconomic factors contributing to the environmental challenges of water include (NCSL 2016):

- Population growth: According to a 2012 United States Census Bureau projection, the U.S. population could reach 400 million people by 2051. Population growth affects energy use through increases in housing, commercial floor space, transportation, and economic activity. With a higher generating capacity, the U.S. will require additional water withdrawals.
- Agriculture: Feeding a growing population may require greater agricultural water use. Agriculture accounts for approximately 37 percent of total freshwater withdrawals in the U.S., and 81 percent of water consumption.
- Geographical water demand: Water supply and demand are not geographically linked. From 1990 to 2010, the second largest regional population growth, 13.8 percent, occurred in the west, one of the

most water deficient regions in the United States. Additionally, water consumption in the western U.S. is much higher than other regions due to agricultural demands. It is estimated that it takes over 1 million gallons of water a year to irrigate one acre of farmland in arid conditions. In other words about 86 percent of irrigation water withdrawals were in western states in 2000.

- Climate change: Climate change is already beginning to affect water supply and electricity use. Warmer or colder weather patterns result in increases or decreases in energy use, which then affects water use. Changes in precipitation in a region could increase or decrease the ability to store water, agricultural production and water use, and overall water supply.

The crucial nature of water sustainability in an increasingly adverse environmental environment reinforces the conclusion that water utilities must increase their investments in infrastructure. To meet the major sustainability challenges facing the industry in the next fifty years, utilities large and small must find and develop new solutions to the water scarcity problem, repair and replace crumbling infrastructure, and deal with the effects of climate change. In markets where these factors have pushed water sustainability initiatives high up the utility management agenda, the need for infrastructure investment funds has become one of the most pressing challenges identified by utility operators and administrators.

Sources of Groundwater Contamination

The activities that make it possible for people to live well, have mobility, and enjoy the natural environment are increasingly endangered by the same things people enjoy. Both the surface and ground supplies of potable water are subject to many different contaminants. Although originally aimed at describing the sources of contaminants in groundwater, the explanation by The Groundwater Foundation (TGF) of Lincoln, Nebraska is applicable to both sources. This foundation is a nonprofit educational organization formed to educate the public and inspire everyone to take action that will ensure sustainable, clean groundwater for future generations. Founded in 1985, TGF provides educational programs and projects for people and communities to learn more about groundwater and how to help protect it. The following discussion on the sources of groundwater is available on their website.

More than half of the population of the United States depends on groundwater for drinking water. Groundwater is also one of our most important sources of water for irrigation. Unfortunately, groundwater is susceptible to pollutants. Groundwater contamination occurs when man-made products such as gasoline, oil, road salts and chemicals invade the water source, making it unsafe and unfit for human use. In addition, contaminants from the land's surface can move through the soil and end up in the groundwater. For example, pesticides and fertilizers can find their way into groundwater supplies over time. Road salt, toxic substances from mining sites, and used motor oil also may seep into groundwater. In addition, it is possible for untreated waste from septic tanks and toxic chemicals from underground storage tanks and leaky landfills to contaminate groundwater. Sources of groundwater contaminants include the following:

- Abandoned storage tanks: There are estimated to be over 10 million storage tanks buried in the United States and over time the tanks can corrode, crack and develop leaks.
- Onsite wastewater disposal systems: Buildings that are not connected to a city sewer system. An improperly designed, located, constructed, or maintained septic system can leak bacteria, viruses, household chemicals, and other contaminants into the groundwater.
- Uncontrolled hazardous waste: There are thought to be over 20,000 known abandoned and uncontrolled hazardous waste sites and the numbers grow every year. If there is a leak, these contaminants can eventually make their way down through the soil and into the groundwater.
- Landfills: Landfills are supposed to have a protective bottom layer to prevent contaminants from getting into the water. However, if there is no layer or it is cracked, contaminants from the landfill (car battery acid, paint, household cleaners, and so on) can make their way down into the groundwater.
- Chemicals and road salts: The widespread use of chemicals and road salts, including chemical products used on lawns and farm fields to kill weeds and insects and to fertilize plants, and other products used in homes and businesses.
- Atmospheric contaminants: Since groundwater is part of the hydrologic cycle, contaminants in other parts of the cycle, such as the atmosphere or bodies of surface water, can eventually be transferred into groundwater supplies.

Groundwater Pollution Concerns

In addition to the non-commercial sources of groundwater contamination, two relatively new sources of water resource pollution are discharged pharmaceuticals into the nation's streams, rivers and other water courses and the use of chemicals and other pollutants in oil and gas well practices known as fracturing or *fracking*.

Pharmaceuticals found in surface waters include prescription and non-prescription human and veterinary drugs. One particularly problematic family, endocrine disrupting chemicals (EDCs), have been common in municipal wastewater treatment effluents and surface waters in which effluents end up. Although current treatments are able to remove EDCs and other pharmaceuticals during the wastewater treatment process, chemicals that resist treatment may be discharged in the effluent that enters surface waters. A long list of these contaminants have been found in very small quantities in America's drinking water, some of which are: caffeine, analgesics and anti-inflammatories, anti-convulsants, anti-anxiety medication, x-ray contrast media, lipid regulators (for cholesterol reduction), and metabolites of nicotine and a hypertensions medication. The National Institute of Environmental Health Sciences (NIEHS 2015) defines EDCs and their potential damage to humans and wildlife as:

> Endocrine disruptors are chemicals that may interfere with the body's endocrine system and produce adverse developmental, reproductive, neurological, and immune effects in both humans and wildlife. A wide range of substances, both natural and man-made, are thought to cause endocrine disruption, including pharmaceuticals, dioxin and dioxin-like compounds, polychlorinated biphenyls, DDT and other pesticides, and plasticizers such as *biphenyl A*. Endocrine disruptors may be found in many everyday products—including plastic bottles, metal food cans, detergents, flame retardants, food, toys, cosmetics, and pesticides. The NIEHS supports studies to determine whether exposure to endocrine disruptors may result in human health effects including lowered fertility and an increased incidence of endometriosis and some cancers. Research shows that endocrine disruptors may pose the greatest risk during prenatal and early postnatal development when organ and neural systems are forming.

In its June 2015 draft report on the findings of a study of potential aquifer contamination caused by the hydraulic fracturing the EPA described the process as use of fluids under pressures great enough to fracture (crack or break open) oil- and gas-producing formations. The fluid injected is usually a mix of water, chemicals, and sand. The draft concluded that, while some alleged pollution damage has been substantiated, the investigators did not find evidence that these activities have resulted in systemic impacts on drinking water resources in the United States. Several specific instances where one or more of these injections did have an impact on drinking water resources, including contamination of drinking water wells, were found. According to the report, (1) the cases took place during both routine activities and accidents and resulted in impacts to surface or groundwater; (2) spills of hydraulic fracturing fluid in some cases reached both surface and ground drinking water resources; (3) the discharge of treated hydraulic fracturing wastewater has increased contaminant concentrations in receiving surface waters; (4) below ground movement of fluids, including water laced with natural gas chemical pollutants, have contaminated drinking water resources; and (5) in some cases, hydraulic fracturing fluids have also been directly injected into drinking water resources, as defined in this assessment, to produce oil or gas that co-exists in those formations.

The EPA draft concluded that the number of identified cases where drinking water resources were impacted are small relative to the number of hydraulically fractured wells, ant there was not enough pre- and post-hydraulic fracturing data on the quality of drinking water resources in areas where the process occurs for a final decision to be reached. Other factors that could have a limiting effect include the presence of other causes of contamination, the short duration of existing studies, and inaccessible information (legitimate industrial secrets) pertaining to hydraulic fracturing activities.

Oil and gas drilling and fracturing is not the only source of widespread pollution of a region's groundwater resources. Box 18.2 is a brief description of how decades of inattention to the value of maintaining a water resource pure has come home to affect many of the highly populated communities of Southern California. The decades of mishandling of groundwater resources has resulted in a major problem for many municipal water utilities and points to one of the unexpected consequences of the region's decades long population growth and years-long drought. The traditional dependence upon imported water supplies is no longer sustainable; many communities have had to return to groundwater to meet the needs of their communities. Pollution has made this alternative highly problematic in many locations. As municipal distribution utilities have found they can no longer depend upon imported water, they were forced to return to the old groundwater wells to make up the discrepancies in supplies. The problem is that many of the wells are polluted and the groundwater is contaminated.

Environmental Impact of the Clean Water Act

The Water Quality Act of 1987 amendments made several changes: (1) eliminating excess toxic pollutants in some waters and (2) controlling pollution of the river or lake by discharge of pollutants from offsite sources. An earlier construction grant program was phased out and replaced by financing projects with revolving funds and low-interest-rate loans. The amendments also addressed storm-water controls and permits, regulation of toxic pollutants in treated sewer sludge, and pollution problems

---

BOX 18.2 GROUNDWATER CONTAMINATION IN L.A. COUNTY WELLS

The following *Los Angeles Times* story excerpt has been edited somewhat and reduced in length:

Decades ago, industrial pollution began fouling some groundwater wells throughout Los Angeles County. That prompted water officials to stop using the most polluted wells and rely more on water from Northern California and the Colorado River. But as this imported water becomes scarcer and more expensive, some water agencies are again looking underground for water. However, contaminated wells are an increasing problem in Los Angeles County.

Most large community drinking water systems in the region rely at least partially on contaminated groundwater sources. Aquifers underneath the ground in the San Fernando and San Gabriel valleys have been polluted with industrial flows and dirty stormwater runoff. The region's underground plumes of pollution are steadily expanding; within five to eight years, the plumes will become so dense and permanent that the rest of the wells in that area would need to be shut down unless the agency can begin purifying more contaminated well water.

The Los Angeles Department of Water and Power (DWP) plans to build the world's largest groundwater treatment center in the San Fernando Valley. State officials, however, have warned that smaller water systems sometimes serve contaminated water when they are unable to treat polluted water or find alternative clean sources. A report written by the State Water Resources Control Board to the California Legislature in 2013 said that smaller water systems in some cases cannot afford to treat or find alternative supplies for a contaminated drinking water source. These small community water systems may be more vulnerable to serving contaminated groundwater to their customers than larger water systems, the report said. About 2 million Californians rely on groundwater from private domestic wells or other well water systems not regulated by the state, which does not require these well owners to test water quality.

Source: Lin and Krishnakumar (2015).

---

in estuaries. Penalties were added for discharge permit violations. Also initiated were sewage sludge-disposal regulations and funding for studies relative to nonpoint and toxic pollution sources.

What has been called one of the most significant pieces of environmental regulations ever enacted, the Federal Clean Water Act of 1972, was prompted by growing national concern for the environment in the late 1960s, fueled by such concerns as the burning Cuyahoga River in Ohio, an unfishable, unswimmable Potomac River, and a nearly dead Lake Erie. National goals and objectives were established to "restore and maintain the chemical, physical, and biological integrity of the Nation's waters." The law had two major goals: (1) eliminate the discharge of *all* pollutants into navigable waters of the United States; and (2) achieve an interim level of water quality that provided for the protection of fish, shellfish, and wildlife and recreation.

To help do this, the following programs were established: A state grant program to support the construction of sewage treatment plants; the NPDES program, whose goal was to eliminate discharges to U.S. waters; and technological standards or discharge limits that had to be met, based on water-quality standards set by the states. A minimum required percent removal of pollutants had been added in 1985. Secondary treatment of sewage was required, and limits were set for three major effluent parameters: biological oxygen demand, suspended solids, and pH (acidity or alkalinity of the effluent).

The 1972 Clean Water Act made a number of improvements to the nation's environmental control policy, but still had farther to go. Forty percent of waters assessed by states do not meet water-quality standards, mostly due to pollution from nonpoint sources. Other than from storm or combined storm sewer overflows, most of the remaining problem is not from pipes (point sources) but from sources such as farming and forestry runoff, construction sites, urban streets (storm water), automobiles, and atmospheric depositions, such as from power-plant air emissions (nonpoint sources). Current approaches to addressing nonpoint pollution include targeting and permitting by given watersheds and TMDL (total maximum daily load for a river stretch) assessments. Many of the facilities funded by federal construction grants, which make up the wastewater collection and treatment infrastructure, were phasing out or were undersized.

Conservation and the Environment

The effects of global warming on the environmental ecosystem in which utilities must operate are creating environmental challenges for all sectors of the utility industry. Drought has caused deep cuts in the water available for all purposes, bringing on mandated conservation measures in much of the west and southwest. Conservation has resulted in reductions in earnings for many utilities, this in turn has reduced their ability to invest in the repair and replacement of old and outdated critical infrastructure. One water industry expert has described the economic effects of conservation this way:

> Conservation is, indeed, an important and valuable endeavor for all utilities, including those in seemingly "water rich" regions. The least expensive drop of water is the drop of water not used. When consumers use less water, utilities pump less through the system, process less water and generally spend less within the overall operations and maintenance of the system. At the same time, customer understanding of the true value of water and the costs associated with

providing even that first drop is critical to gaining acceptance to rate-impacting capital improvement programs. (Wallis-Lage 2014)

Wastewater Environmental Challenges

Despite the many advances in secondary and tertiary wastewater treatment technology, the despoliation of waterways with untreated or partially treated wastewater continues to be a major environmental problem. For example, in 2014, the city of Montreal, Canada announced it was planning to discharge up to eight billion liters of *untreated* sewage into the St. Lawrence River some time in 2015. The discharge was said to be necessary because of sewer pipe replacements in a highway rehabilitation project.

A number of important laws were passed to end pollution of the country's surface waters beginning in the late 1950s: In 1956 Congress passed the Water Pollution Control Act, in 1961 the Clean Water Act, and in 1965 the Water Quality Act, setting standards for states. In the 1970s, beginning with establishment of the EPA in 1970, the regulatory attack on water pollution picked up steam. Congress passed the Federal Water Pollution Control Act (the "Clean Water Act") in 1972. EPA established the National Pollutant Discharge Elimination System (NPDES) permit program in 1973, to regulate industrial point sources and concentrated animal feeding operations that discharge into other wastewater collection systems, or that discharge directly into receiving waters (more than 200,000 sources are regulated by NPDES permits nationwide); and, Congress passed the Safe Drinking Water Act in 1974. These and subsequent adjustments and amendments, plus state and local regulations, continue to place a highly challenging course of regulatory control through which operators of wastewater utilities must navigate.

The Environmental Challenge of Stormwater

A combination of heavy downpours brought about by climate change and aging infrastructure contributes to one of the wastewater sector's greatest environmental challenges. The volunteer river system protection organization *American Rivers,* released a report on the environmental damage caused by sewage pollution of the nation's rivers, streams and lakes. They determined that the damage caused by sewage effluent was caused by several factors, including failing and outdated infrastructure. Failing infrastructure is also the number one challenge for much of the public utility industry. This problem is exacerbated by population increases that lead to sprawling development that paves over the farms, forests, and wetlands that naturally soak up stormwater. As a result, rain and snow that would have naturally drained into the ground or slowly run off the land into streams now gets diverted through ditches and storm sewer pipes systems. In times of excessive rain or snow melt off, the stormwater has no place to go but often be discharged directly into public sewage systems. Even cities with separate sanitary sewers find that stormwater can flow through cracks and broken sewer lines and manhole covers into pipes that carry human waste. The result is sewer overflows of untreated effluent into natural watercourses. Several of these types of overflows were discussed earlier in this chapter.

The report noted that overflows, backflows and stormwater incursion into wastewater pipes increases the volume of wastewater that must be treated. Community sewage treatment facilities that are often already struggling to keep up with the wastewater discharged by rapidly growing populations are often overwhelmed and must release the untreated or only partially treated effluent. Box 18.3 is an excerpt from the report that describes the health damage that can be caused by untreated sewage.

BOX 18.3   HEALTH DAMAGE FROM SEWAGE OVERFLOWS

The following health damage description is taken from the 2014 American Rivers report on sewage overflow discharges into rivers and streets:

The public health and environmental implications of sewage overflows are tremendous. Sewage pollutes our waters with pathogens, excess nutrients, heavy metals, and other toxins. It kills aquatic life and creates algal blooms that can suffocate fisheries. Even worse, sewage carries pathogens that can end up in our drinking water supplies and swimming areas. These disease-causing microorganisms cause diarrhea, vomiting, respiratory, and other infections, hepatitis, dysentery, and other diseases. Common illnesses caused by swimming in and drinking untreated or partially treated sewage include gastroenteritis, but sewage is also linked to long-term, chronic illnesses such as cancer, heart disease, and arthritis.

Experts estimate that there are 7.1 million mild-to-moderate cases and 560,000 moderate-to-severe cases of infectious waterborne disease in the United States each year and the Environmental Protection Agency estimates that between 1.8 and 3.5 million people are estimated to get sick from recreational contact with sewage from sanitary sewer overflows annually. While most people recover from these diseases, they can be deadly for children, the elderly, and other patients with weakened immune systems who comprise approximately 30 percent of our population at any one time.

Source: American Rivers (2014).

ENVIRONMENT CHALLENGES IN THE SOLID WASTE SECTOR

How a society treats its solid waste is a reflection of the mores of the culture within which it appears. A rural culture with little concern for the latest consumer fad may have a distinctly different attitude for the waste that is generated and the way it is disposed than residents of an urban society. People in lesser developed societies who are concerned with scratching a living out of a poor soil or living under a despotic government with little opportunity for lifting themselves out of poverty are as likely to look upon a solid waste landfill as a resource rather than an eyesore or a danger to their health. On the other hand, people living in advanced society in which plastic and electronic consumer products abound might consider yesterday's products just something to be disposed of when something new appears. As the world continues to rapidly urbanize, not only are cities growing in size, people are throwing away greater quantities of waste.

The cities to which people are moving are tasked to manage this waste and do so in a socially and environmentally acceptable manner. However, the battle they are fighting appears to be a losing one. Stopping the growing mountains of municipal waste cannot be resolved by recycling or reuse alone. In some cases, recycling and reuse has a greater negative impact on the environment than when the material was first produced. And, it appears as if reversing the speed at which climate change is occurring is equally problematic. Waste has become what has been described as being "among the most urgent of society's challenges, threatening biodiversity and human security, and causing increases in temperature, extreme weather, sea-level rise and melting glaciers, among other impacts" (Vergara and Tchobanoglous 2012: 297). Table 18.1 is a list of the pollutants emitted from some waste treatment technologies collected from various sources and included in a comprehensive analysis carried out by Vergara and Tchobanoglous in 2012.

Cities are being forced to ship their solid waste miles from where it is collected. Even more important, solid waste production in the form of plastics and other material that do not decompose and the techniques used to collect and dispose of the waste result in the emission of greenhouse gases and other pollutants that add to climate change and are harmful to the environment and people. Solid waste impacts the environment through these emissions to the air, to land and water. The techniques used to dispose of waste—incineration and depositing in landfills—both result in greenhouse gas emissions, and/or toxic and acidic leaching into groundwater, add to the environmental problem of solid waste.

America's solid waste sector faces a number of very strict environmental rules and regulations. Every organization involved in dealing with the waste

Table 18.1   Impact of pollutants emitted from major waste disposal approaches

Disposal Method	Environmental Component		
	Atmosphere	Soil	Water
Landfilling	CO_2, CH_4, VOCs, GHGs, noxious odors	Heavy metals, organic compounds. leachate	Leachate, heavy metals, organic compounds
Incineration	SO_2, N_2O, HCI, CO, CO_2, dioxins, furans, PAHS, VOCS, GHGS, Mercury (Hg)	Fly ash, slag	Fallout of atmosphere pollutants
Composting	Odor, GHGS (minor)	Minor impact	Leachate
Recycling	GHGs (minor)	Need for landfilling of residues	Wastewater from processing

Notes:
VOCs: volatile organic compounds from cleaning products.
GHGs: greenhouse gases.
PAHs: polycyclic aromatic compounds from incomplete burning of coal, oil or natural gas.
HCI: hydrochloric acid.
Dioxins and furans: highly toxic chemicals formed during waste incineration.

Source: Adapted from Vergara and Tchobanoglous (2012).

stream, public or private, must follow EPA and state rules and operational methods. Despite the great strides Americans have made in reducing the amount of solid waste they generate each year; the increase in population simply exceeds the benefits accruing from their decrease. Globally, waste generation increases with population expansion and economic development. Improperly managed solid waste poses a risk to human health and the environment. Uncontrolled dumping and improper waste handling causes a variety of costly environmental problems, including contaminating water, attracting insects and rodents, and increasing flooding due to blocked drainage canals or gullies. In addition, it may result in safety hazards from fires or explosions. Improper waste management also increases greenhouse gas (GHG) emissions, which contribute to climate change. Planning for and implementing a comprehensive program for waste collection, transport, and disposal—along with activities to prevent or recycle waste—can help eliminate these problems. The next section uses the EPA's description of their recommended approach for dealing with solid and hazardous waste.

Integrated Solid Waste Management

The EPA's recommendation to the states and local communities for dealing with this growing amount of solid waste is a program they term *Integrated Solid Waste Management* (ISWM). This is a comprehensive waste prevention, recycling, composting, and disposal program. An effective ISWM system considers how to prevent, recycle, and manage solid waste in ways that most effectively protect human health and the environment. ISWM involves evaluating local needs and conditions, and then selecting and combining the most appropriate waste management activities for those conditions. The major ISWM activities are waste prevention, recycling and composting, and combustion and disposal in properly designed, constructed, and managed landfills. All of these activities require careful planning, financing, collection, and transport, all of which were discussed in Chapter 8.

ENVIRONMENT CHALLENGES IN THE TRANSIT SECTOR

Modern urbanized civilization depends upon transportation for its very survival. The global economy depends upon international travel and trade made possible by aviation and ocean shipping, just as the urban economy depends upon local streets and highways for its motor vehicles and rails for its mass transit. Nearly all carriers, where moving globally or locally, depend upon carbon-based fuels for motive power. But as they make transportation possible, they are also having a devastating effect upon on the global environment. Relatively cheap and plentiful petroleum products have made it possible for people, firms, armies and navies, and other stakeholders to move around the world and to benefit from the last century's great technological advances in transportation (Banister et al. 2011).

Among the problems caused by the great increases in transportation are traffic congestion in most urban areas, injury and death from transportation-related accidents, urban sprawl, concerns for fuel resource security, and possibly most damaging of all, the highly destructive damage to the environment, noise and air pollution, and the ecosystem impacts of acid rain and dying forests from the greenhouse gases that are a product of burning carbon based fuels. Climate warming and other environmental problems resulting from greenhouse gas emissions have been described as society's most pressing environmental challenges.

Benefits of Public Transportation

Public transportation provides benefits of mobility and even contributes to reductions in traffic congestions. However, public transportation is largely fueled by petroleum products, thus contributing its share to the greenhouse gas emission problem. This is even true for rail systems that run on electric power; very large coal-fired generating plants provide much of the nation's electric power. Transport overall is reported to be the only major economic sector in which greenhouse gas emissions continue to grow. The share contributed by automobiles is growing in leaps and bounds as private ownership of automobiles expands in China and India and the BRIC nations. Global trade continues to increase the need for ocean transportation and commercial aviation greenhouse gases. With road freight and private automobile growth, hope for slowing climate change by curtailing the release of greenhouse gases into the atmosphere is weak at best.

SUMMARY

Managers and administrators of public utilities have had to cultivate the knowledge, skills and willpower to survive and thrive in the face of a host of challenges based in our natural environment. Coping with increasingly restrictive environmental regulations is an ongoing challenge to the sustainability of public utilities large and small. Mandated regulations and standards form the basic operational framework and the range of options available to the utility manager. Power utilities face air, water and land pollution restrictions. Water utilities face similar pollution restrictions but must also ensure their products are safe for human consumption. Wastewater utilities must be sure their treated effluent does not harm the water courses into which that effluent is released. Sanitary landfills have clearly identified requirements for their locating and to ensure toxic wastes do not enter the natural environment. Effort to increase rates of recycling is a challenge for which there are no easy solutions or quick fixes. Public transit systems add to traffic congestion and add to the emission of greenhouse gases even while they take large numbers of passengers out of their cars and reduce the overall extent of air pollution.

This chapter examined some of the ways in which public utility organizations are coping with a growing list of increasingly stringent environmental operations regulations in a time when it is becoming more and more difficult to acquire the funds necessary to comply with those rules. At the same time, utilities must acquire the funds needed to repair and replace deteriorating infrastructures. Utility operators and managers know how to deal with operational problems; however, they are finding it increasingly difficult and costly to do so with the environmental challenges associated with global climate change. An example is the modifications which were required with passage in August 2015 of the emissions limitations by the Clean Power Plan. The final version of the country's Clean Power Plan approved in August 2015 was designed to reduce carbon pollution from all sources, but particularly from fossil-fueled electric power plants. The final plan was designed to support and strengthen the trend toward the use of cleaner and lower-polluting fuels in the country. When fully implemented, it is expected to reduce carbon dioxide emissions in 2030 by 32 percent below levels in 2005. The rule also set a target emissions rate or for the amount of carbon dioxide that could be emitted per megawatt-hour of electricity produced for each state.

Water and wastewater utilities, both separately and together, are faced with equally problematic environmental challenges, among which are finite limits to the availability of fresh water resources, pollution of supply sources, aging infrastructure needed to acquire, collect process and distribute supplies and services, the still not completely understood or agreed upon impact of climate change and the effects of new methods of oil and gas exploration upon groundwater, and the need to expand services to a growing and aging population.

Utilities in the water industry face several major environmental challenges, the impacts of which are beginning to be felt across both the water and wastewater segments of the industry. Among the most pressing are increasing water scarcity, aging infrastructure, climate volatility, maintaining sustainable water quality, and rising water-related energy risks. The water and wastewater sectors must develop and implement new water and wastewater sustainability strategies such as generating the public's acceptance of otherwise wasted alternative water as a sustainable potable water resource. More than half of the population of the United States depends on groundwater for drinking water. Groundwater is also one of our most important sources of water for irrigation. Groundwater contamination occurs when man-made products such as gasoline, oil, road salts and chemicals invade the water source, making it unsafe and unfit for human use. In addition, contaminants from the land's surface can move through the soil and end up in the groundwater; pesticides and fertilizers can find their way into groundwater supplies; road salt, toxic substances from mining sites, and used motor oil can also pollute groundwater. In addition, it is possible for untreated waste from septic tanks and toxic chemicals from oil and gas production and underground storage tanks and leaky landfills to contaminate groundwater.

Dealing with the effects upon the world's air, ground and water resources resulting from pollutants emitted from the growing mountain of solid and toxic waste is also a critical challenge for the nation's public utilities. The very methods used to deal with waste—incineration, landfill disposal, and recycling—are sources of the same toxic emissions and greenhouse gases that are responsible for the fabrication and use of the products that end up in the refuse pick-up trucks. The EPA with the participation of the waste industry has come up with a recommended plan for attacking the waste problem: integrated solid waste management. The plan includes developing and implementing procedures for cutting waste at the source, removing organic materials from the waste stream and composting where possible, and recycling, reclaiming and reusing metals and durable products.

Solid waste impacts the environment through these emissions and discharge of pollutants into the air, to land and water. Waste in the form plastics and other material that do not decompose and the techniques used to collect and dispose of the waste result in the emission of greenhouse gases and other pollutants that add to climate change and are harmful to the environment and people. The techniques used to dispose of waste—incineration and depositing in landfills—both result in greenhouse gas emissions, and/or toxic and acidic leaching into groundwater, add to the environmental problem of solid waste.

Environmental problems caused by the great increases in transportation include traffic congestion in most urban areas, injury and death from transportation-related accidents, urban sprawl, concerns for fuel resource security, and the highly destructive damage to the environment. This damage includes noise and air pollution, ecosystem impacts such as acid rain and dying forests, from the greenhouse gases that are a product of burning carbon based fuels.

ADDITIONAL READING

Baker, Lawrence A. (ed.) (2009), *The Water Environment of Cities*. St. Paul, MN: University of Minnesota.

Dow, Kirstin and Thomas E. Downey (2011), *Environmental Politics and Policy*. Washington, DC: CP Press.

Fiorino, Daniel J. (2006), *The New Environmental Regulation*. Cambridge, MA: MIT Press.

Layzer, Judith A. (2011), *The Environmental Case* (3rd edn). Washington, DC: CP Press.

Tammemagi, Hans Y. (1999), *The Waste Crisis: Landfills, Incinerators and the Search for a Sustainable Future*. Oxford, UK: Oxford University.

19. Public utility physical and cybersecurity challenges

In 2010, a large communications services provider described the security threat to U.S. and other nations' utilities as placing them in *the crosshairs of many forces in the world today*. Among the threats they saw on the horizon with the potential physical damage to utility infrastructure was the growing incidence of cyberattacks on the computer and communications systems of public utilities. These systems make up the electronic nerve system that must be protected against internal and external threats of malicious damage to utilities' operations and distributions systems. The service provider added that the federal government has evidence that shows that many utilities' computer systems have already have been breached, and that bits of code left behind can be activated in time of war or a terrorist attack to bring down major portions of the U.S. electric grid, water and transportation systems and other essential infrastructure and public service systems. This chapter looks at ways utilities plan for the operational crises caused by these man-made hazards along with the many natural disasters that they must deal with on a regular basis. The crisis amelioration methods already in place are equally valuable for dealing with crises caused by terrorists.

Environmental hazards can be any situation or state of events that pose a threat to the surrounding work, community or natural environment, and which adversely affect people's health. Categories are shown in Figure 19.1. This term includes topics like pollution and natural disasters such as storms and earthquakes and many more. Environmental hazards can be categorized in six types: natural, chemical, physical, mechanical, biological and psychosocial.

Examples of each category are included in Table 19.1. An operational crisis resulting from one or more of these hazards has been defined as: "a low-probability, high-impact event that threatens the viability of the organization and is characterized by ambiguity of cause, effect, and means of resolution, as well as by a belief that decisions must be made swiftly" (Pearson and Clair 1998: 60). Natural disasters can be and often are highly destructive of critical infrastructure and essential services. Natural disasters typically occur more often than man-caused disasters. Moreover, the damage they cause, while great to life and property, are often predictable.

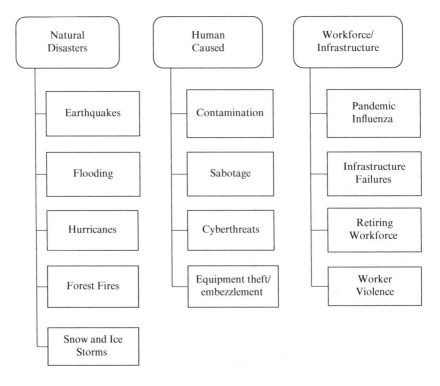

Figure 19.1   Categories and types of utility security threats

Man-made disasters such as the unexpected and unpredicted September 11, 2001 terrorist attack in Washington DC and New York City often result in as much or even greater damage to life and property than a natural event might produce. They are harder to plan for because they occur without warning.

Utilities and the federal, state, and local governments have become accustomed to dealing with damage caused by such natural disasters as hurricanes and earthquakes and regularly practice dealing with such physical phenomena. It is difficult to practice dealing with a sneak terrorist attack on isolated infrastructure or a cyberattack on a utility's computer system. The many variations of terrorist attacks are often aimed at disrupting the command and operations of critical infrastructure, with harm to civilians a secondary effect. Just the threat of such an attack can have far-reaching effects on society. However, utilities must plan to defend against both types of disasters as discussed.

Table 19.1   Categories and examples of environmental hazards

Class of hazard	Discussion
Natural hazards	Natural hazards are natural events that threaten lives, property, and other assets. Often, natural hazards can be predicted. They tend to occur repeatedly in the same geographical locations because they are related to weather patterns or physical characteristics of an area. Natural hazards that can have a major effect on utility operations include floods, fires, earthquakes, tornados, hurricanes, torrential rainstorms, snow and sleet storms, and windstorms.
Chemical hazards	Chemical hazards are present when people are exposed to any chemical preparation (solid, liquid or gas) in the workplace. Examples include: cleaning products and solvents, vapors and fumes, carbon monoxide or other gases, gasoline or other flammable materials.
Physical hazards	Physical hazards are the most common hazards in the workplace, but can also have an effect on utility operations. Workplace examples include: frayed electrical cords, unguarded machinery, exposed moving parts, constant loud noise, vibrations, working from ladders, scaffolding or heights, spills, tripping hazards.
Mechanical hazards	Mechanical hazards refer to moving machinery that can cause injury or death. Mechanical hazards occur in three basic areas: at the point where work is performed, in the power transmission apparatus and in other moving parts.
Biological hazards	Biological hazards come from working with people, animals or infectious plant material. Examples include: blood or other bodily fluids, bacteria and viruses, insect bites, animal and bird droppings.
Psychosocial hazards	Psychosocial hazards include but are not limited to stress, violence and other workplace stressful acts or situations. Examples include bullying, sexual or social harassment; occupational violence, customer aggression, and exposure to alcohol and drug misuse, poor design of work and jobs, poor communication and interpersonal relationships, and fatigue.

Source: FEMA and other government organizations.

NATURAL DISASTERS AND CRISIS MANAGEMENT

Disasters such as the Indian Ocean tsunami in 2004; the Tohoku earthquake, tsunami and subsequent Fukushima Daiichi nuclear accident in

2011; Hurricane Katrina in 2005 and Hurricane Sandy in 2012; and the vast 2015 forest fires in northwestern U.S. and Canada are examples of the increasing severity and occurrence of highly destructive natural disasters affecting U.S. and other nations' public utilities. These incidents have all contributed to making crisis planning and management a major concern of utility managers and the governments of the states and local regions in which they operate.

Among the variety of natural and man-made disasters that can result in a crisis for a public utility are such events as fires and floods, droughts, snow or ice storms, downed power lines and poles from windstorms and hurricanes, broken water mains, backed up sewage systems, power blackouts, terrorist bombings of public events and places, and simply failure of the utility infrastructure due to old age. Utilities employ tried and proved crisis management procedures for dealing with these disasters.

CRISIS MANAGEMENT

Crisis management is a management tool defined as the systematic effort that involves the prompt and effective handling of unusual, unanticipated, and serious problems that all utilities face. Utility crisis planning involves programming the combined tools of analysis, forecasting, and planning in order to be prepared to deal with unexpected crises and disasters. Measuring the effectiveness of prior planning for the wide range of potential crises is problematic if not impossible. Without proper metrics, it has been common for utility managers to point to an after-the-fact word of a potential crisis having been averted as a measure of the effectiveness of their crisis management programs. However, as destructive weather events grow in severity and rate of occurrence, a greater emphasis on crisis preparation is needed.

Crisis Management at the Global Level

Regardless of where an operational crisis occurs, effective crisis management is all about minimizing potential risk before a triggering event. In response to a triggering event, effective crisis management involves improvising and interacting by key stakeholders so that individual and collective sense making, shared meaning, and roles are reconstructed. Following a triggering event, effective crisis management entails individual and organizational readjustment of basic assumptions, as well as behavioral and emotional responses aimed at recovery and readjustment. The International Organization for Standardization (ISO) has prepared a number of recommendations for utilities and other organizations on the adoption of crisis management processes and procedures; its latest in-depth publication, ISO 24, was published in 2015.

The Paris-based Organization for Economic Cooperation and Development (OECD 2012) published a summary of agreements that were reached at an international conference on crisis management policies and procedures, the 2012 Workshop on Inter-Agency Crisis Management. The conference was jointly organized by the OECD and the Swiss Federal Chancellery. Representatives from 40 European countries, academia, the private sector and international organizations met to share the challenges they face in dealing with crisis management. The conference was held as part of the OECD's ongoing High-Level Risk Forum. The essential need for greater cooperation and joint-planning was spelled out in the early pages of the working session report. Moreover, despite their leaning toward a trans-European solution, the concepts addressed are equally applicable for the U.S. federal state and local governments and public utilities:

> The complexities of modern crises often require the involvement of many actors, above and beyond emergency services, and this demands effective co-ordination for a successful outcome. The need for co-ordination also raises significant public governance challenges, as crisis management functions are often exercised at sub-national levels, but coordinated at the centers of governments. The capacity to coordinate crisis management is a fundamental element of good governance, as it tests governments' capacity to provide the appropriate responses at the right time, in order to protect their citizens and businesses and mitigate the impact of disasters. Ensuring that national authorities have the right tools and institutional framework for coordinated action is critical. (Baubion 2013: 4)

A number of social forces have contributed to the changes now occurring in the type and severity of operational challenges. Among these are urbanization and globalization, the increasing complexity and interconnected character of modern society, and the increasing severity and frequency of extreme weather events and rising sea levels, and changing nature and severity of international terrorist activity have led to greater emphasis on the need for multilevel and trans-border crisis management planning and action.

Crisis Management at the Federal Level

In February 2003, President George W. Bush signed Homeland Security Presidential Directive 5 as the key element in the government's plan to "enhance the ability of the United States to manage domestic incidents by establishing a single, comprehensive national incident management system" (DHS 2015b). The President's action made DHS the lead agency for guiding the federal government's coordinated program for dealing with terrorist attacks and natural disasters as called for in the Homeland Security Act of 2002. DHS became responsible for federal preparations, response and recovery from terrorist attacks, major disasters and other designated emergencies (incidents). Two programs were created to aid federal, state and local governments and public utilities in designing and implementing crisis and emergency programs: the National Incident Management System (NIMS), and the National Response Plan (NRP). According to the Federal Emergency Management Agency (FEMA), NIMS is intended to be used by all governments and all response agencies, including all individuals, families, communities, the private and nonprofit sectors, faith-based organizations, and local, state, tribal, territorial, insular area, and government agencies. The National Response Plan (NRP), implemented in February 2004, integrates prevention, preparedness, response and recovery plans into an all discipline, all hazards approach. The NRP is also intended to identify and locate the structure and mechanisms for national level policy and operational direction for federal support to state, local and tribal incident managers.

The National Interagency Incident Management System

The National Interagency Incident Management System (NIIMS) was developed after 9/11 to provide a common system that emergency service agencies can employ at local, state, and federal levels. NIIMS consists of these five major subsystems that together form a total systems approach to all risk incident management:

- An incident command system (ICS)—that includes operating requirements, interactive components and procedures for organizing and operating an on-scene management structure.
- Standardized training that supports the effective operation of NIIMS.
- A qualifications and certification system that meets standard personnel training, experience, and physical requirements to fill specific positions in the Incident Command System.
- Publications management that includes development, publication, and distribution of NIIMS materials.
- Supporting technologies—such as satellite remote imaging, sophisticated communications systems, geographic information systems, and so on that support NIIMS operations.

Local governments have traditionally been responsible for responding to and managing emergency and disaster incidents. The 2002 Act required the DHS to provide to public and private employees from all local response agencies the necessary training and other assistance to prevent, prepare for and respond to all types of incidents. The DHS/FEMA Emergency Management Institute (EMI) offers a wide variety of free independent study courses on the basic and advanced concepts of Emergency and Disaster Management.

A national incident management system (NIMS) became the core guiding document for all interagency incident management. This system was intended to provide a standard system for federal, state, local and tribal governments to work together to prepare for and respond to incidents. NIMS is based on six steps for agencies to follow that are based on the NIIMS program: (1) Command and Management, (2) Preparedness, (3) Resource Management, (4) Communications and Information Management, (5) Support Technologies, and (6) Ongoing Management and Maintenance. Command and Management is the key component in NIMS. This component mandates the use of the Incident Command System (ICS) by all entities and their personnel involved in local incident management, including public and private public works agencies and utilities. Preparedness is the second most important element. This component recognizes that responder ability is significantly enhanced if the agency personnel and the agency as a whole has worked with other relevant agencies prior to an incident. NIMS outlines advance preparedness measures such as planning, training, exercises, qualifications and certification of personnel, and equipment acquisition.

The National Integration Center (NIC) at FEMA develops national standards for education and training, communications and equipment, typing of resources, and the qualifications and credentialing of response and management personnel, each of which has a significant impact on public works agencies and employees across the United States.

National Response Plan

A new feature of the NRP establishes a national framework for assessing incidents and for coordinating interagency management efforts in events that are considered incidents of national significance. These include:

- Credible threats, indications or acts of terrorism within the U.S.
- Major disasters and emergencies as defined by the Stafford Act.
- Catastrophic incidents—incidents with extraordinary levels of casualties and damage that severely disrupt the population, economy, infrastructure or environment.

- Unique situations, such as when a federal agency acts under its own authority or the event exceeds the parameters of other established federal plans, events of regional or national importance that involve one or more federal agencies, such as use of the National Contingency Plan.
- National Special Security Events (for example, Super Bowl, World Series, political conventions).

NIMS-NRP Relationship

Together NIMS and the NRP "provide a standardized framework that ensures that federal, state, local and tribal governments, the private sector and non-governmental organizations, work in partnership to support domestic incident management regardless of cause, size, or complexity (all-hazards). Using NIMS as a foundation, NRP establishes the national organization structure and the procedures for activation and application of federal resources during "Incidents of National Significance" (Lux 2005). A brief description of how a New England gas and electric power utility follows the NIMS procedure in preparing its annual emergency plan is included Box 19.1.

PHYSICAL ATTACKS ON UTILITY INFRASTRUCTURE

There are two broad classes of physical human-caused crises in the utility industry. One is damage to life and property perpetrated with malicious intent or intentional malfeasance and criminal activity; the other is damage brought about through unintentional accidents or lack of knowledge of the consequences of a human act. Among the malicious human generated reasons that result in a need for crisis management are extortion, malevolent product tampering (such as injecting water supplies with toxic substances), civilian deaths caused by vehicle mishandling or tampering, environmental damage from hazardous chemical spills, control tampering, security breaches, workplace violence, plant explosions or fires, release of toxic chemicals, and the physical destruction of iconic or operational infrastructure. Physical attacks carried out by known or suspected belligerents are difficult to predict but many have been prevented as a result of good human intelligence gathering. Cyberattacks are even harder to predict where and when they will occur, primarily because the source is often unknown or suspected; teenaged playful perpetrators have often been identified as creators of very damaging malware.

BOX 19.1 GAS AND ELECTRIC LIGHT COMPANY'S EMERGENCY RESPONSE PLANNING

The Fitchburg Gas and Electric Light Company, doing business as *Unitil*, distributes electricity and natural gas to approximately 170,000 customers through its subsidiaries in Maine, Massachusetts, and New Hampshire. The company annually publishes an updated emergency response plan (ERP) that includes descriptions of the company's System Emergency Operations Center (S-EOC) and its regional emergency operations centers. The purpose of the plan is to "ensure the effective implementation and coordination of the corporate emergency response actions under adverse conditions." Emergencies can be declared by senior officers when weather or other natural or man-made causes such as equipment failures, civil unrest, terrorism, wildfires, snow storms and the like result in a substantial loss of service that cannot be rectified by normal operating procedures.

Unitil uses the NIMS system to guide its emergency response preparedness. The role of NIMS was described in the emergency response plan this way: [NIMS] improves the effectiveness of emergency response providers and incident management organizations across a full spectrum of potential incidents and hazard scenarios. NIMS relies on the Incident Command system (ICS) to coordinate and manage the response of an organization.

The utility has formed its response team around the ICS, combining facilities, equipment, personnel, procedures, and communications to operate within a broad mix of emergencies from small to complex incidents, both natural and man-made including actions of catastrophic terrorism and major equipment failures . . . Unitil's planning follows that of the recommended ICS protocol and is organized around the five major functional areas: Command staff, Operations, Planning, Logistics and Administration/Finance.

Source: Unitil (2012).

Examples of relatively recent physical attacks on the electricity grid, while apparently planned, were not considered to be actions by terrorist groups. An attack on an electric substation in California in April 2013 was later described by an industry spokesman as the most significant incident of domestic terrorism involving the grid that had to that time ever been observed. In that attack, one individual broke into an underground vault and cut fiber optic cables. Then, one or more persons fired their rifles on the aboveground substation, destroying 17 transformers before fleeing. Although the attack appeared to have been planned as opposed to a random act of vandalism, FBI investigators denied the involvement of a terrorist organization. The perpetrators were never caught and no one claimed responsibility (Tweed 2014).

Such vandalism was not an isolated occurrence. A December newspaper article stated that federal energy records indicated the U.S. power grid is the victim of either a cyber or a physical attack about every four days (Reilly 2015). There were in the neighborhood of 360 reported attacks on electric infrastructure from 2011 to 2014, 14 of which were cyberattacks. The physical damage caused by the attacks was usually small, and not nearly as costly as the 2003 cascading electric power blackout that left much of the U.S. northeast and eastern Canada without power for some customers for several days. That outage was caused by a branch falling over wires in Ohio.

CYBERATTACKS ON UTILITY OPERATIONS

The Department of Homeland Security's Industrial Control Systems Cyber Emergency Response Team (ICS-CERT) strongly encourages all utilities to take immediate defensive action to secure ICSs by following the program it terms "defense in depth principles." This includes regular audits of the utility's networks for Internet facing devices, weak authentication methods, and component vulnerabilities. It is also necessary to understand the usage of tools, such as Google and SHODAN (a search engine that tells the user what devices are hooked into the Internet). These platforms can be leveraged to improve awareness of the Internet-accessible devices that might exist within the utility's information system infrastructure. ICS-CERT also recommends that users take defensive measures to minimize the risk of exploitation as follows:

- Minimize network exposure for all control system devices. In general, locate control system networks and devices behind firewalls and isolate them from the business network. When remote access is required, employ secure methods, such as Virtual Private Networks (VPNs), recognizing that VPNs may have vulnerabilities and should be updated to the most current version available. Also recognize that VPN is only as secure as the connected devices.
- Remove, disable or rename any default system accounts wherever possible.
- Implement account lockout policies to reduce the risk from brute forcing attempts.
- Establish and implement policies requiring the use of strong passwords.
- Monitor the creation of administrator level accounts by third-party vendors.
- Apply patches in the ICS environment, when possible, to mitigate known vulnerabilities. Organizations that observe any suspected

malicious activity should follow their established internal procedures and report their findings to ICS-CERT for incident response support and correlation with other similar incidents.

Government, trade associations and state utility commissioners agree that the information (IT) systems of all utilities are vulnerable to cyberattacks. This includes all the business process and systems and networks that connect data and perform intelligent tasks with that data can be and have been subject to data theft and misinformation. According to the National Association of Regulatory Utility Commissioners (NARUC), this vulnerability includes both components, such as individual workstations, and networks that allow interoperability between components:

"IT security begins by protecting the network that enables the flow of data through the system, as well as by protecting the data itself. . . . IT connects all systems, from simple to complex, including communications between systems like the hub or the switch all the way to the firewall and the server . . .. IT, cybersecurity not only includes software and hardware strategies–passwords, antivirus systems, firewalls, logical and physical separation of servers, for example–but also training personnel and creating policies so that their interaction with the IT system enhances, rather than erodes, cybersecurity. Because of this human element, simply upgrading or making hardware more obscure does not equal improved cybersecurity. (NARUC 2013)

Control Systems Security

SCADA systems are automatic control devices and software that provide simple functions such as "on/off" water purification applications, processed wastewater sensor capability, communications capability and human–machine interface (HMI) software applications that provide machine information for human use. In short, secure SCADA assures that the process equipment does what it is supposed to do and does it accurately. NARUC (2013: 7) described the security concern this way:

With a secure SCADA system, you can trust what your machine is telling you . . . these systems more and more often have connections to Internet Protocol (IP) networks, including the Internet in some cases. Even those physically and logically disconnected from other systems may be locally or remotely accessible and have vulnerabilities to be exploited [through cyberattack]. SCADA access and control points are also frequently located in remote and unmanned areas of the utility system, and therefore may require either increased physical security or the ability to isolate those points from the overall system if they become compromised.

SECTOR SECURITY PLANNING

The U.S. Department of Homeland Security (DHS) has warned the public that critical infrastructure such as power, water, oil, and natural gas utilities are all at risk of both physical and cyberattack (Brocklehurst 2014). Utility companies' vulnerability to cyber threats has been a particular worry for the electric grid. Power companies use Supervisory Control and Data Acquisition (SCADA) systems to control their operations and to keep the grid operating efficiently. However, these do not render the systems secure. One reason why is because many of the SCADA systems were developed before security became such a concern. Another is that many utilities have not addressed their security threat as much as they might have. The DHS Industrial Control Systems Cyber Emergency Response Team (ICS-CERT) recommended utilities make the cyber security arrangements listed in the security alert in Box 19.2.

Crossborder Cybersecurity Vulnerability

The vulnerability of the nation's utility systems and networks has made security an increasingly important aspect of crisis management. For example, the Department of Homeland Security, British Columbia Gas; British Columbia Hydro; Duke Energy; Pacific Gas and Electric; Williams Gas Pipeline; Puget Sound Energy; the Port of Seattle; the Idaho Bureau of Disaster Services; the U.S. Navy; the National Infrastructure Protection Administration: these are some of the typical organizations monitoring and preparing to deal with disasters and terrorist attacks on the public utilities of North America. Network security managers find they must now plan on a regional basis and work with a wide variety of public and private stakeholders to develop and manage preparedness strategies. These strategies must include protection, severity reduction, response, recovery, training, and disaster management research and development.

The Pacific Northwest Partnership for Regional Infrastructure Security (PNPRIS) is an example of a successful utility security cooperative association. One of the training exercises sponsored by PNPRIS involved a disaster scenario devised by representatives from the Bonneville Power Center; telecommunications companies Telus, Verizon, and Qwest; the Federal Emergency Management Agency (FEMA); the British Columbia Provisional Emergency Program; and the Canadian Office of Critical Infrastructure Protection and Emergency Preparedness (OCIPEP). The scenario theme was a disruption to the northwest's electric power grid. It also included terrorist and nonterrorist disruptions of natural gas transmission and distribution systems, municipal water systems, regional ports,

---

BOX 19.2   CYBER SECURITY PROTECTION STEPS UTILITIES SHOULD TAKE NOW

The Department of Homeland Security's Industrial Control Systems Cyber Emergency Response Team (ICS-CERT) strongly encourages taking immediate defensive action to secure ICSs by using what it terms "defense in depth principles." These include the following advice:

Audit your networks for Internet facing devices, weak authentication methods, and component vulnerabilities. Understand the usage of tools, such as SHODAN [a search engine that tells the user what devices are hooked into the Internet] and Google, and leverage those platforms to enhance awareness of the Internet accessible devices that might exist within your infrastructure. ICS-CERT also recommends that users take defensive measures to minimize the risk of exploitation as follows:

- Minimize network exposure for all control system devices. In general, locate control system networks and devices behind firewalls and isolate them from the business network. When remote access is required, employ secure methods, such as Virtual Private Networks (VPNs), recognizing that VPNs may have vulnerabilities and should be updated to the most current version available. Also recognize that VPN is only as secure as the connected devices.
- Remove, disable or rename any default system accounts wherever possible.
- Implement account lockout policies to reduce the risk from brute forcing attempts.
- Establish and implement policies requiring the use of strong passwords.
- Monitor the creation of administrator level accounts by third-party vendors.
- Apply patches in the ICS environment, when possible, to mitigate known vulnerabilities.

Organizations that observe any suspected malicious activity should follow their established internal procedures and report their findings to ICS-CERT for incident response support and correlation with other similar incidents. We urge critical infrastructure operators . . . to ensure that they are not directly accessible from the Internet.

Source: ICS-CERT (2014).

---

and telecommunications systems. Disruptions of those critical public services affected other independent infrastructures, including transportation systems, emergency services, public safety services, hospitals, and cross-border cooperation. A chief result of the training session was that many participants discovered that their organizations' contingency plans were negated by the cross-border interdependencies that exist among the region's public services.

Table 19.2   Steps for establishing or improving a cybersecurity program

Step	Steps	Discussion
1	Prioritize and Scope	Identify business/mission objectives and high-level organizational priorities; make strategic decisions regarding cybersecurity implementations and determine scope of systems and assets that support the selected business line or processes that may have different business needs and associated risk tolerance.
2	Orient	Identify related systems and assets, regulatory requirements, and overall risk approach; identify threats to, and vulnerabilities of, those systems and assets.
3	Create current profile	Develop a current profile by indicating which category and subcategory outcomes from the Framework Core are currently being achieved.
4	Conduct risk assessment	Create a target profile that focuses on the assessment of the framework categories and subcategories of the desired cybersecurity outcomes; consider influences and requirements of external stakeholders such as sector entities, customers when creating a profile.
5	Create a target profile	Compare the current profile and the target profile to determine gaps; prioritize action plan to address those gaps that draws upon mission drivers, a cost–benefit analysis, and understanding of risk; determine resources necessary to address the gaps.
6	Determine, analyze, and prioritize gaps	Compare the current profile and the target profile to determine gaps; prioritize action plan to address those gaps that draws upon mission drivers, a cost–benefit analysis, and understanding of risk; determine resources necessary to address the gaps.
7	Implement action plan	Determines which actions to take in regards to the gaps, if any, identified in the previous step; monitor current cybersecurity practices against the target profile.

Source: NIST (2014).

Energy Sector Cross-Border Concerns

Cybersecurity concerns have long been more focused on the security of the nation's electric grid than on other sectors of the utility industry. In 2014, the Bipartisan Policy Center released a detailed report that echoes that focus: *Cybersecurity and the North American Electric Grid: New Policy Approaches to Address an Evolving Threat.* However, despite this traditional focus the increasing numbers of reports of cyberattacks upon the U.S. government, financial institutions, and businesses being reported in the media have helped commissioners and administrators of all sector utilities recognize that the threat is as much their concern as it is for the energy sector utilities.

Security Planning at State and Local Levels

Following federal guidelines, each state has engaged in some level of planning for and implementing physical cybersecurity measures for some or all the public utility sectors operating in their states. This is in addition to their already comprehensive regional approach to preparing for any damage to their utility systems brought on by natural disasters. Preparing for natural disaster and cyberattack and other actions also occurs at the interstate and international level. The Partnership for Regional Infrastructure Security (PNPRIS) is typical of the cooperative problem-solving environment of water and wastewater operations at the state and regional levels. One of the training exercises sponsored by PNPRIS involved a disaster scenario devised by representatives from the Bonneville Power Center; the telecommunications companies Telus, Verizon, and Qwest; the Federal Emergency Management Agency (FEMA); the British Columbia Provisional Emergency Program; and the Canadian Office of Critical Infrastructure Protection and Emergency Preparedness (OCIPEP).

The scenario theme was a hypothetical disruption to the northwest's electric power grid. It also included terrorist and nonterrorist disruptions of natural gas transmission and distribution systems, municipal water systems, regional ports, and telecommunications systems.

Connecticut and Pennsylvania are among the states that have taken a proactive position regarding protecting their utilities against cyberattack, malware, and overt terrorist action.

Security at the Utility Level

Public utilities, like all branches of public services are subject to the same type and scope of cybersecurity attacks as are other government agencies. Moreover, an attack on their operations has a direct impact upon citizens and civil institutions. Small utilities in all sectors tend to not be as prepared as major federal and state agencies to counter attacks on their information systems. Many, if not most, of the thousands of small local distribution utilities have no cybersecurity plans whatsoever. Utilities are responsible for maintaining the viability of critical infrastructures, information systems and assets. The incapacity or destruction of water, energy and transportation systems, for example, would have an exceedingly harmful impact on national security, economic well-being, and public health or safety. As these critical services are dependent on computer systems and networks, the interconnectivity between information systems, the Internet, and other infrastructures, opportunities for attackers to disrupt critical systems, with potentially harmful effects have become commonplace. This list of cyber security weakness in agencies can be said to apply with equal import to federal agencies and local utilities (GAO 2015):

- System-access controls that ensure only authorized individuals can read, alter, or delete data, remain weak.
- Configuration management controls that provide assurance that only authorized software programs are implemented are still to be fully implemented.
- Segregation of duties, decentralization and weak supervision that can reduce the risk that one unauthorized individual can perform inappropriate cyber actions without detection are restricted by the lack of funds for employing adequate professional and supervisory personnel.
- Planning for continuity of operations so that significant disruptions in computer-dependent operations are avoided is seldom carried out to the extent needed.
- Organization-wide information security programs that provide a framework for ensuring that risks are understood and that effective controls are in place and implemented are not adequate or not yet designed.

Local utilities and associated government departments and agencies such as public utility commissions hold potentially sensitive information about individuals and businesses such as trade secrets, enforcement data, social security numbers, credit card numbers, and home addresses, to name just some. This sensitive information in electronic form is held in laptops, thumb drives, PDAs (personal digital assistants), backup tapes, emails and other electronic media. This makes it accessible to hackers and cyber terrorists. What some utility sectors are doing to protect themselves against cyberattack is discussed in the next sections. A seven-step process for developing a utility's cybersecurity plan is shown in Table 19.2.

Energy sector security

Constant attention paid to cybersecurity has become critical to maintaining the security and reliability of the nation's electric grid. In response to the growing cyberattack threat, the U.S. Department of Energy's (DOE) Office of Electricity Delivery and Energy Reliability (OEDER) released its final version of its Energy Sector Cybersecurity Framework. This framework is designed to assist energy sector organizations in the voluntary implementation of their security plans and programs. The DOE's role in ensuring a secure electric grid is considered to be particularly important because it is the most complex, extensive and critical infrastructure that other sectors depend upon to deliver essential services. Since the 1990s, the roles of the electricity sector have changed significantly: generation, transmission, and delivery functions are now separated into distinct markets; many customers have become generators using distributed generation technologies; and distribution utilities have been forced to take on new responsibilities to provide advanced technologies and improve security. Importantly, providing better security is not an idle exercise; the U.S. electric grid has been hit by at least 15 cyberattacks since 2000, according to the U.S. Department of Energy. The U.S. Industrial Control System Cyber Emergency Response Team said 32 percent of its responses to threats against critical infrastructures in 2014 happened in the energy sector.

Executive Order 13636 of February 2014 provided encouragement and direction for the energy sector to strengthen its cybersecurity ability. It was designed to help make it possible for utilities of all sizes and degree of cybersecurity risk or sophistication to apply the tested principles and procedures of risk management in order to improve the security of their critical infrastructure. Its use is not voluntary and not designed to replace any existing security arrangements. The DOE framework identified three classes of cybersecurity risk management approaches, one for the energy industry in total, and one each for the electricity and the natural gas sectors. A brief list of examples of cybercrime tactics are shown in Table 19.3.

Water and wastewater sector security
The U.S. Department of Homeland Security (2010) has warned that along with the rest of the country's critical infrastructure, the water and wastewater systems sector is vulnerable to a variety of attacks, including contamination with deadly agents, physical attacks such as the release of toxic gaseous chemicals and cyberattacks. If these attacks occur:

Table 19.3   Examples of cyberattack tactics

Type of threats	Discussion
Malware	Malware presents a direct threat to a utility's daily operations, directly impacting the availability of critical assets and data. DHS and the U.S. Computer emergency Readiness Team (US-CERT) encourage organizations to evaluate their planning, preparation, detection, and response for such an event. Destructive malware will use popular communications to spread, including worms sent through email and instant messages.
Social Engineering and Phishing	A social engineering attacker uses human interaction (social skills) to obtain or compromise information about an organization or its computer systems. An attacker may seem unassuming and respectable, possibly claiming to be a new employee, repair person, or researcher and even offering credentials to support that identity. By asking questions, he or she may be able to piece together enough information to infiltrate an organization's network. Phishing is a form of social engineering. Phishing attacks use email or malicious websites to solicit personal information by posing as a trustworthy organization.
Spyware	This is malware designed to spy on the victim's computer. When installed on your computer, spyware may send pop-up ads, redirect your browser to certain websites, or monitor the websites that you visit. Some extreme, invasive versions of spyware may track exactly what keys you type. Attackers can use spyware for malicious purposes.
Trojan	Trojan horses have the ability to hide from antivirus detection and steal important financial and other data. Most of the popular threats come from the Trojan family such as Zeus and SpyEyeIt. If the Trojan is really powerful, it can take over a utility's entire security system. As a result, a Trojan can cause many types of damage starting from personal computers to the organization's online accounts.
Rootkits and botnets	A rootkit is software that can be installed and hidden on computer without a user's knowledge. It may be included in a larger software package or installed by an attacker who has been able to take advantage of vulnerability on your computer or has convinced you to download it, enabling it to access information, monitor your actions, modify programs, or perform other functions on your computer without being detected. A botnet is an automated computer program, or "robot." Bots refer to computers that can be controlled by one, or many, outside sources. An attacker usually gains control by infecting the computers with a virus or other malicious code that gives the attacker access to your system.

Source: United States Computer Emergency Readiness Team (US-CERT 2013).

The result could be large numbers of illnesses or casualties and/or a denial of service that would also impact public health and economic vitality. Critical services such as firefighting and healthcare (hospitals), and other dependent and interdependent sectors, such as Energy, Food and Agriculture, and Transportation Systems, would suffer negative impacts from a denial of service in the Water and Wastewater Systems Sector. (DHS 2010)

In 2015, the International Standards Organization released ISO 24518 to serve as a guideline that water and wastewater utility operators can use to ensure a sufficient and safe water supply and a sanitary wastewater system is available during a natural or human instigated crisis.

Water utility concerns
The American Water Works Association (AWWA) compiled a list of five areas of concern for water utilities that also apply to energy, refuse and transportation utilities. They described these concerns as the "key drivers" of utility security: physical security, cyber security, security laws, executive orders, and emergency preparedness. The physical security of water utilities is the concern that led to the passage of the Bioterrorism Act of 2002. However, physical security was thought to not be adequately addressed beyond the traditional concept of more gates and guards. The AWWA recommended that the U.S. Department of Homeland Security's utility safety recommendations be considered areas of special concern.

The physical security of water utilities was the nation's concern that led to the passage of the Bioterrorism Act of 2002. However, physical security is not adequately addressed through the traditional concept of more gates and guards. It is better characterized in two security standards developed by AWWA in collaboration with various stakeholders that have received Safety Act designation by the U.S. Department of Homeland Security. These standards include updating the utility's vulnerability assessment no less than every five years, updating emergency response plans and business continuity plans as appropriate. The EPA and utility operator associations have developed physical security guidelines for drinking water and wastewater utilities. While the design-basis threat approach has been superseded, the fundamental elements for physical security consideration during design and construction of utility facilities remain sound as originally proposed. Resources dedicated to security and preparedness needs should be included in the annual operational plan as well as the utility's strategic plan. Provisions for contamination monitoring and surveillance must be a constant operational element, with defensive shields never let down.

Waste collection and disposal security

The nation's highly urbanized society cannot function without adequate systems for the collection and disposal of the mountains of solid waste generated each day and the vast amounts of hazardous and toxic wastes produced by industry and commerce. Anyone living in a city where these services are interrupted even for one or two weeks in a labor dispute knows how disruptive piles of uncollected trash on the sidewalks and spilling into the streets can be. Uncollected waste attracts insects and rodents that in turn can spread disease among humans.

To ensure that the waste collection and disposal system functions as designed requires the same type of electronic SCADA systems that energy and water utilities employ. The information such systems carry is typically transmitted over the Internet and as a result, subject to hacking and malware. Information about employees and customers is also maintained in electronic records, again subject to hacker activity.

PUBLIC TRANSIT SYSTEM SECURITY

The American Public Transportation Association (APTA) has made a concerted effort to warn its transit system members that cybersecurity is a concern that affects all transit agencies from large to small, and one that systems must plan for and take action to ensure their critical operations are not threatened by. The increasing occurrence and complexity of cyberattacks have required transit system operators to take action to protect their critical operating information and maintain the ability to supply service to their riders. The vulnerability of their systems to cyberattacks on information technology (IT) has been a common strategy used by hackers and terrorists. Big and small transit systems are heavily dependent on information technology systems and are, therefore, targets in a wide variety of cyberthreats. Cyberattacks can destroy a transit agency's operation systems, overload them to the point where they become inoperable, or pass control of those systems to outside intruders. This has become a common path for collecting private data on employee or customer data.

Despite the undeniably costly effects of a cyberattack, the mass destruction and loss of life as a result of physical terrorist attacks on transit systems can be even more destructive. Since the 9/11 attacks, terrorists have plotted more than 700 attacks on surface transportation systems internationally. In the U.S., the FBI and other security agencies have stopped more than 50 of these attacks before the damage took place. New York police uncovered a 2003 plot to release cyanide gas in the city's subway system. In 2006, the FBI discovered a plan to place suicide bombers on a

PATH train and to destroy the retaining wall separating the Hudson River from the World Trade Center site in a plan to cause massive flooding in the city's financial district. In 2013, police in Cleveland arrested five would-be terrorists accused of plotting to blow up a four-lane highway bridge. In 2009, seven men came within days of executing a plot to conduct coordinated suicide bombings in the New York City subway system.

Growing Intensity of Transit Attacks

Examples of successful attacks on public transit systems include the deadly nerve gas attack on the Tokyo subway system in March 1995, the damage to New York's subway system and surface transit operations as a result of the September 11, 2001 terrorist attack on New York's World Trade buildings, and the 2005 subway and bus bombings in London. These three disasters illustrate the carnage that result from such attacks on mass transit systems.

On March 20, 1995, members of a Japanese religious cult dropped five plastic bags of liquid sarin on subway trains packed with rush-hour commuters in the Japanese capital. This coordinated attack, at the height of the morning rush hour, was carried out by five two-man terrorist teams from the cult, riding on separate subway trains. As the trains converged at the station the terrorists pierced their packets of liquid sarin with metal-tipped umbrellas, releasing deadly nerve gas. They then took a sarin antidote and escaped while the commuters, blinded and gasping for air, fled to the exits. Twelve people died, and 5,500 were treated in hospitals, some in a comatose state. Most of the survivors recovered, but some victims suffered permanent damage to their eyes, lungs, and digestive systems. Experts later agreed that if the sarin gas had been disseminated more effectively at the station at the major hub of the Tokyo subway system, tens of thousands might have been killed.

Almost 3,000 lives were lost in the 9/11 New York City aircraft attack; extensive damage to the city's transportation and communications infrastructure also occurred. The destruction included collapsing of subway tunnels for Lines 1 and 9, destruction of the New York Port Authority's Trans-Hudson (PATH) train station at the World Trade Center, bus facilities on the streets surrounding the attack site, and important parts of the telecommunications and power infrastructure in Lower Manhattan, including a switching facility and substations.

In the midst of the morning commute of Thursday, July 7, 2005, three bombs exploded simultaneously, destroying sections of three different London Underground train lines. One bomb was detonated just outside Liverpool Street station, a second outside the Edgware Road and the third between Kings Cross and Russell Square. An hour later an explosion on the top level of a double-decker bus in Tavistock Square near Kings Cross was caused by a device similar to the ones used on the underground. The explosions left 52 innocent people dead and over 700 injured. The attacks brought the city's public transport network to a standstill, with the complete closure of the underground system and Zone 1 bus networks forcing thousands of commuters to find other ways home.

To be effective, a transit agency's system security and cybersecurity strategy must be an integral part of the organization's operations at all levels. While eliminating cyber threats is impossible, transit agencies can take a risk-based approach. No longer is mainlining system sustainability in the event of physical damage and cybersecurity just an IT department problem. It has become a critical management element that requires involvement at all levels of the organization. In 2013, the APTA released a document meant to guide operators in maintaining security that all transit agencies, large or small, can use: the *Cybersecurity Considerations for Public Transit Recommended Practice.*

SUMMARY

On November 20, 2015, the Federal Energy Regulatory Commission (FERC) approved a proposal to enhance the physical and cyber security for most-critical bulk-power system facilities and reduce the overall vulnerability of the grid to physical and cyberattacks. FERC approved a physical security Reliability Standard submitted by the North American Electric Reliability Corporation (NERC). The new reliability standard requires owners and operators of the bulk-power system to perform a risk assessment of their systems to (1) identify critical facilities; (2) evaluate potential threats to, and vulnerabilities of, those facilities; and (3) develop and implement a security plan to protect against attacks on those facilities. While not directly attributed to any specific identified threat to the system, the action occurred at a time of heightened threats from international terrorist organizations, social unrest among groups in several urban areas, and physical violence.

This chapter looked at ways utilities plan for the operational crises caused by human actions along with the many natural disasters that they already deal with on a regular basis. The crisis amelioration methods already in place are equally valuable for dealing with crises caused by terrorists. Hazards that result in operational crises can be grouped into four main categories: natural, technological, societal and security. Natural disasters can be, and often are, highly destructive of critical infrastructure and essential services. Natural disasters typically occur more often than man-caused disasters. Moreover, the damage they cause, while great to life and property, are often predictable or come with some warning that give utility managers time to prepare the resources necessary to deal with the crisis. Man-made disasters such as the unexpected and unpredicted September 11, 2001 terrorist attack in Washington DC and New York City seldom occur with advance warning. When they do they result in as much or even greater damage to life and property than a typical natural event might produce. Man-made hazards are harder to plan for because they occur without warning.

Federal, state, and local government agencies and the utilities for which the agencies provide regulatory oversight have become accustomed to dealing with damage caused by such natural disasters as hurricanes and earthquakes and regularly practice dealing with such physical phenomena. It is extremely difficult to practice dealing with a sneak terrorist attack of an unknown type on an isolated utility infrastructure or a cyberattack on a utility's computer system. The many variations of terrorist attacks are often aimed at disrupting the command and operations of critical infrastructure, with harm to civilians a secondary effect. Just the threat of such an attack can have far-reaching effects on society. However, utilities must plan to defend against both types of disasters.

ADDITIONAL READING

Clark, R.M., S. Hakim and A. Ostfeld (eds) (2011), *Handbook of Water and Wastewater Systems Protection*. New York: Springer-Scientific.

Gordon, Lawrence A. and Martin P. Loeb (2006), *Managing Cybersecurity Resources: A Cost–Benefit Analysis*. New York: McGraw-Hill.

Lewis, Ted G. (2014), *Critical Infrastructure Protection in Homeland Security: Defending a Networked Nation*. New York: Wiley.

Mullen, Samuel (2013), *Emergency Planning Guide for Utilities* (2nd edn). Boca Raton, FL: CRC Press.

Ness, Larry (2006), *Securing Utility and Energy Infrastructure*. Hoboken, NJ: Wiley-Interscience.

Singer, Peter, W. and Allan Friedman (2014), *Cybersecurity and Cyberwar: What Everyone Needs to Know*. Oxford, UK: Oxford University.

States, Stanley (2009), *Security and Emergency Planning for Water and Wastewater Utilities*. Denver, CO: American Water Works Association.

20. Sustainability: the core challenge facing public utilities

The public utility sector of the U.S. utility industry is in many ways in the best shape it has been for a long time as a result of intense study and investment that occurred in the last two decades of the last century. The private versus public ownership battle has been put to rest; privatization and other industry restructuring has been shown to not always provide the tremendous cost savings promised since the 1990s; the financial status of both the investor-owned and publicly owned utilities have emerged from the deepest recession since that of the 1930s capable of carrying them through most of the challenges facing them in the next quarter-century. Prices for the newly discovered accessible sources of carbon-based energy have dropped precipitously from their historic highs, making it far less costly to generate electricity and heat homes and offices, cutting heating and air-conditioning bills for much of the nation. The uncharacteristically warm early 2015–2016 winter in the eastern United States resulted in the lowest prices for natural gas in more than a dozen years. Water conservation efforts of states and local communities are working; all sectors of the economy seem to be using less water. Amounts of solid waste generated by households and businesses continue to decline while recycling percentages grow. A decade of investment in public transportation has brought dependable, low-cost mobility to thousands in both urban and rural regions of the country.

Yet, despite all these accomplishments, the public utility future is not all as rosy as it appears. As managers and administrators in the public utility industry approach the last years of the first quarter of the increasingly turbulent twenty-first century the challenges before them are exacerbated by human and natural events and conditions not previously encountered. The combination of climate change, security threats, population growth, urbanization and road congestion, and infrastructure deterioration is building a set of challenges for utility managers that promise to severely strain their financial resources. Lower gas and electricity prices means lower revenues for the necessary repair and modernization of utility product delivery infrastructure.

THE NATURE OF UTILITY SUSTAINABILITY

All sectors of the public utility are increasingly concerned about their sustainability, their ability to meet their mandates to provide dependable services at affordable prices. The problem is that traditional definitions of sustainability have focused on development more than continuity. There are many different definitions of sustainability, but the formal definition cited most often is the 1987 Brundtland Report definition for sustainable development:

> Sustainable development is development that meets the needs of the present without compromising the ability of future generations to meet their own needs. It contains within it two key concepts: (1) the concept of 'needs', in particular the essential needs of the world's poor, to which overriding priority should be given; and (2) the idea of limitations imposed by the state of technology and social organization on the environment's ability to meet present and future needs. (WCED 1987: 43; cited in Twink.org 2015 online)

A number of critics have objected to the Brundtland Report's emphasis on development, focusing instead on the long term viability of a behavior, policy or activity. Examples of definitions more applicable for public utilities pay less attention to development and more to continuing to function in a changing economic, environmental and political environment include this definition in the online *Oxford Dictionary*: If something is sustainable it is "able to be maintained at a certain rate or level; conserving an ecological balance by avoiding deletion of natural resources; able to be upheld or defended, as in *sustainable definitions of* [a] *good . . . practice.*" An earlier example was provided by a *Center for Sustainability* in Great Britain: Sustainability is "the capacity for continuance into the long term future. Anything that can go on being done on an indefinite basis is sustainable. Anything that cannot go on being done indefinitely is unsustainable" (cited in Twink.org online 2015). Perhaps the briefest is this definition from Canada's transport policy institute: "Sustainability is the ability to continue a defined behavior indefinitely" (Litman and Burwell 2006: 333). The American Public Transportation Association defines sustainability as "at its core, a way to make our communities more livable by integrating and balancing economic, social and environmental needs" (APTA 2015).

Although each sector of the industry has its own list of the challenges that the individual sector considers to be the major barriers to its own sustainability over the remaining first half of the twenty-first century, a number of issues are common to the industry as a whole. Table 20.1, for example, is a list of the top ten issues deemed important by the managers in all sectors of the public utility industry in 2015. The list of challenges

Table 20.1   Top ten challenges facing managers in all utility sectors

Challenge	Discussion
Aging infrastructure and rising operating costs	The great majority of expansion to the electric, water, wastewater, and solid waste infrastructure was put into place in the decade preceding and the three decades following the Second World War. As a result, time, heavy use and the effects of corrosive environment influence has rendered much if not most of that infrastructure obsolete and subject to failure.
Finding financing for repairs and replacement of critical system components	The decades of significant federal investments in utility infrastructure are long gone. Utilities must find new sources of financing improvements and replacement of failing infrastructure.
Aging and retiring workforce	Much of the utility industry's skilled workforce has reached the age of retirement and there are few properly trained and educated replacement workers available.
Effects of climate change on supply	Climate change is having a significant impact on the already stressed utility infrastructure. Parts of the country are experiencing dramatic increases in severe storms while others are suffering from severe drought conditions. Repair and replacement requirements far exceed strategic plans for meeting the demands from the adverse climate.
Environmental restrictions	Damage to the environment from decades of carbon-based fuel for power generation, over-use of groundwater resources, and pollution of many surface water resources has resulted in transformative changes in utility operations and mitigation of past damage.
Increasingly stringent regulatory environment	Decades of utility regulatory standards have resulted in a growing load of compliance requirements. And, the federal and state governments are adding to utility's mandated compliance with stricter standards.
Difficulty in securing needed rate increases	The general public, long having benefited from some of the lowest costs for utilities services, are finding it difficult in reconciling the shift for full cost of service rate increase with older subsidized rates.
Demographic changes	The aging general population has placed a heavier responsibility upon public utilities for reduced cost services. At the same time, population growth has resulted in greater demand for services, often in areas of the nation where service is more difficult to supply.
Combating cyber and physical threats	Cyberthreats and physical attacks to existing infrastructure, along with more destructive severe weather, places greater need for security planning and implementation upon utilities.

Table 20.1   (continued)

Challenge	Discussion
Changing demand structure	The movement of large numbers of citizens from the northeastern and north central sections of the nation to the west and other sunbelt states has resulted in stagnant or declining demand (and revenue) for some utilities while placing heavy demand for new infrastructure to supply needed service, often where supply is limited.

Source: Author's conclusions from diverse sources.

identified by representatives of the electric utility sector in 2014 and 2015 seen in Table 20.2 show how the relative importance of the issues shift in importance from year to year. Underlying all these specific challenges is the absolute necessity for retaining operational sustainability. Society requires energy, water, and other public services to survive. Governments will do whatever is necessary to ensure those services are safe and reliably provided. The problem for utilities is balancing the sustainability requirement with the need for complying with societal demands as interpreted by legislators and mandated by oversight agencies.

This chapter looks at five of the major sustainability challenges that face utility managers and administrators in the next fifty years. These include repairing and replacing aging infrastructure; dealing with the increasingly stringent regulatory environment; meeting operation changes necessitated by climate change and its related repercussions; securing the necessary funding for capital improvements; and protecting utility infrastructure and operations against physical and cyberattacks. The order presented is not the same order of important challenges reported by responders from all sectors, but one in which all five factors are found high in the list for all sectors.

THE INFRASTRUCTURE CHALLENGE

In a 2015 report by the National Academy of Engineering (NAE), restoring and improving the nation's deteriorating infrastructure was rated high on a list that the association termed the "14 grand challenges for engineering in the twenty-first century." Infrastructure consists of the combination of physical and managerial structures and systems that support an institution, an industry, community, region, or country. It includes everything from water and sewer systems to road and rail networks to the national power and

Table 20.2 Shifting challenges in the electric utility industry, 2014–2015

Rank	2014 Challenge Category	% Ranked Critically Important	2015 Challenge Category	% Ranked Critically Important
1	Old infrastructure	48	Old infrastructure	47
2	Current regulatory model	32	Aging workforce	39
3	Aging workforce	31	Current regulatory model	38
4	Distributed generation	30	Stagnant load growth	28
5	Flat demand growth	28	Federal emissions standards	25
6	Smart grid deployment	23	Physical and cyber grid security	24
7	Grid reliability	21	Distributed energy resources	23
8	Coal plan retirements	17	Coal plant requirements	21
9	Groundwater pricing	17	Grid reliability	17
10	Renewable portfolio standards	17	Smart grid deployments	16
11	Energy efficiency mandates	16	Renewable portfolio standards	13
12	Emission standards	12	Energy efficiency mandates	9
13	Cybersecurity	11	--	--

Source: Utility Dive (2014, 2015).

natural gas grids. In a word, it describes the nation's utilities. The size of the problem and its costs for just one large U.S. city are described in Box 20.1.

 In its broadest sense, the water supply infrastructure includes surface and groundwater sources, the groundwater wells, and surface-water intake facilities and equipment, reservoirs of untreated water for municipal, industrial, agricultural and household needs, the dams and water supplies stored behind the dams, the reservoirs of finished water, aqueducts and pipes, storage tanks, treatment plants, pumping stations, systems that distribute water to users, and the wastewater collection and treatment facilities that process the treated water prior to release into wetlands or water courses. In the continental U.S., there are close to 77,000 dams and reservoirs, 168,000 utilities that treat and distribute fresh water, and somewhere

BOX 20.1   REPLACING AGING WATER PIPES; A MULTI-
             BILLION DOLLAR DILEMMA

A water main break in 2013 sprayed water a foot in the air through a hole in the buckled asphalt that left residents in the Venice neighborhood of Los Angeles without water service for hours. The break was just another in an increasingly common pattern for the aging waterworks of the California city. The pipe was more than 80 years old; it was rusted out; and, it was buried in corrosive soil. About one-fifth of the city's 6,730 miles of main water pipes were installed before 1931 and nearly all will reach the end of their useful lives over a 15-year period. The breaks are responsible for close to half of all water main leaks, and replacing them is a $1-billion problem for the city. According to the Los Angeles Department of Water and Power, replacing just 435 miles of deteriorating pipe by 2025 is expected to cost $1.3 billion. But, finding the money for the repairs and whether the utility can ever catch up with its aging infrastructure are questions still not answered.

Los Angeles water officials estimate that about eight billion gallons of water are lost each year to leaky pipes, firefighting, evaporation, theft and other unaccounted losses, though they emphasize that the leak rate has been in decline over the last decade, and is about half the industry average. But the lost water is enough to supply an almost 50,000 households for a year. In Los Angeles in 2014, a water main estimated to be 93 years old broke wide open, causing severe flooding on the campus of UCLA.

Future funding for the plan will depend on a combination of higher water rates, bond sales and other department revenue.

Researchers estimate as much as 2.1 trillion gallons of treated water is lost each year in the U.S. because of aging and leaky pipes, broken water mains and faulty meters. Fixing that infrastructure won't be cheap, which is something every water consumer is likely to discover.

The Chicago-based Center for Neighborhood Technology, a nonprofit organization focused on sustainability, has estimated about six billion gallons of water is lost each day in the U.S., much of it just leaking out of old iron pipes and water mains that crack and break.

Source: Poston and Stevens (2015); Schaper (2014).

near 16,000 publicly owned wastewater treatment facilities. All of these facilities operate day and night, every day of the year, year after year. And most are vulnerable to some type of infrastructure failure. As noted earlier, the nation's public utilities as a group could be given no higher grade of a D+ by the civil engineers association for the failure to make the repairs and renewals of their infrastructure.

Three sectors of the public utility industry have been identified by DHS as part of the nation's critical infrastructure: water, telecommunications, and energy (DHS, 2015a). These utility sectors are all highly reliant on one another for their operations and in some instances they are co-located at the same geographic location (that is, hydroelectric dams, pipes secured to bridges, and telecommunications antennas on water tanks and standpipes). In addition, an outage in any one of these sectors could have a significant impact on the other DHS-identified 17 critical infrastructures.

THE REGULATORY CHALLENGE

The Federal Power Act (FPA) of 1935 established the regulatory system of the federal government regulating interstate wholesale electric transactions and state regulatory organizations being responsible for intrastate retail transactions. Under FPA, FERC oversees the rates, terms and conditions of sales of electricity for resale (wholesale transactions) and transmission service in interstate commerce. FERC regulates primarily investor-owned utilities and does not have jurisdiction over federal entities, such as the Bonneville Power Administration (BPA) or the Tennessee Valley Authority (TVA), cooperatives, municipalities, or the Electric Reliability Council of Texas (ERCOT). States are responsible for regulating intrastate retail transactions, including the distribution of electricity. Most state regulatory commissions have major responsibility to assure that retail electric consumers have adequate and reliable electric service. The Energy Policy Act of 1992 (EPAct) introduced wholesale competition in the electric power industry, and subsequent FERC orders have encouraged the formation of regional transmission organizations to facilitate access to the transmission system. In addition, many states have moved to allow competition on the retail level. Reliability and infrastructure protection were not addressed in federal and state restructuring legislation, and there is currently no federal regulation of electric network security. Until recently, impacts of competition on physical and cyber-security of the electric power industry were not part of the congressional debate.

The close regulatory oversight of the nation's water sector can be said to have begun with the Federal Water Pollution Control Act of 1948, the first major U.S. law to address water pollution. Growing public awareness and concern for controlling water pollution led to sweeping amendments in 1972. As amended in 1972, the law became commonly known as the Clean Water Act (CWA). Provisions of the Water Act formed the basic structure for regulating pollutant discharges into the waters of the United States, gave EPA the authority to implement pollution control programs, reinforced existing requirements for water quality standards for all contaminants in surface waters, and made it unlawful to discharge any pollutant from any source into navigable waters, unless a permit was obtained under its provisions. Revisions in 1981 streamlined and improved the construction process and capabilities of municipal treatment plants built under the program. Changes in 1987 phased out the construction grants program, replacing it with the State Water Pollution Control Revolving Fund, more commonly known as the Clean Water State Revolving Fund. Additional laws and amendments have altered parts of the Clean Water Act and added others, although the basic provisions remain in place.

The nation is far better off as a result of the Clean Water Act and its follow-on standards and the implementation of those standards by state and local environmental and public health agencies. However, meeting the health and safety requirements by utilities has not always been a simple task. As more and more stringent requirements are added, adjustments and clarifications to the CWA continue. On August 5, 2015, for example, the EPA administrator signed a final rule updating six key areas of the federal water quality standards regulation to help implement the Clean Water Act. The final revisions are said to "provide a better-defined pathway for states and authorized tribes to improve water quality, protect high quality waters, increase transparency and enhance opportunities for meaningful public engagement at the state, tribal and local levels" (EPA 2015g). The previous regulation had been in place since 1983. These program areas were addressed in the final rule: (1) the EPA's determinations that new or revised water quality standards are necessary, (2) designated uses for water bodies, (3) triennial reviews of state and tribal water quality standards, (4) antidegradation requirements, (5) water quality standards variances, and (6) provisions authorizing the use of schedules of compliance for water quality-based effluent limits in NPDES permits.

The determination statement explained that the changes were needed to allow the EPA and states and tribes to communicate directly and specifically on areas where water quality standards improvements should be considered and for the EPA to announce determinations made under relevant sections of the CWA. The alteration was made to comply with the rule that all compliance standards applicable to water utilities must be reviewed triennially. The final rule requires that if a state or tribe chooses not to adopt new or revised criteria for any parameters for which EPA has published new or updated criteria recommendations under the CWA, they must explain their decision when reporting the results of their triennial review to the EPA.

THE CLIMATE CHANGE CHALLENGE

Although there may be a few critics who still discount the possibility of global warming, the scientific community is in general agreement that the earth is getting hotter. In the 2015 annual state-of-the climate report of the National Oceanic and Atmospheric Administration (NOAA) and the American Meteorological Society it was reported that ocean surface temperatures in 2014 were the warmest in 135 years of recordings and sea levels reached record highs (NOAA 2015). The year was also the hottest year on record at the earth's surface; many locations reported extreme heat waves; the world's glaciers and Arctic and Antarctic sea ice continue to melt. Scientists from the U.S. Geological Survey reported extreme soil shoreline erosion taking place in regions of northern Alaska. Box 20.2 describes how climate change is expected to affect different regions of the U.S.

Greenhouse Gas Concentrations

Carbon dioxide, methane, and nitrous oxide—the major greenhouse gases released into the atmosphere—once again all reached record high average concentrations in 2014. Carbon dioxide increased by 1.9 parts per million (ppm), reaching a global average of 397.2 ppm for the year. Altogether, the contributions of 5 major and 15 minor greenhouse gases were 36 percent greater than they had been just 25 years ago. Europe had its warmest year on record, with close to two dozen countries breaking their previous national temperature records. Many countries in Asia had annual temperatures among their 10 warmest on record. Africa reported above-average temperatures across most of the continent throughout 2014. Australia recorded its third warmest year on record, following record heat there in 2013. Mexico had its warmest year on record, and Argentina and Uruguay each had their second warmest year on record. Eastern North America was the only major region to observe a below-average annual temperature.

It was the oceans that drove the record global surface temperature increase in 2014; the globally average sea surface temperature (SST) was the highest on record. This was particularly noticeable in the North Pacific Ocean, where unusually warm water in the northeast Pacific occurred over the winter of 2013–2014. The report added that because of ocean warming and ice melts, upper level ocean waters reached record highs for the year, "reflecting the continued increase of thermal energy in the oceans, which absorb over 90% of Earth's excess heat from greenhouse gas" (Blunden and Arndt 2015). The global mean sea level in 2014 was 67 millimeters

BOX 20.2   HOW CLIMATE CHANGE WILL EFFECT
DIFFERENT REGIONS OF THE U.S.

According to the Intergovernmental Panel on Climate Change (IPCC), the extent of climate change effects on individual regions of the United States will vary geographically and over time. The IPCC predicts that increases in global mean temperature of less than 1.8 to 5.4 degrees Fahrenheit (1 to 3 degrees Celsius) above 1990 levels will produce beneficial impacts in some regions and harmful ones in others. Some of the impacts that can be seen now and will continue to impact these regions in the future as published by the National Aeronautics and Space Administration are included below.

Northeast. Heat waves, heavy downpours, and sea level rise pose growing challenges to many aspects of life in the Northeast. Infrastructure, agriculture, fisheries, and ecosystems will be increasingly compromised. Many states and cities are beginning to incorporate climate change into their planning.

Northwest. Changes in the timing of stream flow reduce water supplies for competing demands. Sea level rise, erosion, inundation, risks to infrastructure and increasing ocean acidity pose major threats. Increasing wildfire, insect outbreaks, and diseases are causing widespread tree die-off.

Southeast. Sea level rise poses widespread and continuing threats to the region's economy and environment. Extreme heat will affect health, energy, agriculture, and more. Decreased water availability will have economic and environmental impacts.

Midwest. Extreme heat, heavy downpours, and flooding will affect infrastructure, health, agriculture, forestry, transportation, air and water quality, and more. Climate change will also exacerbate a range of risks to the Great Lakes.

Southwest. Increased heat, drought, and insect outbreaks, all linked to climate change, have increased wildfires. Declining water supplies, reduced agricultural yields, health impacts in cities due to heat, and flooding and erosion in coastal areas are additional concerns.

Source: NASA (2014).

higher than the 1993 average level. Figure 20.1 shows which areas in the nation are predicted to have more and which will have less rainfall in the next decades.

Climate change is having a negative effect on the environment from which America's utilities acquire or produce, use and distribute the resources considered vital for modern society. A group of a scientists and government agency personnel working together in the Intergovernmental Panel on Climate Change (IPCC) released their third climate change impact assessment in 2014. The chapter on climate change impacts in the United States produced the following 12 key messages that public utility managers and administrators should be aware of and plan for (Walsh et al. 2014, 20–21):

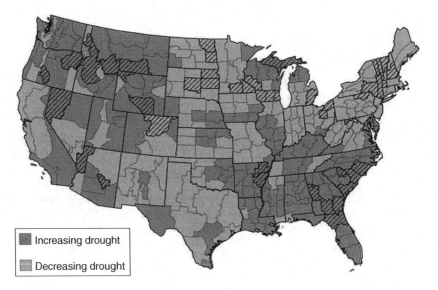

Notes: Hatching in regions indicated severe changes in drought conditions.

Source: USCGRP photo printed in EPA (2015a).

*Figure 20.1   Expected patterns of climate change-related drought
conditions in the U.S.*

1. The global climate is changing. That change is apparent in a wide
    range of phenomena. Change that has occurred since the 1950s is
    primarily due to human activities.
2. Global climate change is expected to continue over the rest of this
    century and beyond. The amount of change occurring over the
    next several decades depends on how much heat-trapping gases are
    emitted globally and how the Earth reacts to the increases.
3. U.S. average temperatures have increased by 1.3° F. to 1.9° F since
    record keeping began in 1895; most of this increase has occurred
    since 1970. The decade 2000 to 2010 was the warmest on record.
    Temperatures are expected to continue to rise, but the effects of the
    rise will differ from region to region (Box 20.1 explains the differences).
4. The frost-free season has lengthened, particularly since the 1980s,
    resulting in a longer growing season, mostly in the western U.S. The
    growing season length is expected to continue to grow.
5. While average precipitation has increased since 1900, the increases
    have not been the same across the country. More winter and spring
    precipitation is projected for the northeast and less for the southwest.

6. Very heavy downpours are occurring more often and are expected to occur more often over the rest of the century. The largest increases have occurred and are expected to continue to do so in the Midwest and northeast.

7. Extreme weather events are occurring more often. Heat waves become more frequent, are hotter, and last longer, especially in the western regions. Cold waves have occurred less often and are less severe. Droughts in the southwest are expected to last longer and be more intense.

8. North Atlantic hurricanes have increased in intensity, frequency and duration since the early 1980s. The length of the season is expected to increase in the future.

9. Winter storms in general have increased in frequency and intensity since the 1950s. The patterns of frequency and intensity of tornados, hail storms and damaging thunderstorm winds are still uncertain.

10. Global sea levels have risen about eight inches since record keeping began in the 1880s. They are expected to rise another one to four feet by the end of the century.

11. Ice volume and the surface extent of ice on land, lakes and seas is decreasing as a result of rising overall temperatures. The Arctic Ocean is projected to be essentially ice free during the winter months before 2050.

12. The world's oceans now absorb about 25 percent of the emitted carbon dioxide annually and are becoming more acidic as a result. This is intensifying impacts on marine ecosystems.

For the electric and natural gas energy sector of the industry, increases in domestic supply and resulting declining energy prices are straining profits needed to fund the infrastructure replacement needs; climate change is causing changes in weather patterns that are resulting in warmer winters, stronger rainstorms in some regions and huge drought-caused fires and parched fields in others; the security threat is greater than ever; and environmental and health concerns are resulting in ever-greater health and safety regulations. Warmer temperatures are changing the seasonal demand structure for electricity and natural gas from winter heating to summer air conditioning. At the same time, conservation of resources has helped to reduce the total demand for energy and water, thus reducing the income streams needed to fund critical infrastructure repairs and new construction. Much if not most of the utility distribution infrastructure in both the publicly owned and investor owned sectors of the utility industry suffer from a heightened degree of aging along with their inefficient and or obsolescent physical plants. Lower levels and warmer surface water makes it harder and more costly to cool electricity generating equipment. Blackouts that darken the northeastern United states and Canada, toxic algae blooms that force utilities to cut tap water supplies to a half million or more residents in the American Midwest, long-term droughts with higher temperatures that severely reduce the supplies of water available in a dozen or more western states: these are just a few of the mega-challenges facing utility managers.

Effects on the Energy Sectors

Climate change is the chief environmental factor seen as having a significant impact on the generation and use of electricity and production and distribution of natural gas. Warming across the nation is increasing electricity demand for cooling in the summer while decreasing demand for electricity, natural gas, heating oil and wood products for heating during the winter.

Although there still may be a few critics who discount the possibility of global warming, the scientific community is in general agreement that the earth is getting hotter. In the 2015 annual state-of-the-climate report of the National Oceanic and Atmospheric Administration (NOAA) and the American Meteorological Society it was reported that ocean surface temperatures in 2014 were the warmest in 135 years of recordings and sea levels reached record highs. The year was also the hottest year on record at the earth's surface; many locations reported extreme heat waves; the world's glaciers and Arctic and Antarctic sea ice continue to melt. Scientists from the U.S. Geological Survey reported extreme soil shoreline erosion taking place in regions of northern Alaska. This is resulting in significantly lower consumption rates for winter heating and record demand for air conditioning use in the warmer months.

Effects on the Water and Wastewater Sectors

Climate change is having a significant impact on the amount and distribution of water available for human and agricultural use in the United States. Records of rainfall since 1950 reveal that the amount of rain falling during the most intense one percent of storms has increased by nearly 20 percent (USGCRP 2009). Warmer winter temperatures are causing more rain to fall over ocean areas and some land regions, and less snow to accumulate. Snow accumulations are beginning to melt earlier in the year, thereby changing the streamflow patterns. Normally arid regions are receiving less precipitation, with droughts increasing in length.

The experience of an Ohio public water system is included here to illustrate how warming affects water systems. America's Great Lakes are estimated to hold 20 percent of the entire world's supply of freshwater. The problem with that supply is that much of it is become polluted. The latest consequence of that pollution occurred in Lake Erie in the summer of 2014 when the City of Toledo and western Ohio was forced to warn roughly a half million residents of the region not to drink the water (Arenschield 2014). In what was a repeat version of the toxic algae bloom that threatened Cleveland in 2011, a large concentration of algae came together where Toledo draws its water from the lake. Algae flourish in warm shallow waters; Lake Erie is the shallowest of the Great Lakes. The blue-green algae (microcystis) produce microcystin, a toxin that not even boiling removes from the water; all boiling does is concentrate the toxin, making it more harmful to humans and animals. Microcystin is not the only bacteria found in the lake; traces of E. coli bacteria have also been found on the beaches of Lake Erie and other lakes in the region.

Water utility administrators in Toledo and other utilities in the region were reluctant to seek other locations in the lake for water intakes because as of 2014 the Environmental Protection Agency (EPA) has not yet approved a standard for testing the presence of the toxin. After missing for twenty years, low levels of the toxin were again found inside the water processing plant since 1995. However, those low levels of the toxin were effectively removed during the plant's multi-stage treatment process (Henry 2014). That is no longer the case.

A consultant's audit report of the Toledo water utility completed after a 10-month study criticized the utility for such weaknesses as not having a strategic plan, experiencing more workplace injuries than the industry average, salaries below the industry average, supervisors who don't supervise anyone or anything, a weak and inefficient customer call center, slow follow through on repair orders, and slow replacement of damaged water mains and sewer lines.

Modern agriculture benefits greatly from the use of phosphorus as fertilizer and is a contributor to the economy of Middle America. However, heavy winter rains resulted in major fertilizer runoff during the previous several years. That runoff of phosphorus is considered the major cause of the algae bloom, while the use of nitrogen fertilizer contributes to the size and make-up of the annual bloom. The affected water cannot be used for cooking or food processing, only adults were supposed to use the tainted water for bathing, although no one was permitted to swim in the polluted region of the lake.

THE FINANCING CHALLENGE

Public utilities are similar in many ways. They all provide a necessary public service; they are all rather heavily regulated and monitored by regulators in one or more levels of government. They are either departments of government organizations (state and local), quasi-government organizations in that they exist as independent nonprofit organizations, or they are investor-owned companies that are constantly and closely monitored at both the federal and state levels of government. They are also similar in their search for innovative solutions to all types of managerial and operation problems, including finding the affordable financing needed to make required capital improvements. Because of this close association with government that finds itself in a similar situation, this discussion focuses on funding innovation in the public sector. A center of research on this field is the Ash Center for Democratic Governance and Innovation of Harvard University's Kennedy School of Government.

The search for innovative solutions to major funding needs may be the greatest challenge facing all utilities in the remaining first half of the twenty-first century. Aging infrastructure, changing weather conditions, heightened security concerns, rapidly changing technology, and retaining qualified professional personnel all make demands for funding that cannot be met by rate increases. Hence, utilities are examining new and better ways of operating, including examining new approaches to governance.

Adopting alternative forms of governance has been a solution to the funding difficulty that has been tried extensively in Europe and to an increasing degree in the United States. This change has entailed privatizing publicly owned utilities. A number of privatized failures has curtailed this approach. Another model that has been tested and found to have greater promise is what is known as the collaborative or cooperative innovation model. For investor-owned utilities, innovation is spurred by the quest for maintaining and improving profits through new, creative and better ways of operating. For government and nonprofit utilities, the profit motive does not exist. Hence, public and nonprofit sector utilities depend on innovative ways of solving their daily policy and management problems. Borins (2014: 6) has explained the growing acceptance of cooperative innovation in the public sector as a natural product of what he saw as an underlying willingness to innovate among public servants:

> The urge to innovate is ... born of a belief in government as a solution, a belief that government can find better ways to deliver services [including public utilities]. Innovators share a conviction that creative problem solving, inspired

improvisation, experimentation, and risk-taking within their organizations are possible.

The commitment to innovation continues to grow, as is the willingness to embrace open innovation through inter-organizational collaboration. It is happening in all sectors of the utility industry and all sizes of organizations. And, it is not happening just in the United States: innovation at all levels of government is now a global phenomenon.

Public service organizations have been forced to change the way they operate. Political pressures and the need to fund wars in the Middle East have made it more and more difficult for governments, including utilities, to secure the funds needed to operate, repair weather damage and aging infrastructure, let alone grow to meet the mandate to serve all comers. Innovative solutions to old problems have become a necessity. Innovation begets transformational change in all types of organizations. Jonathan Breul (2006: 7) described the need for greater inter-organizational cooperation in innovation this way:

> Rising public expectations for demonstrable results and enhanced responsiveness will require fundamental *transformation* of government—where roles and even continued existence of some organizations and functions will be at stake .... Government organizations need to pick up the pace to become less hierarchical, process-oriented, stovepiped [i.e., single-purpose], and inwardly focused. They will need to become more partnership-based, results-oriented, integrated and externally focused. (Breul 2006: 7)

Abramson, Breul and Kamensky (2006) outlined six broad categories of innovative solutions that utility managers must develop and adopt in response to the pressures for change they face (McNabb 2009). Collectively, responses to these and other demands for change are spurring greater and inter-organizational transformation. They include:

1. Changes in the rules of government, in the way public work takes place.
2. Changes in the management of government operations through implementation of performance management practices.
3. Changes from bureaucratic to market-based governance.
4. Changes that enable agencies to provide services on demand.
5. Changes from tolerating citizen participation to encouraging and re-engaging the electorate and encouraging greater volunteer involvement.
6. Changes in the structure of services delivery to include collaboration, public–private teamwork, networks, partnerships, and coalitions.

Collaboration in seeking and applying innovative solutions to problems has become increasingly the norm among organizations providing public services. Borins (2014) found a wide shift over a 15-year period in the sources and characteristics of innovative programs among the many public service organizations applicants to the Harvard University Kennedy School's Innovations in American Government awards. The number of organizations reporting they collaborated with external organizations increased from 28 percent of the 1990–1994 pool of applicants to 65 percent of the semifinalists in 2010. Collaboration with other government organizations similarly grew from 21 percent in the early 1990s to 58 percent of the applicants in 2010. Decreases were reported in just two of the eight categories of characteristics mentioned: process improvement, 34 percent in the early 1990s pool to 29 percent in 2010, and in citizen empowerment, from 26 percent in 1990–1994 to 16 percent in 2010 (Borins 2014: 10).

THE SECURITY CHALLENGE

Security attacks on public utilities come from a variety of causes, including bad weather, disgruntled employees, vandalism and terrorist activity. In the electric and natural gas energy sectors, physical attacks might target transformers, transmission towers, substations, control centers, power plants (including nuclear reactors or dams), or, gas wells, collection and processing centers, pipelines and fuel delivery systems. Terrorist threats to the public utilities of the United states include physical attacks, as well as attacks on computer systems, or cyberattacks (this section draws heavily on the congressional report on cyberwarfare by Abel, Parfomak and Shea 2004). Cyberattacks could include attempts to interrupt power plant and transmission system operations, including interrupting normal water flow at hydroelectric facilities. Each of these components are vulnerable to a variety of threats that range from weather-related incidents and vandalism to more infrequent, but potentially more devastating, acts of terrorism (Seger 2003).

There are two broad classes of physical human-caused crises in the utility industry: damage to life and property perpetrated with malicious intent or intentional malfeasance and criminal activity; and damage brought about through unintentional accidents or lack of knowledge of the consequences of a human act. Among the malicious human generated reasons that result in a need for crisis management are extortion, malevolent product tampering (such as injecting water supplies with toxic substances), civilian deaths caused by vehicle mishandling or tampering, environmental damage from hazardous chemical spills, control tampering, security breaches, workplace violence, plant explosions or fires, release of toxic chemicals, and the physical destruction of iconic or operational infrastructure. Physical attacks carried out by known or suspected belligerents are difficult to predict but many have been prevented as a result of good human intelligence gathering. Cyberattacks are even harder to predict where and where they will occur, primarily because the source is often unknown or suspected; teenaged playful perpetrators have often been identified as creators of very damaging malware, for example.

Security in the Energy Sector

Service disruptions are the result of physical attacks on electric power targets, including power lines, substations, transformers, and central power stations. Usually, electric outages are caused by use of a weapon to shoot out transformers or use of simple tools to take down transmission towers, sometimes with the intention of causing outages but usually as a result of mischief. Most utilities and regional transmission organizations have crisis management and recovery plans in place to minimize the effect of an outage. However, a planned terrorist attack could damage the electric power system well beyond the level of normal design criteria for maintaining reliability and recovery. Under extreme scenarios, large portions of the United States could be without power for several months. The potential for terrorist attacks has pushed the topic of reliability into the federal policy arena from its traditional venue of being an industry responsibility, subject to state regulatory authority.

Beginning in the 1990s, federal policies began emerging to ensure the protection of the nation's infrastructure, including the electric system, from terrorist activities. The potential for terrorist attacks on the electric and natural gas energy system has pushed reliability into the federal policy arena from its traditional position as an industry responsibility. In 1996, the President's Commission on Critical Infrastructure Protection was created to address concerns relating to the vulnerability of critical national infrastructures. The President's Commission's report stated that: "Of particular concern are the bulk power grid (consisting of generating stations, transmission lines with voltages of 100 kV or higher, plus 150 control centers and associated substations) and the distribution portion of those electric power systems where interruption could lead to a major metropolitan outage" (Whitehouse 1996). On December 17, 2003 the Department of Energy (DOE) was identified as the lead agency with which the energy industry must coordinate responses to energy emergencies. However, DOE had only limited authority in the energy infrastructure security area. The

North American Electric Reliability Council (NERC) assumed coordination responsibilities for the private electric utility sector. NERC retains
responsibility for promulgating and overseeing reliability guidelines for the
electric power industry but NERC does not have enforcement authority;
industry compliance remains voluntary for electric utilities. Portions of
DOE's energy infrastructure security and assurance activities, including
parts the Office of Energy Assurance and the National Infrastructure
Simulation and Analysis Center, were transferred to the Department of
Homeland Security (DHS). In March 2003, the Department of Energy
(DOE) was assigned responsibility for all energy supply and demand
issues; energy reliability; energy emergencies; technology; training and
support; coordination; and energy policy. The critical infrastructure protection functions of the DHS are generally expected to include: security issues; threats and terrorism; and critical infrastructure protection.
However, according to both DOE and DHS, their responsibilities overlap
on some energy security issues, including emergencies, vulnerability and
critical assets. Even though DHS and DOE have various responsibilities
for infrastructure protection the agencies do not have regulatory authority to force utilities to implement security initiatives (Abel, Parfomak and
Shea 2004).

Security in the Water and Wastewater Sector

Drinking water and wastewater utilities have been included as a single
sector in the Department of Homeland Security's 18 critical infrastructure sectors that must be protected against natural and terrorist damage.
Water systems are vulnerable to a variety of natural and human-caused
threats (Van Leuven 2011). Over the first ten years of the twenty-first
century, growing concerns about critical infrastructure becoming potential
targets by terrorist attacks in the United States have forced the water and
wastewater utility sector to focus greater attention upon real and potential
security threats. These utilities, with those of the energy sectors, make up a
considerable portion of the nation's critical infrastructure. Figure 20.2 lists
the categories and examples of the three types of threats to public utilities.
   Physical or cyberattacks to any of the systems of the water or wastewater sectors could have ramifications far beyond the public's understanding. Disruption of operating or distribution system elements, power or
communications systems, electronic SCADA systems, and damage to
reservoirs or pumping stations could result in a loss of treatment and flow
to customers and make firefight efforts difficult. Destruction of a large
dam would result in catastrophic flooding and death, as well as cost of
the water stored in the reservoir. Bioterrorism or chemical attacks could

Example threats to utilities' operations		
Natural Disasters	**Physical Incidents**	**Cyberthreats**
• Blizzards	• Hazmat spills/releases	• Malware
• Floods	• Physical breaches	○ Viruses
• Droughts	• Vandalism	○ Spyware
• Hurricanes	• Arson	○ Worms
• Fires	• Laptop theft	• Password attacks
• Tornadoes	• Workplace violence	• Denial-of-service
• Earthquakes	• Mechanical failures	• Cyber theft
• Power outages		

Figure 20.2   Classes and types of threats to utility operations

cheaply and rapidly deliver contamination from small amounts of micro-biological agents or toxic chemicals. Cyberattacks on computer operations could shout down an entire network, curtail the flow of water and result in sewer system back-ups and discharge of untreated wastewater into surface water supplies.

The ramifications of damage from wastewater collection treatment facilities can impact more than the environment. A 2010 report to Congress noted that explosives placed in large underground collector sewers could destroy buildings and transportation networks; explosions in the sewers can cause collapse of roads, sidewalks and structures. A city's underground pipeline network could function as weapons by the introduction of highly flammable substances through a manhole or stormwater inlet. Destruction of wastewater treatment chemical stores could result in release of toxic chemicals such as chlorine gas (Copeland 2010).

Security for Public Transit Systems

The U.S. Department of Transportation is responsible for operational oversight of the mass transit and passenger rail sector including service by buses, rail transit (commuter rail, heavy rail—also known as subways or metros—and light rail, including trolleys and streetcars), long-distance rail (Amtrak and Alaska Railroad) and other, less common types of service (cable cars, inclined planes, funiculars, and automated guideway systems).

The Department of Homeland Security has security oversight responsibility for the this and all other sectors of the transport system, including aviation, highway infrastructure and motor carrier, maritime transportation system, the pipeline system, freight rail, and the postal and shipping system.

Public transit safety and security planning was included in a 2003 *Security and Emergency Preparedness Planning Guide* issued by the U.S. Department of Transportation's Federal Transportation Administration (FTA) shortly after the September attacks. Recognizing that public transit systems exist to move people quickly and safely to and from and through rural and urban areas, the report was founded on the idea that transit must provide unimpeded, easy access to passengers in all environments and all conditions. Public transit must provide low-cost transportation alternatives available to everyone, and, therefore, must support a cost structure that enables affordable transportation. To achieve required gains in protection and preparedness the industry has had to participate in interagency coordination, and make financial investments for the safety and security of their systems. At many agencies, major projects and ongoing programs for maintenance and operational upgrades had to be delayed or re-directed to provide the resources and personnel necessary to address security and preparedness requirements.

FTA also reminded readers that defending against terrorism is not new to the industry. The nation's largest rail and bus operations have worked to address the credible threat from terrorism since the early 1990s. Bombings and assaults in Europe, the Middle East, India, and Latin America demonstrated the inherent susceptibility of the public transportation infrastructure to a broad range of terrorist methods and weapons. The experiences in those regions formed the plans, training, and exercises which sustained industry preparedness.

The Federal Transportation Administration supports industry programs for security and preparedness through training, research, guidelines and even regulation. All rail transit agencies are required to document their security and preparedness programs in System Security Program Plans, reviewed and approved by State Oversight Agencies. Ongoing FTA auditing of this requirement ensures that agency plans and procedures are up-to-date and address a range of contingencies. Small and medium-sized bus systems are encouraged to do and often participate in programs administered at the state program level.

Working with the U.S. Department of Transportation's Office of Intelligence and Security, FTA has also coordinated closely with national domestic preparedness programs developed after the 1995 sarin release on a Tokyo subway killed 12 and sent thousands of others to local hospitals.

The Defense Against Weapons of Mass Destruction Act of 1996 initiated programs to provide training and equipment for first responders to deal with terrorist incidents, including those involving weapons of mass destruction (WMD), in 120 of the highest risk cities in the country. The presence of public transportation infrastructure was a critical element in the assessment of risk.

THE SUSTAINABLE FUTURE FOR UTILITIES

Throughout the preceding chapters it was apparent that a number of the operational challenges before public utilities were common to the industry in general. However, it was also apparent that the managers, operators and administrators in their governing bodies in each sector of the utility industry face a variety of policy and operations challenges that are unique to their sector of the industry. In the following pages the key issues that representatives of each sector see as having an impact on their sector are presented, beginning with what managers in the electric utility think are likely to be the most pressing challenges they face from now until at least 2050.

Sustainability of the Energy Sector

The remaining years in the first half of the twenty-first century are going to be difficult for the nation's public utilities. Each year, the editors of *Utility Drive*, a utility industry daily news source, asks a spectrum of large and small, public and private electric utilities in all the fifty states what they believe are going to be the biggest problems facing the industry. More than 60 percent of responses were from investor-owned utilities. In returns from the more than 500 respondents for 2014 and 2015, respondents appeared to be most concerned over the problem of replacing and upgrading an aging infrastructure.

An aging workforce and the problems associated with finding qualified replacements for their many retirees, the third most pressing issue in 2014, was identified as the second most pressing challenge in 2015. With the declining income stream resulting from static demand growth (28 percent in both years), it is clear that financial and human resources issues are having and will continue to have a large impact on electric utilities for some time to come. Also noteworthy was the more than doubling from 11 percent in 2014 to 24 percent in 2015 of utilities' concern over physical and cyber security. On a positive note, the nearly 50 percent cut in respondents' concerns over actions needed to meet mandated efficiency mandates declined from to 16 percent in 2014 who saw this as a challenge, to just 9 percent who said so in 2015. A second positive change was the one year decline from 23 to 16 percent of respondents reporting concern for the work necessary to establish greater smart grid reliability. This suggests that more utilities have completed the installation of smart grid meters and other information technology necessary for smart grid operations.

The survey editors ended the 2015 survey report with a conclusion that utilities will have to deal with the regulatory requirement to produce more "clean" energy from now on. This means they will have to close more coal-fired generation facilities and install equipment to use more solar, wind, and natural gas for power generation. Box 20.3 describes how some industry analysts view the major transformation occurring in the public power industry and the challenges that the transformation is setting before industry administrators and managers. The changes described are having the same impact upon investor-owned power utilities.

While not the major concern that characterized earlier responses, the changing nature of the energy sector's regulatory environment remains an issue among survey respondents. The decline in growth and greater pressure for including environmental and social benefits in utility operations has resulted in many utilities pressing their state commissions for changes in the traditional rate of return (ROR) mechanism for rate determinations. Under the leadership of principal researcher Ken Costello, the National Regulatory Research Institute (NRRI) has published several studies on the efficacy of alternative rate mechanisms. In an April, 2014 NRRI report, 18 of the alternative rate basing mechanisms proposed were evaluated to determine their compatibility with state utility commission rate-case determination objectives. The report also described the experiences of seven different state commissions with different variations of alternative rate mechanisms.

Sustainability in the Water and Wastewater Sector

The California-based Pacific Institute is a global water think tank that seeks to influence local, national, and international efforts in developing sustainable water policies. The Institute publishes a series of volumes with articles by researchers on the state of the global water crisis. Volume 7, published in 2012, carried a paper by the editors on the need for reform in the U.S. water policy. The introduction of that paper is included here in order to emphasize the challenges facing the sustainability of the nation's water systems:

> The United States faces a bevy of persistent and emerging water challenges in the 21st century. Many key water laws and policies are outdated or not effectively or

---

BOX 20.3   CHALLENGES IN THE PUBLIC POWER UTILITY
SECTOR

Major changes occurring in the public power utility industry were described in a 2013 article in the sector's journal, *Public Power*. A portion of that analysis is included here:

"The [electric power] utility industry is in a period of dramatic transformation with no end in sight. Utility boards and management are increasingly challenged with cutting back or tightening budgets, filling gaps in their leadership and workforce due to retirements, making infrastructure upgrades, staying up with beneficial new technology and market opportunities, and addressing new regulatory mandates and concerns from the public and ratepayers. Moreover, to offer competitive rates, utilities must be increasingly efficient."

"The utility business is fundamentally changing. The model of generating electricity in a large plant, delivering it to homes and businesses on poles and wires and then communicating with customers once a month through a billing statement is not sustainable. Changes in environmental regulations, customer interest in renewable energy and the need to take advantage of technological developments are requiring electric utilities to rethink not only how they create and distribute power, but also to reassess the ideal relationship with their customers."

"Historically, utilities have had limited communications with their customers, and customers have thought about their utility provider only in the event of an outage or when their bill arrived. Although this limited communication was adequate in the past, many customer service experts believe it is no longer enough—and that a more personalized approach is necessary. Several external factors create opportunities for utilities to personalize their communications with customers, such as the availability of individual communication and interaction preferences or more energy usage information via smart grid technology."

Source: Shiflea and Jensen (2013).

---

equitably enforced. An increasing number of aquatic ecosystems are in danger of collapse. Many cities, businesses, and farms are not taking advantage of existing, cost-effective water conservation technologies and practices. Much of the nation's infrastructure is outdated and will become increasingly obsolete as climate change alters the timing and magnitude of water supplies. Rising energy demands and shifts in energy sources, such as increased ethanol and natural gas production, are putting additional pressure on the nation's water resources. In turn, increased water demand for growing populations will have important energy implications. (Christian-Smith, Gleick, and Cooley 2012: 143)

Other important water utility organizations support the conclusions of the Pacific Institute authors. For example, every year since 2004 the American Water Works Association (AWWA) surveys a random sample of water industry utilities to learn their projections of the state of the industry. Respondents include operational and management personnel at large and small public and private water-related industries. A total of 1,747 surveys were returned during the 2015 study. Respondents rated the state of the industry at 4.5 on a seven-point scale, down slightly from the 2014 mean of 4.6. This is consistent with the range of ratings from 4.5 to 4.9 over the 11-year period. Respondents were also asked to indicate what will be the soundness of the state of the industry in 2010. That prediction was 4.4 on the seven-point scale, down from 4.5 in the previous year study. The major barriers to sustainability are highlighted in results of water industry surveys conducted by the American Water Works Association in 2014 and 2015. The need to replace deteriorating water and wastewater infrastructure was ranked first in importance in both years (Table 20.3).

Respondents were also asked to indicate what they believed were the most important challenges facing the industry in 2015 and beyond. The top five issues believed to be most important for the sustainability of the industry and their mean rating on a five-point scale were:

1. Renewal and replacement of aging water and wastewater infrastructure   4.59
2. Financing for capital improvements   4.46
3. Long-term water supply availability   4.44
4. Public understanding of the value of water systems and services   4.37
5. Public understanding of the value of water resources   4.28

The next five issues deemed important were watershed/source protection, cost recovery (pricing water to accurately reflect its true cost), emergency preparedness, water conservation/efficiency, and compliance with future regulations. Cyber security issues were not considered to be very important; rated 24 of 34 items with a mean score of 3.77. Other items often cited in the literature as important utility management issues were climate risk and resiliency rated 29 of 34 with a mean score of 3.47, and fracking/oil and gas activities, rated next to last with a mean score of 3.34. The issue respondents considered to be most important, renewal and replacement of aging infrastructure, was also rated highest in the 2014 study. New to the top ten list in 2015 were water conservation/efficiency and compliance with future regulations. Items dropped from the top ten were groundwater management and overuse and drought or periodic water shortages.

Similar results were found in the 2015 Black and Veatch *Strategic Directions: U.S. Water Industry* survey. In that study, the need for maintaining or expanding the life of existing physical assets was considered to be the greatest barrier to their ability to sustain their operations in the future. This factor was seen as having the greatest potential for limiting

Table 20.3   *Top 15 challenges in all water utility industry sectors, 2014 and 2015*

Rank	2014	Rank	2015
1	State of water and sewer infrastructure	1	Renewal and replacement of aging water and wastewater infrastructure
2	Long-term water supply availability	2	Financing for capital improvements
3	Financing for capital improvements	3	Long term water supply availability
4	Public understanding of the value of water resources	4	Public understanding of the value of water systems and services
5	Public understanding of the value of water systems and services	5	Public understanding of the value of water resources
6	Groundwater management and overuse	6	Watershed/source water protection
7	Watershed protection	7	Cost recovery
8	Drought or periodic water shortages	8	Emergency preparedness
9	Emergency preparedness	9	Water conservation/efficiency
10	Cost recovery	10	Compliance with future regulations
11	Acceptance of rate increases	11	Groundwater management and overuse
12	Talent attraction and retention	12	Compliance with current regulations
13	Compliance with current regulations	13	Drought or periodic water shortages
14	Compliance with future regulations	14	Asset management
15	Water conservation/recovery	15	Acceptance of future water and wastewater rate increases

Source: American Water Works Association (AWWA 2014b, 2015).

their sustainability in all sectors of the water industry: Water only utilities, 58.8 percent; wastewater only, 67.3 percent; water or wastewater, 48.2 percent; water, wastewater and stormwater, 52 percent; and combined utilities, 63.8 percent. The issue that the second largest number of water-only utilities rated as a significant barrier to sustainability was problems

Table 20.4   Water industry management's groundwater challenges in 2015

Rank	Challenge Category	2015 Mean Score	% Ranked Critically Important
1	Declining groundwater levels	4.09	41
2	Watershed/groundwater protection	4.01	34
3	Groundwater regulations	3.82	26
4	Agricultural use of groundwater	3.79	27
5	Monitoring and reporting groundwater withdrawals	3.75	23
6	Restrictions on groundwater pumping	3.72	24
7	Oil and gas exploration and processing activities	3.63	28
8	Reclaimed water for groundwater recharge	3.55	17
9	Groundwater pricing	3.35	11

Source: American Water Works Association (AWWA 2014b, 2015).

with customer rates; 43.4 percent rated it a significant limitation to their sustainability. For wastewater only organizations, 47.3 percent mentioned energy efficiency problems as a critical barrier to sustainability. Industry concerns over the state of the nation's groundwater resources in 2015 indicated that the threat resulting from over-withdrawals of existing aquifers was the most important challenge to their sustainability (Table 20.4).

Sustainability in the Solid Waste Sector

The solid and hazardous waste collection and disposal industry has a wide variety of barriers to its continued sustainability. Foremost of these is the growing mountain of waste expected from population growth and the declining numbers of locations and methods for disposing of that waste. The waste consists of paper, glass, metals, yard waste, wood, and plastic, plus a host of other items including liquid and solid hazardous products. The removal and transport of this waste is carried out by public and private organizations, with the majority consisting of highly regulated private businesses. Disposal is also a public–private mix, but with most disposal landfills in public ownership and most incinerating facilities in private sector hands. Recycling and reuse is usually a mixed operation. Disposal of hazardous waste is almost exclusively a private operation.

Sustainability barriers affect both sectors equally. They include the heavy cost of complying with safety and public health requirements, the difficulty of locating new disposal sites and the transportation and processing equipment used in handling solid waste. Transportation is another barrier to sustainability. All waste is transported on public streets and highways, with additional amounts moved by special refuse trains that transport waste from local transfer stations to disposal or incineration sites as much as 300 or more miles from where its is generated. Road congestion is the main problem, and is probably going to become an even greater problem in the near future.

Security is usually not a major worry for this segment of the public utility industry. There is little to be gained by setting off a bomb in a landfill, although operations have been adversely affected in the past by striking refuse truck drivers and other workers. Such labor action can result in refuse piling up on curbs and alleys, with rodents and other animals spreading the waste in yards and on sidewalks. These actions do not occur often and are usually settled without long delays.

Sustainability in the Public Transit Sector

Sustainability problems in the transit sector of the industry are the opposite of what characterizes the solid waste sector. Transit operations are highly vulnerable to all types of security breaches, violence and vandalism, and terrorist actions. A train or bus wreck can result in large numbers of casualties and disrupt movement in the corridor for a long period of time. A list of issues affecting the sustainability of public transportation in the United States identified by one respected analyst is shown in Table 20.5.

Possibly the biggest barrier to public transit sustainability is the world's love affair with the automobile. Transportation infrastructure improvements are paid for mostly by state and national taxes on fuels, and are usually earmarked for repairs and improvements to roads and bridges. Financial support for transit improvements does not have the same lobbying support as automobile manufacturers, oil companies, and construction firms give to legislatures for roads and bridges. Only recently has support for a broader view of sustainable development included economic and social welfare, population equity, human health and ecological integrity. Solutions to traffic congestion, lack of parking, and environmental damage from engine exhausts can no longer just involve technological considerations, but instead must include more integrated solutions that include travel choices, land use changes as well as technical innovation (Litman and Burwell 2006). Meanwhile, most automobiles carry a single passenger, traffic congestion is getting more frustrating and costly, and support for public transit systems remains stagnant or is declining.

Table 20.5   Some key challenges facing the public transportation industry

Transport Problem	Discussion
Funding for public transit to mitigate traffic congestion and increasing urbanization	The urban problem that stands out in the minds of most commuters in regions of the country is the traffic congestion that threatens to clog movement in and out of city centers. The result is a dilution of the benefits or urban concentration and time-loss penalties for non-urban commuters. Funding for the projects needed to meet transit projects comes from public funds allocated by federal, state and local governments, with system operations revenue. In 2008, federal funds met nearly 40 percent of the total transit agency capital expenditures; state funds provide 12 percent, and local funds met the remaining 48 percent. Federal funds for these investments come from the Highway Trust Fund which receives its funding from motor fuel and other highway use taxes. However, federal duel tax revenues have not increased since 1993, in part as a result of greater vehicle fuel efficiency. The fund will need $132 billion more than it is expected to take in between 2015 and 2022.
Improving public transport fleet adequacy and balance against declining resources for investments in maintaining aged equipment while gearing up for meeting growing demand	Improved transit asset management is needed because (1) much of the buses, rail cars are already beyond their useful lives and must be replaced, (2) additional equipment is needed to meet growing demand for transit services, and (3) continued fare increases and decreasing state and local funding are placing greater pressures on the general ridership. Moreover, many of the nearly 700 public transit agencies are struggling to maintain their road and rail assets in acceptable condition.
Coordinating transit service for disadvantaged population and improving services for bicycle riders and walkers	Public transit systems must be designed to provide maximum availability during morning and evening commuting hours, while meeting the special needs of disadvantaged and public transit-dependent populations. However, they must also contend with little need for rider service during off-commuting times and weekends. Systems must balance need with limited resources, often resulting in inadequate capability in peak demand periods and for non-motorized transportation needs. To meet these needs transit authorities are forced to maintain a variety of services, at various times, for various human needs. Greater federal support for services for transportation of disadvantaged populations is needed.

Source: Federal Transit Administration (FTA 2015b).

SUMMARY

In many ways, the public utility industry is in the best condition it has ever been. However, many problems continue to plague utility managers and administrators; the challenges they face are exacerbated by human and natural events and conditions not previously encountered. The combination of climate change, security threats, population growth, urbanization and road congestion, and infrastructure deterioration form a set of challenges for utility managers that promise to severely strain their financial and operational resources. This chapter looked at five of the major challenges that utilities must surmount over the next twenty-five years and beyond, including making the repairs and replacements necessary in large segments of the industry's infrastructure, dealing with an increasingly stringent regulatory environment, climate change related environmental repercussions, securing the necessary funding for capital improvements, and protecting against physical and cyberattacks.

The entire public utility industry faces these serious challenges together; all are critical elements in a complex system of public service; we cannot function as a nation without them. Among the most pressing is finding affordable funding for making the repairs and replacements and other capital improvements needed to serve their growing customer base, and at the same time investment in security measures that includes preparing for the increasing likelihood of physical and cyberattacks on their operations.

Utilities' ability to defend against intensive weather events, physical disasters such as earthquakes, infrastructure destruction and cyberattacks was discussed as barriers to utilities' sustainability, beginning with natural disasters and the crisis management procedures in place to deal with them. Among the variety of natural and man-made disasters that can result in operational and/or a management crises for a public utility are such events as fires and floods, droughts, snow or ice storms, downed power lines and poles from windstorms and hurricanes, broken water mains, backed up sewage systems, power blackouts, terrorist bombings of public events and places, and simply failure of the utility infrastructure due to old age. Utilities employ crisis management procedures for dealing with these disasters.

Crisis management describes the systematic efforts that make possible the prompt and effective handling of unusual, unanticipated, and serious problems that all utilities face at one time or another. Utility crisis planning involves programming the combined tools of analysis, forecasting, and planning in order to be prepared to deal with unexpected crises and disasters. Effective crisis management begins with proactive actions designed to minimize potential risk before a triggering event occurs. Response to a triggering event then involves response improvising and interacting by key stakeholders so that individual and collective sense making, shared meaning, and roles are known in advance.

The National Incident Management System (NIMS) the core guiding document for incident management, was developed with the aid of FEMA to provide a standard system for federal, state, local and tribal governments to work together to prepare for and respond to incidents. NIMS is based on the National Interagency Incident Management System (NIIMS) which was developed to provide a common system that emergency service agencies can employ at local, state, and federal levels.

ADDITIONAL READING

Chang, Ni-Bin and Ana Pires (2015), *Sustainable Solid Waste Management: A Systems Engineering Approach*. New York: Wiley.

Herring, Horace and Steve Sorrell (2009), *Energy Efficiency and Sustainable Consumption: The Rebound Effect (Energy, Climate and the Environment)*. Basingstoke: Macmillan.

Jones, J.A.A. (2011), *Water Sustainability: A Global Perspective*. New York: Routledge.

Lassiter, Allison (ed.) (2015), *Sustainable Water: Challenges and Solutions from California*. Oakland, CA: University of California.

Patterson, Walt (2009), *Keeping the Lights On: Towards Sustainable Electricity*. London: Earthscan.

Rada, Elena C. (2015), *Biological Treatment of Solid Waste: Enhancing Sustainability*. Boca Raton, FL: CRC Press.

Robertson, Margaret (2014), *Sustainability, Principles and Practice*. London: Earthscan.

Schiller, Preston, Eric Bruun and Jeffey Kenworthy (2010), *An Introduction to Sustainable Transportation: Policy, Planning and Implementation*. London: Earthscan.

Spellman, Frank R. (2013), *Water and Wastewater Infrastructure: Energy Efficiency and Sustainability*. Boca Raton, FL: CRC Press.

Sutton, John C. (2015), *Gridlock: Congested Cities, Contested Policies, Unsustainable Mobility*. New York: Routledge.

Bibliography

AAR (2015), 'U.S. rail crude oil traffic,' Association of American Railroads, accessed December 6, 2015 at www.aar.org/todays-railroads/what-we-haul/crude-oil-by-rail.

Abel, Amy, Paul W. Parfomak and Dana A. Shea (2004), *Electric Utility Infrastructure Vulnerabilities; Transformers, Towers and Terrorism.* Washington, DC: Congressional Research Service, accessed June 8, 2016 at www.fas.org/sgp/crs/homesec/R42795.pdf.

Abramson, Mark A., Jonathan D. Breul and John M. Kamensky (2006), *Six Trends Transforming Government.* Washington, DC: IBM Center for The Business of Government.

Afullo, Augustine (2014), *Integrated Solid Waste Management Handbook: For Engineers, Planners, Environmentalists, Students and Policy Makers.* Nairobi, Kenya: I. Wamra Technoprises.

Agranoff, Robert and Michael McGuire (2001), 'American federalism and the search for models of management,' *Public Administration Review*, 61 (November/December), 671–681.

Alauer, William C. (ed.) (2001), *Excellence in Action: Water Utility Management in the 21st Century.* Denver: American Water Works Association.

Alvey, Jennifer (2003), 'The CIO forum: budgets byte back,' *Public Utilities Fortnightly*, 141 (October 1): 24–28.

American Rivers (2014), 'Sewage problems and solutions,' accessed November 20, 2015 at www.americanrivers.org/initiative/stormwater-sewage/projects/sewage-problems-and-solutions/.

Anderson, Terry L. and Peter J. Hill (1996), *Water Marketing: The Next Generation.* Lanham, MD: Rowman and Littlefield.

APPA (2010), '2010 Governance Survey,' American Public Power Association, accessed October 9, 2015 at www.publicpower.org/files/PDFs/2010GovernanceSurvey.pdf.

APPA (2015), '2015 Governance survey,' American Public Power Association, accessed October 21, 2015 at www.csu.org/CSUDocuments/appagovernancesurvey2015.pdf.

APTA (2014a), *Public Transportation Fact Book*, American Public Transportation Association, accessed September 1, 2015 at www.apta.

com/resources/statistics/Documents/FactBook/2014-APTA-Fact-Book. pdf.

APTA (2014b), *Public Transportation Yearbook*. American Public Transportation Association, accessed June 28, 2016 from www.apta. com/resources/statistics/Pages/transitstats.aspx.

APTA (2015), 'Millennials and mobility: understanding the millennial mindset,' accessed June 22, 2016 at APTA-Millinnials-and-Mobility.pdf.

APTA (2016), 'Public transportation ridership report,' accessed June 22, 2016 at www.metrotransit.org/metro-transit-ridership-tops-858-million-in-2015.

Arenschield, Laura (2014), 'Toledo bearing full brunt of Lake Erie algae bloom,' *The Columbus Dispatch* (August 4), accessed August 19, 2015 at www.dispatch.com/content/stories/local/2014/08/04/this-bloom-is-in-bad-location.html.

Artesian Resources Corporation (2002), *Annual Report*. Newark, DE.

ASCE (2013), 'Annual report card for America's infrastructure: waste-water,' American Society of Civil Engineers, accessed October 19, 2015 at www.infrastructurereportcard.org/wastewater/.

AWWA (2014a), Water Utility Capital Financing. Denver, CO: American Water Works Association.

AWWA (2014b), AWWA State of the Water Industry Report. Denver, CO: American Water Works Association, accessed June 29, 2016 at AWWA-State–of-the- Water-Industry-Report-2014.pdf.

AWWA (2015), AWWA State of the Water Industry Report. Denver, CO: American Water Works Association, accessed June 29, 2016 at AWWA-State–of-the-Water-Industry-Report-2015.pdf.

AWWA and EPA (2008), 'Workforce planning for water utilities— successful recruiting, training, and retaining of operators and engineers,' accessed June 26, 2008 at www.waterrf.org/PublicReportLibrary/91237. pdf.

Bakker, Karen (2003), *Good Governance in Restructuring Water Supply: A Handbook*. Ottawa: Federation of Canadian Municipalities.

Bakker, Karen (2010), *Privatizing Water: Governance Failure and the World's Urban Water Crisis*. Ithaca, NY: Cornell University Press.

Bakker, Karen (2015), 'The business of water: market environmentalism in the water sector,' *Annual Review of Environment and Resources*, 2015 (39): 469–494.

Ballaglio, Randy P. (2014), *Public Human Resource Management*. Thousand Oaks, CA: CQ Press.

Banister, David, Karen Anderson, David Bonilla, Moshe Givoni and Tim Schwanen (2011), 'Transportation and the environment', *Annual Review of Environment and Resources*, 2011 (36): 247–270.

Barnes, Irston R. (1942), *The Economics of Public Utility Regulation.* New York: F.S. Crofts.

Barzelay, Michael (2001), *The New Public Management: Improving Research and Policy Dialogue.* Berkeley, CA: University of California Press.

Basin Electric Power Cooperative (2004), 'What we do,' assessed June 6, 2004 at www.basinelectric.com.

Bason, Christian (2011), *Leading Public Sector Innovation: Co-Creating for a Better Society.* Chicago, IL: Policy Press.

Baubion, C. (2013), 'OECD risk management: strategic crisis management,' *OECD Working Papers on Public Governance*, 23, OECD Publishing, accessed December 11, 2015 at http://dx.doi.org/10.1787/5k41rbd1lzr7-en.

Bauer, John (2010), *Effective Regulation of Public Utilities.* Boston, MA: Gale (Cengage Learning).

Beder, Sharon (2003), *Power Play: the Fight to Control the World's Electricity.* New York: New Press.

Berry, Kate and Eric Mollard (2009), *Social Participation in Water Governance and Management: Critical and Global Perspectives.* London: Routledge.

Bellenger, Gail (2002), *What is the Clean Water Act*, accessed February 21, 2004, www.pa.essortment.com/cleanwateract_ rgrl.htm.

Berman, Evan M., James S. Bowman, Johnathan P. West and Montgomery R. Van Wart (2012), *Human Resources in Public Service: Paradoxes, Processes, and Problems* (4th edn). Thousand Oaks, CA: Sage.

Bezdek, Roger H. and Robert M. Wendling (2004), 'The case against gas dependence: greater reliance on gas-fired power implies serious economic, technical, and national security risks,' *Public Utilities Fortnightly*, 142 (April): 43–47.

Bipartisan Policy Center (2014), 'Cybersecurity and the North American electric grid: new policy approaches to address an evolving threat,' accessed October 14, 2015 at http://bipartisanpolicy.org/wp-content/uploads/sites/default/files/Cybersecurity%20Electric%20Grid%20BPC.pdf.

Birchall, Johnston (2002), 'Mutual, non-profit or public interest company? An evaluation of options for the ownership and control of water utilities,' *Annals of Public and Cooperative Economics*, 72 (2): 181–213.

Bloetscher, Fred (2011), *Utility Management for Water and Wastewater Operators.* Boulder, CO: American Water Works Association.

BLS (Bureau of Labor Statistics) (2015a), 'Waste Management and Remediation Services: NAICS 562,' accessed June 22, 2016 from www.bls.gov/iag/tgs/iag562.htm.

BLS (2015b), 'Industries at a glance: waste management and remediation,' Bureau of Labor Statistics, accessed June 28, 2016 at www.bls.gov/iag/tgs/iag562.htm.

Blunden, Jessica and Derek S. Arndt (eds) (2015), 'State of the Climate in 2014,' *Bulletin of the American Meteorological Society*, 96 (7): S1–S267.

Boone, Louis E. and David L. Kurtz (2015), *Contemporary Marketing* (17th edn). Boston, MA: Cengage Learning.

Borenstein, Severin and James Bushnell (2015), *The U.S. Electricity Industry after 20 Years of Restructuring*. Energy Institute working paper. Berkeley, CA: University of California.

Borins, Sanford (2014), *The Persistence of Innovation in Government: A Guide for Innovative Public Servants*. Washington, DC: IBM Center for the Business of Government.

Bozeman, Barry and Jeffrey D. Straussman (1991), *Public Management Strategies*, San Francisco, CA: Jossey-Bass.

Bradley, David (2015), 'NatGas marketers' 2014 downward spiral continued in final quarter,' *Natural Gas Intelligence* (March 16) accessed September 21, 2015 at www.naturalgasintel.com/articles/101677-natgas-marketers-2014-downward-spiral-continued-in-final-quarter.

Bradley Jr., Robert L. (2011), *Edison to Enron: Energy Markets and Political Strategies*. Salem, MA: Scrivener.

Brennan, Timothy J., Karen L. Palmer and Salvador A. Martinez (2002), *Alternating Currents: Electricity Markets and Public Policy*. Washington, DC: Resources for the Future.

Breul, Jonathan D. (2006), 'What is transformation?' In Mark A. Abramson, Jonathan D. Breul and John M. Kamensky (eds), *Six Trends Transforming Government*, Washington, DC: IBM Center for The Business of Government.

Brocklehurst, Katherine (2014), 'DHS confirms US public utility's control system was hacked,' *The State of Security* (May 21) accessed September 5, 2015 at www.tripwire.com/state-of-security/incident-detection/dhs-confirms-u-s-public-utilitys-control-system-was-hacked/.

Brown, Matthew H. and Richard P. Sedano (2003), *A Comprehensive View of U.S. Electric Restructuring with Policy Options for the Future*. Washington, DC: National Council on Electricity Policy.

Bruchey, Stuart (1990), *Enterprise: The Dynamic Economy of a Free People*. Cambridge, MA: Harvard University Press.

Bruun, Eric C. (2013), *Public Transit Systems: Analyzing Investments and Performance*. New York: Routledge.

Bryant, Keith L. Jr. and Henry C. Dethloff (1990), *A History of American Business* (2nd edn). Englewood Cliffs, NJ: Prentice Hall.

Bryson, John M. (2011), *Strategic Planning for Public and Nonprofit Organizations* (4th edn). New York: Wiley.

Buffington, Jack (2015), *The Recycling Myth: Disruptive Innovation to Improve the Environment*. Santa Barbara, CA: Praeger.

Bui, Ann T. (2012), *Financial Management for Water Utilities: Principles of Finance, Accounting, and Management Controls*. Denver, CO: American Water Works Association.

Bureau of Labor Statistics (BLS) (2015), 'Employment by major industry sector,' accessed June 8, 2016 at www.bls.gov/news.release/ecopro.t02.htm.

Burgelman, Robert A., Clayton M. Christensen and Steven C. Wheelwright (2004), *Strategic Management of Technology and Innovation* (4th edn). Boston, MA: McGraw-Hill Irwin.

Burkhart, Lori A. (2004), 'CIS: the new profit machine,' *Public Utilities Fortnightly*, 142 (May): 31–37.

Burr, Michael T. (2004), 'Consolidating Co-Ops,' *Public Utilities Fortnightly*, 142 (June): 71–76.

Burr, Michael T. (2013), 'Big data, big change,' *Fortnightly Magazine* (August), accessed June 24, 2016 at www.fortnightly.com/fortnight nightly/2013/08/big-data-big-change.

BusinessDictionary.com (2015a), 'Electronic commerce (E-Commerce),' accessed December 8, 2015 at www.businessdictionary.com/definition/electronic-commerce-E-Commerce.html.

Businessdictionary.com (2015b), 'Definition of an environmental problem,' accessed September 27, 2015 at www.businessdictionary.dom/definition/environmental-problem.html.

Ceccato, Vania and Andrew Newton (2015), *Safety and Security in Transit Environments: An Interdisciplinary Approach*. New York: Palgrave Macmillan.

Ceder, Avishai (2015), *Public Transit Planning and Operation: Modeling, Practice and Behavior* (2nd edn). Boca Raton, FL: CRC Press.

CenterPoint Energy (2014), '2014 Annual Report,' accessed June 29, 2016 at investors.centerpointenergy.com/secfiling.cfm?filingID=1130310-14-5&CIK=1130310.

Cervery, Robert (2013), 'Transport infrastructure and the environment: sustainable mobility and urbanism,' accessed December 16, 2015 at iurd. berkeley.edu/wp/2013-03.pdf.

Chandler, Alfred D. and Richard S. Tedlow (1985), *The Coming of Managerial Capitalism*. Homewood, IL: Irwin.

Chandler, Alfred Jr. (1990), *Scale and Scope: The Dynamics of Industrial Capitalism*. Cambridge: Harvard University.

Chandrappa, Ramesha and Jeff Brown (2012), *Solid Waste Management: Principles and Practice*. Berlin: Springer.

Chang, Ni-Bin and Ana Pires (2015), *Sustainable Solid Waste Management: A Systems Engineering Approach*. New York: Wiley.

Chesbrough, Henry W. (2003a), *Open Innovation: The New Imperative for Creating and Profiting at Technology*. Boston, MA: Harvard Business School Press.

Chesbrough, Henry W. (2003b), *Open Business Models: How to Thrive in the New Innovation Landscape*. Boston, MA: Harvard Business School Press.

Chesbrough, Henry W. (2003c), 'The era of open innovation,' *MIT Sloan Management Review*, 44 (3): 35–41.

Chesbrough, Henry W. (2011a), *Open Services Innovation*. San Francisco, CA: Jossey-Bass.

Chesbrough, Henry W. (2011b), 'Bringing open innovation to services,' *MIT Sloan Management Review*, 52 (2): 85–90.

Christensen, Thomas, H. (ed.) (2010), *Solid Waste Technology and Management*. New York: Wiley.

Christensen, Tom and Per Lægreid (2002), 'New Public Management—Undermining Political Control?', in T. Christensen and P. Lægreid (eds), *New Public Management. The Transformation of Ideas and Practice*. Burlington, VT: Ashgate, pp. 93–120.

Christian-Smith, Juliet, Peter H. Gleick and Heather Cooley (2012), 'U.S. water policy reform,' in Peter H. Gleick, Lucy Allen, Michael J. Cohen, Heather Cooley, Matthew Heberger, Jason Morrison, Meena Palaniappan and Paul Schulte (eds), *The World's Water*, Vol. 7. Washington, DC: Island Press, pp. 143–155.

CH2M HILL (2009), 'Transportation and sustainability best practices background,' accessed December 16, 2015 at environment.transportation.org/PDF/sustainability_peer_exchange/AASHTO_SustPeerExh_BriefingPaper.pdf.

Ciolik, Mark, Wallace Jones and William Wilson (2003), 'Utility ratemaking and ROE: thinking the tools of the trade,' *Public Utilities Fortnightly*, 141 (October 15): 24–29.

City of Austin (2012), *Governance Study of Public Power Utilities for the City of Austin*, accessed December 24, 2015 at https://austinenergy.com/wps/wcm/connect/f3bb639b-6433-4dfb-a687-b0c0376ed3b1/governanceStudy.pdf?.

City of Riverside (2015), 'Public utilities: strategic goals,' accessed September 8, 2015 at www.riversideca.gov/utilities/admin-strategicplan.asp.

Clough, Shepard B. and Theodore F. Marburg (1968), *The Economic Basis of American Civilization*. New York: Cornwell.

Cochran, Clark E., Lawrence C. Mayer, T.R. Carr and N. Joseph Cayer (2015), *American Public Policy* (11th edn). New York: St. Martin's Press.

Coe, Charles K. (2015), *Urban Services: A Basic Guide for Local Governments*. New York: Routledge.

Cohen, Steve (2008), 'Wasted again: What can we do with all that garbage?' accessed December 6, 2015 at http://observer.com/2008/07/wasted-again-what-can-we-do-with-all-of-that-garbage/.

Colburn, David R. and George E. Pozzetta (eds) (1983), *Reform and Reformers in the Progressive Era*. Westport, CT: Greenwood Press.

Colorado Springs Independent (October 23, 2014), 'Another look at utilities governance,' accessed December 24, 2015 at www.csindy.com/IndyBlog/archives/2014/10/23/another-look-at-utilities-governance.

Colorado Springs Utilities (2011), 'Governance alternatives white paper,' accessed December 24, 2015 at www.csu.org/CSUDocuments/governancealternatives2011.pdf.

Commonwealth of Massachusetts (2015), 'Overview of electricity and natural gas rates,' accessed December 8, 2015 at www.mass.gov/ago/doing-business-in-massachusetts/energy-and-utilities/energy-rates-and-billing/electric-and-gas-rates.html.

Conant, Jeff (2010), 'Beyond public vs. private,' in Tara Lohan (ed.), *Water Matters*. San Francisco, CA: Alternet Books, pp. 77–87.

Cooper, Terry L. (2012), *The Responsible Administrator: An Approach to Ethics for the Administrative Role* (6th edn). San Francisco, CA: Jossey-Bass.

Copeland, Claudia (2010), *Terrorism and Security Issues Facing the Water Infrastructure Sector*. Washington, DC: Congressional Research Service.

Costello, Kenneth W. and Robert Burns (2003), 'Era of low gas prices may be behind us,' *NRRI Networker* (Summer), 1.

Costello, Ken (2014), *Alternative Rate Mechanisms and the Compatibility with State Utility Commission Objectives*. Silver Springs, MD: National Regulatory Research Institute.

CPUC (2012), 'Trends in Utility Infrastructure Financing,' San Francisco, CA: California Public Utilities Commission.

CPURA (Connecticut Public Utilities Regulatory Authority) (2014), *Cybersecurity and Connecticut's Public Utilities*, accessed October 14, 2015 at www.ct.gov/pura/lib/pura/electric/cyber_report_041414.pdf.

CSCMP and Nada Sanders (2014), *The Definitive Guide to Manufacturing and Service Operations*. Council of Supply Chain Management Professionals. Upper Saddle River, NJ: Pearson FT Press.

CTTA (2015), 'A platform for rural transportation,' Community Transportation Association of America, accessed September 7, 2015 at Platform_for_Rural_Transportation (2).pdf.

CWRCB (2016), 'Laws and regulations.' California Water Resources

Control Board, accessed June 28, 2016 at www.waterboards.ca.gov/ laws_regulations/.

Davis, Aaron C. (2015), 'American recycling is stalling, and the big blue bin is one reason why,' accessed December 6, 2015 at www.washingtonpost. com/local/dc-politics/american-recycling-is-stalling-and-the-big-blue-bin-is-one-reason-why/2015/06/20/914735e4-1610-11e5-9ddc-e33535 42100c_story.html?hpid=z3.

Davis, Michelle and Steve Clemmer (2014), *Power Failure: How Climate Change puts our Electricity at Risk—and What we Can Do.* Union of Concerned Scientists, accessed August 20, 2015 at www.ucsusa.org/ global_warming/science_and_impacts/impacts/effects-of-climate-change-risks-on-our-electricity-system.html#.VdYWg_nF8Uo.

Deason, Jonathan P., Theodore M. Schad and George W. Sherk (2001), 'Water policy in the United States: a perspective,' *Water Policy* 3 (2001): 175–192.

Deder, Avishai (2015), *Public Transit Planning and Operations: Modeling, Practice and Behavior* (2nd edn). Boca Raton, FL: CRC Press.

Denardt, Janet V. and Robert B. Denhardt (2011), *The New Public Service.* New York: Taylor & Francis.

DHS (2015a), 'Critical Infrastructure Sectors.' Department of Homeland Security. Accessed June 27, 2016 at www.dhs.gov/critical-infrastruc ture-sectors.

DHS (2015b), 'Homeland Security Presidential Directive-5,' accessed June 26, 2016 at www.dhs.gov/sites/default/files/publications/Home land.

Dimock, Marshall E. (1935), *Business and Government.* New York: Henry Holt.

Dominion Resources (2002), *Annual Report.* Richmond, VA.

Donaldson, Thomas and Thomas W. Dunfee (1999), *Ties That Bind: A Social Contracts Approach to Business Ethics.* Boston, MA: Harvard Business School Press.

Donnelly, Kristina and Juliet Christian-Smith (2013), *An Overview of the "New Normal" and Water Rate Basics* (White Paper). Oakland, CA: Pacific Institute, accessed August 30, 2015 at pacinst-new-normal-and-water-rate-basics.pdf.

Dornbier, David (2015), 'Creative tools to fund water infrastructure,' *Water World,* accessed November 24, 2015 at www.waterworld.com/ articles/print/volume-28/issue-6/water-utility-management/creative-financing-tools-to-fund-water-infrastructure.html.

Drinan, Joanne E. and Frank Spellman (2012), *Water and Wastewater Treatment: A Guide for the Nonengineering Professional* (2nd edn). Boca Raton, FL: CRC Press.

Drummond, Jim and Fred Hanna (2006), *Selling Power: Marketing Energy Under Deregulation*. Victoria, Canada: Traffard.

Eadie, Douglas C. (1983), 'Putting a powerful tool to practical use: the application of strategic planning in the public sector,' *Public Administration Review*, 43(5): 447–452.

Eadie, Douglas C. (1999), 'Putting a powerful tool to practical use,' in Richard C. Kearney and Evan M. Berman (eds), *Public Sector Performance: Management, Motivation, and Measurement*. Boulder, CO: Westview Press, pp. 133–147.

EIA (1996), 'Service report: an analysis of FERC's final environmental impact statement for electricity open access and recovery of stranded costs,' accessed June 21, 2016 at www.osti.gov/nle/topicpages/s/strand ed+cost+recovery.html.

EIA (2004), 'The basics of underground natural gas storage,' Energy Information Administration, accessed September 19, 2015 at www.eia. gov/pub/oil_gas/natural_gas/analysis_publications/storagebasics/stor agebasics.html.

EIA (2006), 'Natural gas processing: the crucial link between natural gas production and its transportation to market,' accessed September 19, 2015 at www.eia.gov/pub/oil_gas/natural_gas/feature_article/2006/ ngprocess/ngprocess.pdf.

EIA (2009), 'About U.S. natural gas pipelines,' accessed September 18, 2015 at www.eia.gov/pub/oil_gas/natural_gas/analysis_publications/ng pipeline/interstate.html.

EIA (2011), 'Natural gas processing plants in the United States in 2010,' accessed September 19, 2015 at www.eia.gov/pub/oil_gas/natural_gas/ feature_articles/2010/ngpps2009/.

EIA (2012), 'Municipal solid waste plants convert garbage to electricity,' accessed June 22, 2016 at www.eia.gov/todayinenergy/detail. cfm?id=7990.

EIA (2013), 'Annual Energy Outlook – 2013.' U.S. Energy Information Administration, accessed June 28, 2016 at www.eia.gov/forecasts/aeo/ pdf/0383(2013).pdf.

EIA (2014), 'Number of natural gas customer participating in customer choice program is increasing,' accessed October 3, 2015 at www.eia.gov/ todayinenergy/detail.cfm?id=19031.

EIA (2015a), 'U.S. remained world's largest producer of petroleum and natural gas hydrocarbons in 2014,' accessed September 21, 2015 at www. eis.gov/todayinenergy/detail.cfm?id=20192.

EIA (2015b), 'Natural gas consumption by end use,' accessed September 19, 2015 at www.eia.gov/dnav/ng/ng_cons_sum_dcu_nus_a.htm.

EIA (2016), 'Average price of electricity to ultimate consumers by end-use sector,' U.S. Energy Information Administration, accessed June 28, 2016 at www.eia.gov/electricity/monthly/epm_table_grapher. cfm?t=epmt_5_6_a.

EIR (Environmental Information Regulations) (1976), Resource Conservation and Recovery Act. Accessed June 22, 2016 at elr.info/sites/default/files/docs/statutes/full/rcra.pdf.

ELP (2010), 'E Source announces top utilities in business customer satisfaction,' *Electric Light and Power*, accessed June 29, 2016 at www.elp.com/articles/2010/09/e-source-announces-top-utilities-in-business-customer-satisfaction.html.

Ely, Richard T. (1900), *Monopolies and Trusts*. London: Macmillan.

EMRF (2013), 'Evolution of the electric industry structure in the U.S. and resulting issues,' Electric Markets Research Foundation, Washington, DC: Navigant, accessed August 14, 2015 at evolution_of_the_electric_industry_for_emrf_10_8_13(2).pdf.

Encyclopedia Britannica (2015), 'Riparian rights,' accessed December 20, 2015 at www.britannica.com/topic/riparian-right.

EPA (1993), 'Criteria for solid waste disposal facilities: a guide for owners/operators', Environmental Protection Agency, accessed August 9, 2015 at www.epa.gov/osw/nonhaz/municipal/landfill/criteria/landbig.pdf.

EPA (2013a), 'Solid waste laws and regulations,' accessed August 9, 2015 at www.epa.gov/region9/waste/solid/laws.html.

EPA (2013b), 'Municipal solid waste,' accessed October 8, 2015 at www3.epa.gov/epawaste/nonhaz/municipal/.

EPA (2015a), 'Climate impacts on water resources,' accessed August 20, 2015 www.epa.gov/climatechange/impacts-adaptation/water.html.

EPA (2015b), 'Climate impacts on Energy,' accessed August 20, 2015 at www.epa.gov/climatechange/impacts-adaptation/energy.html.

EPA (2015c), 'Fact sheet: overview of the clean power plan,' accessed October 7, 2015 at www2.epa.gov/cleanpowerplan/fact-sheet-overview-clean-power-plan.

EPA (2015d), 'Summary of the Clean Water Act,' accessed August 28, 2015 at www2.epa.gov/laws-regulations/summary-clean-water-act.

EPA (2015e), 'Advancing sustainable materials management: facts and figures 2013,' accessed October 8, 2015 at www.epa.gov%2Fepawaste%2Fnonhaz%2Fmunicipal%2Fpubs%2F2013_advncng_smm_rpt.pdf&urlHash=hNrW.

EPA (2015f), 'What is integrated solid waste management?' accessed November 20, 2015 at www3.epa.gov/epawaste/nonhaz/municipal/pubs/ghg/f02026.pdf.

EPA (2015g), 'Final rulemaking to update the national water quality standards regulation,' accessed November 29, 2015 at www2.epa.gov/wqs-tech/final-rulemaking-update-national-water-quality-standards-regulation.

EPA (2015h), 'Energy and the environment,' accessed June 25, 2916 at www.epa.gov/energy/learn-about-energy-and-environment.

EPA (2016a), 'Municipal Solid Waste, Environmental Protection Agency,' accessed February 15, 2016 at www3.epa.gov/epawaste/nonhaz/municipal/.

EPA (2016b), 'Watershed Academy Web: Introduction to the Clean Water Act,' accessed June 21, 2016 at https://cfpub.epa.gov/watertrain/module-Frame.cfm?parent_object_id=1972.

EPA (2016c), 'Hazardous waste,' accessed June 22, 2016 at www.epa.gov/hw.

EPE (2002), '2002 Annual Report', El Paso Electric, Co., accessed June 29, 2016 at www.getfilings.com/o0000930661-03-001165.html.

Farris, Martin T. and Roy J. Sampson (1973), *Public Utilities: Regulation, Management and Ownership*. Boston, MA: Houghton Mifflin.

FBI (2010), 'Pine Ridge woman sentenced for theft from tribal organization,' U.S. Federal Bureau of Investigation, accessed June 29, 2916 at www.fbi.gov/minneapolis/press-releases/2014/pine-ridge.

FEA (Federal Energy Administration) (1975), 'The natural gas shortage: a preliminary report,' Washington, DC: U.S. Department of Energy.

FERC (2015), 'Liquefied natural gas,' Federal Energy Regulatory Commission, accessed October 3, 2015 at www.ferc.gov/industries/gas/indus-act/lng.asp.

FERC (2016), 'LNG,' Federal Energy Regulatory Commission, accessed June 29, 2016 at www.ferc.gov/industries/gas/indus-act/lng.asp.

FGU (2014), '2014 Annual Report,' Florida Gas Utilities, accessed June 29, 2016 at flgas.com/wp-content/uploads/2014-annual-report-final.pdf.

Finon, Dominique, Tor A. Johnsen and Atle Midttun (2004), 'Challenges when electricity markets face the investment phase,' *Energy Policy*, 32 (12): 1355–1362.

Fox, Mary F. and John M. Braxton (1994), 'Misconduct and social control in science: issues, problems, solutions,' *Journal of Higher Education*, 65 (May/June): 373–383.

Fox-Penner, Peter and James E. Rogers (2014), *Smart Power (Anniversary Edition): Climate Change, the Smart Grid, and the Future of Electric Utilities*. Washington, DC: Island Press.

Frenzel, Carroll W. (1999), *Management of Information Technology*. Cambridge, MA: Course Technology (ITP).

FTA (2015a), 'About the FTA and our history,' Federal Transportation Administration, accessed August 29, 2015 at www.fta.dot.gov/about/14103.html.

FTA (2015b), 'Public transit challenges: funding, investing in systems and coordinating services.' Testimony of Dave Wise of the Federal Transit Administration before the U.S. Senate Committee on Banking, Housing and Urban Affairs, January 16, 2015.

GAO (2015), 'Cybersecurity.' U.S. Government Accountability Office, accessed June 26, 2016 at www.gao.gov/key_issues/cybersecurity/issue_summary.

Gardiner, Jim (2014), 'Environmental challenges facing United States utility commissions,' Paper presented at the May 13–14 11th EU–US Energy Regulators Roundtable, Boston, MA, accessed September 27, 2015 at www.naruc.org/international/Documents/2Gardner_SesI_EnvironmentalChallenges.pdf.

Garofalo, Charles and Dean Geuras (1999), *Ethics in the Public Service: The Moral Mind at Work*. Washington, DC: Georgetown University Press.

Geddes, Rick (1999), 'Public utilities.' *Encyclopedia of Law and Economics*. Accessed November 14, 2015 at encyclo.findlaw.com/5940book.pdf.

Genieser, Kevin (2004), 'Boardroom evolution,' *Public Utilities Fortnightly*, 142 (June): 67–70.

Gent, Chris (2004), 'KUA manager of corporate communications,' personal email correspondence with the author.

Geuras, Dean and Charles Garofalo (2010), *Public Ethics in Administration* (3rd edn). Vienna, VA: Management Concepts.

Giuliano, Genevieve (2012), 'Transportation policy: public transit, settlement patterns, and equity in the United States,' in Nancy Brooks, Kieran Donaghy and Gerrit-Jan Knaap, (eds), *The Oxford Handbook of Urban Economics and Planning*. Oxford: Oxford University Press, pp. 562–579.

Glaeser, Martin G. (1957), *Public Utilities in American Capitalism*. New York: Macmillan.

Goetz, Melanie (2014), *Communicating Water's Value: Talking Points, Tips and Strategies*. Denver: American Water Works Association.

Gomez-Mejia, Louis R., David B. Balkin and Robert L. Cardy (2011), *Managing Human Resources* (7th edn). Upper Saddle River, NJ: Prentice Hall.

Gordon, Lawrence A. and Martin P. Loeb (2006), *Managing Cybersecurity Resources*. New York: McGraw-Hill.

Goss, Robert P. (1996), 'A distinct public administration ethics?' *Journal of Public Administration Research and Theory*, 6 (October): 573–98.

Grabar, Henry (2015), 'American mass transit is dying,' *Solon* (March 1), accessed August 17, 2015 at www.salon.com/2015/03/01/american_mass_transit_is_dying/.

Griff, Neil S. (2011), *Water Finance: Public Responsibilities and Private Opportunities*. Hoboken, NJ: Wiley.

GSA (2016), Sustainable Facilities, Solid Waste System Overview, General Services Administration, accessed February 18, 2016 at https://sftool. gov/explore/green-building/section/57/solid-waste/system-overview.

Gunawansa, Asanga and Lovleen Bhullar (eds) (2013), *Water Governance: An Evaluation of Alternative Architectures*. Cheltenham, UK and Northampton, MA, USA: Edward Elgar Publishing.

Halfman, John D. (2009), 'Landfills: where does our trash go,' accessed October 7, 2015 at people.hws.edu/halfman/Data/PublicInterestArticle/ Landfills.pdf.

Hampton, Howard (2003), *Public Power: The Fight for Publicly Owned Electricity*. Toronto: Insomniac Press.

Hayne, Robert L. and Gregory E. Aliff (2014), *Accounting for Public Utilities*. Dayton, OH: LexisNexis.

Heller, Miriam, Eric W. Von Sacken and Richard L. Gerstberger (2001), 'Water utilities as integrated businesses,' in William C. Lauer (ed.), *Excellence in Action: Water Utility Management in the 21st Century*. Denver, CO: American Water Works Association, pp. 275–300.

Hemily, Brendon (2004), 'Trends affecting public transit's effectiveness,' American Public Transportation Association, accessed August 30, 2015 at http://community-wealth.org/content/trends-affecting-public-transits-effectiveness-review-and-proposed-actions.

Hempling, Scott (2015), *Regulating Public Utility Performance: The Law of Market Structure, Pricing and Jurisdiction*. Chicago, IL: American Bar Association.

Henry, Tom (2014), 'Water crisis grips hundreds of thousands in Toledo area, state emergency declared,' *Toledo Blade* (August 3), accessed August 20, 2015 at www.toledoblade.com/local/2014/08/03/Water-crisis-grips-area.html.

Herring, Horace and Steve Sorrell (2009), *Energy Efficiency and Sustainable Consumption: The Rebound Effect (Energy, Climate and the Environment)*. Basingstoke: Palgrave Macmillan.

Hill, Peter J. (ed.) (1997), *Water Marketing: The Next Generation*. Lanham, MD: Rowman and Littlefield.

Hinckley, Elias (2014), 'Why utility downgrades are a big deal,' in *Breaking Energy*, September 13, 2014. Accessed June 23, 2016 at http://breaking-energy.com/2013/09/13/why-utility-downgrades-are-a-big-deal/.

Hodgkinson, Christopher (1983), *The Philosophy of Leadership*. New York: St. Martin's Press.

Hughes, Owen E. (2003), *Public Management and Administration*. Basingstoke: Palgrave Macmillan.

Hull, William J. and Robert W. Hull (1967), *The Origin and Development of the Waterways Policy of the United States*. Washington, DC: National Waterways Conference.

Hyman, Leonard S. and Public Utilities Reports (1998), *The Water Business: Understanding the Water Supply and Wastewater Industry*. Reston, VA: Public Utilities Reports.

Hyman, Leonard S., Andrew S. Hyman and Robert C. Hyman (2005), *America's Electric Utilities: Past, Present, and Future* (8th edn). Reston, VA: Public Utilities Reports.

ICS-CERT (2014), 'Internet accessible control systems at risk.' *ICS-CERT Monitor*, Industrial Control Systems Cyber Emergency Response Team, accessed September 5, 2015 at ICS-CERT_Monitor_Jan-Spril2014(2). pdf.

Ilic, Marija (2001), 'Understanding demand: the missing link in efficient electricity markets,' unpublished working paper No. MIT EL 01-014WP. Cambridge, MA: MIT Energy Laboratory.

Inofina.com (2015), 'Structure of the natural gas industry,' accessed September 18, 2015 at www.iofina.com/iofina-natural-gas/overview.

ISRI (Institute of Scrap Recycling Industries) (2014), '2014 Yearbook,' accessed June 30, 2016 at www.isri.org/docs/default-source/commodities/2014-scrap-yearbook.

ISRI (2015), 'ISRI scrap yearbook,' Institute of Scrap Recycling Industries, accessed June 28, 2016 at www.scrap2.org/yearbook/index.html#17.

itscolumn.com (2012) accessed June 8, 2016 at www.itscolumn.com/2012/03/28-types-of-computer-security-threats-and-risks/.

Jacobson, Charles D. (2000), *Ties that Bind: Economic and Political Dilemmas of Urban Utility Networks, 1800–1990*. Pittsburgh, PA: University of Pittsburgh Press.

Johnson, Michael D. and Fred Seines (2004), 'Customer portfolio management: toward a dynamic theory of exchange relationships,' *Journal of Marketing*, 68 (April): 1–18.

Jones, J.A.A. (2011), *Water Sustainability: A Global Perspective*. New York: Routledge.

Joseph, Sarah, Jenny Schultz and Melissa Castan (2000), *The International Covenant on Civil and Political Rights*. Oxford: Oxford University Press.

Joskow, Paul L. (2003), *The Difficult Transition to Competitive Electricity Markets in the U.S.* Washington, DC: AIE-Brookings Joint Center for Regulatory Studies. Paper prepared for the *Electricity Deregulation: Where at Here?* Conference at Texas A&M University, accessed April 4, 2015 at www.aei-brooking.org/admin/authirpdfs/page.php?id=271.

Jung, Helen (2014), 'Clatskanie utility female employees win $1.3 million settlement in sex-harassment case,' *The Oregonian* (June 13) online, accessed November 18, 2015 at www.oregonlive.com/pacific-northwest-news/index.ssf/2014/06/clatskanie_utility_female_empl.html.

Kahn, Bob (2012), *Governance Study of Public Power Utilities for the City of Austin*, accessed August 15, 2015 at cleanenergyforaustin.org/downloads/governanceStudy.pdf.

Katz, Sara M. (2002), 'Don't confuse marketing with public participation,' *American Water Works Association Journal*, 94 (7): 38–39.

KBC Advance Technologies (2003), *Annual Report*. Houston, TX.

Kearns, G.S. and A.L. Lederer (2003), 'A resource-based view of strategic IT alignment: how knowledge sharing creates competitive advantage,' *Decision Sciences* 34(1): 1–29.

Keeter, Scott and Paul Taylor (2009), *The Millennials*, accessed October 28, 2015 at www.pewresearch.org/2009/12/10/the-millennials/.

Kent, Calvin A. (1993), *Utility Holding Company Act of 1935: 1935–1992*. Washington, DC: Energy Information Administration.

Keohane, Robert O. and Joseph Nye (2002), 'Governance,' in Robert O. Keohane and John D. Donahue (eds), *Governance in a Globalizing World*. Washington, DC: Brookings Institution Press.

Kettl, Donald F. (2002), *The Transformation of Governance*. Baltimore, MD: Johns Hopkins University Press.

Kidder, Ben (2006), 'The challenges of rural transportation,' Logan, UT: Western Rural Development Center (WRDC) at Utah State University. Accessed September 5, 2015 at wrdc.usu.edu/htm/publications/file=8263.

Kidnay, Arthur J., William R. Parrish and Daniel G. McCartney (2011), *Fundamentals of Natural Gas Processing*, Boca Raton, FL: CRC Press.

Kitterman, Brad and Jack Dugan (2006), 'The disappearing utility workforce,' accessed June 26 2016 at http://electricenergyonline.com/show_article.php?mag=&article=261.

Knickmeyer, Ellen and Scott Smith (2015), 'Fear at the tap: uranium contaminates water in the West,' accessed December 8, 2015 at www.aol.com/article/2015/12/08/fear-at-the-tap-uranium-contaminates-water-in-the-west/21280444/?icid=maing-grid7|main5|d11_11|sec1_1nk3%26pLi d%3D-1760862028.

Kolb, Robert W. (2014), *The Natural Gas Revolution: At the Pivot of the World's Energy Future*, Upper Saddle River, NJ: Pearson.

Koontz, Harold D. (1941), *Government Control of Business*. Boston, MA: Houghton-Mifflin.

Kraft, Michael E. and Scott R. Furlong (2015), *Public Policy: Politics, Analysis and Alternatives* (5th edn). Thousand Oaks, CA: Sage.

Krier, Robert (2012), 'U.S. paying a price for lack of water policy,' *InsideClimate News*, accessed December 20, 2015 at http://insideclimate-news.org/news/20120917/us-paying-price-lack-water-policy.

Lambert, Jeremiah D. (2015), *The Power Brokers: The Struggle to Shape and Control the Electric Power Industry*. Cambridge, MA: Massachusetts Institute of Technology.

Lashgari, Malek (2004), 'Corporate governance: theory and practice,' *Journal of American Academy of Business*, 5 (September): 46–51.

Lassiter, Allison (ed.) (2015), *Sustainable Water: Challenges and Solutions from California*. Oakland, CA: University of California.

Laudon, Kenneth C. and Carol Travor (2013), *E-Commerce 2014* (10th edn). Upper Saddle River, NJ: Prentice Hall.

Laudon, Kenneth C. and Jane P. Laudon (2014), *Management Information Systems* (14th edn). Upper Saddle River, NJ: Prentice Hall.

Lauer, William C. (ed.) (2001), *Excellence in Action: Water Utility Management in the 21st Century*. Denver, CO: American Water Works Association.

Lee, Sang M., Taewon Hwang and Donghyun Choi (2012), 'Open innovation in the public sector of leading economies,' *Management Decision*, 50 (1): 147–162.

Lewis, Peter (2003), 'Texas utility billing company told to quit doing business in the state,' *Seattle Times* (September 4): B3.

Lewis, J. (1985), 'History of the EPA,' *EPA Journal*, accessed August 7, 2015 at www2.epa.gov/aboutepa/birth-epa.

Lin, Rong-Gong II and Priya Krishnakumar (2015), 'Groundwater contamination a growing problem in L.A. County wells,' accessed November 19, 2015 at www.latimes.com/visuals/graphics/la-me-g-drought-wells-20150520-htmlstory.html.

Litman, Todd and David Burwell (2006), 'Issues in sustainable transportation,' *International Journal of Global Environmental Issues*, 6 (4): 331–347.

Lombardi, Kristen (2015), 'Duke Energy fined $25.1 million for groundwater damage at coal ash,' accessed November 19, 2015 at www.publicintegrity.org/2015/03/11/16868/duke-energy-fined-251-million-groundwater-damage-coal-ash.

Lovelock, Christopher H. and Jochen Wirtz (2014), *Services Marketing: People, Technology, Strategy* (7th edn). Upper Saddle River, NJ: Prentice Hall.

Lusk, Sean and Nick Birks (2014), *Rethinking Public Strategy*. Basingstoke: Palgrave Macmillan.

Lux, Larry (2005), 'The Impact of Homeland Security Presidential Directive 5 on the Public Works Community,' accessed June 26, 2016 at www.apwa.net/

Resources/Reporter/Articles/2005/1/The-impact-of-Homeland-Security-Presidential-Directive-5-on-the-public-works-community.

MacAvoy, Paul W. (2000), *The Natural Gas Market: Sixty Years of Regulation and Deregulation*. New Haven, CT: Yale University Press.

McCann, Justin C. (2004), *Industry Profiles: Standard & Poor's Industry Survey*, accessed May 13, 2004 at www.netadvantage.stadardAndpoorts. com/docs/industr////elu_0204/elu30204.htm.

McLean-Conner (2004), *Customer Service: Utility Style*. Tulsa, OK: PennWell.

McLeod, Raymond Jr. and George Schell (2006), *Management Information Systems* (13th edn). Upper Saddle River, NJ: Prentice Hall.

McNabb, David E. (1968) *Pubic vs. Private Power Fight*. Unpublished Master's thesis. Seattle, WA: University of Washington.

McNabb, David E. (2009), *The New Face of Government: How Public Managers Are Forging a New Approach to Governance*. New York: CRC Press.

Maine Public Service Company (2002), *Annual Report*. Presque Isle, ME.

Marshall, Christine, Robert Blair, Jonathan Abe and Christopher Clark (2001), 'FERC Order 2000 drives RTO initiatives; ISOs, Transcos prevail,' *Electric & Power*, May 1, accessed June 21, 2016 at www.elp.com/articles/print/volume-79/issue-5/industry-news/ferc-order-2000-drives-rto-initiatives-isos-transcos-prevail.html.

Mason County Public Utility District No. 3 (n.d.), *Annual Report*. Shelton, WA.

Mattoon, Richard (2002), 'The electricity system at the crossroads,' *Society*, 40 (1): 64–79.

MDLS (Maryland Department of Legislative Services) (2012), 'Financing options for transit expansion,' accessed November 24, 2015 at dls.state.md.us/data/polanshare.polanshar_natresenvntra/Financing-Options-for-Transit-Expansion-Report.pdf.

Menzel, Donald C. (2012), *Ethics Management for Public Administration* (2nd edn). New York: Taylor & Francis.

Mills, Robin M. (2008), *The Myth of the Oil Crisis*. Westport, CT: Praeger.

Minnesota PUC (2010), 'Utilities rate study June 2010,' accessed December 8, 2015 at mn.gov/puc/assets/012854_tcm14-5188.pdf.

Mishra, Amareshwar and R.K. Mishra (2014), *Financing Patterns for Infrastructure Projects*. New Delhi: Academic Foundation Press.

Mokhatab, Saeid, John Y. Mak, Jaleel V. Valappil and David Atwood (2013), *Handbook of Liquefied Natural Gas*. Amsterdam: Elsevier.

Morgan, C.S. (2010), *Regulation and the Management of Public Utilities*. Boston, MA: Gale (Cengage Learning).

MPUC (2012), 'Xcel Energy's application for approval of its 2008–2022

Resource Plan,' Minnesota Public Utility Commission, accessed June 29, 2016 at www.edockets.state.mn.us/EFiling/edockets/search Documents.

Mullin, Megan (2009), *Governing the Tap: Special District Governance and the New Local Politics of Water*. Boston, MA: MIT Press.

NAE (2015), '14 grand challenges for engineering in the 21st century: restore and improve urban infrastructure,' National Academy of Engineering, accessed November 21, 2015 at www.engineeringchallenges.org/challenges/infrastructure.aspx.

Nanus, Burt (1996), *Leading the Way to Organizational Renewal*. Portland, OR: Productivity Press.

Napolitano, Frank A. (2004), 'Banking on predictability,' *Public Utilities Fortnightly*, 142 (April): 53–56.

NARUC (2013), 'Cybersecurity for state regulators 2.0 with sample questions for regulators to ask utilities (Primer),' accessed June 26, 2016 at energy.gov/oe/downloads/cybersecurity-state-regulators-naruc.

NASA (2014), 'Climate change: vital signs of the planet,' accessed June 30, 2016 at http://climate.nasa.gov/effects/.

NaturalGas.org (2013), 'Overview of natural gas: marketing,' accessed September 21, 2015 at http://naturalgas.org/naturalgas/marketing/.

NCSL (2016), 'Water and natural resources.' National Conference of State Legislatures, accessed June 26, 2016 at www.ncsl.org/research/environment-and-natural-resources/adapting-to-climate-change.aspx.

New Jersey Future (2015), 'Complex web of jurisdictions in New Jersey's CSO municipalities,' accessed June 26, 2016 at www.njfuture.org/wp-content/uploads/2014/06/Water-and-Sewer-System.

New York State Inspector General (2012a), 'Investigation of employee misconduct at the Department of Public Service,' accessed December 11, 2015 at ig.state.ny.us/pdfs/PSCPublicReport.pdf.

New York State Inspector General (2012b), 'Inspector General report faults utility gifts to Department of Public Service staff investigating safety issues; utility to pay fine of $1.167 million,' accessed June 26, 2016 at pulpnetwork.blogspot.com/2012/07/inspector-general-report-faults-utility.html.

NGI (2015), 'Top North American gas marketers,' *Natural Gas Intelligence*, accessed June 29, 2016 at www.naturalgasintel.com/marketer_rankings/2015.

NIEHS (2015), 'Endocrine disruptors.' National Institute of Environmental Health Sciences, accessed June 26, 2016 at www.niehs.nih.gov/health/topics/agents/endocrine/.

NIST (2014), 'Update on the cybersecurity framework,' National Institute of Standards and Technology, accessed October 14, 2015 at www.

nist.gov/cyberframework/upload/nist-cybersecurity-framework-update-120514.pdf.

NOAA (2015), 'International report confirms: 2014 was Earth's warmest year on record,' National Oceanic and Atmospheric Administration, accessed September 4, 2015 at www.noaanews.noaa.gov/stories2015/071615-international-report-confirms-2014-was-earths-warmest-year-on-record.html.

NWRA (2014), 'Begin with the bin,' National Waste & Recycling Association, accessed November 2, 2014 at http://beginwiththebin.org/resources/for-education.

NYC (2015), New York City's wastewater treatment system,' accessed October 20, 2015 at www.nyc.gov/html/dep/html/wastewater/wwsystem-process.shtml#top.

OECD (2012), 'Strategic crisis management,' accessed December 11, 2015 at www.oecd.org/officialdocuments/publicdisplaydocumentpdf/?

Olsen, Audrey B. (1999), *North Dakota Small Community Water System's Handbook on Developing and Setting Water Rates.* Revised edition, accessed June 27, 2016 at www.map-inc.org/pdf/pub_water_rates.pdf.

Orth, Mike (2015), 'Resilience questions expose gaps, opportunity for water industry,' *Opflow*, 41 (12): 8–9.

Osborne, David and Peter Plastrik (1992), *Banishing Bureaucracy*. Reading, MA: Addison-Wesley.

OSHA (2015), 'National Transit Systems Security Act (NTSSA) 6 U.S.C. §1142,' accessed June 22, 2016 at www.whistleblowers.gov/acts/ntssa.html.

Otenyo, Eric E. and Nancy S. Lind (2011), *E-Government: The Use of Information and Communication Technologies in Administration*. New York: Teneo Press.

Oxford Dictionaries on line (2015), 'Sustainable,' accessed December 18, 2015 at www.oxforddictionaries.com/us/definition/american_english/sustainable.

Ozan, Turgut M. (1972), 'Controls for operations management,' *Journal of the American Water Works Association*, 64 (2): 74–81.

Patterson, Walt (2009), *Keeping the Lights On: Towards Sustainable Electricity*. London: Earthscan.

Pearce, Fred (2006), *When the Rivers Run Dry*: Water—*the Defining Crisis of the Twenty-first Century*. Boston, MA: Beacon Press.

Pearce, John A. and Richard B. Robinson (2014), *Strategic Management* (14th edn). Burr Ridge, IL: Irwin.

Pearson, Christine and Judith A. Clair (1998), 'Reframing crisis management,' *Academy of Management Review*, 22 (January): 59–76.

Petrick, Joseph A. and John F. Quinn (1997), *Management Ethics: Integrity at Work*. Newbury Park: CA: Sage.

Pew Research Center (2014), 'Millennials in adulthood,' accessed October 28, 2015 at www.pewsocialtrends.org/2014/03/07/millennials-in-adulthood/.

Pond, Oscar L. (2012), *Municipal Control of Public Utilities; A Study of the Attitude of Our Courts Toward an Increase in the Sphere of Municipal Activity*. Lenox, MA: HardPress.

Porter, Richard C. (2002), *The Economics of Waste*. Washington, DC: Resources for the Future.

Poston, Ben and Matt Stevens (February 16, 2015), 'Replacing L.A.'s aging water pipes; a $1-billion dilemma,' *Los Angeles Times*, accessed November 28, 2015 at http://graphics.latimes.com/la-aging-water-infrastructure/.

Pynes, Joan (2013), *Human Resources Management for Public and Nonprofit Organizations* (4th edn). San Francisco, CA: Jossey-Bass.

Pyper, Julia and ClimateWire (2011), 'Does burning garbage to produce electricity make sense?,' accessed December 6, 2015 at www.scientificameri can.com/article/does-burning-garbage-to-produce-energy-make-sense/.

PwC (PricewaterhouseCoopers, LLP) (2013), *Guide to Accounting for Utilities and Power Companies*, accessed August 13, 2015 at www.pwc.com/us/en/cfodirect/publications/accounting-guides/guide-to-accounting-for-utilities-and-power-companies-2013.jhtml.

Rachman, David J., Michael H. Mescon, Courtland L. Bovée and John V. Thill (1993), *Business Today* (7th edn). New York: McGraw-Hill.

Rada, Elena C. (2015), *Biological Treatment of Solid Waste: Enhancing Sustainability*. Boca Raton, FL: CRC Press.

Rainey, Hal G. (2014), *Understanding and Managing Public Organizations*. San Francisco, CA: Jossey-Bass.

Reamer, Adam (2012), *U.S. Water Policy: Trends and Future Directions*, National Agricultural and Rural Development Policy Center (NARDeP), accessed December 20, 2015 at www.nardep.info/uploads/WaterPolicy_Reimer.pdf.

Reed, William L. (2003), 'Competitive electricity markets and innovative technologies: hourly pricing can pave the way for the introduction of technology and innovation,' Rand Corporation working papers, accessed February 20, 2004 at www/rand.org/scitech/stpi/Evision/Supplement/reed.pdf.

Reilly, Steve (2015), 'Bracing for a big power grid attack,' *US Today* (March 24). Accessed June 26, 2016 at www.usatoday.com/story/news/2015/03/24/power-grid-physical-and-cyber-attacks-concern-security-experts/24892471/.

Richardson, Whit (November 18–19, 2013), 'New name, same

commitment—Bangor Hydro, Maine Public Service to become Emera Maine.' *Bangor Daily News*, accessed August 19, 2015 at http://bangordailynews.com/2013/11/18/business/new-name-same-service-bangor-hydro-maine-public-service-to-become-emera-maine/.

Riggins, Frederick J. and Hyen-Suk Rhee (1998), 'Toward a unified view of electronic commerce,' *Communications of the ACM*, 41 (October): 88–95.

Rizak, Samantha and Steve E. Hurdey (2007), 'Achieving safe drinking water—risk management based on experience and reality.' *Environmental Reviews*, 15 (2007): 169–174.

Robertson, Margaret (2014), *Sustainability, Principles and Practice*. London: Earthscan.

Robinson, Colin (ed.) (2002), *Utility Regulation and Competitive Policy*. Cheltenham, UK and Northampton, MA, USA: Edward Elgar Publishing.

Rodrique, Jean-Paul, Claude Comtois and Brian Slack (2013), *The Geography of Transport Systems* (3rd edn). New York: Routledge.

Rogoff, Mark J., Jon Kennedy, Augusto Rodriquez and Ralph Lassiter (2002), 'Optimizing public utility operations with performance evaluation and business planning,' *Opflow*, accessed March 16, 2004 at www.hdrinc.com/architecture/consulting/EngArticles/OptimizingPublicUtilityOps(7).html.

Rohr, John A. (1998), *Public Service, Ethics & Constitutional Practice*. Lawrence, KA: University Press of Kansas.

Rosenthall, Stephen R. (1981), 'Teaching public sector operations management,' *Policy Analysis*, 7 (2): 245–258.

Rothstein, Eric and Donna Kiyosaki (2003), 'Portfolio management for public utilities: development of a strategic plan,' *American Water Works Association Journal*, 95 (1): 52–65.

Royte, Elizabeth (2005), *Garbage Land*. New York: Little, Brown.

RPU (2014), 'Power resources risk management policies,' City of Riverside Public Utilities, accessed June 29, 2016 at www.riversideca.gov/utilities/pdf/2015/PRRMP-Final-20140429.pdf.

Schaper, David (2014), 'As infrastructure crumbles, trillions of gallons of water lost,' accessed November 28, 2015 at www.npr.org/2014/10/29/359875321/as-infrastructure-crumbles-trillions-of-gallons-of-water-lost.

Scharfenberg, David (February 15, 2015), 'The MBTA's long, winding infuriating road to failure,' *Boston Globe*, accessed September 1, 2015 at www.bostgonglobe.com/metro/2015/02/14/transportation/U7vqP861gKQFRly2jmjdL/story.html.

Schiller, Preston, Eric Bruun and Jeffrey Kenworthy (2010), *An Introduction to Sustainable Transportation: Policy, Planning and Implementation*. London: Earthscan.

Schwarzenbach, René, Thomas Egli, Thomas B. Hofstetter, Urs von Gunten and Karl S. Zimmer (2010), 'Global water pollution and human health,' *Annual Review of Environment and Resources*, 2010 (35): 109–136.

Sedlak, David L. (2015), 'One type of water: potentially drinkable,' *Journal of the American Water Works Association*, 107 (9): 18–24.

Seger, Karl A. (2003), *Utility Security: The New Paradigm*. Tulsa, OK: PennWell.

Seidenstat, Paul, Michael Nadol and Simon Hakim (2000), *America's Water and Wastewater Industries*. Washington, DC: Public Utilities Reports.

Senn, James A. (2003), *Information Technology in Business* (3rd edn). Englewood Cliffs, NJ: Pearson.

Shere, Craig (2004), *Natural Gas. Standard & Poor's Industry Surveys*, accessed May 13, 2005 at www.netadvantage.standardandpoors.com/docs/indsur///ngd_0504/ngd4054.htm.

Shiflea, Rebecca and Thomas Jensen (2013), 'Future utility success: top 10 practices,' *Public Power*, 71(4), accessed June 29, 2016 at www.publicpower.org/Media/magazine/ArticleDetail.cfm?ItemNumber=37816.

Shively, Bob and John Ferrare (2011), *Understanding Today's Natural Gas Business* (6th edn). Self-published.

Smart Insights (2014), 'The challenges and opportunities of CRM in 2014,' accessed June 24, 2016 at www.smartinsights.com/customer-relationship-management/e-crm-strategy/crm-2014/.

Smeloff, Edward and Peter Asmus (1997), *Reinventing Electric Utilities: Competition, Citizen Action, and Clean Power*. Washington, DC: Island Press.

Smil, Vaclav (2015), *Natural Gas: Fuel for the 21st Century*. New York: Wiley.

Sneider, Gary P. (2014), *Electronic Commerce*. Boston, MA: Course Technology.

South Jersey Industries (2002), *Annual Report*. Folsom, NJ.

Sparks, William Q. (1964), 'J.D. Ross and Seattle City Light, 1917–1932,' unpublished master's degree thesis, Seattle: University of Washington.

Spellman, Frank R. (2013), *Water and Wastewater Infrastructure: Energy Efficiency and Sustainability*. Boca Raton, FL: CRC Press.

Spillane, Robert and Jean-Etienne Joullié (2015), *Philosophy of Leadership: The Power of Authority*. Basingstoke: Palgrave Macmillan.

Stell, Jeannie (2015), 'Top five gas processers eye additional expansion,' *Gas Processing* online, accessed June 28, 2016 at www.gasprocessingnews.com/features/201402/top-five-us-gas-processers-eye-additional-expansions.aspx.

Stoft, Steven (2002), *Power System Economics*. Piscataway, NJ: IEEE Press.

Stone, Madeline (2014), 'The US cities with the best public transportation systems,' accessed November 3, 2015 at www.businessinsider.com/cities-with-best-public-transportation-systems-2014-1.

Storey, Michael, Bram van der Gaag and Brenden P. Burns (2011), 'Advances in on-line drinking water quality monitoring and early warning systems,' *Water Research*, 45 (2): 741–747.

Stucki, Andrea (2009), 'Open innovation models in public utilities as an option to react on reform process: the case of the postal sector.' Paper presented at the Second Annual conference on Competition and Regulation in Networked Industries. Brussels, Belgium, accessed August 9, 2015 at infoscience.epfl.ch/record/151576/files/astruckipaper-CRN109.pdf.

Sun, Jinping and Thomas D. Lynch (2008), *Government Budget Forecasting: Theory and Practice*. Boca Raton, FL: Taylor & Francis.

Sustainable Thurston (2012), 'Solid waste work group white paper,' Thurston County, Washington, accessed December 15, 2015 at www.trpc.org/DocumentCenter/Home/View/1507.

Sutton, John C. (2015), *Gridlock: Congested Cities, Contested Policies, Unsustainable Mobility*. New York: Routledge.

Suzuki, Hiroaki and Robert Cervero (2013), *Transforming Cities with Transit: Transit and Land Use Integration for Sustainable Urban Development*. Washington, DC World Bank.

Sweet, Cassandra (2015), 'Pepco sale blocked by regulators,' *The Wall Street Journal* (August 26): B6.

Teske, Paul (2003), 'State regulation: captured Victorian-era anachronism or 'reinforcing' autonomous structure?,' *Perspectives on Politics*, 1 (June): 291–306.

The Groundwater Foundation (2015), 'Potential threats to our groundwater: groundwater contamination,' accessed November 19, 2015 at www.groundwater.org/get-informed/groundwater/contamination.html.

Thomas, Arthur A. and A.J. Strickland III (2003), *Strategic Management* (13th edn). Chicago, IL: Irwin.

Thompson, Lynn (March 2, 2012), 'Former city employee arrested in $1 million theft at Seattle public Utilities' *Seattle Times* online, accessed November 18, 2015 at www.seattletimes.com/seattle-news/former-city-employee-arrested-in-1-million-theft-at-seattle-public-utilities/.

Turban, Efraim, Ephraim McLean and James Wetherbe (2015), *Information Technology for Management: Making Connections for Strategic Advantage* (10th edn). New York: Wiley.

Tweed, Katherine (2014), 'Attack on California substation fuels grid security debate,' accessed June 26, 2016 at http://spectrum.ieee.org/energywise/

energy/the-smarter-grid/attack-on-california-substation-fuels-grid-security-debate.

Twenty-first Century Power Partnership (2013), 'Market evolution: wholesale electricity market design for 21st century power systems,' Produced under the guidance of the Department of Energy and the Clean Energy Ministerial by the National Renewable Energy Laboratory under Interagency Agreement S- OES-12-IA-0010 and Task Number WFH1.2010. October 7, 2013, accessed December 8, 2015 at www.hks.harvard.edu/hepg/rlib_rp_wholesale.html.

Twink.org (2015), 'Finding and resolving the root causes of the sustainability problem,' accessed December 18, 2015 at www.thwink.org/sustain/glossary/Sustainability.htm.

UACOG (2008), *Effective Utility Management: A Primer for Water and Wastewater Utilities*, Utility Advisors and Collaborating Organization Group, accessed August 12, 2015 at 2008-06EUMprimer.pdf.

UACOG (2013), *Rural and Small Systems Guidebook to Sustainable Utility Management*, Environmental Protection Agency, accessed August 12, 2015 at water.epa.gov,infrastructure/sustain/upload/SUSTAINABLE_ MANAGEMENT_ OF_ RURAL_ AND_ SMALL_ SYSTEMS_ GUIDE_ FINAL_ 10-24-13.pdf.

Uchimura, Keiichi, Takashi Saitoh and Hiro Takahashi (1999), 'The dial-a-ride problem in a public transit system,' *Electronics and Communications in Japan*, Part 3, 82 (7): 30–38.

UCS (2014), 'How climate change puts our electricity at risk,' Union of Concerned Scientists, accessed August 20, 2015 at www.ucsusa.org/global_warming/science_and_impacts/impacts/effects-of-climate-change-risks-on-our-electricity-system.html#.VdYWg_nF8Uo.

Unitil (2012), 'Electric Emergency Response Plan,' Fitchburg Gas and Electric Light Company, accessed June 29, 2016 at c2pr4+Nn.pdf.

US-CERT (United States Computer Emergency Readiness Team) (2013), Cyber threat protection tip, accessed February 23, 2016 at www/us-cert.gov/ncas/tips#attacks-and-threats.

USDA and EPA (2016), *Rural and Small Systems Guidebook to Sustainable Utility Management*, accessed June 25, 2016 from RuralandSmallSystemsGuidebook2016.pdf.

USDHS (2010), 'Water Sector-Specific Plan,' US Department of Homeland Security, accessed October 19, 2015 at www.dhs.gov/xlibrary/assets/nipp-ssp-water-2010.pdf.

USDHS (2011), 'Pipeline threat assessment,' US Department of Homeland Security, Transportation Security Administration, Office of Intelligence, accessed December 5, 2015 at https://publicintelligence.net/ufouo-tsa-liquid-and-natural-gas-pipeline-threat-assessment-2011/.

USDOS (2011), *U.S. Water Policy Brief: the Global Water Challenge*, Washington, DC: U.S. Department of State, accessed December 20, 2015 at www.state.gov/e/oes/rls/other/2011/158419.htm.

USDOT (2013), *Transportation Systems Security and Emergency Preparedness Planning Guide*. Cambridge, MA: U.S. Department of Transportation, Research and Special Programs Administration.

USGCRP (U.S. Global Change Research Program) (2009), *Global Climate Change Impacts in the United States*. U.S. Global Change Research Program. New York: Cambridge University.

US Government (2011), US Government Water Policy Brief, March 4, 2011. US State Department. Accessed June 20, 2016 at http://www.state.gov/e/oes/rls/other/2011/158419.htm.

USGS (2014), *Estimated Use of Water in the United States in 2010*. United States Geological Survey Circular 1405. Reston, VA: U.S. Department of the Interior.

USGS (2015), 'A visit to a wastewater-treatment plant: primary treatment of wastewater,' accessed October 20, 2015 at http://water.usgs.gov/edu/visit.html.

Utility Dive (2014), 'State of the Electric utility survey results,' accessed October 10, 2015 at www.utilitydive.com/library/2014-state-of-the-electric-utility/.

Utility Dive (2015), 'State of the Electric utility survey results,' accessed October 10, 2015 at www.utilitydive.com/library/the-state-of-the-electric-utility-2015/.

VanGuilder, Cliff (2011), *Hazardous Waste Management: An Introduction*. Dulles, VA: Mercer Learning and Information.

Van Leuven, Laurie J. (2011), 'Water/wastewater infrastructure Security: threats and vulnerabilities,' in R.M. Clark, S. Hakim and A. Ostfeld (eds), *Handbook of Water and Wastewater Systems Protection*. New York: Springer-Scientific, pp. 27–46.

Velasquez, Manuel (2011), *Business Ethics: Concepts and Cases* (7th edn). Upper Saddle River, NJ: Prentice Hall.

Vergara, Sintana E. and George Tchobanoglous (2012), 'Municipal solid waste and the environment: a global perspective,' *Annual Review of Environment and Resources*, 2012 (37): 277–309.

Vital, Tina (2004), *Oil and Gas: Production and Marketing*. Standard & Poor's Industry Surveys, accessed April 22, 2004 at www.netadvantage.standardandpoors.com/docs/indsur///ogp_0404/ogp50404.htm.

WADoE (1987), *Solid Waste Landfill Design Manual*. Olympia, WA: Washington State Department of Ecology, accessed December 20, 2015 at https://fortress.wa.gov/ecy/publications/documents/87013.pdf.

Walker, Jarrett (2011) *Human Transit: How Clearer Thinking about Public Transit can Enrich our Communities and our Lives*. Washington, DC: Island Press.

Wallis-Lage, Cindy (2014), 'Strategic directions: U.S. Water Industry report,' accessed June 26, 2016 from bv.com/docs/default-source/ reports-studies/2014-sdr-water-industry.

Walsh, J., D. Wuebbles, K. Hayhoe, J. Kossin, K. Kunkel, G. Stephens, P. Thorne, R. Vose, M. Wehner, J. Willis, D. Anderson, S. Doney, R. Feely, P. Hennon, V. Kharin, T. Knutson, F. Landerer, T. Lenton, J. Kennedy and R. Somerville (2014), 'Our changing climate,' *Climate Change Impacts in the United States: The Third National Climate Assessment*, J.M. Melillo, Terese (T.C.) Richmond and G.W. Yohe (eds), U.S. Global Change Research Program, 19–67, accessed December 19, 2015 at doi: 10.7930/J0KW5CXT.

Warren, Charles (1928), *The Supreme Court in United States History*. Boston, MA: Little, Brown.

Watkins, Sherron (2003), 'Former Enron vice president Sherron Watkins on the Enron collapse,' *Academy of Management Executive*, 17 (4): 119–125.

WCED (1987), *Our Common Future*. United Nations World Commission on Environment and Development.

WCF (Water Governance Facility) (2016), 'What is water governance,' accessed June 25, 2016 at http://watergovernance.org/governance/ what-is-water-governance/.

Weiss, Carol H. (1998), *Evaluation* (2nd edn). Upper Saddle River, NJ: Prentice Hall.

Westar Energy (2002), *Annual Report*. Topeka, KS.

WGL (2013), '2013 Annual Report,' accessed June 26, 2016 at www.wgl holdings.com/secfiling.cfm?filingID=1193125-13-447277.

WGL Holdings (2002), *Annual Report*. Washington, DC: WGL Hold ings.

The Whitehouse (1996), 'Executive Order EO 13010: Critical Infrastructure Protection,' accessed June 27, 2016 at http://fas.org/irp/offdocs/eo13010. htm.

Wickwar, W. Hardy (1938), *The Public Services: A Historical Survey*. London: Cobden-Sanderson.

Woller, Gary M. and Kelly D. Patterson (1997), 'Public administration ethics: a postmodern perspective,' *American Behavioral Scientist*, 41 (1): 103–108.

World Bank (2015), 'Introduction to wastewater treatment processes,' accessed October 20, 2015 at www.worldbank.org/en/topic/water.

WPTA (2015), 'Sustainability,' American Public Transportation

Association, accessed December 18, 2015 at www.apta.com/resources/hottopics/sustainability/Pages/default.aspx.

WSDOH (2011), 'Water use efficiency.' Washington State Department of Health, accessed June 28, 2016 at www.doh.wa.gov/CommunityandEnvironment/DrinkingWater/WaterSystemDesignandPlanning/WaterUseEfficiency.

WSDOT (2015), 'Mason transit authority honored as 2015's best rural transit system in America,' Washington State Department of Transportation, accessed August 29, 2015 at http://wsdotblog.blogspot.com/2015/06/mason-transit-authority-honored-as.html.

Yoshimura, Henry (2013), 'Wholesale/retail pricing: can the disconnected realities be bridged?,' Harvard Electricity Policy Group 70th Plenary Session, Dana Point, CA, March 7–8, 2013. Harvard Electricity Policy Group, wholesale and retail competition, accessed December 8, 2015 at www.hks.harvard.edu/hepg/rlib_rp_wholesale.html.

Zeithalm, Valerie and Mary Jo Bitner (2012), *Services Marketing* (6th edn). New York: McGraw-Hill.

Glossary and useful definitions

This section is a list of words, phrases, and technical terminology that frequently appear in the utilities industry and associated literature. A number of them, but not all, are used in this volume. The definitions are collected and edited from industry, government, and utility literature.

Acid rain: Precipitation containing harmful amounts of nitric and sulfuric acids formed primarily by nitrogen oxides and sulfur oxides released into the atmosphere when fossil fuels and some solid waste components are burned.

Active solar energy: Solar radiation used to provide space and water heating, or to produce electricity.

Aerobic: Decomposition process in the presence of oxygen (see "composting").

Aggregator: A commercial entity that purchases electric or natural gas energy in bulk for a group of customers, thereby receiving quantity discounts from suppliers.

Anaerobic: Decomposition process in the absence of oxygen (see "methane").

Ancillary services: Additional services necessary to support the transmission of energy from sources to loads; natural gas processors are an example.

Aquaculture water use: Water used in raising and processing finfish and shellfish in captivity.

Aquifer: A geologic formation with enough saturated porous and permeable material to maintain and transmit matter at a rate sufficient to feed a spring or well.

Barrel: A volume unit of measurement for crude oil and processed petroleum products; it is equivalent to 42 U.S. gallons. The abbreviation for barrel is 'Bbl.'

Base bill: A charge for energy or water calculated by multiplying the appropriate schedule rate by the level of consumption. Use over the schedule rates are added to the base bill.

Baseload: The minimum amount of electric power delivered or required over a given period of time at a study rate. The lowest level of power needed during a time period (usually a season or a calendar year).

Baseload plant: The capacity of the generating equipment normally operated to serve loads on an around-the-clock basis.

Biomass: A waste organic material that can be used as a fuel for generating electricity. It includes such material as dead trees and branches, yard and garden waste, left-over food crops, wood chips, bark, and sawdust from lumber mills. It also includes combustible material found in household, commercial and industrial waste.

British thermal unit (BTU): A standard unity for measuring the quantity of heat energy equal to the quantity of heat required to raise the temperature of one pound of water by one degree Fahrenheit.

bsf: The abbreviation for 1 million cubic feet, commonly used for measuring amounts of natural gas.

Coal ash: Impurities containing silica, iron, alumina, and other noncombustible matter contained in coal. Ash increases the weight of coal, adds to the cost of handling and can affect its burning characteristic. Coal ash is often stored in ponds to let contaminants settle; it is sometimes used in sanitary landfills as a waste layer covering product. Also see fly ash.

Cogenerator: A generating facility that produces electricity and another form of useful energy (such as heat or steam) that is used for industrial, commercial, heating or cooling purposes. To be identified as a qualified facility (QF), the facility must meet certain ownership, operating, and efficiency criteria established by FERC.

Combined cycle: An electric generating technology in which electricity is produced from otherwise waste heat exiting from one or more gas combustion turbines. The exiting heat is routed to a conventional boiler or to heat recovery steam unit for use to produce electricity. The process increases the efficiency of the electric generating unit.

Combustion: Refers to controlled burning of waste with environmental control technology to reduce the waste volume and often to generate energy.

Commercial sector: The economic sector that includes all non-manufacturing business establishments, including hotels, motels, restaurants, wholesale and retail trade, and health, social, and educational institutions.

Commercial water use: Water used by hotels and motels, restaurants, office buildings and other commercial facilities, military and civilian institutions. This water may be acquired from a public utility system or may be self-supplied.

Commission: A public body with power to regulate or oversee the activities of one or more type of public utilities. Examples include the Federal Energy Regulatory Commission (FERC) and all state and local management or regulatory commissions.

Composting: The controlled aerobic biological decomposition of organic matter, such as food scraps and plant matter, that produces humus, a soil-like material.

Conservation: The demand-side management that represents the amounts of reduction in consumer peak load use of energy or water at the time of system peak from programs that reduce consumer load (see "demand-side management").

Construction and demolition (C&D) waste: Waste products from the construction and demolition industry that are considered recyclable; they include stone, brick, concrete, windows, metal, lumber, and shingles.

Contract price: The price of fuels or other utility products marketed on a contract basis and covering a period of one or more years. Contract prices reflect market conditions at the time the contract was negotiated and therefore remain constant over the life of the contract (or adjusted by inclusion of a clause in the contract).

Conventional power: Power produced from non-renewable fuels such as coal, oil, gas, and nuclear; also known as traditional power.

Cooperative electric utility: A utility legally established to be owned and operated for the benefit of those using its service in an area not served by another utility. Most cooperative utilities were initially financed by the Rural Electrification or Rural Water office of the U.S. Department of Agriculture.

Demand-side management (DSM): The planning, implementation and monitoring of utility activities designed to encourage customers to modify their patterns of usage; demand-side management activities time of use rates, incentive payments to consumers to install DSM appliances, fuel substitutions, measurement and evaluation and others designed to reduce demand and/or use.

Deregulation: The process of changing the laws and regulations that control sectors of the public utility industry and allow competition of services and sales, allowing customers to choose their provider.

Distribution: Distribution companies are the utilities that deliver product to homes and businesses over wires, pipelines, motor vehicles and other means. They are also referred to as local distribution companies or LDCS.

Distribution system: The portion of a total utility operation that is dedicated to delivering the final product or service to an end user.

Domestic water use: Water used for indoor household purposes such as drinking, food preparation, bathing, washing clothing and dishes, flushing toilets, and outdoor purposes such as watering lawns and gardens. This water may be supplied by a public utility or self-supplied as from private wells.

Electric plant: A facility containing electric generators and auxiliary equipment for converting mechanical, chemical, and/or fission energy into electric energy.

Electric rate schedule: A statement of the electric rate and terms and conditions governing its application, including contract terms and conditions that have been accepted by a regulatory agency or other body with appropriate oversight authority.

Electric utility: A corporation, person, agency, authority, or other legal entity or instrumentality that owns and/or operates facilities for the generation transmission, distribution, or sale of electric energy primarily for use by the public.

Energy: Energy is the capacity of doing work; it is measured in two different ways: (1) as the inherent capability within a fuel of carrying out work, or (2) by the actual conversion of this capability to motion (kinetic energy). Most of the world's energy at this time comes from fossil fuels that are burned to produce heat that is then used as a transfer medium to mechanical work or other processes in order to accomplish tasks.

Fly ash: Particle matter from coal ash. Fly ash is removed from flue gas using flue gas particulate collectors such as fabric filters and electrostatic precipitators.

Fossil fuel: Any naturally occurring organic fuel, such as petroleum, coal, and natural gas which was formed from the remains of prehistoric life.

Freshwater: Water that contains less than 1,000 milligrams of dissolved solids.

Garbage: Solid waste disposed of in a landfill or other non-productive use; it is also known as refuse.

Gas: Gas is a fuel burned for heat, to generate electricity, or by internal combustion engines for electric generation or transportation. Gases for these purposes include natural gas, manufactured gas, gas from waste decomposition, coal gas, propane, and methane.

Gasification: The process of producing power from biomass gas containing hydrogen, methane, carbon monoxide, nitrogen, water and carbon dioxide. The term also refers to the production of synthetic gas from coal.

Gas turbine: A gas turbine typically consists of an axial flow air compressor, one or more combustion chambers where fuel is burned and the hot gases are passed to the turbine where the gas expands to drive the generator or to run the air compressor.

Generating unit: Any combination of physically connected generators, reactors, boilers, combustion turbines, or other prime mover operated together to produce electric power.

Geothermal plant: A plant in which the prime mover is a steam turbine. The turbine is driven either by steam produced from hot water or by natural steam that derives its energy from heat found in rocks or fluids of various depths beneath the surface of the earth.

Gigawatt (GW): One billion watts of electricity.

Gigawatt hour: One billion watt-hours.

Global climate change: Gradual changing of global climate due to buildup of carbon dioxide and greenhouse gases in the earth's atmosphere. Also referred to as global warming.

Governance: The process by which stakeholders communicate their interests and concerns, their input is absorbed, management decisions are taken and implemented, and decision-makers are held accountable.

Governance model: A description of the principles of the type of governance model employed, and of the allocation of responsibilities and relationships between stakeholders for tasks and practices required for governance of an institution or an enterprise.

Hazardous materials: Chemicals or substances that are physically hazardous or health hazards as defined and classified in Article 80 of the Uniform Fire Code, whether the materials are in useable or waste condition.

Hazardous waste: Any waste or combination of wastes that are corrosive, ignitable, toxic, or persistent in the environment and may cause irreversible illness, and increase in mortality, or pose a substantial threat to human health or the environment.

Household hazardous waste: Hazardous wastes generated by households rather than by businesses, industries or institutions.

Industrial water use: Water used for fabrication, processing, washing, and cooling, including processes carried out by chemical and allied products, food processing, mining, paper production, petroleum refining and iron and steel production.

Irrigation water use: Water that is applied by an irrigation system to assist crop and pasture growth, or to maintain vegetation on recreational lands such as parks and golf courses, and water that is used for frost protection, chemical application, weed control, field preparation, crop cooling, harvesting, dust suppression, leaching of salts from the root zone and other uses.

Landfill: Disposal site for nonhazardous solid wastes. The waste is spread into layers, compacted to reduce its volume, and covered by material such as clay or soil, which is applied at the end of each operating day.

Methane: Gas generated when wastes in a landfill decompose anaerobically; comprises approximately 50 percent of the gases emitted from landfills.

Municipal solid waste (MSW): All wastes generated by residential, business, industrial and institutions.

Public–private partnership: Private-sector involvement in designing, building, operating or managing aspects of public utility services and supply systems.

Public-supply water use: Water withdrawn by public and private water suppliers that furnish water to at least 25 people or have a minimum of 15 connections.

Public water use: Water supplied from a public utility for such purposes as firefighting, street washing, flushing of water lines, and maintaining municipal parks and swimming pools.

Reclaimed wastewater: Wastewater treatment plant effluent that has been diverted for beneficial uses such as irrigation, industry, or thermoelectric power cooling.

Recovery: The process of removing materials from the waste stream for purposes of recycling or composting.

Recycling: The act of collecting, reprocessing, and/or recovering certain waste materials to make new materials or products; separating a given waste material from the waste stream and processing it so that it may be used again as a useful material for products that may or may not be similar to the original. DOE defines recyclable material as generally including paper, metal, glass, plastic and organic substances.

Restructuring: Changes in management systems, or to the organizational and institutional dimensions of management systems. In simple terms, restructuring results in changes in who does what.

Rural water use: Water used in suburban or farm areas for domestic and livestock needs. This water is generally self-supplied and includes such use as drinking water for livestock, dairy sanitations, cleaning, and waste disposal.

Self-supplied water use: Water withdrawn from a groundwater or surface water source by a user rather than being obtained from a public-supply source.

Solid waste: Garbage, rubbish, refuse, swill, ashes, industrial wastes, sewage sludge, demolition and construction wastes, abandoned vehicles and parts of abandoned vehicles.

Thermoelectric power water use: Water used in the process of generating electricity with steam-driven turbine generators.

Transfer station: A facility where wastes are transferred from smaller vehicles into larger transport trailers prior to movement to a landfill or to a rail facility for further transportation to a landfill or other disposal.

Waste prevention: The act of substituting durable goods and materials for disposables or less durable materials; also includes seeking for new ways to reuse goods.

Waste reduction: The process of consuming or discarding less material by redesigning products to use fewer raw materials in production or for a longer shelf life, or so they can be used again after original use.

Wastewater: Water which is of no further value to the purpose for which it was used because of its quality, quantity or time of occurrence. However, wastewater from one user can be a potential supply to a user elsewhere.

Wastewater collecting system: A system of conduits which collect and conduct wastewater. Collecting systems are often operated by public authorities or semi-public associations.

Wastewater treatment: All treatment processes of wastewater in wastewater treatment plants. Wastewater treatment plants are usually operated by public authorities or by private companies working by order of public authorities. Includes wastewater delivered to treatment plants by trucks.

Watershed: A river basin; the total area from which a single river collects surface runoff.

Water use: Water that is withdrawn for a specific purpose, such as for public supply, domestic use, irrigation, thermoelectric power generation, and other uses.

Yard debris: Plant material commonly created in the course of maintaining yards and gardens and through horticulture, gardening, landscaping or similar activities; includes but not limited to grass clippings, leaves, branches, brush, weeds, flowers, roots, windfall fruit, and vegetable garden debris.

Index